fun with the family
Massachusetts

Help Us Keep This Guide Up to Date

We would love to hear from you concerning your experiences with this guide and how you feel it could be improved and kept up to date. Please send your comments and suggestions to:

editorial@GlobePequot.com
Thanks for your input, and happy travels!

FUN WITH THE FAMILY SERIES

fun with the family
Massachusetts

hundreds of ideas for day trips with the kids

Eighth Edition

Marcia Glassman-Jaffe

travel

Guilford, Connecticut

All the information in this guidebook is subject to change. We recommend that you call ahead to obtain current information before traveling.

To buy books in quantity for corporate use or incentives, call **(800) 962-0973** or e-mail **premiums@GlobePequot.com**.

Editor: Amy Lyons
Project Editor: Lynn Zelem
Layout: Joanna Beyer
Text Design: Nancy Freeborn and Linda R. Loiewski
Maps: Rusty Nelson © Morris Book Publishing, LLC
Spot photography throughout © Photodisc and © RubberBall Productions

ISSN 1537-291X
ISBN 978-0-7627-9675-5

Printed in the United States of America

To Mark, Ian, Morgan, Mallory, Marisa, Justin, and Chase.

Thank you for helping me see the wonders around us as we travel life's many paths. I am truly blessed with a wonderful and loving family. Thank you for your understanding and support; I always sensed your pride in me for my determined perseverance. And lastly, I would like to thank the Walter Mitty's of this world, no matter what their age, who dare to dream.

This book is dedicated to the beloved memories of my late parents, Natalie and Cyril Glassman, who inspired my love of travel, discovery, and nature.

About the Author

Marcia Glassman-Jaffe received a B.A. in Psychology from the University of Massachusetts in Amherst and a Masters in Education and Human Development with a concentration in Travel and Tourism Administration and Policy from George Washington University in Washington, DC. Marcia got her start in the travel industry as a travel agent and eventually worked as part of a management team. She later performed tourism research for the Boston Organizing Committee on the viability of Boston as a host city for the Summer Olympics. Marcia also served as a Research Associate for an adventure travel book before authoring *Fun with the Family Massachusetts* and *Are We Almost There? Where to Go and What to Do with the Kids in Boston* (GPP Travel). Marcia lives on the North Shore of Massachusetts with her husband Mark. They are the proud parents of Ian, Morgan, Mallory, Marisa, and Marisa's husband, Justin, and grandparents of Chase.

Acknowledgments

Thank you to the members of the Massachusetts Office of Travel and Tourism, the regional travel offices, and the chambers of commerce throughout the state, the National Park Service visitor centers, and the sites and attractions contained in this book for their time and cooperation in making this book as accurate and informative as possible. I would further like to thank Morgan and Mallory Jaffe and Marisa Jaffe Gelfand for their technological assistance and Morgan Jaffe and Kirsten Williamson for all their proofreading work and support.

My gratitude, too, to my many friends who put friendship on hold so I could follow my writing dream and for their discoveries and tips that they shared with me.

To my dear friend Diane Bair: This project wouldn't have happened without you—many thanks.

I would like to thank Amy Lyons, my editor, for her encouragement, guidance, and wonderful conversations. Amy, you've been lovely to work with. Thank you also to Lynn Zelem, project editor at GPP.

Contents

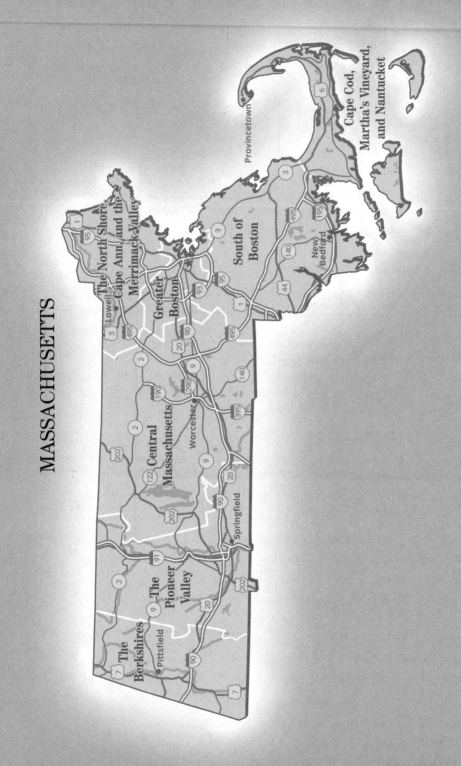

MASSACHUSETTS

The North Shore, Cape Ann, and the Merrimack Valley

Lowell

Greater Boston

South of Boston

Provincetown

Cape Cod, Martha's Vineyard, and Nantucket

New Bedford

Central Massachusetts

Worcester

Springfield

The Pioneer Valley

The Berkshires

Pittsfield

Introduction

Massachusetts was settled in 1620 by a brave band of 101 men, women, and children. From that initial Plimoth outpost in the "wilds of Massachusetts" grew the state that has garnered a worldwide reputation for its educational institutions, medical facilities, unique sites and culture, rich history, and physical beauty. Boston, the state capital, is considered the gateway to New England and is popular with both domestic and international tourists because of the breadth of its attractions—performing and visual arts, sports facilities, and cultural institutions.

The book is arranged from the western part of the state toward the eastern end, and then proceeds down the Massachusetts coast. Each entry includes an address, telephone number, website, and description. Where possible, hours, prices, and directions have been added to the entries. The suggested age ranges for a particular site are just that, suggested guidelines. Parents or caregivers must use their own judgment and experience based on the maturity of the child to determine whether a particular site is appropriate.

The maps in the beginning of each chapter are designed to orient you to a particular area, but they are in no way intended to be a substitute for a detailed state road system map.

The following key indicates pricing by dollar sign instead of a numerical rate for lodgings and restaurants. Lodging prices fluctuate depending on location and time of year. Please be aware that lunch is usually a better value at an establishment than dinner. Be sure to inquire about family rates or discounts where indicated in this text.

RATES USED IN THIS GUIDE

Rates for places to stay and eat are represented with dollar signs and offer a sense of the price ranges at press time.

Rates for Accommodations

| $ | up to $125 | $$$ | $226 to $325 |
| $$ | $126 to $225 | $$$$ | more than $325 |

Rates for Restaurants

$	most entrees under $15	$$$	most $25 to $35
$$	most $15 to $24	$$$$	most over $35

SPECIAL NOTES OF INTEREST

The **Massachusetts Office of Travel and Tourism** is eager to send information packages to prospective tourists. The Massachusetts Office of Travel and Tourism can be contacted at the State Transportation Building, 10 Park Plaza, Suite 4510, Boston, MA 02116; (617) 973-8500 or (800) 227-MASS (US or Canada); massvacation.com. To reserve a stay at any one of the **Massachusetts state campgrounds,** contact **Reserve America** toll-free at (877) 422-6762 or online at reserveamerica.com. Individual state parks will no longer make reservations. The entire state park system consists of state reservations, parks, and forests, which for the most part charge entry fees. It may be more economical to buy a season pass for $35 if you're a Massachusetts resident ($45 for out-of-staters) at the parks or by telephone or online with Reserve America. The national parks, refuges, monuments, and sanctuaries offer the Golden Eagle Pass, a season pass that allows entry to multiple sites.

Attractions Key

The following is a key to the icons found throughout the text.

SWIMMING		**FOOD**	
BOATING / BOAT TOUR		**LODGING**	
HISTORIC SITE		**CAMPING**	
HIKING / WALKING		**MUSEUM**	
FISHING		**PERFORMING ARTS**	
BIKING		**SPORTS/ATHLETICS**	
AMUSEMENT PARK		**PICNICKING**	
HORSEBACK RIDING		**PLAYGROUND**	
SKIING / WINTER SPORTS		**SHOPPING**	
PARK		**PLANTS/GARDENS/NATURE TRAILS**	
ANIMAL VIEWING		**FARM**	

The Berkshires

C overing the western end of Massachusetts, Berkshire County changes dramatically, from the high mountains and isolated valleys in the north to the hilly forests and farmland of the area along the Connecticut border. A magnet for leaf-peeper pilgrimages, the color is brilliant in autumn, sweeping over the knolls and rises of the landscape. Tell the kids to keep an eye out for the carved wooden Indians that "guard" the tourist shops along the Mohawk Trail; they are a nod to the native peoples who once frequented this road when it was just a path. Williamstown, found in the westerly end of the Mohawk Trail, is known for **Williams College** and its world-class art museums set in a classic New England village of white churches and clapboard houses along the edges of the town green. To the southeast of North Adams is Mt. Greylock, the state's highest mountain, part of a huge park full of hiking trails of varying difficulties, as well as waterfalls, fishing areas, and campgrounds.

The southern Berkshire area is gentler in topography and more cultural in nature. The region abounds with museums, theaters, and outdoor classical music venues, the most famous of which is Tanglewood, summer home of the Boston Symphony Orchestra. Kids will marvel at the round stone barn at Hancock Shaker Village outside Pittsfield. Farther south, in Stockbridge, take the time to walk along the long porch and through the enormous lobby area of the rambling old Red Lion Inn. During the winter Berkshire County is a mecca for skiing families.

The **Berkshire Visitor Bureau,** 66 Allen St., Pittsfield, MA 01201, can be contacted at (413) 743-4500 or (800) 237-5747; berkshires.org. They are extremely helpful if you want information or hot tips on Berkshire County.

THE BERKSHIRES

Williamstown

(8)

Florida

North Adams

(7)

(2)

New Ashford

Mount
Greylock

Adams

(43)

Cheshire

(8)

(9)

Hancock

Windsor

Lanesborough

Dalton

Pittsfield

Hinsdale

(20)

(7)
(20)

(8)

Lenox

(90)

Lee

Becket

Stockbridge

(20)

Housatonic

Tyringham

(90)

South
Egremont

Great
Barrington

East
Otis

(23)

Monterey

(23)

(41)

(8)

Sheffield

(7)

Mount
Washington

New Malborough

Ashley Falls

Mohawk Trail

The Mohawk Trail, Route 2, is the highway version of the path that Native Americans used to travel from the Connecticut River Valley to the Hudson River Valley. Sixty-seven miles long, the road is only partially in the Berkshires, since it begins in the Connecticut River Valley. Near the town of Florida, the trail passes by the entrance to the **Hoosac Tunnel,** which at 25,081 feet (or 4.82 engineering miles) was the longest railway tunnel in the country when it was completed in 1875. An engineering marvel in its time, the Hoosac Tunnel was the first construction to use nitroglycerin. Stop at the Wigwam Western Summit Gift Shop not for the shop—it's closed and shuttered—but for the telescope (25 cents for about 3 minutes) on the edge of the steep hill that overlooks the northern Berkshires. Other viewing areas on Route 2 with telescopes are located at the Golden Eagle Restaurant in Clarksburg and near the **Eastern Summit Gift Shop** in Florida. The highest point on the trail is the **Whitcomb Summit** at 2,240 feet. To the east of the summit is the **Elk Memorial,** the second-most photographed statue on the Mohawk. The elk, sculpted by **Eli Harvey,** serves as a memorial to the fallen members of the Order of Elks in World War I. ***Trail warning:*** The trail makes several hairpin turns on its way into North Adams. For more information on the Mohawk Trail, contact the **Mohawk Trail Association**, PO Box 1044, North Adams, MA 01247; (413) 743-8127; mohawktrail.com.

TopPicks in the Berkshires

- **Hancock Shaker Village and the Berkshire Museum,** Pittsfield

- **Mt. Greylock State Reservation,** Lanesborough

- **Mohawk Trail**

- **Sterling and Francine Clark Art Institute,** Williamstown

- **Tanglewood Music Festival,** Lenox

North Adams

The City of Spires, as residents like to call it, is a bit run-down nowadays; the beautiful old brick factories and warehouses that produced paper, textiles, and leather goods are mostly empty now. Several of these buildings are the home of the Massachusetts Museum of Contemporary Art, which everyone calls Mass MoCA.

Massachusetts Museum of Contemporary Art aka Mass MoCA (all ages)

1040 MASS MoCA Way, North Adams; (413) 662-2111; massmoca.org. Open daily July 1 through Labor Day 10 a.m. to 6 p.m., after Labor Day through June 25, Wed through Mon 11 a.m. to 5 p.m. (closed Tues). Admission: $15 for adults, $10 for college students, $5 for children 6 to 16, free for children under 5. Combination tickets are available with other area museums.

A rising Phoenix from its former factory setting, MASS MoCA is one of the liveliest and largest centers for making and showing the best art and music of our time. Three floors in a building at the campus center house a retrospective of more than 100 Sol Lewitt wall drawings in a variety of mediums, showing the breadth and depth of his career—there's over an acre of his work on display. A 10,000-square-foot repurposed water tank on the museum campus is dedicated to the work of German artist Anselm Kiefer. It's open in warm months. Kidspace is MASS MoCA's child-centered gallery, complete with art-making activities on weekends, holidays, and in the summer. The museum stages over 40 nights of dance, music, theater, and film throughout the year, including two major music festivals on indoor and outdoor stages. Call for public hours, programs, and a family activity schedule. Try the lobby cafe, Lickety Split, for a snack.

North Adams Historical Society Museum of History and Science (all ages)

Route 8, Western Gateway Heritage State Park, Building 5A, North Adams; (413) 664-4700; northadamshistory.org. Open May 1 through Oct, Thurs through Sat from 10 a.m. to 4 p.m. and Sun from 1 to 4 p.m. Limited hours Nov through Apr, Sat 10 a.m. to 4 p.m. and Sun 1 to 4 p.m. Closed on holidays. Admission and parking are free; donations accepted.

With more than 25 permanent exhibits and a temporary gallery within a 6,000-square-foot space, the museum details the history and natural environment of North Adams and the region on three amazing floors. Kids will be attracted to the history of North Adams and its agrarian and industrial past. Other kid-friendly exhibits are Grandma's Attic, the Barracks Room containing a replica of Fort Massachusetts (which was located in North Adams), and the Blacklight Gallery. On the second floor is the Science Discovery Center with a cool hands-on area.

Western Gateway Heritage State Park and Tourism Information Center (all ages)

Route 8, 115 State St., Building 4, North Adams; (413) 663-6312; mass.gov/eea/ agencies/dcr/massparks/region-west/western-gateway-heritage-state-park-generic .html. Open daily mid-May through mid-Oct 10 a.m. to 5 p.m., mid-Oct through mid-May Thurs to Mon 10 a.m. to 4 p.m. Due to staff limitations, call before arrival to verify hours. Free; donations accepted.

If your family includes a railroad buff or two, visit the Western Gateway Heritage State Park, a former railroad yard. An introductory 30-minute video sets the tone, along with interesting tidbits about North Adams's history as a bustling rail-road town (changing historical and seasonal exhibits), the growth of the railroad industry, and the construction of the Hoosac Tunnel. There are family programs throughout the year. Kids like the working scale-model railroad that depicts North Adams in the 1950s and the Junior Explorers Program. There are free lectures on Sat; consult the website for the weekly topic.

Where to Eat

Brewhaha, 437 West Main St., North Adams; (413) 664-2020. Open 7 a.m. to 5 p.m. Thurs through Tues (closed Wed). Try the orange almond French toast or one of their specialty coffees or teas. $

Freight Yard Restaurant and Pub, 1 Furnace Park, Western Gateway Heritage State Park, North Adams; (413) 663-6547; freightyardpub.com. Open year-round for lunch and dinner. Serving burgers, pasta, steak, and seafood. Kids' menu. $–$$$

Golden Eagle Restaurant, Route 2, 1935 Mohawk Trail (at the hairpin turn), Clarksburg; (413) 663-9834; thegoldeneaglerestaurant.com. Open Memorial Day through mid-Nov and winter weekends, serving lunch and dinner. Good old-fashioned American cooking and fabulous sunsets from the seasonal outdoor patio. Reasonably priced. $–$$$

Down the **Road!**

Seven Western Massachusetts Scenic Byways were created to help point the way to the best discoveries in the western Massachusetts region; bywayswestmass.com.

Gramercy Bistro (at MASS MoCA campus), 87 Marshall St., North Adams; (413) 663-5300; gramercybistro.com. Open year-round Wed through Mon, for dinner only, lunch is offered Wed through Sat Memorial Day through the end of Oct. Upper-scale fine dining in a casual atmosphere. Sunday brunches popular with families. $–$$$

Where to Stay

Blackinton Manor, 1391 Massachusetts Ave., North Adams; (413) 663-5795; blackinton-manor.com. Former mill owner's home. Lovely antique building tastefully furnished. Close to Mass MoCA and Williams College. Children 12 and up. $$–$$$

The Porches Inn, 231 River St., North Adams; (413) 664-0400; porches.com. Forty-seven rooms and suites in six connecting Victorian-era row houses that have been renovated. Outdoor heated pool, many rooms with Jacuzzi-style tubs. Room includes continental breakfast. *Condé Nast* award winner. Seasonal assortment of treats in the lobby. Cribs. $$–$$$$

Williamstown

Williamstown hasn't changed much since the late 19th century—it's a quintessential New England town. It's home to one of New England's best small liberal arts colleges, Williams College, and to two exceptional art museums: the Sterling and Francine Clark Art Institute and the Williams College Museum of Art. For more information on Williamstown, contact the **Williamstown Chamber of Commerce,** PO Box 357, 7 Denison Park Dr., Williamstown, MA 01267; (413) 458-9077 or (800) 214-3799; williamstownchamber.com.

Sterling and Francine Clark Art Institute (all ages)

225 South St., Williamstown; (413) 458-2303; clarkart.edu. Open year-round, Tues through Sun 10 a.m. to 5 p.m. with the addition of Mon from 10 a.m. to 5 p.m. in

July and Aug. Closed Thanksgiving, Christmas, and New Year's Day. Admission: $15 June through Oct; the rest of the year it is free for adults; children under age 18 and full-time students are free year-round. Combo tickets with other museums are available.

The Sterling and Francine Clark Art Institute, fondly known locally as "the Clark," has a world-class collection of late 19th-century paintings by Renoir, Monet, Corot, Pissarro, and Degas, among others. Also of interest is a room with paintings by the American artists Sargent, Remington, Inness, and Homer, admired American painters of the late 19th and early 20th centuries. They were contemporaries, and all were celebrated in their time for very different styles and subject matter: Sargent for his exquisite portraits of high-society figures; Remington for his depictions of cowboys and western life; Inness for his ethereal landscapes; and Homer for his haunting New England sea and mountain scenes. July 2014 marked the grand reopening of the original 1955 building (where the permanent collection is housed), which was closed for renovation and expansion of a brand-new visitor, conference, and exhibition center.

The beautiful grounds are a great spot for a picnic and the band concerts every Tues in July. Call for the schedule of children's special events. An extremely popular event with families is the annual Summer Family Day, with free admission and family fun activities. Two dining options will please any palate.

Play **Time**

From late June through Aug, the **Williamstown Theatre Festival,** PO Box 517, 1000 Main St., Williamstown, MA 01267; (413) 597-3399 (schedules and information) or (413) 597-3400 (box office); wtfestival .org, one of the country's preeminent theater groups, presents musicals, dramas, children's theater, and special events. Most performances are at Williams College's Adams Memorial Theater or the '62 Centre for Theatre and Dance.

Williams College Museum of Art (all ages)

15 Lawrence Hall Dr. (off of Route 2, Main Street), Williamstown; (413) 597-2429;
wcma.williams.edu. Open Mon through Sat 10 a.m. to 5 p.m. (closed Wed), Sun 1
to 5 p.m. Closed Thanksgiving, Christmas, and New Year's Day. Free.
The Williams College Museum of Art is one of the best college art museums in
the country in terms of the breadth of its collection, which spans antiquity to the
present, including contemporary, modern American, and non-Western art. The
museum encourages multidisciplinary learning through encounters with works of
art that traverse time periods and cultures. Good traveling exhibitions stop here
too. The museum offers free public performances and lectures, as well as summer education programs.

Other Things to See & Do

Natural Bridge State Park, McCauley Road off Route 8, North Adams; (413) 663-
6392 or (413) 663-8469 (off-season); mass.gov/eea/agencies/dcr/massparks/region-
west/natural-bridge-state-park-generic.html. Open daily 9 a.m. to 5 p.m. Memorial
Day through Columbus Day. White marble natural bridge that was formed 550 million
years ago by glacial retreat. Summer interpretive programs. Parking fee: $2 per car.

Old Hopkins Observatory and Mehlin Museum of Astronomy, Williams College, Williamstown; (413) 597-2188; astronomy.williams.edu/hopkins-observatory/
milham-planetarium. Oldest astronomical observatory in the US. Planetarium.

Steeple Cats, PO Box 540, Joe Wolfe Field, North Adams; (413) 652-1031; steeple
cats.com. Member of the New England Collegiate Baseball League.

Williamstown Rural Land Foundation at Sheep Hill, 671 Cold Spring Rd., Williamstown; (413) 458-2494; wrlf.org. Fifty-acre preserved property land trust with
additional trails on other properties in Williamstown. Summer interpreter, hiking trails,
children's programs, special events. Most events are free; donations welcome.

Where to Eat

Hobson's Choice, 159 Water St., Williamstown; (413) 458-9101; hobsonsrestaurant
.com. Homemade soups and abundant salad bar. Kids can order a half plate. $–$$$

Water Street Grill, 123 Water St., Williamstown; (413) 458-2175; waterstgrill.com.
Open for lunch (burgers, sandwiches, seafood) and dinner (pasta, steaks, seafood) in
the comfortable dining room or the tavern. Kids' menu. $–$$

Where to Stay

House on Main Street B&B, 1120 Main St., Williamstown; (413) 458-3031; houseonmainstreet.com. Three rooms with private baths; 3 others share 1 full and 1 half bath. The big screened-in porch is a nice spot to relax. Wonderful breakfasts. Caters to food allergies. $–$$

The Orchards, 222 Adams Rd., Williamstown; (413) 458-9611 or (800) 225-1517; orchardshotel.com. Antiques, four-poster beds, fireplaces, pond, outdoor pool, Jacuzzi, exercise room. Complimentary cookies and beverages every day. Great restaurant (**Gala Steakhouse and Bistro,** $–$$$$) serving elegant specialties. Cribs. $–$$$$

Adams, Lanesborough & Hancock

Adams is the birthplace of **Susan B. Anthony,** the suffragist who led the struggle to gain the vote for women and is still remembered with an annual summer festival in July called Susan B. Anthony Days. Adams is set peacefully along the banks of the Hoosic River and shadowed by Mt. Greylock. The southern entrance to Mt. Greylock is in Lanesborough. Due west is the town of Hancock; blink and you are in the state of New York! Hancock is noted for being a quiet and peaceful place. For information on Adams, contact the **Adams Visitor Center,** 3 Hoosick St., Adams, MA 01220; (413) 743-8356; town.adams.ma.us/Public_Documents/ AdamsMA_CommDev/AdamsMA_Planning/visitorsctr. Contained in the same building is the Thunderbolt Ski Museum with a video and historical displays.

Ashuwillticook Rail Trail Bike Path (all ages)

Current access is at Cheshire Lake in Cheshire, at the Berkshire Mall in Lanesborough, and in Russell Fields in Adams and in Adams Center; (413) 442-8928 (DEM Region 5 Headquarters); mass.gov/eea/agencies/dcr/massparks/region-west/ ashuwillticook-rail-trail.html. Open all year. Free.

The Ashuwillticook Rail Trail Bike Path is an 11.2-mile trail (a former rail bed) that is fairly flat for an easy ride. The Massachusetts State Park Rail Trail extends from Lanesborough to Cheshire to Adams. There are beautiful vistas (a good leg of the trail is on Cheshire Lake) with potentially great views of fall foliage and mountainscapes. All the rail trails can be used for jogging, walking, snowshoeing, and

Amazing
Massachusetts Facts

Mt. Greylock, at 3,491 feet, is the highest point in the state.
Incorporated in 1898, it was the first state park in Massachusetts.

cross-country skiing. Forgot your bike? Call **Berkshire Outfitters,** 169 Grove St.
in Adams, at (413) 743-5900; berkshireoutfitters.com. They are 300 yards from
an access point and 1 mile from the northern entrance to the trail. Rent hybrid
bikes with comfort saddles as well as tag-along trailers and half bikes for older
children. Helmets are included!

Mt. Greylock State Reservation (all ages)

Visitor Center, 30 Rockwell Rd., Lanesborough; (413) 499-4263 or (413) 499-4262;
mass.gov/eea/agencies/dcr/massparks/region-west/mt-greylock-state-reservation-
generic.html. The park is open from sunrise until a half hour before sunset. The
Visitor Center is open daily year-round, 9 a.m. to 4:30 p.m., with extended hours
Memorial Day through Columbus Day. There are several ways to approach the
mountain. One is following the Western Massachusetts Scenic Byway from West-
ern Gateway Heritage State Park in North Adams (take the Furnace Street bypass,
which merges to Reservoir Road, follow to Notch Road through a residential
area that turns into woody hills; signs will direct you from there). The other is via
Route 7 in Lanesborough (follow the signs). TIP: **The auto road is open to the sum-**
mit late May through Oct (weather depending). Recreational vehicles over 13 feet
and tour buses aren't permitted. Free; however, there is a $2 parking fee in
season at the summit.

Mt. Greylock State Reservation is an enormous park (more than 12,500 acres)
with 70 miles of hiking trails of varying difficulties, as well as backpack camping
(contact Reserve America at 877-422-6762 or reserveamerica.com for one of the
sites that can accommodate families or groups), nature viewing, fishing, cross-
country skiing, and snowmobiling. The visitor center in Lanesborough is an excellent first stop; be sure to get a map. A large tabletop relief map shows the park's
layout and topography. Even if your family hasn't done a lot of hiking, don't be
discouraged. Many of the park's trails leave from the parking area on top of the
mountain (this is one of the reasons it's such a terrific family place; you can drive

right to the best part). One of the routes suggested by the rangers is a 4-mile round-trip hike from the summit down Overlook Trail to Hopper Trail, then on to March Cataract Falls.

Note: The weather can change quickly and unexpectedly on Mt. Greylock. Every year a few experienced hikers find themselves stranded. Get a map and talk to rangers in the visitor center before you begin your hike.

Whether or not you hike, don't end your visit to Mt. Greylock without climbing the War Memorial Tower. On a clear day you'll be able to see Mt. Monadnock in New Hampshire, 56 miles away, as well as the full Berkshire range, the Taconics in New York, southern Vermont, deep into Connecticut, Mount Wachusett in Central Massachusetts, and the southern part of the Appalachians for a five-state view. The tower is open 9 a.m. to 5 p.m. daily, late May through mid-Oct, weather permitting. When the wind picks up from the east, hang gliders and parasailers can be seen launching off the east side of the mountain, and it is a spectacular sight! October is the busiest month to visit because of the brilliant foliage views.

On Columbus Day the town of Adams sponsors the Mt. Greylock Ramble, an annual trek to the mountain summit from the Cheshire Harbor Trailhead on West Mountain Road, a great family event 3.3 miles one-way to the summit.

Other Things to See & Do

Bakers Miniature Golf, 658 South Main St., Lanesborough; (413) 443-6102; bakers golfcenter.com. Miniature golf and driving range. Next door is a Pitch 'n' Putt and go-karts. Open seasonally.

Ioka Valley Farm, 3475 Route 43, Hancock; (413) 738-5915; iokavalleyfarm.com. An agritourism four-season destination. Petting farm (Uncle Don's Barnyard), pick-your-own Indian corn and pumpkins, maple-sugaring demonstrations and tastings,

Take Me Out **to the Fair!**

The only major agricultural fair in the Berkshires, the **Adams Fair** takes place during the last days of July/first days of Aug at Bowe Field off Route 8 (Old Columbia Street). Call (413) 663-3977 or visit aafadams.tripod.com for more information.

recycled-farm-equipment playground, and hayrides at pumpkin time. Choose and cut your own holiday tree. The Calf-A (pun on *cafe*!) is open in the spring, serving home-made pancakes, waffles, and French toast with their own maple syrup.

Susan B. Anthony Birthplace and Museum, 67 East St., Adams; (413) 743-7121; susanbanthonybirthplace.com. Susan B. Anthony was a suffragist, early feminist, and social reformer; the museum's exhibits revolve around her life and times. Admission fee.

The East Hoosuck Quaker Meeting House, corner of Notch Road and Maple Street, Maple Street Cemetery, Adams; (413) 743-1799; adamshistorical.us/collections/quaker_house/index.html. Open Sun afternoons 1 to 4 p.m. between the Fourth of July and Columbus Day.

Where to Eat

Greylock's Bascom Lodge, Summit Road, Lanesborough; (413) 743-1591; bascom lodge.net. The lodge, built in the 1930s, sits atop Mt. Greylock. Run by the Bascom Lodge Group. Many renovations and upgrades have occurred. Open June to late Oct. Gift shop and cafe. Reservations required for dinner (not for breakfast or lunch). $–$$$

Where to Stay

Greylock's Bascom Lodge, Summit Road, Lanesborough; (413) 743-1591; bascomlodge.net. The eight rooms are rustic but comfortable and vary in size, from dormitory-style rooms that sleep 8 people to private doubles. All rooms share baths and are provided with linens. $–$$

Florida, Dalton & Hinsdale

It's rumored that the small village of Florida is the most frigid spot in the state because of its location, not quite the tropical picture its name would suggest. But in the summer months, with refreshing waters and cooling falls, Savoy State Park in Florida is a hidden jewel. Dalton is home to the Crane Paper Company, which has bragging rights as the only supplier of paper for US currency. Hinsdale takes great pride in native son Israel Bissell, who gave Paul Revere a run for his money.

The Midnight Ride of **Israel Bissell?**

A few miles southeast of Dalton is the small town of Hinsdale, whose claim to fame is Israel Bissell. Bissell is the man who outdid Paul Revere: In five days he rode from Hinsdale through Connecticut to New York and on to Philadelphia to carry the news of the colonists' confrontation with the British in 1775. Bissell is buried in the Maple Street Cemetery (take Route 143 east; the cemetery is at the top of the first small hill after Route 8).

Crane Museum (all ages)

Housatonic Street, off Route 8, Dalton; (413) 684-2600; crane.com (click on "About Us" and then on "Crane Museum of Papermaking"). Open June through mid-Oct, Mon through Fri 1 to 5 p.m. Free.

Crane Paper Company makes the paper on which all US currency is printed. Tour the museum to learn how paper is made and see a display about the history of paper money. Crane papers are used for currency, bonds, stock certificates, and fine stationery.

Savoy Mountain State Forest (all ages)

260 Central Shaft Rd., Florida; (413) 663-8469; mass.gov/eea/agencies/dcr/ massparks/region-west/savoy-mt-state-forest-generic.html. From Route 2 in Florida, turn onto Central Shaft Road. Open year-round dawn to dusk. Day-use fee $5. *TIP:* **This is black bear country, so store food properly.**

Savoy Mountain State Forest, on 11,000 acres, is a less crowded version of Mt. Greylock State Reservation. The park is especially appealing to children because of the good swimming in North Pond (there isn't much legal swimming on Greylock). The hiking is less challenging too, and the pleasant trek to Tannery Falls brings you to one of the nicest falls in the Berkshires. There are four cabins (rentable year-round) on the banks of South Pond and forty-five campsites available Memorial Day to Columbus Day; contact Reserve America at (877) 422-6762; reserveamerica.com.

Berkshire **Skiing Meccas**

During the winter Berkshire County is a mecca for skiing families. Some of New England's best small-scale, family-oriented downhill and cross-country ski areas are here. All can boast of excellent ski schools, family packages, and reasonably priced accommodations either at the base of the mountain or within a few miles.

- **Bousquet Ski Area,** 101 Dan Fox Dr., Pittsfield; (413) 442-8316; bousquets.com. Downhill skiing (day and night), snow tubing, and snowboarding. There are 20 trails. Summer fun at Play Bousquet.

- **Butternut Basin,** Route 23, 380 State Rd., Great Barrington; (413) 528-2000 or (800) 438-SNOW; skibutternut.com. Downhill skiing (1,000-foot vertical drop), 12 lifts (3 quads), 2 terrain parks with jumps and moguls, 2 lodges, 4 magic carpets for beginners, a 7-lane tubing park, and rentals. Fifth-graders ski free weekdays with an accompanying adult skier ticket purchase (non-holiday weeks only).

- **Canterbury Farm,** 1986 Fred Snow Rd., Becket; (413) 623-0100; canterbury-farms.com. Cross-country skiing and snowshoeing. Beautiful setting. Bed-and-breakfast on the property. One fee rental for cross-country skiing, ice skating, or snowshoeing—switch them out anytime from 9 a.m. to 5 p.m.!

- **Catamount,** Route 23, South Egremont; (413) 528-1262; catamount ski.com. A 1,000-foot vertical drop; longest run is 2.5 miles, the longest in the Berkshires. Six lifts, 34 trails. Ski school, nursery, rentals, night skiing, and a snowboard megaplex consisting of 2 parks. Off-season, try the Catamount Aerial Adventure Park.

- **Cranwell Resort,** Route 20, 55 Lee Rd., Lenox; (413) 637-1364 or (800) CRANWELL; cranwell.com. Cross-country skiing; 114 deluxe rooms; gourmet dining in Wyndhurst Restaurant in a historic setting. Amenities include an 18-hole PGA golf course, tennis courts, ice skating, and 1 indoor and 1 outdoor heated pool.

- **Jiminy Peak,** 37 Corey Rd., Route 43 to Brodie Mountain Road, Hancock; (413) 738-5500 or (800) 882-8859 (lodging); jiminypeak

.com. Self-contained resort with nice condominiums and a slope-side inn. The state's first 6-passenger lift is here, along with 8 other lifts. There are 3 snowboard terrain parks and 45 trails, 22 of which are lit for night skiing. Challenging steep intermediate runs and black-diamond slopes deserve their rating. There's a kids-only area for KidsRule with lessons, and the day-care center takes kids from 6 months up. Jiminy Peak has gone green and is the first resort in the nation to generate its own energy, saving about one-third of its output. During the summer the Mountain Adventure Park is a popular attraction for the kids. It includes an alpine slide, mountain coaster (which is also open in the winter), a giant swing, a rock-climbing wall, 4 Euro-bungee trampolines, jousting, a spider web, a bouncy bounce, and a rope adventure. The Aerial Adventure Park is a challenge course offering zip-lining fun and rope bridges through the trees. Scenic rides and mountain biking round out your day.

- **Notchview Reservation,** 83 Old Route 9, Windsor; (413) 684-0148 or (413) 298-3239; thetrustees.org. Free for Trustees of Reservations members weekdays during the summer and winter; a fee is charged winter weekends. Nonmembers are charged at all times. Trustees of Reservations property with more than 3,000 acres for hiking and cross-country skiing (with 25 kilometers of groomed trails in the winter out of 40 kilometers of trails). The base elevation is 2,000 feet, which translates to more snowfall than other cross-country ski areas located at lower elevations. Facilities include a lodge, 2 trailside picnic shelters, and rentals for snow-shoes (they are considering having cross-country ski rentals—check before you go!)

- **Otis Ridge,** Route 23W, Otis; (413) 269-4444; otisridge.com. A small downhill ski area oriented to families. The vertical drop is only 400 feet, and there are just 11 runs. An overnight camp is offered in the winter during school vacations. Come here if you want your kids to learn to ski in an intimate setting; experienced skiers will be bored.

Where to Stay

Maplewood Bed & Breakfast, 435 Maple St., Hinsdale; (413) 655-8167; maple woodbandb.com. Three rooms, one being a two-room suite popular with families. Kids are welcome, however, the house isn't childproof. $–$$

Pittsfield

The residents of Pittsfield are extremely dedicated to preserving the contributions of the Shakers to the American lifestyle at Hancock Shaker Village. Pittsfield offers many recreational and cultural opportunities, with its many lakes, museums, and parks. Great sources of information are the **Berkshire Chamber of Commerce,** Central Station, 66 Allen St., Pittsfield, MA 01201 (413-499-4000; berkshirechamber.com) and the Town of Pittsfield, 70 Allen St., Pittsfield (413-499-9321; pittsfield-ma.org).

Berkshire Museum (all ages)

Route 7, 39 South St., downtown Pittsfield; (413) 443-7171; berkshiremuseum.org. Open Mon through Sat 10 a.m. to 5 p.m., Sun noon to 5 p.m. Admission: $13 for adults, $6 for ages 4 to 18, free for under 4.
An eclectic museum that is a little bit of everything, the Berkshire Museum is a diamond in the rough; it surprises and amazes you, drawing you right in to its varied collection. Somehow the museum combines a hands-on aquarium with science and history exhibits, paintings, sculpture, and decorative arts. A cinema runs a selection of first-rate films (call for a schedule). Children's programs crowd the galleries; the museum specializes in blockbuster interactive family exhibitions year-round. Changing exhibitions are always participatory to engage visitors of all ages. A new interactive space focuses on innovation and creativity.

Hancock Shaker Village (all ages)

1843 West Housatonic St., Route 20 just west of the Route 41 Junction, Pittsfield; (413) 443-0188 or (800) 817-1137; hancockshakervillage.org. Self-guided tour mid-Apr through June, 10 a.m. to 4 p.m. and July through Nov 10 a.m. to 5 p.m. Admission: $18 adults, $8 kids 13 to 17, free for kids 12 and under. Closed Nov through Mar.
Our culture reveres the Shakers for their simple, beautiful furniture and building designs. What most people don't know is that their crafting skill was a direct

Fish Tales or **Fantastic Fishing Spots?**

Grab your fishing license and bring the kids to one of these tried-and-true fishing holes:

- **Ashmere Lake,** Hinsdale
- **Benedict Pond,** Monterey
- **Benton Pond,** East Otis Reservoir, Otis
- **Berry Pond,** Pittsfield State Forest, Pittsfield
- **Center Pond and Yokum Pond,** Becket
- **Cheshire Reservoir,** Cheshire
- **Goose Pond and Laurel Lake,** Lee
- **Onota and Pontoosuc Lakes,** Pittsfield
- **Prospect Lake,** Egremont
- **Stockbridge Pond,** Stockbridge
- **Thousand Acre Swamp,** New Marlborough
- **Windsor Pond,** Windsor

expression of their religious devotion to express their reverence to God by making their environment a "heaven on earth." Hancock Shaker Village was the third of 19 Shaker communities established in the US. Its heyday was in 1830, just after the round stone barn was completed, when 300 Shakers lived, worked, and worshipped here. They farmed, sold seeds and herbs, manufactured medicines, and made and sold all types of goods, from boxes to textiles. Eventually their population dwindled, and in 1960 the Shaker ministry in Canterbury, New Hampshire, sold the Hancock property to a group of Pittsfield residents. The following year they opened Hancock Shaker Village as a museum. The entire property consists of 20 restored buildings and is open to the public. Kids learn how the Shakers spun wool, made furniture, cooked, and performed such crafts as basket making. The staff is knowledgeable, dedicated, and enthusiastic; tour guides welcome and encourage questions. The kids really enjoy the reenactment of a Shaker classroom with a costumed staff person acting as the Shaker school-teacher, Shaker suppers during fall weekends, and the Discovery Room, with hands-on activities such as looms for weaving, spinning wheels, and a dress-up corner. Classes are offered in organic gardening and oval box making (prior registration required). The visitor center has changing exhibits from Memorial Day through Oct. The Village Harvest Cafe is open in season.

Other Things to See & Do

Arrowhead, 780 Holmes Rd., Pittsfield; (413) 442-1793; mobydick.org. Open daily Memorial Day through Columbus Day and select dates year-round. Home of Herman Melville, author of *Moby Dick*.

Hebert Arboretum at Springside Park, Route 7, 874 North St., Pittsfield; (413) 443-5348; hebertarboretum.org. Two hundred thirty one acres with native trees, woodland, meadows, formal landscapes, ponds, and streams. Open daily dawn to dusk. **Free.**

Onota Boat Rentals and Livery, on Lake Onota, 463 Pecks Rd., Pittsfield; (413) 442-1724; onotaboat.com. Rent canoes, pedal boats, pontoon boats, and kayaks. Day use only.

Pittsfield State Forest, 1041 Cascade St., Pittsfield; (413) 442-8992; mass.gov/eea/agencies/dcr/massparks/region-west/pittsfield-state-forest-generic.html. Hiking, cross-country skiing, snowmobiling, camping, canoeing, and fishing on more than 10,000 acres. $2 per day use fee.

Wahconah Park and the Pittsfield Sun, 105 Wahconah St., Pittsfield; (413) 236-2961; pittsfieldsuns.pointstreaksites.com. Players are from the Futures Collegiate Baseball League, which draws the top Division 1 players, half of which are from New England. Firework displays after some of the games.

Where to Eat

Bagels Too, 166 North St., Pittsfield; (413) 499-0119. Specializing in bagels and sandwiches, eat in or take out. Open daily from 6 a.m. to 4 p.m. $

Mad Jack's BBQ, 295 North St. Pittsfield; (413) 442-2290; madjacksbbqonline.com. Open Tues to Sat for lunch and dinner, Sun dinner only. Great Southern-style pulled pork and BBQ ribs. Large portions. $–$$

Misty Moonlight Diner, 565 Dalton Ave., Pittsfield; (413) 499-2483; mistydiner .com. Classic diner. Great prices. $–$$

Where to Stay

Hollyhock House, 1130 Barker Rd., Pittsfield; (413) 443-6901; hollyhockbb.com. Charming B&B with lovely gardens, no minimum stay requirements. Ask for the master bedroom. $–$$

White Horse Inn, 378 South St., Routes 7 and 20, Pittsfield; (413) 442-2512; white horsebb.com. Gracious, pristine bed-and-breakfast with mature plantings and well-appointed rooms. Children over 12 are welcome. Full breakfasts are prepared daily. $–$$$

Southern Berkshires

The southern Berkshires have been a haven for the wealthy for well over a century, and the cultural life in the towns of Lenox and Stockbridge reflects their passions: music and theater. During the high season of July and August, kids can see more live performances here than they could in many large cities—and much of it goes on outdoors. There are several excellent museums; gracious historic inns for families with well-behaved children; and parks, wildlife sanctuaries, and decent skiing.

Lenox

The summer home of the Boston Symphony Orchestra, Lenox has become a tourism magnet for lovers of fine music, theater, and dance. Home to wealthy New York aristocrats at the turn of the 20th century, many Lenox mansions are experiencing a rebirth as some of the finest hostelries in the area.

A potpourri of information on Lenox is found at the **Lenox Chamber of Commerce, 18 Main St (inside the Lenox Library)**; (413) 637-3646; lenox.org.

Tanglewood Music Festival (all ages) ♫

297 West St., Lenox; (413) 637-5165, toll-free (888) 266-1200 (box office), or (617) 266-1492 (off-season); bso.org or tanglewood.org. Shed and Hall tickets range from $15 to $125. Lawn tickets are $10 to $30, depending on the event; lawn tickets for children under 12 are free (four per family, unless there is a special guest artist). Children under 5 are not allowed in the Shed or the Hall during concerts. Write ahead for a full summer schedule: Symphony Hall, 301 Massachusetts Ave., Boston, MA 02115.

Tanglewood is the summer home of the Boston Symphony Orchestra, whose members, on summer weekends, perform concerts from the afternoon into the evening, often with the assistance of internationally known musicians and conductors. Most people who come to hear them sit outside on the lawn, arriving early with elaborate picnics and making a day of it. Some devotees choose to sit "inside," which means under the roof of one of the two buildings: the Shed (which is anything but), with seating for more than 5,000, and Seiji Ozawa Hall, with seating for 1,054. If your kids are lucky enough to have music lovers for parents, your entire family will enjoy an outing to Tanglewood, especially on a warm summer evening when the BSO plays the *1812 Overture,* complete with fireworks under the stars.

Tanglewood on Parade

Tanglewood on Parade is a daylong outdoor celebration in midsummer featuring both the BSO and the Boston Pops, finishing with a gala evening performance topped off with fireworks.

Other Things to See & Do

Berkshire Horseback Adventures, 293 Main St., Route 7A, Lenox; (413) 637-9090; berkshirehorseback.net. Open mid-May through Oct. All ability levels, ages 10 and up, and adults weighing less than 250 pounds. Can arrange 1-hour, half-day, or overnight trips.

Berkshire Scenic Railway and the Railway Museum, off Routes 7 and 20, Willow Creek Road, Lenox; (413) 637-2210; berkshirescenicrailroad.org. A restored 1902

Lenox railway station and the Railway Museum. Travel one-way or round-trip from Adams to North Adams. Weekends and holidays only May through Oct.

Berkshire Scenic Treks and Canoe Tours, 320 New Lenox Rd. (off of Rte. 7), Deckers Landing, Lenox; (413) 442-2789; berkshirecanoetours.org. Guided trips on the gentle Housatonic River.

Edith Wharton's Estate and Gardens, The Mount, 2 Plunkett St., Routes 7 and 7A, Lenox; (413) 637-1899; edithwharton.org. House and gardens designed by Edith Wharton open daily May through Nov and weekends through mid-Dec. Look closely— things aren't what they seem.

Frelinghuysen Morris House and 1930 Studio, 92 Hawthorne St., Lenox; (413) 637-0166; frelinghuysen.org. Housing abstract and cubist art of George L. K. Morris and Suzy Frelinghuysen. Open late June to Columbus Day. Call for schedule.

Kennedy Park, Routes 7 and 20, Pittsfield Road, Lenox; (413) 637-3646; lenox.org. Hiking, picnicking, cross-country skiing on 15 miles of groomed trails. Trail maps available.

Pleasant Valley Wildlife Sanctuary, 472 West Mountain Rd., Lenox; (413) 637-0320; massaudubon.org. Seven miles of walking trails with pretty water features. Canoe trips are offered.

Undermountain Farm, 400 Undermountain Rd., Lenox; (413) 637-3365; undermountainfarm.com. Ride on horseback through lush meadows and old-growth forests with mountain views as a backdrop. All levels.

Ventfort Hall, Museum of the Gilded Age, 104 Walker St., Lenox; (413) 637-3206; gildedage.org. Open daily May through Oct (except major holidays). Magnificent mansion undergoing restoration; built by the Morgan family. Set location for the movie *The Cider House Rules.*

Where to Eat

Chocolate Springs Cafe, Route 7, 55 Pittsfield/Lenox Rd., Lenox; (413) 637-9820; chocolatesprings.com. Dessert cafe specializing in pastries, chocolates, ice cream, and hot beverages. Open daily. $

Church Street Cafe, 65 Church St., Lenox; (413) 637-2745; churchstreetcafe.biz. Pasta and grilled fish specialties. Dine under the stars in season Thurs through Mon. $$–$$$

Perfect **Picnics**

Sit on the lawn listening to the fortissimo crescendo of a Tchaikovsky piece while having a gourmet experience to the max courtesy of **Haven Cafe and Bakery,** 8 Franklin St., Lenox; (413) 637-8948, havencafebakery.com. All the fixin's included. Just order 24 hours ahead and bring to your favorite performance. Bravo! Magnifico!

Firefly Restaurant, 71 Church St., Lenox; (413) 637-2700; fireflylenox.com. Call for hours. Recommended by those in the know as fun and family friendly, serving comfort food. Owner studied under James Beard, author of many highly regarded cookbooks. $$–$$$

Rumplestiltzkin's Restaurant at the Village Inn, 16 Church St., Lenox; (800) 253-0917; villageinn-lenox.com. Favorites are the gingerbread pancakes for breakfast and the Shaker-style cranberry pot roast for dinner. Yummy. $$–$$$

Where to Stay

Apple Tree Inn and Restaurant, 10 Richmond Mt. Rd., Lenox; (413) 637-1477; appletree-inn.com. Open year-round. Thirty-four rooms on lovely 22-acre estate. Family friendly, heated pool, tennis, complimentary continental breakfast. Near Tanglewood. Additional charge for cribs. $–$$$$

Harrison House, 174 Main St., Lenox; (413) 637-1746; harrison-house.com. A wide porch beckons you inside this centrally located Victorian charmer. $$–$$$$

Rookwood Inn, PO Box 1717, 11 Old Stockbridge Rd., Lenox; (413) 637-9750 or (800) 223-9750; rookwoodinn.com. Charming and comfortable Victorian-style inn, half a block from Lenox center and 1 mile from Tanglewood. Afternoon tea (iced tea and lemonade in the summer) and a sweet. Children welcome for an additional fee. Cribs available. $$–$$$$

Stockbridge & Lee

Authentic New England charm permeates the town of Stockbridge, which was home to Norman Rockwell and where he drew his inspiration for his scenes of Americana. The Red Lion Inn's long wraparound porch is a town fixture for a welcoming cool summer drink and is a local landmark showcasing typical Rockwellian subject matter. Due north of Stockbridge is Lee, with early 20th-century appeal; its downtown is listed in the National Registry of Historic Areas.

Berkshire Botanical Garden   (all ages)

5 West Stockbridge Rd., Junction of Routes 102 and 183, Stockbridge; (413) 298-3926; berkshirebotanical.org. Open daily May through mid-Oct 9 a.m. to 5 p.m. Admission: $15 for adults, $12 for students and seniors, free for children under 12. Gift shop with snacks.

Berkshire Botanical Garden offers 15 acres of gardens that vary from herbs to lilies to vegetables of all kinds. This is a different kind of green space that young children will enjoy; it's accessible to them because the plants are just their size! Picnicking is encouraged here. Children's summer programs and rotating exhibits.

Norman Rockwell Museum   (all ages)

9 Route 183, Stockbridge; (413) 298-4100; nrm.org. Open daily, 10 a.m. to 5 p.m. May through mid-Nov. Open mid-Nov through Apr, 10 a.m. to 4 p.m. weekdays and 10 a.m. to 5 p.m. weekends and holidays. Extended hours during school vacation periods; closed Thanksgiving, Christmas, and New Year's Day. The studio building is open from May through Oct. Admission: $16 for adults, $10 for students, $5 for ages 6 to 18, free for children under 6. Combination tickets with other museums are available.

Rockwell, chronicler of life in America for seven decades, lived in Stockbridge for the last twenty-five years of his life. The Norman Rockwell Museum holds the largest collection of original Rockwells, including *Saturday Evening Post* favorites depicting American values and strength of character. Changing exhibits feature works of other illustrators. Allow up to 1.5 hours to enjoy this museum, and ask for the family guide upon entry. The museum has special family days, programs, and art activities (the children's activity room is on the lowest level). The grounds are a pleasant spot for a walk or a picnic. Outdoor sculptures are by Rockwell's son Peter.

"Sedgewick **Pie**"

Found alongside Route 102 in Stockbridge is the village cemetery, where, among other local notables, the Sedgewick family is buried. In 1781 Thomas Sedgewick, a lawyer, successfully defended Elizabeth "Mum Bett" Freeman, who became the first slave freed by law in the US. Elizabeth sued and won on the inherent rights of man that "all men [and women!] are created equal." The trial also rendered slavery illegal in Massachusetts. Mum Bett is buried with the Sedgewick family in the "Sedgewick Pie," the family grave plot, so called because family members are buried in a circle with their feet in the center. Why? They hoped that when they sit up on Judgment Day, they will see one another before they see anything else. The Sedgewick plot is toward the rear of the cemetery, surrounded by trees and shrubs.

October Mountain State Forest (all ages)

256 Woodland Rd., Lee; (413) 243-1778; mass.gov/eea/agencies/dcr/massparks/region-west/october-mountain-state-forest-generic.html. Open year-round dawn to dusk. Free except for campsites. Call Reserve America at (877) 422-6762 or visit reserveamerica.com. Camping is seasonal.

Covering more than 16,500 acres, October Mountain is the largest of the state forests in Massachusetts. Most people come here to hike (the Appalachian Trail is one of the best known trails), fish, ATV, dirt-bike, or boat, but in the winter cross-country skiing, snowmobiling, and snowshoeing trails (ungroomed) reign supreme. There are 47 campsites including 3 yurts and a bathhouse with flush toilets and showers. No swimming. *TIP:* Watch out—you are in bear country!

Other Things to See & Do

Animagic—Museum of Animation, Special Effects and Art, 135 Main St., Lee; (413) 243-2051 or (413) 841-6679; mambor.com/animagic/museum.htm. The name says it all! Hands-on activities and workshops for kids. By donation.

Chesterwood, off Route 183, 4 Williamsville Rd., Stockbridge; (413) 298-3579; chesterwood.org. Estate of sculptor Daniel Chester French.

Lee Premium Outlets, 17 Premium Outlet Blvd., Lee; (413) 243-8186 or (877) GO-OUTLETS; premiumoutlets.com/Lee. Savings on designer brands.

Mission House, 19 Main St., Stockbridge; (413) 298-3239, ext. 3000; thetrustees .org. Built in 1742. Home of John Sargent, first missionary to the Mohican Indians.

Naumkeag, 5 Prospect Hill Rd., Stockbridge; (413) 298-3239; thetrustees.org. Joseph Hodges Choate's summer home, designed by Stanford White (of McKim, Mead, and White fame) in the Shingle style. Gardens by Fletcher Steele, famous landscape architect. Open daily late May to mid-Oct 10 a.m. to 5 p.m. Fee.

Winter Activities (Cross-Country & Downhill Skiing, Hiking, or Snowshoeing) Safety Tips

1. **Dress warmly.** Layer your clothes for best protection.

2. **Use a helmet,** no matter what your age.

3. **Carry a backpack with emergency supplies** when cross-country skiing, hiking in winter, or snowshoeing.

4. Use the **buddy system.**

5. **Check for frostbite** on frigid or windy days. If a spot appears, immediately address it by going inside as quickly as possible. Watch for a drop in temperature and changes in the weather. When in doubt, don't go out!

6. **Always have a trail map.** Consider buying an inexpensive compass. Choose appropriate trails for your skill level.

7. **Carry a set of matches,** which could be indispensable.

8. **To help prevent injuries,** stretch out to warm up.

9. **Be fully aware of your surroundings,** and turn off the iPod!

Where to Eat

Elm Street Market, 4 Elm St. (off Main Street), Stockbridge; (413) 298-3634; elm streetmarket.com. Breakfast and lunch only. An old-fashioned general store with a lunch counter serving plain food—eggs, bacon, pancakes, sub sandwiches—and lots of local gossip. $

Joe's Diner, 85 Center St., Lee; (413) 243-9756. Open daily except for Thanksgiving, Christmas and New Year's. year-round. Serving classic diner food—open-faced sand-wiches, fries and gravy, and the like. *The Runaway,* Norman Rockwell's painting of a boy seated next to a policeman on a diner stool was rendered with Joe's Diner as the backdrop. $

Red Lion Inn Dining Room and Tavern, 30 Main St., Stockbridge; (413) 298-5545; redlioninn.com. Open for breakfast, lunch, and dinner. Traditional decor, lots of antiques. Food is contemporary regional cuisine. $–$$$$

Where to Stay

Historic Merrell Inn, 1565 Pleasant St., South Lee; (413) 243-1794 or (800) 243-1794; merrell-inn.com. Original wide-plank floors, fireplaces, and antiques. Breakfasts are delicious and filling. Not appropriate for young children. $–$$$

Red Lion Inn, 30 Main St., Stockbridge; (413) 298-5545; redlioninn.com. Open year-round (very crowded in July and Aug). Treat yourselves to a stay at this quintessential rambling New England inn that many others try to emulate. Rooms vary in size, from quite small to almost palatial. Families will be happiest in the suites with connecting bathroom. The annex buildings tend to be quieter than the main inn building. $–$$$$

Santarella Estate and Gardens, 75 Main Rd. (3.5 miles from Route 102 in Lee), Tyringham; (413) 243-2819; santarella.us. Gingerbread house and gardens of sculptor Sir Henry Hudson Kitson. Stay in the silo tower or four-bedroom house. No breakfast. $$–$$$

Hidden Berkshires

Picturesque towns and villages near the corner of the state bordering Connecti-cut and New York are a bit off the beaten path but not to be overlooked. Local resources such as Butternut Basin and Catamount are nice beginner downhill ski areas for families (see sidebar on "skiing meccas" in this chapter). Many properties managed by the Trustees of Reservations are found here, as well as many wilderness areas.

Mt. Washington State Forest (all ages)

43 East St., Mt. Washington; (413) 528-0330; mass.gov/eea/agencies/dcr/mass parks/region-west/mt-washington-state-forest-generic.html. Directions: Take the Mass Pike to exit 2, take Route 102 West to Stockbridge for about 4.5 miles, then take Route 7 South to Route 23 West for approximately 7.5 miles, take Route 41 South, then take a quick right onto Mt. Washington Road (which becomes East Street) for about 9 miles to the park entrance. Turn into the second parking area. Open daily, dawn to dusk. Free.

Mt. Washington State Forest has over 30 miles of trails. A favorite trail is the hike to Bash Bish Falls, a great name for a great place. From the Massachusetts parking area, you can hike 0.3 mile, then clamber, climb, or walk down a stone stairway to see the 60-foot waterfall that plunges into a churning pool. Unfortunately, you can't swim here—too dangerous—but the boulders that border the falls are still a cool spot to relax on a hot day. The Appalachian Trail crisscrosses the state forest. *TIP:* The hike from the New York parking lot is 0.6 mile but is much less steep!

Great Barrington, Monterey, Housatonic & East Otis

Imagine an area that is mall-free, clean, and quaint—a Norman Rockwell snippet of New England charm. A great source of information on such a place is the **Southern Berkshire Chamber of Commerce,** 362 Main St., Great Barrington, MA 01230; (413) 528-1510 or (800) 269-4825; southernberkshirechamber.com.

Beartown State Forest (all ages)

69 Blue Hill Rd., Monterey; (413) 528-0904; mass.gov/eea/agencies/dcr/massparks/
region-west/beartown-state-forest.html. Open year-round dawn to dusk. Parking
is $5 for day use in season. Call Reserve America for one of the 12 campsites
(877) 227-MASS or visit reserveamerica.com.

Crossed by the Appalachian Trail, the park has good hiking, snowshoeing, ice
fishing, snowmobiling, and cross-country skiing, but its highlight is Benedict
Pond, one of the regions' best swimming holes. On a lazy summer day, the pond
is dotted with boats and fishermen. *Caution:* This state forest was given the
name Beartown for a reason, but sightings could also include deer, bobcat, beaver, and other wildlife.

Monument Mountain Reservation (all ages)

Stockbridge Road, Route 7, Great Barrington; (413) 298-3239, ext. 3020; thetrustees
.org. Open dawn to dusk. Closed in winter. **Free**.

Noted for its easy hiking trails and outcrops of quartzite rock, Monument Mountain has a colorful history. Squaw Peak at the summit got its name from an Indian
maiden who wasn't allowed to marry her lover and plunged to her death from
this spot. A cluster of rocks mark where she landed, put there as a tribute to her
by members of her tribe. It is also the spot where famous writers Herman Melville and Nathaniel Hawthorne were introduced, a meeting arranged by a group
of friends. They enjoyed a picnic, drank champagne, and became lifelong friends.
Owned by the Trustees of Reservations.

Other Things to See & Do

Bidwell House Museum, Art School Road, Monterey; (413) 528-6888; bidwell
housemuseum.org. Historical home of the local vicar. Period antiques, hiking trails,
and gardens. Family programs. Seasonal. Open Thurs through Mon, hourly tours 11
a.m. to 4 p.m. (last tour at 3 p.m.)

Cove Lanes, 109 Stockbridge Rd., Great Barrington; (413) 528-1220; covelanes.com.
Twenty-four lanes of bowling, minigolf, snack bar, and arcades.

Housatonic Riverwalk, downtown Great Barrington, Great Barrington; (413) 528-
3391; gbriverwalk.org. Designated a National Recreation Trail along the Housatonic
River. The W.E.B. Du Bois River Garden Park along the trail is inspired by native son Du
Bois. Visit spring through fall during daylight hours. **Free.**

A Day at the **Beach**

Lake Garfield, Tyringham Rd., Monterey; (413) 528-3831 (be sure to go to Lake Fest)
Lake Mansfield, Lake Mansfield Road, Great Barrington

Mahaiwe Performing Arts Centre, 14 Castle St., Great Barrington, (413) 528-6415 or (413) 528-0100 (box office); mahaiwe.org. Historic theater. View performing acts, speakers, comedy, dance, music, theater, and opera.

Tolland State Forest, 410 Tolland Rd., East Otis; (413) 269-6002; mass.gov/eea/agencies/dcr/massparks/region-west/tolland-state-forest-generic.html. Call Reserve America for one of the 93 campsites (877) 227-MASS or online at reserveamerica .com. Highly regarded for its great fishing, Tolland State Forest has a multitude of water-based activities such as swimming and boating. Other popular recreational opportunities are hiking, mountain biking, cross-country skiing, and snowshoeing.

Upper Housatonic Valley African American Heritage Trail, Great Barrington; (413) 528-3391; africanamericantrail.org. More than 29 sites of historical significance stretching from Massachusets to Connecticut.

Where to Eat

Four Brothers, 100 Stockbridge Rd., Route 7, Great Barrington; (413) 528-9684; fourbrotherspizzainn.com. Part of a chain of Greek pizza places that covers upstate New York and the Berkshires, serving delicious pizza and eggplant dishes. $–$$

Martin's and Staax, 49 Railroad St., Great Barrington; (413) 528-5455; martinsgreat barrington.com; staaxburgers.com. Martin's serves breakfast as well as lunch specials from 6 a.m. to 3 p.m. Try the omelet made with Monterey chèvre, the strawberry-banana pancakes, or the lentil stew. The same location becomes Staax from 5 to 9:30 p.m. and specializes in great burgers. $

Route 7 Grill, Route 7, 999 Main St., Great Barrington; (413) 528-3235; route7grill .com. Open 7 days a week for lunch and dinner. Pig roasts and BBQ specialties. $–$$

TopEvents in the Berkshires

- **Maple Sugaring,** late Feb through Apr, various locations; (413) 628-3912; massmaple.org

- **Butternut Basin Family Fun Day,** Mar, Great Barrington; (413) 528-2000; skibutternut.com

- **Sheep Shearing Days at Hancock Shaker Village,** Apr, Pittsfield; (413) 443-0188; hancockshakervillage.org

- **Berkshire International Film Festival,** May, Great Barrington; (413) 528-8030; biffma.com

- **Barrington Stage Company,** May through Aug, 30 Union St., Pittsfield; (413) 236-8888; barringtonstageco.org

- **Wilco's Solid Sound Music and Art Festival,** June, 87 Marshall St., North Adams; (413) 662-2111; massmoca.org

- **Tanglewood Music Festival,** June through early Sept, Lenox; (413) 637-5165, (617) 266-1492, or (888) 266-1200; bso.org or tanglewood.org

- **Berkshire Theatre Group,** peak season June through early Sept and during the Christmas holidays, Stockbridge and the Colonial Theatre in Pittsfield; (413) 298-5576; berkshiretheatregroup.org

- **Williamstown Theatre Festival,** June through Aug, Williamstown; (413) 597-3400 (box office), (413) 597-3399 (info line); wtfestival.org

- **Jacob's Pillow Dance Festival,** mid-June through late Aug, 358 George Carter Rd., Becket; (413) 243-0745 or (413) 243-9919; jacobspillow.org

- **Berkshire Choral Festival,** July and Aug, 245 North Undermountain Rd., Sheffield; (413) 229-8526; choralfest.org

- **Berkshire Summer Arts Festival,** Butternut Basin, July, Great Barrington; (800) 834-9437; americanartmarketing.com

- **Shakespeare and Company,** year-round, 70 Kimball St., Lenox; (413) 637-3353 (box office) or (413) 637-1199; shakespeare.org

- **Robbins-Zust Family Marionettes,** summer, 29 Main St., St. Paul's Church, Stockbridge; (413) 698-2591 or (413) 822-0663; berkshire web.com/zust

- **Annual Monument Mountain Climb,** first Sun in Aug, Great Barrington; (413) 442-1793; mobydick.org

- **Pittsfield Ethnic Fair,** first Sun in Aug, Pittsfield; (413) 443-6501; downtownpittsfield.com

- **Annual Stockbridge Summer Arts and Crafts Show,** mid-Aug, Main St., Stockbridge; (413) 298-5200; stockbridgechamber.org

- **Country Fair Weekend,** last weekend in Sept, Hancock Shaker Village, Pittsfield; (413) 443-0188; hancockshakervillage.org

- **FreshGrass Festival of Bluegrass and Roots Music,** Sept, 87 Marshall St., North Adams; (413) 662-2111; massmoca.org

- **Apple Squeeze,** fourth weekend of Sept, Village of Lenox; (413) 637-3646; lenox.org

- **Great Josh Billings Runaground,** triathlon, mid-Sept, Great Barrington to Lenox; (413) 637-6913; joshbillings.com

- **Fall Foliage Festival,** late Sept through early Oct, North Adams; (413) 663-3735; berkshirechamber.com or fallfoliageparade.com

- **Spinning and Weaving Week,** early Oct, Hancock Shaker Village; Pittsfield; (413) 443-0188; hancockshakervillage.org

- **Mount Greylock Ramble,** Oct, Adams; (413) 743-8300; celebrate adams.com

- **Berkshire Museum Festival of Trees,** mid-Nov through Dec, 39 South St., Pittsfield; (413) 443-7171; berkshiremuseum.org

- **Mt. Dew Vertical Challenge,** December, Butternut Basin, Route 23, 380 State Rd., Great Barrington; (413) 528-2000; www.skibutternut. com

- **Main Street at Christmas,** first weekend in Dec, Main St., Stockbridge; (413) 298-5200; stockbridgechamber.org

Where to Stay

The Wainwright Inn, 518 South Main St., Great Barrington; (413) 528-2062; wain wrightinn.com. Old fashioned country elegance awaits. Be sure to request a room with a fireplace. $–$$$

Windflower, 684 South Egremont Rd., Great Barrington; (413) 528-2720 or (800) 992-1993; windflowerinn.com. Thirteen rooms, fireplaces, gardens, pool. Children welcome, extra charge for cribs and cots. Full breakfast and afternoon tea and cook-ies. $$–$$$

Ashley Falls

This tiny town near the Connecticut border is the site of two interesting attrac-tions owned by the Trustees of Reservations: the oldest dwelling in Berkshire County, the Ashley House; and Bartholomew's Cobble, a National Natural Landmark.

Ashley House (all ages)

117 Cooper Hill Rd., Ashley Falls; (413) 229-8600 or (413) 298-3239; thetrustees .org. Open summer weekends; please call for tour hours. Admission: $5 for adults, $1 for children, free for under age 5.

Colonel John Ashley House is named for one of the first citizens of the town of Sheffield, which was purchased in 1722 from Native Americans for 460 pounds sterling, three barrels of cider, and 30 quarts of rum. Ashley, a surveyor and lawyer, built his house in 1735. In 1773 the Ashley house was the site of the

signing of the Sheffield Resolve, now considered one of the first "declarations of independence" from Britain. After the Revolutionary War Ashley's slave Elizabeth "Mum Bett" Freeman was freed under the new state of Massachusetts's constitution (see also the "Sedgewick Pie" sidebar in this chapter). Elizabeth successfully sued for her freedom in 1781, and her case was instrumental in ending slavery in the state of Massachusetts. The Ashley House is an anchor site on the Upper Housatonic Valley African American Heritage Trail. The Interpretative Center focuses on the story of Elizabeth Freeman (open year-round). The house features a collection of colonial-era tools and tableware.

Bartholomew's Cobble (all ages)

105 Weatogue Rd. (Route 7A to Rannapo Road to Weatogue Road), Ashley Falls; (413) 229-8600 or (413) 298-3239; thetrustees.org. Museum and information center open daily, 9 a.m. to 4:30 p.m. Closed Sun and Mon Dec through Mar. Trails open from dawn to dusk. Admission: $5 for adults, $1 for children 6 to 12, free for kids under age 6.

Bartholomew's Cobble is an unusual natural and wild, hilly rock garden, studded with limestone outcroppings (the cobbles) and featuring distinctive flora, more than 40 species of ferns, and many wildflowers. Bird watching is excellent here due to the abundant plant life. There are 5 miles of hiking trails (the easygoing Ledges Trail is particularly pleasant for families with younger kids), picnic facilities, nature trails, canoe trips, snowshoe rentals, and a small natural-history museum.

The Pioneer Valley

The Pioneer Valley borders the Connecticut River, which stretches north to south through the state. The river valley is broad and fertile, making it excellent farming country. Many crops are grown here, including corn, tobacco, and sod for golf courses. The area was one of the first regions of inland New England to be secured by English settlers during the turbulent late 17th and early 18th centuries, when they battled Native American tribes and French militia. The town of Deerfield is one of the best sources of information about this early period of colonial history. At Turners Falls there's an interesting underwater view of a fish ladder, where salmon and shad swim during the spring. In Agawam, Six Flags is New England's largest amusement park. It features all the essentials—roller coasters, bumper cars, water rides, and lots of sticky fried food. Finally, for sixteen days every Sept, the **Big E** (the **Eastern States Exposition**), in Springfield, is the biggest annual fair on the East Coast. It's family fare all the way—livestock shows, crafts contests, musical entertainment, a circus, rides, and midways.

The **Greater Springfield Convention and Visitors Bureau,** 1441 Main St., Box 15589, Springfield, MA 01103 (413-787-1548 or 800-723-1548; valleyvisitor .com), has information on the entire Pioneer Valley. For information on Franklin County, contact the **Franklin County Chamber of Commerce,** PO Box 898, 395 Main St., Greenfield, MA 01302; (413) 773-9393 (visitor center) or (413) 773-5463; co.franklincc.org. For information on where to stay in the Five College Area, contact the **Five College Area Bed and Breakfast Association** at fivecollegebb .com. For information on scenic byways in western Massachusetts, click onto bywayswestmass.com.

TopPicks in the Pioneer Valley

- **Historic Deerfield** and **Yankee Candle Company,** Deerfield

- **Six Flags,** Agawam

- **Forest Park,** the **Zoo in Forest Park,** and the **Basketball Hall of Fame,** Springfield

- **Northfield Mountain Recreation** and the *Quinnetukut II,* Northfield and **Kringle Candle Shop,** Bernardston

- **Shelburne Falls** and the **Bridge of Flowers,** Shelburne and Buckland

- **Eastern States Exposition** (The Big E) and the **Storrowton Village Museum,** West Springfield

Mohawk Trail Region

The Mohawk Trail (Route 2) was the first road designated a Scenic Byway. The route is much more dramatic when you drive it from east to west. The trail starts in central Massachusetts and ends on the New York / Massachusetts border. As the road begins climbing into the foothills, look back over the Connecticut River Valley. Contact the **Mohawk Trail Association** at PO Box 1044, North Adams, MA 01247; (413) 743-8127; mohawktrail.com.

Northfield, Bernardston & Gill

The historic village of Bernardston boasts several buildings on the National Register of Historic Places, including the library, the Unitarian Church, the town halls, and the old high school, all of which are on Main Street. The new Kringle Candle Campus is giving Yankee Candle in Deerfield a run for its money. The quaint New England town of Northfield on the banks of the Connecticut River is home to the prestigious private secondary school Northfield / Mt. Hermon. An informative website on the area is visitnorthfieldarea.com.

THE PIONEER VALLEY

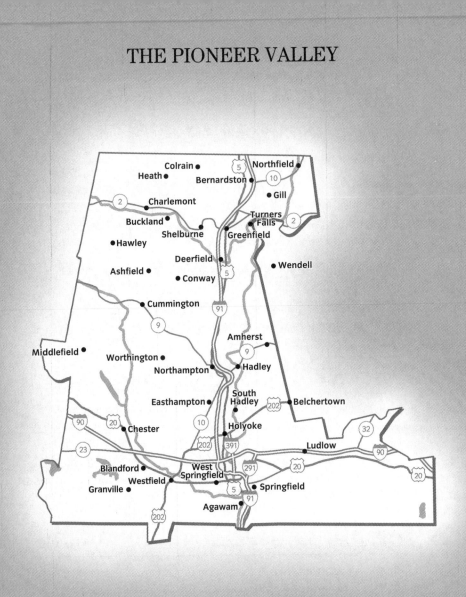

Colrain
Heath
Bernardston
Northfield
5
10
Gill
Charlemont
2
Turners Falls
Buckland
Shelburne
Greenfield
2
Hawley
Deerfield
Wendell
Ashfield
Conway
5
Cummington
91
9
Middlefield
Amherst
9
Worthington
Hadley
Northampton
Easthampton
South Hadley
Belchertown
202
Chester
20
90
Holyoke
10
32
Blandford
202
391
Ludlow
90
23
West Springfield
291
20
20
Westfield
Springfield
Granville
5
Agawam
91
202

Barton Cove and Barton Cove Campground (all ages)

Route 2, Gill; (413) 863-9300 or (800) 859-2960; firstlightpower.com/northfield. Open Memorial Day to Labor Day. Kayak and canoe rentals, which include life vests and paddles, are $25 for 2 hours, $40 for the day. Camping start at $22 per night. There are 31 spacious tent sites; reserve early.

You can rent canoes at Barton Cove (operated by the Northfield Mountain Recreation and Environmental Center) on the Connecticut River. There's a campground with showers (call for reservations and fees). *Warning:* Campers may not bring firewood because of the threat of deadly tree pests to the local trees. Clean wood is available for a fee. A fun camp-over destination is Munn's Ferry (reservations required), reachable by canoe, with primitive facilities and a rustic atmosphere. Barton Cove is home to nesting bald eagles, which can be observed as you paddle by.

Kringle Candle Shop (all ages)

220 South St., Bernardston; (413) 648-3077; kringlecandle.com. The Farm Table (413-648-5200; kringlefarmtable.com), the Chocolate Cottage, and the Country Barn are across the street at 219 South St.

Kringle Candle opened its doors in the sleepy town of Bernardston in 2011. The son of the former owner of Yankee Candle is creating a new candle destination for tourism; the Kringle Candle Shop. Across the street is a large campus featuring a 20,000-square-foot country barn. Found within is a New England country store jam-packed with goods and fragrant candles, a toy loft (Pappa Kringle's Toy Shoppe) with traditional tried and true children's toys and stuffed animals, and a Christmas traditions shop. A separate building houses the Chocolate Cottage, which is full of organic treats for the chocoholic. The Farm Table Restaurant can be pricey, but it's a locavore's dream dining experience (see listing below).

Northfield Mountain Recreation and
Environmental Center (all ages)

99 Millers Falls Rd., off Route 63, Northfield; (413) 659-3714 or (800) 859-2960; first lightpower.com. Cross-country skiing mid-Dec through Mar, Wed through Sun 9 a.m. to 4:30 p.m. Trail fees are $12 for adults, $11 for seniors, $6 for ages 8 to 14, and free for children 7 and under and seniors over 70. Hiking in the off-season is free. The visitor center is open Wed through Sat, 9 a.m. to 4:30 p.m.

Inside Northfield Mountain is Northfield Mountain Power Station and Environmental Center, an enormous power-generating facility that's owned by First

TopEvents in the Pioneer Valley

- **Spaulding Hoop Hall Classic High School Invitational,** Jan, Springfield College, Springfield; (413) 781-6500; hoophall.com

- **Winter Carnival,** Feb, Greenfield; (413) 772-1553; townofgreenfield .org

- **Winterfest,** Feb, Cherry Hill Golf Course, Amherst; (413) 253-0700; winterfestamherst.com

- **American Heritage Chocolate Celebration,** Feb, Historic Deerfield; (413) 774-7476; historic-deerfield.org

- **Holyoke Winter Carnival,** Feb, City-wide, Holyoke; (413) 244-6766; holyokewintercarnival.org

- **Dr. Seuss Birthday,** Mar 2, the Quadrangle, Springfield; (413) 263-6800; springfieldmuseums.org

- **Cardboard Box Race,** end of Mar, Berkshire East, 66 Thunder Mountain Rd., Charlemont; (413) 339-6617; berkshireeast.com

- **NCAA Men's Division II College National Championship,** Mar, Springfield; (413) 781-6500; hoophall.com

- **Holyoke St. Patrick's Day Parade,** Mar, downtown Holyoke; (413) 533-1700; holyokestpatricksparade.com

- **Spring Bulb Show,** Mar, Smith College Lyman Conservatory, Northampton; (413) 585-2740; smith.edu/garden

- **Massachusetts International Festival of the Arts,** Mar, spring, fall, winter, Amherst, Northampton, Holyoke, and Springfield; (800) 224-MIFA; passportholyoke.org

- **Patriots' Day Muster and Parade,** Apr (Patriots' Day), 80 Old Main St., Route 5/The Street, Deerfield; (413) 774-5581; historic-deerfield .org

- **Pentathalon,** Apr, Berkshire East, Charlemont; (413) 339-6617; berkshireeast.com

- **Paradise City Arts Festival,** May and Oct, Northampton Fairgrounds, 54 Ferry Rd., Northampton; (800) 511-9725; paradisecity arts.com

- **Bone Frog Challenge,** May, Berkshire East, Charlemont; (413) 339-6617; berkshireeast.com or bonefrogchallenge.com

- **Fish-spawning migrations,** May/June, Holyoke Dam and Turners Falls; (413) 659-3714; firstlightpower.com/northfield

- **Children's Book Festival,** June, Eric Carle Museum, Amherst; (413) 658-1100; carlemuseum.org

- **Shelburne Falls Riverfest,** June, Shelburne Falls; (413) 625-2544; shelburnefalls.com

- **Taste of Amherst,** June, town common, Amherst; (413) 253-0700; tasteofamherst.com

- **Kidsfest,** June, Six Flags of New England, Agawam; (413) 786-9300 or (800) 370-7488; sixflags.com/newengland

- **Star Spangled Springfield,** July, Memorial Bridge, Springfield; (413) 733-3800; spiritof springfield.org

- **Green River Festival,** July, Greenfield; (413) 773-5463; greenriverfestival .com

- **Indian Motocycle Rally,** mid-July, the Quadrangle, Springfield; (413) 263-6800; springfieldmuseums.org

- **Annual Glasgow Lands Scottish Festival,** mid-July, Look Park, 300 North Main St., Northampton; (413) 862-8095; glasgowlands.org

Tap into **This!**

Many of the maple-sugaring houses in the Pioneer Valley offer tours and dining facilities. For a copy of the *Massachusetts Maple Producers Directory*, contact the **Massachusetts Maple Producers Association,** Watson-Spruce Corner Road, Ashfield, MA 01330; (413) 628-3912; massmaple.org.

Light Power Resources. Atop the mountain is a water reservoir that's used to generate power when consumer demand exceeds supply from other power sources. The property is open to the public for cross-country skiing, hiking, picnicking, mountain biking, snowshoeing, and wildlife viewing. The altitude makes for fairly consistent snow on the 25 miles of cross-country skiing trails (which are groomed regularly) and 6 miles of dedicated snowshoeing trails, which in warm weather are used for hiking. Call (800) 859-2960 for current snow conditions. The lodge offers ski and snowshoe rentals and lessons, a heated lounge, and outdoor picnic tables with a fire pit. *TIP:* People who own snowshoes can snowshoe for **free.**

Quinnetukut II (all ages)

Route 63 (2 miles north of Route 2), Northfield; (413) 659-3714 or (800) 859-2960; firstlightpower.com/northfield. Operates Fri through Sun, late June to mid-Oct (call for a schedule). Admission: $12 for adults, $11 for seniors 55 and over, $6 for children under 14. Reservations are highly recommended. Pick up your tickets 15 minutes prior to departure at the Northfield Mountain Visitor Center, which is across the street from the Riverview Pavilion picnic area.

The *Quinnetukut II* takes up to 44 passengers on a 90-minute, 12-mile round-trip cruise on the Connecticut River between Northfield and Gill. Knowledgeable guides comment on the flora, fauna, and history of the areas. It's a birder's paradise. On a recent trip bird sightings included two eagles, swans, an osprey, a blue heron, and an egret. The highlight of the trip is through the French King Gorge, a spectacular sight. Boats leave from the River View picnic area, across from the entrance to First Light Power Resources. *TIP:* In the fall the river can be much colder than land. You may want to consider taking along hats, gloves, a heavy coat and a blanket.

Other Things to See & Do

Wendell State Forest, 392 Montague Rd., Wendell; (413) 659-3797; mass.gov/eea/
agencies/dcr/massparks/region-central/wendell-state-forest. State park with 10-acre
Ruggles pond, a great place for swimming. Activities at the park also include cross-
country skiing, mountain biking, hiking, and field sports.

Where to Eat

The Farm Table, 219 South St., Bernardston; (413) 648-5200; kringlefarmtable.com.
Open for lunch daily, dinner Thurs through Sat (Sun during ski season), and Sunday
brunch. Locally sourced food and the restaurant is a "green" environment. Considered the best new restaurant in the Pioneer Valley. Eclectic decor; a mix of antique
farm tools and chandeliers made from old bottles with an elegant farmhouse feel.
Children's menu. $–$$$

Four Leaf Clover, Route 5, 19 South St., Bernardston; (413) 648-9514. Family-
oriented restaurant with a U-shaped luncheon counter with a couple of tables scat-
tered about; open for breakfast, lunch, and dinner year-round. $–$$

Gill Tavern, 326 Main Rd., Gill; (413) 863-9006; gilltavern.com. Diverse menu ranging from shepherd's pie to duck confit. Open Wed through Sun for dinner and Sun for
brunch. Reservations highly recommended. $–$$

Where to Stay

Centennial House, Route 63, 94 Main St., Northfield; (413) 498-5921; thecentennial
house.com. Federal-style home with a large rolling lawn, 6 bedrooms (2 are suites
with an extra bedroom) with fireplaces, and brass or sleigh beds; complimentary full
breakfast. Cookies and cocoa upon check-in. No cribs. $–$$$

The Inn at Crumpin-Fox, 71 Northfield Rd., Bernardston; (413) 648-9131; crumpin
foxinn.com. Renovated in 2010, 29-room inn, motel style, sited on 23 acres with ter-
raced flower gardens about a mile from the Crumpin-Fox Golf Course. Family friendly
for those on a budget. Considered a "green" inn. Continental breakfast included in the
room rate. $–$$

Greenfield & Turners Falls

Longview Tower, the tallest steel observation tower in the state, is found along the Mohawk Trail on Route 2 in Greenfield with observation decks that offer views of Massachusetts, Vermont, and New York. Hurricane Irene forced its closure in August of 2011, but repairs should be completed soon. The **Upper Pioneer Valley Visitor Center** (413-773-9393) is open daily year-round from 8:30 a.m. to 6 p.m.; it's a wonderful full-service information center located in Greenfield at 18 Miner St. (at the intersection of I-91 and Route 2). From Greenfield, drive through the town of Montague to reach Turners Falls, the site of the first dam on the Connecticut River.

Cross-Country **Skiing Meccas**

Maple Corner Farm, 794 Beech Hill Rd., Granville; (413) 357-8829 or (413) 357-6697 (snow conditions); xcskimass.com/ski-areas/ about-maple-corner-farm or hidden-hills.com. Open Mon through Fri 10 a.m. to 5 p.m., weekends and holidays 9 a.m. to 5 p.m. A seventh-generation family working farm since 1812; 500 acres of varied terrain with more than 16 miles of groomed trail for all levels of skiers and snowshoers (separate snowshoe trails). Snowshoe and ski rentals lessons, snack bar in fireplaced lodge.

Northfield Mountain Cross-country Ski Area, off Route 63, North-field; (413) 659-3713 or (800) 859-2960 (ski conditions); xcskimass .com or firstlightpower.com. Offers 25 miles of trails. Rentals available. See Northfield Mountain Power Station and Environmental Center.

Stump Sprouts Guest Lodge and Cross Country Ski Center, 64 West Hill Rd., Hawley; (413) 339-4265; stumpsprouts.com. Twenty miles of groomed trails on 450 acres. Instruction and rentals; guided tours available by arrangement. Simple rooms accommodating two to five people can be reserved, but bring your own linens (lodging includes meals). The trails are open weekends, Monday holidays, and school vacations 9 a.m. to sunset.

Cruising Down the River

The Connecticut River Greenway State Park extends from the border with Connecticut (Chicopee) to the New Hampshire/Vermont border. The park encompasses six public boat accesses to the Connecticut River, the Mount Sugarloaf Observation Area, the Norwottuck Rail Trail, and public lands acquired to create a public greenway along the Connecticut River. The gentlest portion of the river for kayaking and canoeing is from Turners Falls in Montague south for 15 miles to Hatfield. The Connecticut River was designated one of fourteen American Heritage Rivers in 1998. For further information, call (413) 586-8706 or visit mass.gov/eea/agencies/dcr/massparks/region-west/connecticut-river-greenway-state-park.html.

Turners Falls Fishway Ladder (all ages)

100 First St. (off Avenue A), left into parking lot, Turners Falls; (413) 659-3714 or (800) 859-2960; firstlightpower.com/northfield. Open mid-May through mid-June, Wed through Sun, 9 a.m. to 5 p.m. Interpreter on-site. Free.

Owned and maintained by First Light Power, the draw here is the underground/under-river viewing facility that allows kids to watch sea lamprey, shad, and other anadromous fish (those that migrate upriver from the sea to breed in freshwater) pass by a window on their way to their favorite spawning grounds upstream. The facility is on the south side of the dam, just upstream of the bridge; look for the sign. Unity Park, just above the dam, is a nice spot for a picnic; there's a playground here, too.

Other Things to See & Do

Great Falls Discovery Center, 2 Ave. A, Turners Falls; (413) 863-3221; greatfalls discoverycenter.org. The Discovery Center focuses on the history of the Connecticut River and its habitat. Outdoor park and play center with views of the canal. Picnic tables.

Old Greenfield Village, 386 Mohawk Trail, Route 2, PO Box 1124, Greenfield; (413) 774-7138. Open by appointment. Wayne Morse's collection of memorabilia and antiques re-creates a New England Village of 1895.

The Covered Bridges of Franklin County!

Scenic covered bridges of interest:

- Colrain—**Arthur Smith Covered Bridge,** Route 112, Main Road, over the North River
- Charlemont—**Bissel Covered Bridge** on Route 8A
- Conway—**Burkeville Covered Bridge** over the South River off Route 116
- Greenfield—**Greenfield Pumping Station Covered Bridge** over the Green River on Leydon Road

Pioneer Valley Symphony, 91 Main St., Greenfield; (413) 773-3664; pvso.org. No concert hall of their own, but they play at different regional venues.

Poet's Seat Tower, Mountain Road and Maple Street, Greenfield; (413) 773-5463; townofgreenfield.org. The tower was named for Frederick Goddard Tuckerman, a poet of sonnets. Hiking, birding (eagles and hawks have been spotted), and views. **Free.**

Where to Eat

Greenfield Grille, 30 Federal St./Route 5, Greenfield; (413) 376-4772; greenfieldgrille .com. Great presentation, wonderful food, large portions. Open Tues through Sun for dinner and Tues through Fri for lunch. Sunday brunch. $–$$

Hope and Olive, 44 Hope St., Greenfield; (413) 774-3150; hopeandolive.com. Fresh locally produced fare uniquely presented and reasonably priced in a philosophically green restaurant. $–$$

Where to Stay

Brandt House Country Inn, 29 Highland Ave., Greenfield; (413) 774-3329; brandt house.com. Estate with 9 guest rooms (some with fireplaces), pretty gardens, billiards, and a wraparound porch. Well-behaved dogs are allowed with prior notice. Rates include breakfast. Children 12 and up. $–$$$

House on the Hill, 330 Leyden Rd., Greenfield; (413) 774-2070; thehouseonthehill bnb.com. Cozy and tasteful rooms. Great wraparound porch with lovely views of the valley. Full breakfast made with locally sourced food. Cribs are available. $–$$

Poetry Ridge Bed and Breakfast, 55 Stone Ridge Ln., Greenfield; (413) 773-5143; rkotours.com. Sitting on 11 acres, the guest rooms were named after famous poets. A total of 7 fireplaces throughout the inn, a dedicated billiards room, hot breakfasts. Trail leading to Poet's Seat Tower. Children over 10 please. $$–$$$

West Winds Bed and Breakfast, 151 Smead Hill Rd., Greenfield; (413) 774-4025; westwindsinn.com. Seven rooms, all attractively decorated in an upscale traditional style with delightful views (especially during foliage season) and extensive grounds (5.5 acres). Children 12 and over. Full breakfast included with lodging. $–$$

Shelburne, Buckland & Charlemont

Not far off of Route 2 and the Mohawk Trail is the village of Shelburne Falls, a business district shared by the towns of Shelburne and Buckland. At Shelburne Falls's Bridge of Flowers, more than 500 varieties of flowers are planted and cultivated. More than 22,000 people a year enjoy this restorative oasis of beauty from the first blush of tulips in the spring through autumn, when mums are the featured plant. Shelburne Falls is considered one of the hundred best small art towns in America; see artists at work creating quilts, glass objects, pottery, and weavings. Be on the lookout for Josh Simpson, a nationally known glass artist and the owner of the **Salmon Falls Art Gallery** (salmonfalls gallery.com). One of Josh's signature themes is paperweights that seem to have a planetary influence, with smaller globes floating inside the larger glass that is encasing them. Maybe his creativity is influenced by his wife, former astronaut Cady Coleman. Hollywood has filmed three movies here recently: Paramount's *Labor Day,* Warner Bros.' *The Judge,* and Char-lemont Pictures's *Then There Was.* The **Shelburne Falls Village Information Center** (open May 1 through Octo-ber 31) can be reached at 75 Bridge St.; (413) 625-2544; shelburnefalls.com.

TopEvents in the Pioneer Valley

August–December

- **Annual Iron Bridge Dinner,** Aug, Shelburne Falls; (413) 625-2544; shelburnefalls.com

- **Greenfield Lightlife Triathalon,** Aug, Greenfield; (413) 772-1553; greenfield-triathlon.com

- **The Great Holyoke Block Party,** Aug, Holyoke City Hall, Holyoke; (413) 322-5510; holyoke.org/events/the-great-holyoke-block-party or passportholyoke.com

- **The Big E (Eastern States Exposition),** Sept, West Springfield; (413) 737-2443; thebige.com

- **Apple Harvest and Crafts,** Festival, Sept, Amherst Town Common, Amherst; (413) 253-0700; amherstarea.com

- **Basketball Hall of Fame Enshrinement,** Sept, Springfield; (413) 231-5514 or (413) 231-5511; hoophall.com

- **History on the Move Car Show,** Sept, the Quadrangle, Springfield; (413) 263-6800; springfieldmuseums.org

- **Old Deerfield Craft Fair,** Sept and Nov, Deerfield; (413) 774-7476; deerfield-craft.org

- **Volleyball Hall of Fame Induction Ceremony,** Oct, Volleyball Hall of Fame, Holyoke; (413) 536-0926; volleyhall.org

- **Blues and BBQ Festival,** Oct, Greenfield; (413) 772-1553; riverside bluesandbbq.com

- **Ashfield Fall Festival,** Oct, Rte. 116 (Main St), Ashfield; ashfieldfall festival.org

- **Frightfest at Six Flags New England,** Oct, Agawam; (413) 786-9300 or (800) 370-7488; sixflags.com/newengland

- **Festival of the Hills,** Oct, Main Street, Conway; (413) 522-7374; festivalofthehills.com

- **Greenfield Lightlife Triathalon,** Aug, Greenfield; (413) 772-1553; greenfield-triathlon.com

- **Trolleyfest,** Oct, Sheburne Falls Trolley Museum, Shelburne Falls; (413) 625-9443; sftm.org

- **Spooky Safari,** Oct, the Zoo in Forest Park, Springfield; (413) 733-2251; forestparkzoo.com

- **Haunted Train Ride,** Oct, Look Park, Northampton; (413) 584-5457; lookpark.org

- **Cider Day,** Nov, Shelburne /Buckland Community Ctr, Shelburne Falls; (413) 773-5463; ciderday.org or franklincc.org

- **Chrysanthemum Show,** Nov, Smith College, Lyman Conservatory, Northampton; (413) 585-2740; smith.edu/garden

- **Moonlight Magic,** late Nov, Shelburne Falls; (413) 625-2544; shelburne falls.com

- **Tower Square Parade of Big Balloons,** Nov, Main Street, Springfield; (413) 733-3800; spiritofspringfield.org

- **Lighting of the Quadrangle,** late Nov, the Quadrangle, Springfield; (413) 263-6800; springfieldmuseums.org

- **Reenactment of a Colonial Thanksgiving,** day after Thanksgiving, Historic Deerfield; (413) 774-5581; historic-deerfield.org

- **Winter Wonderland Holiday Lights,** late Nov to beginning of Jan, Look Park, Northampton; (413) 584-5457; lookpark.org

- **Santa's Arrival,** early Dec, Holyoke Heritage State Park, Holyoke; (413) 534-1723; mass.gov/eea/agencies/dcr/massparks/region-west/holyoke-heritage-state-park

- **First Night Jr.,** New Year's Eve, Holyoke Heritage State Park, Holyoke; (413) 534-1723; mass.gov/eea/agencies/dcr/massparks/region-west/holyoke-heritage-state-park

- **Santa's Trains,** mid-Dec to Christmas Eve, Look Memorial Park, 300 North Main St., Route 9, Florence; (413) 584-5457; lookpark.org

- **Bright Nights,** end of Nov to early Jan, Forest Park, Springfield; (413) 733-2251 or (413) 733-3000; spiritofspringfield.org or bright nights.org

Berkshire East (all ages)

66 Thunder Mountain Rd., Charlemont; (413) 339-6617; berkshireeast.com. Go to their website for schedules and prices. Open daily mid-Dec through mid-Mar. Night skiing is Wed through Sat.

Day and night skiing and snow-tubing opportunities abound here. Berkshire East is where a lot of skiers learn the ropes. Berkshire East has a 1,180-foot vertical drop, a base lodge to warm up in, 5 lifts, and 45 trails ranging from beginner to double black diamond all dumping down into the same base so that you can never lose the kids! For the snowboard enthusiast in your family, try the half-pipe and terrain park. Lessons and rentals are available. There is a cafeteria on the premises. For off-season fun, try the **Zipline Canopy Tour** (berkshirezip.com), which operates on a passive gravity system. Open mid-Apr through Oct. There are weight and age limits (see website) for each of the 3 tours, varying in difficulty and adrenaline rush. Reservations are strongly recommended.

Bridge of Flowers (all ages)

Entrances on Water Street (in the center of town), Shelburne Falls, and State Street in Buckland; (413) 625-2544; shelburnefalls.com. The bridge is in full bloom from late Apr to Oct. Free parking.

In the riverside village of Shelburne Falls, a quick detour off Route 2, see the Bridge of Flowers, which spans the Deerfield River. It's a 400-foot retired trolley bridge that has been planted with flower beds. The best time for viewing the bridge is in July and Aug. Don't miss the nearby Salmon Falls (former Native American fishing grounds) with the country's most glacial potholes, which were formed by retreating ice from the glaciation period. On either side of the falls are the historic mills that once used the falls for power.

Deerfield Valley Canopy Tours (10 years old and up)

7 Main St., Charlemont; (800) 532-7483; deerfieldzipline.com. Open Apr through mid-Nov, weather permitting. Cost: $94 per person (must weigh between 70 and 250 pounds).

Deerfield Canopy Tours are part of Zoar Outdoor, and they pride themselves on being the first canopy tour in New England. Deerfield Valley Canopy Tours are completely built in the trees, distinguishing them from other zip-lining companies that offer a more adrenaline-based experience versus a nature and environment focus. Their guides not only teach you how to use the equipment, properly ride the zips, and to hand-brake, they also offer interpretative information about the canopy and your surroundings. The hand-braking system allows guests to participate more fully in the experience than the passive braking system. Deerfield Valley Canopy tours have 11 zip lines, 2 sky bridges, and 3 rappels. Each group of 8 has 2 guides with them to maximize their experience as well as their safety. The course is fun for all levels. Set aside 3 hours for the Deerfield Valley Canopy Tour.

Shelburne Falls Trolley Museum (all ages)
14 Depot St., Shelburne Falls (cross the Shelburne Falls bridge into Buckland); (413) 625-9443; sftm.org. Open Memorial Day weekend through Oct, weekends and holidays, 11 a.m. to 5 p.m. Open 1 to 5 p.m. on Mon in July and Aug. Price: $4 for adults, $2 for children 6 to 12, free for 5 and under.

The museum is dedicated to preserving the Shelburne Falls and Colrain Railway Combine No. 10, which served the valley for thirty years; over the years other cars have been added to the collection. The route crossed the Deerfield River over the trolley bridge, which has since been converted to the present-day Bridge of Flowers, and delivered passengers, freight, and mail. Still in operation, the combine makes a short journey around its new home in the Buckland Rail Freight Yard. Rides are also given on an old-fashioned pump car, and a caboose is open for exploration. Inside the visitor center there are wooden and electric trains for children to play with, early 1900s pictures of the Shelburne Falls and the trolley, and a gift shop with railroad memorabilia. Allocate about 45 minutes for your visit. *TIP:* For signed copies of Marie Betts Bartlett's book *The Little Yellow Trolley Car,* go to Boswell's Books (see below). This is a great picture book for ages 2 to 8.

Hail to the **Sunrise**

Just beyond Charlemont on Route 2 is a 900-pound bronze statue of a Mohawk Indian chief with his arms and face lifted to the east in praise to the Great Spirit. The piece is called *Hail to the Sunrise* and it's the most photographed statue on the Mohawk Trail. It's one of many statues that you'll see along the trail.

Climbing Up a Wall

Kids ages 2 to 15 who love outdoor challenges will love the vertical challenge of rock climbing or zip lining with **Zoar Outdoor,** Mohawk Trail, 7 Main St., Route 2, Charlemont; (413) 339-4010 or (800) 532-7483; zaroutdoor.com.

Other Things to See & Do

Boswell's Books, 10 Bridge St., Shelburne Falls; (413) 625-9362; boswellsbooks .net. Local favorite for bookworms; cuddle up with Boswell the cat.

Double Edge Theatre, 948 Conway Rd., Ashfield; (413) 628-0277; doubledge theatre.org. Based on their rural 105-acre Farm Center, the internationally acclaimed Double Edge Theatre ensemble creates indoor performances that tour nationally and around the world as well as site-specific indoor/outdoor Summer Spectacles based on classic works of literature (past productions include *The Three Musketeers* and *The Illustrious Don Quixote*), which have drawn thousands of visitors to the Farm Center from around the country.

Mohawk Trail Concerts, 175 Main St., Federated Church, Route 2, Charlemont; (413) 625-9511; mohawktrailconcerts.org. Music program late June to July.

Mohawk Trail State Forest, Route 2, Charlemont; (413) 339-5504; mass.gov/eea/ agencies/dcr/massparks/region-west/mohawk-trail-state-forest.html. Comprises 6,457 acres of old-growth forest and the tallest pine trees in New England. Camping and cabin rentals (contact Reserve America at 877-422-6762 or reserveamerica.com), hiking, fishing, nature programs, swimming, and a good picnic area.

Where to Eat

Baker's Oven Bistro, 24 Bridge St., Shelburne Falls; (413) 489-3110; thebakersoven shelburne.com. Open Thurs through Sun 11 a.m. to 9 p.m. Features sandwiches, burgers, pizzas, and main dishes presented with flair. Local farms and orchards are the main source of the ingredients used, and breads are all baked on the premises. Kids' menu. $–$$

Gould's Sugarhouse, 587 Mohawk Trail, Route 2, Shelburne; (413) 625-6170; goulds-sugarhouse.com. Open daily Mar and Apr and Sept and Oct, 8:30 a.m. to 2 p.m. Good breakfast or lunch stop along the Mohawk Trail, especially if you're into pancakes, waffles, corn fritters, and syrup. $

McCusker's Market and Deli Cafe, 3 State St., Buckland; (413) 625-9411; green fieldsmarket.coop. Open daily 7 a.m. to 7 p.m. Natural gourmet food, including baked goods, and extensive health-food store. Tables are in the rear. $

Where to Stay

Bird's Nest Bed and Breakfast, 2 Charlemont Rd., Buckland; (413) 625-9523; birdsnestbnb.com. TripAdvisor 2013 winner of a certificate of excellence. Historical home filled with family heirlooms and recent acquisitions. Rooms named after birds. Country breakfasts. $$

The Dancing Bear Guest House Bed and Breakfast, 22 Mechanic St., Shelburne Falls; (413) 625-9281; dancingbearguesthouse.com. Historic Moses W. Merrell Victorian home with 3 guest rooms (1 with en suite bath; the rest of the rooms are shared bath). Kid friendly, children of all ages welcome. Family-style full breakfasts are served daily. Minutes to local attractions. $–$$

Deerfield

Deerfield has survived more than just 300 years of farming in New England's unpredictable climate. In 1675 the Bloody Brook Massacre battle of King Philip's War resulted in the deaths of sixty-seven Deerfield residents. In 1704 a band of French and Indian soldiers attacked, killing forty-nine of the inhabitants and carrying off 111 more to Quebec. Miraculously, a few of these people survived and were able to make their way back to Deerfield. Historic Deerfield has an interesting story to reveal about the history and lifestyles of a struggling inland settlement. No longer a struggling settlement today, the Yankee Candle Company of Deerfield is a major destination in the Pioneer Valley. For more information on Deerfield, visit deerfieldattractions.com.

Historic Deerfield (ages 6 and up)

80A Old Main St., Route 5/The Street, Deerfield; (413) 774-5581; historic-deerfield
.org. All of the museum's houses are open daily mid-Apr through Dec, 9:30 a.m.
to 4:30 p.m.; closed Thanksgiving and Christmas. Open weekends Jan through
mid-Apr from 9:30 a.m. to 4:30 p.m. for the Flynt Center of Early New England Life
(although the museum houses can be toured by appointment). Admission: $16 for
adults, $5 for children 6 to 17, 5 and under are **free.**

Eleven of the restored houses along the Street form an association called Historic Deerfield. These spectacular examples of 18th- and 19th-century architecture, design, furnishings, and lifestyles will probably be most interesting to older
kids, who can appreciate the work that has gone into these houses, as well as
the rich history of the town and its inhabitants. Don't try to see more than three
houses in one day; they're all worth visiting, but more than three would be too
much for any but the most ardent historic preservationist, let alone a family with
children. The Flynt Center of Early New England Life is a modern museum building with two floors of exhibits that include the Helen Geier Flynt Textile Gallery
on Fiber Arts that is ever-changing. On weekends and one month of the summer,
there are activities for families (the special activity days are found on their website). A children's history workshop is offered periodically off-season and during
winter vacations. Don't miss the Patriots' Day Muster and Parade.

Up the Creek without a Paddle

Contact these tour companies for whitewater rafting and kayaking
adventures and calmer river trips on the Deerfield, West, and Millers
Rivers. All tours provide lunch, offer instruction and equipment, and
have a variety of trips suited for the neophyte and the old hand alike.

- **Crab Apple Whitewater,** Mohawk Trail, 2056 Mohawk Trail, Route
  2, Charlemont; (800) 553-7238; crabapplewhitewater.com

- **Moxie Outdoor Adventures,** Mohawk Trail, South River Rd., Charlemont: (207) 663-2231 or (800) 866-6943; moxierafting.com

- **Zoar Outdoor,** Mohawk Trail, Route 2, 7 Main St., PO Box 245,
  Charlemont, MA 01339; (800) 532-7483; zaroutdoor.com

Set the **Mood**

Set the mood before going to Deerfield with these books geared toward children in grades five through seven:

- *The Boy Captive in Canada* by Mary Wells Smith
- *The Boy Captive in Old Deerfield* by Mary Wells Smith
- *The Ransom of Mercy Carter* by Caroline Cooney

For younger children, pick up a copy of the *Cobblestone* magazine on Deerfield in the gift shop at Historic Deerfield.

Magic Wings Butterfly Conservatory and Gardens
(all ages)

281 Greenfield Rd., Routes 5 and 10, South Deerfield; (413) 665-2805; magicwings .com. Open daily year-round from 9 a.m. to 5 p.m.; until 6 p.m. from Memorial Day to Labor Day. Closed Thanksgiving and Christmas. Admission is $14 for adults, $12 for seniors, $10 for children ages 3 through 17, **free** for kids under age 3. Admission packages are available. Monarch's Restaurant, with family-friendly prices, serves breakfast, lunch, and dinner; check the website for hours. *TIP:* The last admission is a half hour prior to closing.

The 8,000-square-foot Magic Wings conservatory is planted with exotic vegetation and holds within it butterflies that are both native and tropical. Imagine if you will, hundreds of butterflies (more than 4,000) silently fluttering by, unaware of their grace and beauty and the delight that they bring to all ages. Do not be surprised if a butterfly alights upon you; a truly magical moment. The grounds have 1.5 acres of gardens with native trees and flowers along with quiet little resting places to view nature's bounty. Reptiles, birds, and bugs are recent additions. Children's events and activities are held weekly. This is a great place to hold a kid's birthday party. Full-service restaurant and food court.

The Yankee Candle Company (all ages)

25 Greenfield Rd., Route 5, South Deerfield; (413) 665-2929 or (877) 636-7707 (special event hotline); yankeecandle.com/about-yankee-candle/visit-our-flagship-stores/t. Open daily 9:30 a.m. to 6 p.m.; closed Thanksgiving and Christmas. Admission to all is **free.**

The Yankee Candle Company began in 1969 in a kitchen here, and the rest is history—at least, the company thinks so. At this complex that seems to sprout new buildings every season, you can dip your own candles, visit a Bavarian Christmas village (a toy factory with Santa and Mrs. Claus) where it snows every day every 4 minutes, explore the Wax Works with hands-on wax activities, and tour a museum that demonstrates candle making through history. Of course, selling candles is the main focus of the Yankee Candle Company, and there's a huge variety at the Candle Mountain lodge, which has a bakery, a fudgery, and an animatronics band. Chandler's Restaurant is on-site if you get hungry. Call for a schedule of special events. My family's favorites are the Teddy Bear Tea, the Witches' Ball, the Waxworks Party, the kids' cooking classes, the kids' New Year's Party, and the Fancy Nancy Luncheon.

Other Things to See & Do

Old Deerfield Country Store, 480 Greenfield Rd., Routes 5 and 10, Deerfield; (413) 774-3045; olddeerfieldcountrystore.com. Polished pottery, jewelry, kitchen gadgets, Byers Carolers, toys, candy, and "made in Deerfield" products.

Where to Eat

Champney's Restaurant at the Deerfield Inn, 81 Old Main St., Deerfield; (413) 774-5587 or (800) 926-3865; champneysrestaurant.com. Historic setting for delicious regional dishes. Kids' menu. $$–$$$$

Chandler's Restaurant at Yankee Candle, 25 Greenfield Rd., Yankee Candle Village, Routes 5 and 10, South Deerfield; (413) 665-1277; yankeecandle.com/about-yankee-candle/visit-our-flagship-store/chandlers-restaurant/t. Open for lunch and candlelit dinner Wed through Sun and Mon and Tues for lunch. Traditional yet with a wide range to suit any palate. No dress code. Award-winning kids' menu. $–$$$

Wolfie's, 52 South Main St., South Deerfield; (413) 665-7068. Open for lunch and dinner year-round, Mon through Sat, 11 a.m. to 9:30 p.m. Great sandwiches, huge seafood platters, and a calm atmosphere. Good food for a reasonable price. $–$$

Where to Stay

Deerfield Inn, 81 Old Main St., Deerfield; (413) 774-5587 or (800) 926-3865; deerfield inn.com. With only 24 rooms in this historic setting, make your reservation early (Deerfield Academy parent weekends tend to sell out the inn). Room rates include afternoon tea, a three-month membership to Historic Deerfield, and a country breakfast. $$–$$$

The Five College Area

Families with near-college-age children will find lots to do here, especially if the kids are interested in visiting any of the five colleges—the University of Massachusetts (which everyone calls UMass), Amherst College, Hampshire College, Smith College, and Mount Holyoke College. Campus tours are given several times a week at most colleges, and each has a lovely campus with a different flavor.

Amherst

This quintessential college town is home to **Amherst College, Hampshire College,** and the **University of Massachusetts.** Amherst has everything you would expect a charming New England town to have: a center common, assorted architectural styles from different periods, and a rural setting (until you drive around Route 9 or the university!). College towns attract literati, so it should be no surprise that Amherst boasts two well-known poets: the beloved Robert Frost, who taught poetry at Amherst College, and Emily Dickinson, who was a lifelong resident. The **Amherst Area Chamber of Commerce** is at 28 Amity St., Amherst, MA 01002, and can be contacted at (413) 253-0700; amherst area.com. The chamber shares space with the **Hampshire County Regional Tourism Council,** (413) 253-0700; visithampshirecounty.com.

Emily Dickinson Museum, The Homestead, and The Evergreens (all ages)

280 Main St., Amherst; (413) 542-8161; emilydickinsonmuseum.org. Open Mar to mid-Dec. Check website for schedule and to reserve your spot ahead of time if you are a group of six or more. Admission: dependent upon the tour that you choose.

The Belle of Amherst

Beautifully illustrated and riveting children's bedtime storybooks on Emily Dickinson are *Emily* (Bantam/Doubleday) by Michael Bedard, illustrated by Barbara Cooney, and *The Mouse of Amherst* by Elizabeth Spires. These sweet tales would be a great read prior to a tour of the Emily Dickinson Homestead. For older children, a selection of Emily Dickinson poetry entitled *Final Harvest* is recommended.

If you have a poetry fan in the family, be sure to walk by the Emily Dickinson Homestead near the campus of Amherst College. Dickinson was born and spent most of her life in this house. Her gravesite, at West Cemetery on Triangle Street, is not far from her home. Ask for directions, and recite one of her poems over her grave, as the UMass American poetry students do. Don't forget to go next door to visit the Evergreens, home of Emily's brother, Austin, and sister-in-law, Susan, which remains as it once was, untouched by time. The 45-minute tour of the homestead, entitled "This Was a Poet," is the most captivating for kids. Amherst College acquired both properties.

Jones Public Library (all ages)

43 Amity St., Amherst; (413) 256-4090; joneslibrary.org. Free; call for a schedule.

The library's special collections rooms hold a precious store of handwritten works by Emily Dickinson, as well as a comprehensive collection of papers and other articles owned by Robert Frost, another native of Amherst. An exhibit room showcases Emily Dickinson, Robert Frost and Robert Francis (a friend of Frost's well known regionally for his poetry).

The Eric Carle Museum of Picture Book Art (ages 2 to 10)

125 West Bay Rd., Amherst; (413) 658-1100; carlemuseum.org. Open Tues through Fri 10 a.m. to 4 p.m., Sat 10 a.m. to 5 p.m., and Sun noon to 5 p.m. Closed Mon except summers and select holidays. Open select Massachusetts vacation weeks. Admission: $9 for adults; $6 for seniors, children, and students; free for children younger than 1 year.

This museum contains more than 40,000 square feet and features picture-book art from around the world. Founded by Eric Carle, author and illustrator of the popular and beloved children's books *The Very Hungry Caterpillar* and *The Tiny Seed,* among others, the museum will fascinate your children while subtly encouraging a love of reading. Guest picture-book artist exhibits are on display; see if you recognize any of your favorite books! In each exhibit hall there are books in bins by the featured artist for a quick story time between child and parent. Guest authors (such as Chris Van Allsburg, author of *Jumanji* and *Polar Express*) do presentations and book signings, lectures, creative crafts, and story-telling, which bring the process of illustration and the art of the story to life. Pick up a family guide upon arrival for the best ideas on exploring the museum. There is a library and museum shop on-site.

TIP: Eric Carle still does an annual book signing. Check the museum's website for further information on the exact date as it changes every year.

Other Things to See & Do

Mullins Center, University of Massachusetts, 200 Commonwealth Ave., Amherst; (413) 545-0505 (box office), (800) 745-3000 (Ticketmaster), (413) 545-2751 (ice rink), or (877) 858-0300 (theater); mullinscenter.com. Athletic and training complex.

Yiddish Book Center, 1021 West St., Hampshire College, Amherst; (413) 256-4900; yiddishbookcenter.org. Open Sun to Fri. **Free.** Programs, films, performances, exhibitions, and, of course, books in Yiddish (more than 1.5 million!).

Stone House Museum, 20 Maple St., Route 202, Belchertown; (413) 323-6573; stonehousemuseum.org. Sculpture, antique carriages and sleighs, and late-1700s furnishings. Call for the schedule.

Where to Eat

Judie's, 51 North Pleasant St., Amherst; (413) 253-3491; judiesrestaurant.com. Lunch and dinner. Creative American and continental food with a flair; small full meals are very popular. Home of the popover with apple butter and vegetarian specials. There is art hanging on the walls and hand-painted tables with original art. Kids' menu. $–$$

Johnny's Tavern, 30 Boltwood Walk, Amherst; (413) 230-3818; johnnystavern amherst.com. Hormone-free meat and poultry, lots of fish and seafood selections. Highly acclaimed chef. $–$$

Museums of the Five Colleges of the Pioneer Valley

- **Amherst College's Mead Art Museum,** the **Benenski Museum of Natural History,** and the **Bassett Planetarium,** Amherst College, corner of Route 9 and Route 116, Amherst; (413) 542-2335 for the Mead (amherst.edu/museums/mead); (413) 542-2165 for the Beneski (amherst.edu/museums/naturalhistory/), and (413) 542-2000 for the Bassett (amherst.edu/museums/bassett)

- **Hampshire College Art Gallery,** 893 West St., Amherst; (413) 549-4600; hampshire.edu/library/gallery.htm

- **Mount Holyoke College Art Museum and the Arboretum,** 50 College St. and look for Lower Lake Road, South Hadley; (413) 538-2245 and (413) 538-2085 (art museum); mtholyoke.edu/artmuseum

- **Smith College Museum of Art,** 20 Elm St. (Route 9) opposite Bedford Terrace, Northampton; (413) 585-2760; smith.edu/artmuseum/

- **University Museum of Contemporary Art,** University of Massachusetts Fine Arts Center lower level, 151 President's Dr., Amherst; (413) 545-3670; umass.edu/umca

Pasta E Basta, 26 Main St., Amherst; (413) 256-3550; pastaebastaofamherst.com. Traditional and contemporary Italian cuisine. Casual setting. First-floor counter service, and the second and third floors have waitress service. Great for kids. $

The Amherst Pub, 15 East Pleasant St., Amherst; (413) 549-1200; amherstpub.com. A local icon. Caters to families, popular "Just for Kids" menu. $–$$

Where to Stay

The Lord Jeffery Inn, 30 Boltwood Ave., Amherst; (413) 253-2576 or (800) 742-0358; lordjefferyinn.com. Reopened in 2012 after a full renovation, the 49-room Lord Jeffrey Inn facing Amherst Common is loaded with charm. Highly regarded dining room (**30Boltwood**). $$–$$$$

Stone House Farm Bed and Breakfast, 649 East Pleasant St., Amherst; (413) 549-4455; stonehousefarmbb.com. Stucco and clapboard-style farmhouse, tasteful rooms. Lovely award-winning garden. Children are welcome to visit the barnyard animals or pick berries. Full farm breakfast from homegrown eggs. $$–$$$

Hadley

Don't be surprised if you drive by tobacco drying in the barns at harvest time. Hadley (hadleyma.org) is a sleepy agricultural community bordered by its sophisticated sister communities of Amherst and Northampton.

Skinner State Park (all ages)

Route 47, Hadley; (413) 586-0350 or (413) 253-2883 (visitor center); mass.gov/eea/ agencies/dcr/massparks/region-west/skinner-state-park-generic. Open Memorial Day through Columbus Day; seasonal hours. $2 parking fee on weekends and holidays.

Skinner State Park is located on Mt. Holyoke, part of the **Holyoke Range.** The park is named after Joseph A. Skinner, a successful entrepreneur who donated the hotel and the land to the state. Mt. Holyoke is part of the **M and M Trail** (Mt. Metacomet in Connecticut to Mt. Monadnock in New Hampshire), which snakes for 11 miles through the Holyoke Range and Skinner State Park. A road and several hiking trails lead to the summit of Mt. Holyoke and extend to the Holyoke Range State Park. The summit is a great picnic spot, with tables, a few grills, and a superb view of the Connecticut River Valley. The historic Summit House at Skinner State Park (413-586-0350; open weekends May through Oct) is a restored old mountain inn that's set up like an inn of the early 1900s and staffed by an interpreter.

Other Things to See & Do

Hadley Farm Museum, 147 Russell St. (Junction of Routes 9 and 47), Hadley; (413) 533-2412; hadleyfarmmuseum.org. Open mid-May through mid-Oct, Sat and Sun 2 to 4 p.m. Admission: $5 for adults, $3 for students and seniors, $1 for children under 12. Antique farm tools, equipment, and vehicles in a restored barn.

New England Falconry, 115 River Dr. (Route 47), Hadley; (413) 259-1466; newengland falconry.com. Learn about the handling of this raptor and its ties to the environment. By appointment only.

Where to Eat

Zoe's Fish House, 195 Russell St., Hadley; (413) 387-0700; zoesfish.com. Voted best seafood restaurant by the *Valley Advocate*. The chef was asked to prepare two of his specialties for Julia Child's 80th birthday. $–$$$

Where to Stay

Hadley Meadow Bed and Breakfast, 113 Rocky Hill Rd., Hadley; (413) 549-1937; hadleymeadow.com. Two-room bed-and-breakfast, beautiful views, pastoral setting. Near Norwottuck Rail Trail; easy access for biking, in-line skating, and cross-country skiing. Pool on premises. Children over age 6 welcome. Continental breakfast. $–$$

Ivory Creek Bed and Breakfast, 31 Chmura Rd., Hadley; (413) 587-3115 or (866) 331-3115; ivorycreek.com. Perched on 24 acres of wooded privacy, close access to the M and M Trail. Children welcome. Guest pantry with treats. Gourmet breakfast. $$

Northampton

Northampton, an artsy town, is a cultural hub for this region, influenced by Smith College. For more information on Northampton, contact the **Northampton Chamber of Commerce,** 99 Pleasant St., Northampton, MA 01060; (413) 584-1900; explorenorthampton.com. Don't miss the **Sojourner Truth** memorial statue (sojournertruthmemorial.org) at the corner of Pine and Park Streets in Florence (a village of Northampton). Sojourner Truth, an abolitionist best known for her book *The Narrative of Sojourner Truth: A Northern Slave,* lived

Favorite **Son**

Calvin Coolidge, the 30th president of the US, was mayor of Northampton from 1910 to 1911 and 48th governor of Massachusetts from 1919 to 1920. Although Coolidge was not born in Northampton, he did die here in his beloved town in 1933. In his honor the **Forbes Library** (20 West St., Northampton; 413-587-1011; forbeslibrary.org) houses a museum that has the largest collection of primary source material on the late president.

Norwottuck **Rail Trail** Bike Path

The Norwottuck is an 11.5-mile bike path on the former Boston and Maine Railroad railway bed. The path is a paved 8-foot-wide trail (some sections have been widened to 10 feet) connecting Northampton, Hadley, Amherst, and Belchertown. Run by the Department of Conservation and Recreation (DCR) and part of the **Connecticut River Greenway State Park** (mass.gov/eea/agencies/dcr/massparks/region-west/connecticut-river-greenway-state-park), the path meanders through forest, pastureland, and residential areas. Route highlights include Beaver Pond, with beaver activity in South Amherst, scenic vistas of the Mt. Holyoke Range, and crossing over the Connecticut River on the old railroad bridge. To access the path, enter at **Elwell State Park** on Damon Road in Northampton, behind the Mt. Farms Mall in Hadley and the Whole Foods grocery store, or at Station Road in South Amherst. (**Note:** Public restrooms are at Elwell State Park only.) Bikes can be rented at **Valley Bike and Ski Werks,** 173 Russell St., Hadley; (413) 582-0733; valleybikeandskiwerks.com. For an off-trail bite, try **Sofia's Praises,** 8 Railroad St., Hadley (413-584-2282), for sandwiches, ice cream, and desserts. For a trail map, go to the website for the **Norwottuck Rail Trail** (mass.gov/eea/agencies/dcr/massparks/region-west/norwottuck-rail-trail) or contact (413) 586-8706, ext. 12. The Norwottuck Rail Trail bike path is free.

in Florence in a utopian community called the Northampton Association of Education and Industry. Her statue is the first stop on the **Northampton African American Heritage Trail.**

Smith College Museum of Art, the Lyman Plant House, and the Botanic Gardens (all ages)

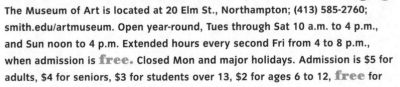

The Museum of Art is located at 20 Elm St., Northampton; (413) 585-2760; smith.edu/artmuseum. Open year-round, Tues through Sat 10 a.m. to 4 p.m., and Sun noon to 4 p.m. Extended hours every second Fri from 4 to 8 p.m., when admission is free. Closed Mon and major holidays. Admission is $5 for adults, $4 for seniors, $3 for students over 13, $2 for ages 6 to 12, free for

ages 5 and under. The Lyman Plant House is located within the campus arboretum, Smith College Campus, 16 College Ln., Northampton; (413) 585-2740; smith
.edu/garden. Open every day 8:30 a.m. to 4 p.m. year-round except for Thanksgiving and Christmas week. The Botanic Gardens are campus-wide and always
accessible. Free.

Art lovers will enjoy a visit to the Smith College Museum of Art and its fine collection of more than 20,000 pieces. Thematic exhibits are drawn from the many
works of art from the museum's holdings displayed in an outstanding building,
the Brown Fine Arts Center. The museum is considered to have a fine collection
of American and European art (including the French impressionists Degas, Corot,
Courbet, Cezanne, and Monet). To support the college's academic offerings, the
collection was expanded to include Islamic, Asian, and African art.

The Lyman Plant House showcases ferns, succulents, camellias, and tropical
and subtropical plants. The Botanic Gardens (which were initially designed by
Frederick Law Olmsted) were created to help in the study of plants by the students. The gardens have systematic beds where plants are classified according
to families. The rock and knot gardens are quite beautiful, as are the Japanese
Garden for Reflection and Contemplation and the formal garden. The green-
houses have annual flower spectaculars in March (spring bulbs) and November
(chrysanthemums). The Smith College campus, covering more than 150 acres, is
a national arboretum.

The Frank Newhall Look Memorial Park (all ages) 🌊🔺🚙🐘

300 North Main St., Route 9, Florence; (413) 584-5457; lookpark.org. Open daily
7 a.m. to dusk Memorial Day to Labor Day, Apr vacation week, and weekends in
Apr, Sept, and Oct. Parking is $5 on weekdays, $7 on weekends and holidays, and
half price on attractions on Wed and off-season. Seasonal hours and activities;
call for a schedule. Separate fees for pedal boats, tennis courts, picnic sites, train
rides, minigolf, and bumper boats.

Look Memorial Park is a 157-acre conservation area with many water activities
available—there is a 5,000-square-foot water-spray park, bumper boats, and
pedal boats—as well as a miniature railroad, an outdoor theater (where summer
concerts are held on most weekends), a smallish zoo, minigolf, tennis courts,
playgrounds, meandering walking and biking paths, and lots of picnic tables and
grills. In the winter other activities include cross-country skiing and snowshoeing in a beautiful natural setting. Don't miss Santa's Trains during mid-December
leading up to Christmas Eve. The Garden House within the park is changed into

a Victorian train station with railroad vignettes, holiday trees, Santa's workshop, Santa and Mrs. Claus, and the elves.

Other Things to See & Do

Arcadia Wildlife Sanctuary, 127 Combs Rd., Easthampton; (413) 584-3009; mass audubon.org. Visitor center; canoeing (by reservation); hiking trails covering 5 miles of wetlands, forest, meadows, and marshland; bird watching; and wildlife on 700 acres.

The Manhan Rail Trail, Easthampton to Northampton; manhanrailtrail.org. Running for 6 miles through the city of Easthampton and connecting onward to Northampton, the Manhan Rail trail will eventually be part of a rail trail system from New Haven, Connecticut, to Northampton. Check the website for numerous access points and a trail map.

Pioneer Valley Balloons, Old Ferry Road, Northampton Airport, Northampton; (413) 218-7823; pioneervalleyballoons.org. Open all year. Sunrise or sunset rides, with complimentary appetizers and champagne for adults. Serving pastries in the morning and European-style picnics in the afternoon.

Where to Eat

Ben and Bill's Chocolate Emporium, 141 Main St., Northampton; (413) 584-5695; benandbills.com. Indulge in handmade chocolate treats from family recipes handed down from generation to generation made right on the premises, ice cream (seasonal), and hot drinks. $

Fitzwilly's, 23 Main St., Northampton; (413) 584-8666; fitzwillys.com. Popular spot for a relaxing dinner for over 40 years. Great appetizers and sliders. $–$$

Miss Florence Diner, 99 Main St., Florence; (413) 584-3137; missflorencediner .com. Affectionately known as Miss Flo's. On the National Register of Historic Places, emblematic of old-time distinctive diners. Great value and down-home cooking. $

Spoleto, 1 Bridge St., Northampton; (413) 586-6313; spoletorestaurants.com. Open for dinner, specializing in Italian cuisine. Will do half portions or pastas for kids. $$–$$$

Where to Stay ⊖

Hotel Northampton and Historic Wiggins Tavern, 36 King St., Northampton; (413) 584-3100 or (800) 547-3529; hotelnorthampton.com. Lovely 106-room hotel, great cafe (Coolidge Park Cafe), and dining room (**The Wiggins Tavern**), centrally located. $$–$$$$

Sugar Maple Trailside Inn, 62 Chestnut St., Northampton; (413) 575-2277 or (866) 416-2753; sugar-maple-inn.com. Featured on HGTV's *Restore America,* as well as accolades in *Yankee Magazine* and the *Boston Globe.* Great access to the rail trail. Two rooms. Children welcome. Continental breakfast. For a heartier breakfast, go to the Miss Florence Diner next door. $

South Hadley & Granby

A charming, quieter college town very proud of the Mt. Holyoke campus, South Hadley is between Northampton and Springfield. Neighboring Granby has a quaint small-town atmosphere with a town green and many period Greek Revival homes.

Other Things to See & Do

Brunelle's Marina, 1 Alford St., South Hadley; (413) 315-6342; brunelles.com. Forty-nine-seat interpreted cruise on the Connecticut River on the *Lady Bea* from the marina to Northampton.

Joseph Skinner Museum at Mt. Holyoke College, 33 Woodbridge St., South Hadley; (413) 538-7127 or (413) 538-2085; mtholyoke.edu/artmuseum/skinner. Shells, watches, eyeglasses, Native American objects, armor and weapons, ancient artifacts, farming equipment, minerals, glassware, and Early American regional furnishings representing the varied collecting interests of Joseph Skinner. The majority of the 7,000-piece collection is on view. Open May through Oct, Wed and Sun from 2 to 5 p.m. **Free.**

Nash Dinosaur Tracks, 594 Amherst Rd., off Route 116, South Hadley; (413) 467-9566; nashdinosaurtracks.com. Open Apr through Thanksgiving. Admission: $3 for adults, $2 for kids. Museum featuring dinosaur tracks and fossils. The gift shop sells minerals, fossils, and dinosaur tracks.

Holyoke

Like Lowell, Holyoke is a mill city, planned around the canals built in the mid-19th century as the power source for the Holyoke Water Power Company. The 150-year-old system still generates hydroelectric power and supplies process water to manufacturing companies that occupy the old mill buildings. The **Holyoke Chamber of Commerce,** 177 High St., Holyoke, MA 01040, can be reached at (413) 534-3376. For more information on Holyoke events, visit passportholyoke.org or holyokechamber.com.

Holyoke Heritage State Park (all ages)

221 Appleton St., Holyoke; (413) 534-1723 (visitor center); mass.gov/eea/agencies/dcr/massparks/region-west/holyoke-heritage-state-park.html. The visitor center is open Tues through Sun noon to 4 p.m. The visitor center features historical exhibits on the history of Holyoke and revolving contemporary exhibits showcasing local artists. There is loads of children's programming throughout the year focusing on history, environmental education, and family entertainment.

Holyoke Heritage State Park is a 7-acre complex of enormous mill buildings and outdoor spaces, with exhibits about the city's growth. There are three main attractions for families here: the Holyoke Merry-Go-Round, the Children's Museum, and the Volleyball Hall of Fame.

- Children's Museum (age 8 and under), 444 Dwight St. (or can be accessed from within the park), Holyoke; (413) 536-KIDS or (413) 536-7048; childrensmuseumholyoke.org. Open Tues through Sat 10 a.m. to 4 p.m. and Sun noon to 4 p.m. (closed during Sept). Admission: $7 per person, free for children under 1. The Children's Museum emphasizes family participation in educational games and interactive exhibits. Make your own paper or try your hand at one of the mock-ups of local businesses, including a miniature Big Y grocery store, the mail room, the fire station, the ambulance, and the vet clinic. The Air Maze and the Light Bright exhibits are also very popular.

- Holyoke Merry-Go-Round, 221 Appleton St., Holyoke; (413) 538-9838; holyokemerrygoround.org. Open weekends noon to 4 p.m. from Sept through June; daily from noon to 4 p.m. in summer (check the website for extended hours during Holyoke school vacations and July and Aug). Closed Mon except for school vacations. Price: $2 per ride. The antique merry-go-round was built in 1929 by the Philadelphia Toboggan Company. Housed in a colorful new building near the entrance to the park, the large carousel has 48 horses and 2 chariots, all carved by hand, plus a loud, cheerful band organ. Private parties by arrangement.

- Volleyball Hall of Fame, 444 Dwight St. (can be accessed from within Heritage State Park), Holyoke; (413) 536-0926; volleyhall.org. Open Thurs through Sun from noon to 4:30 p.m. year-round. Admission is $3.50 for adults, $2.50 for ages 7 through 17 and seniors, and free for ages 6 and under. A look at this sport's history, from its inception at the Holyoke YMCA in 1895 to the present.

Other Things to See & Do

Holyoke Blue Sox, MacKenzie Stadium, Holyoke; (413) 533-1100; holyokesox.com. Member of the New England Collegiate Baseball League.

Holyoke Civic Symphony, Leslie Phillips Theater (the Forum) at Holyoke Community College, 303 Homestead Ave., Holyoke; (413) 256-1760; holyokecivicsymphony .org. Most concerts are free. Delighting Holyoke area residents since 1966.

Mt. Tom State Reservation, 125 Reservation Rd., off Route 5, Holyoke; (413) 534-1186; mass.gov/eea/agencies/dcr/massparks/region-west/mount-tom-state-reservation.html. Twenty miles of hiking, natural-history museum, wildlife watchtower with beautiful views. Canoeing and fishing in the summer. Popular winter activities are ice skating, snowshoeing, and cross-country skiing. Seasonal hours.

Wistariahurst Museum, 238 Cabot St., Holyoke; (413) 322-5660; wistariahurst .org. Mansion of silk manufacturer William Skinner. Guided tour through the 26-room mansion Sat through Mon noon to 4 p.m. **Caution:** Borders a questionable section of town.

The Holyoke **Dam and Fishway**

Located on Route 116N (which turns into Canal Street; take a left at the fishway sign just before the South Hadley Falls Bridge), the **Holyoke Dam** and the **Robert E. Barrett Fishway** have a viewing window and observation platform for watching more than a quarter of a million migrating shad and salmon in mid-May to mid-June. Staffed with informative guides. Call (413) 536-9474 or (800) 859-2960 or visit hged.com/html/hadley_falls_fish_lift for more information.

Where to Eat

Delaney's Grille, 3 Country Club Rd. (Route 5), Holyoke; (413) 532-1800; logcabin-delaney.com. Great Sunday brunches. Elegant setting. $$–$$$$

JP's Restaurant, 200 Whiting Farms Rd., Holyoke; (413) 532-9444; jpsrestaurant.com. Reasonably priced burgers, pizzas, sandwiches, salads, and entrees. $

Where to Stay

The D. Hotel and Suites, 1 Country Club Rd., Holyoke; (413) 533-2100; stayatthed.com/contact. Studio suites come with a king bed, a pullout, and a kitchenette. Pool and hot tub on the premises. Cribs. Full breakfast is included. $$–$$$

Greater Springfield

Springfield is the largest city in the Greater Springfield region (valleyvisitor.com), as well as in the entire Pioneer Valley. It is also considered the gateway to western Massachusetts and Connecticut. Dr. James Naismith invented basketball here when he made a game of throwing a soccer ball into a peach basket at Springfield College in 1891. The Naismith Basketball Hall of Fame is a family favorite, as are the museums of the Quadrangle, where Theodor Seuss Geisel (better known as Dr. Seuss) has a national memorial in tribute to his work. Six Flags, the largest amusement park in New England, is found down the road in Agawam.

Forest Park and the Zoo in Forest Park (all ages)

302 Sumner Ave. (Route 83, off Route 21), Springfield; (413) 787-6441 (park), www3.springfield-ma.gov/park; or (413) 733-2251 (zoo), forestparkzoo.com. Forest Park is open 8 a.m. to dusk ($3 fee). The zoo is open on a seasonal schedule; check the website. Admission: $9 for adults, $6 ages 5 to 12, $4 ages 1 to 4, free for under age 1. Train rides $3.25; $2 for the animal food.

Forest Park is a beautifully maintained large city park with a small zoo, easily navigated nature trails by picturesque ponds and lakes, picnic spots, swimming pools, ice skating, and other recreational activities. The centerpiece of Forest Park is its Aquatic Gardens, with tendrils of land jutting out into the ponds for closer observation of the birds that call this park home. Don't miss the Carriage House, a Victorian charmer overlooking a rolling lawn (a great place to hold a wedding), with the Mausoleum Bridge and the Three Sister's statue close by. During the late Nov through Dec holidays, the park has several drive-through lighting displays called Bright Nights with various themes such as the North Pole Village, Barney's Mansion, and the Victorian Village (admission is $18 Mon through Thurs, $21 Fri through Sun per car).

Leave a leisurely hour and a half for the small but appealing Zoo in Forest Park which has native wildlife, barnyard animals, and an exotic animal collection (some of whom are on the endangered or threatened list); the children's playground at the entrance; and the 1.3-mile train tour around the outside perimeter of the zoo (extra fee). A Discovery program allows you to interact and touch many of the animals that are featured in the presentations. The zoo store carries grain cones and cookies (fee) for the kids to feed the animals. During Halloween the Spooky Safari, held at night, is a child favorite. The only disappointment for your family may be the spotty signage identifying the animals within the exhibits. *TIP:* A Bright Night's discount coupon can be found on brightnights.org.

Naismith Memorial Basketball Hall of Fame (all ages)

1000 Hall of Fame Ave., Springfield; (413) 781-6500 or (877) 4-HOOPLA; hoophall .com. Open 10 a.m. to 4 p.m. Sun through Fri and 10 a.m. to 5 p.m. Sat. Extended summer hours. Closed select Mondays, Thanksgiving, and Christmas. Admission: $21 for adults, $17 for seniors, and $15 for children 5 to 15; free for children under 5 accompanied by a parent.

The Naismith Memorial Basketball Hall of Fame is an entertainment center/ museum that will be interesting to any visitor who's ever had even a remote connection to the game. A state-of-the-art museum that doubled its size opened in 2002. The exterior architecture of the museum is a sphere with a tower beside it. On top of the tower is a perpetually lit orange ball that serves as a beacon to beckon and attract those traveling down I-91 to visit. The main showpiece of the museum is the Center Court, which features a full-size basketball court and scoreboard visible from balconies on each of the museum's three levels. All of your favorite Hall of Famers are on display, timelined with world history and great moments in basketball. The second floor features a coach's gallery honoring high school, college, national, and international teams. The Game Gallery is very interactive and showcases the game and the evolution of the equipment from its earliest humble beginnings to the present. The Media Gallery allows you to relive broadcasts, have a photo of you e-mailed, or act out an interview and be taped. Challenge your basketball knowledge. Shoot hoops of various shapes, sizes, and heights. Play Jason Kidd or Dawn Staley in the virtual-reality game. Or compare your height and arm span to those of the game's biggest players. Legends of the game will be brought in to lecture and conduct clinics. The basketball theme carries over to the Museum Store. A multitude of restaurants are found on-site, ranging from simple fare like subs to fine dining. A hotel is conveniently located on the campus (the Hilton Garden Inn). Enshrinement into the Basketball Hall of Fame is in September.

TIP: Tickets to the Basketball Hall of Fame Enshrinement are for sale to the public but sell out very quickly. Act fast!

Six Flags New England (all ages)

1623 Main St. (Route 159), Agawam; (413) 786-9300 or (800) 370-7488; sixflags .com/newengland. Open mid-Apr through end of Oct. Admission is $54.99 for adults, $49.99 for kids up to 54 inches, **free** for kids under 2. Special VIP Tours and Flash passes to help you get to the front of the line can be reserved. There is a charge for parking and special event attractions within the park. *TIP:* Look for special pricing online. Visitation is lower in the spring, fall, and midweek, which may translate to shorter lines if you visit during those times. Start your day at rides farthest from the park entrance and try to ride the more popular rides during off-peak times (when the park opens and from dinner time onward).

Six Flags of New England has spared no expense ($200 million in renovations) to give you a "high." There are four areas dedicated to children: Whistlestop Park, Looney Tunes Movie Town, Kidzopolis, and Splash Island. With the number-one steel roller coaster Bizarro (a distinction bestowed by *Amusement Today*, winning the Golden Ticket Award), Six Flags is home to the largest water park in New England. With 60 rides (46 dry rides and 14 water rides), shows, and attractions spread over 235 acres, Six Flags can be crowded on summer weekends, but the tumult can add to the experience. There are 3 water rides in the theme park, 11 roller coasters (3 are inverted), 4 Kiddieland areas, and a nice old merry-go-round on the grounds. Favorite rides for those with nerve and verve are the Scream (3 Scream towers; the ride starts on the bottom and shoots you up prior to a 20-story free-fall drop), Buzzsaw (a wooden boat on a platform with pivoting arms that swing like a clock's pendulum that eventually does a 360. Don't forget to keep your hands up!), and the Typhoon Water Coaster (a raft ride that goes both uphill and downhill—the only one in New England!). New in 2014 is the New England Screamer swing ride. If you are not an acrophobe, this ride is for you! The ride is over 400 feet tall (which translates to approximately 40 stories in height!) and circles at speeds up to 40 mph. There are daily performances to let your "thrill be chill" and give your overworked adrenalin rush a break. The Hurricane Harbor Waterpark has seven complexes with two sandy beaches, water slides (the Bonzai Pipelines Waterslide sends you on a thrilling 257-foot, 40-mph drop full of twists and turns), a lazy river, and two wave pools. Note that one price admits you to both Six Flags of New England and Hurricane Harbor Waterpark (the water park is within the theme park). Check the website for special events and festivals.

The Springfield Museums at the Quadrangle and the Dr. Seuss National Memorial Sculpture Garden (all ages)

21 Edwards St., Springfield; (413) 263-6800 or (800) 625-7738; springfieldmuseums .org or catinthehat.org. Open Tues through Sat 10 a.m. to 5 p.m., Sun 11 a.m. to 5 p.m. Closed Mon except holidays and summertime. Admission (includes entry to all museums): $15 for adults, $10 for seniors, and $8 for children 3 to 17, free for children under 3. Museum cafe, fully stocked gift shop, and weekend family programs and activities.

Winner of the "Best Rainy Day Place for the Family" by the *Springfield Republican*, the Springfield Museums at the Quadrangle, a complex that incorporates four museums and the Dr. Seuss National Memorial Sculpture Garden, is a nice place to spend some time. Parking is **free** at the museums' lots on Edwards Street. The Dr. Seuss National Memorial Sculpture Garden (open daily 9 a.m. to 5 p.m.) includes 18 bronze sculptures (created by his stepdaughter Lark Grey Dimond-Cates), which are a tribute to native son Theodor Geisel, author of the Dr. Seuss books. Keep your fingers crossed: A permanent exhibit or museum at the Quadrangle dedicated to Dr. Seuss is in the initial planning stages. Museums at the Quadrangle include:

- George Walter Vincent Smith Art Museum: A Victorian-era collectors' museum containing Middle Eastern rugs, the largest collection of Chinese cloisonné in the West, Japanese arms and armor, a Shinto shrine, Chinese jade, 19th-century American paintings, and the Hasbro Games Art Discovery Center for Families. *TIP:* Make a point of noticing the windows—a vast majority were made by Tiffany.

- Michelle and Donald D'Amour Museum of Fine Arts: European and American paintings, sculpture, and paper mediums. Largest permanent collection of Currier and Ives prints in the country. A vast collection of Japanese woodblock prints.

- Springfield Science Museum: The R.E. Phelon African Hall focuses on the diverse wildlife of the African continent, and Dinosaur Hall (the kids' favorite) includes a full-size replica of a towering tyrannosaur. Other attractions include a hands-on Exploration Center with live animals, the Native American Hall with artifacts and lifestyles of Native Americans, Earth Hall with hundreds of unique specimens of rocks and minerals, an observatory, and the Seymour Planetarium (planetarium program on weekends). The Seymour Planetarium is the oldest continuously operating planetarium in the country.

- The Lyman and Merrie Wood Museum of Springfield History: History of Springfield and the region from pre–Civil War to the present. The collection includes the Indian Motocycle collection, Springfield-built automobiles starting with the Duryea (including two Rolls Royces), a Gee Bee aircraft, the largest Smith & Wesson gun collection in the world, and other inventions by local inventors.

Major Agricultural Fairs in the Pioneer Valley (mafa.org)

- **Belchertown Fair,** late Sept, Main Street at the Town Common, Belchertown; (413) 323-7210; belchertownfair.com

- **Blandford Fair,** early Sept, 10 North St., Blandford; (413) 848-2888; theblandfordfair.com

- **Cummington Fair,** late Aug, 97 Fairgrounds Rd., Cummington; (413) 238-7724 or (413) 634-5091; cummingtonfair.com

- **Eastern States Exposition (The Big E),** Sept, 1305 Memorial Ave. (Route 107), West Springfield; (413) 737-2443 or (413) 205-5115 (info line); thebige.com

- **Franklin County Fair,** early Sept, 89 Wisdom Way, Greenfield; (413) 774-4282; fcas.com

- **Heath Fair,** mid-Aug, 9 Hosmer Rd., Heath; (413) 337-4733 or (413) 337-5716; heathfair.org

- **Littleville Fair,** early Aug, 15 Kinne Brook Rd., Chester; (413) 667-3193; hidden-hills.com/littlevillefair

- **Middlefield Fair,** mid-Aug, 7 Bell Rd., Middlefield; (413) 623-5350 or (413) 623-6027; hidden-hills.com/middlefieldfair

- **Three-County Fair,** early Sept, 54 Fair St., Northampton; (413) 584-2237; 3countyfair.com

- **Westfield Fair,** mid-Aug, 137 Russellville Rd., Westfield; (413) 562-3001; thewestfieldfair.com

Other Things to See & Do

Amelia Park, Amelia Park Museum, and the Ice Arena, 21 South Broad St., Westfield; (413) 572-4014 (museum) or (413) 568-2503 (ice arena); ameliaparkmuseum .org or ameliaparkice.org. The Amelia Park Museum is great for children under 12, with many hands-on exhibits (open Thurs though Mon 9 a.m. to 4 p.m.). Indoor ice arena, outdoor in-line skating rink. Garden with summertime concerts.

Lupa Zoo, 62 Nash Hill Rd., Ludlow; (413) 589-9883 (administration) or (413) 583-8370 (general information); lupazoo.org. Open seasonally. Barnyard and exotic animals.

MassMutual Center, 1277 Main St., Springfield; (413) 782-6610 (main line) or (413) 787-6600 (box office) or (800) 639-8602; massmutualcenter.com. Sports and entertainment venue.

Riverfront Park, 1200 West Columbus Ln. (foot of State Street), Springfield; (413) 787-6440; www3.springfield-ma.gov/park/riverwalk. Seven-acre park with playground. The park is adjacent to the Connecticut River Walk and Bikeway and covers 3.7 miles along the Connecticut River. **Caution:** Be aware of your surroundings.

Springfield Armory National Historic Site, 1 Armory St. #12, Springfield; (413) 734-8551; nps.gov/spar. Open daily 9 a.m. to 5 p.m. Free. National armory, site chosen by General Washington. Museum features huge firearm collection, interactive exhibits, introductory film, and bookstore.

Springfield Falcons, Mass Mutual Center, 45 Falcons Way, Springfield; (413) 739-4625 or (413) 787-6600 for tickets; falconsahl.com. American Hockey League team, an affiliate of the NHL Colombus Blue Jackets.

Stanley Park, 400 Western Ave., Westfield; (413) 568-9312; stanleypark.org. A 300-acre park consisting of lush gardens, a bell tower, trails, and sporting facilities. Open May through Nov 7 a.m. to dusk.

Storrowton Village Museum, Eastern States Exposition, 1305 Memorial Ave., West Springfield; (413) 205-5051; thebige.com. Re-created 19th-century New England village within the Big E fairgrounds. Open year-round.

Titanic Historical Society, 208 Main St., Indian Orchard; (413) 543-4770; titanic historicalsociety.org. Artifacts and displays from the *Titanic* and its survivors. Fee for nonmembers $4; children $2, under 6 **free.** Open Mon through Fri 10 a.m. to 4 p.m., Sat 10 a.m. to 3 p.m.

Oh What a **Fun Thing to Do!**

For me—and for you—
To read all of Dr. Seuss's stories
At the Springfield Quadrangle in all their glory
While looking at bronze sculptures of Theodor Geisel.
It's more fun—believe me—than riding on a carousel!
Green Eggs and Ham, The Cat in the Hat can only be beat
by *And to Think That I Saw It on Mulberry Street*.

Worthington Ballooning, 159 Huffington Hill Rd., Worthington; (413) 238-5514; worthingtonballoning.com. Hot-air balloon rides by reservation only.

Where to Eat

The Fort, 8 Fort St., Springfield; (413) 788-6628; studentprince.com. Paneled walls lined with German plates. One of the largest stein collections in the US. Local icon serving German and American dishes. Children's menu. $–$$

Red Rose Pizzeria, 1060 Main St., Springfield; (413) 739-8510; redrosepizzeria .com. Regarded as the best pizza in Springfield. Kids are given pizza dough to play with while waiting for their dinner. $–$$

Storrowton Tavern and the Carriage House, 1305 Memorial Ave., West Springfield, (413) 732-4188; storrowtown.com. Open for lunch and dinner. Antique tavern from the 19th century serving hearty New England fare. $$–$$$

Where to Stay

Naomi's Inn, 20 Springfield St., Springfield; (413) 433-6019, (413) 732-3924, or (888) 762-6647; naomisinn.net. Three suites with sitting area and private bath. Snacks served. Toys and games available, very family friendly. Full breakfast. $–$$

Central Massachusetts

Central Massachusetts is the geographic center of the Commonwealth of Massachusetts. Rolling hills run through most of this peaceful area, a region that Boston families treasure as a nearby source of seasonal rural activities. In spring, pastures are full of young animals kicking up their heels. Clear lakes and large parks welcome picnickers on summer afternoons. Orchards provide hours of fun for enthusiastic apple-pickers from late Aug through late Oct. Quiet country roads lead to the hiking and cross-country skiing trails that crisscross the region. But when you are looking for something to do on an inclement day, the city of Worcester has several good family-oriented museums. The **Central Massachusetts Convention and Visitors Bureau,** 30 Elm St., Worcester, MA 01609 (508-755-7400 or 866-755-7439; centralmass .org), is a helpful resource. South of Worcester, Old Sturbridge Village is an early 19th-century "village" that was constructed in 1946. Unpaved roads, costumed interpreters, and working artisans give kids a flavor of what it might have been like to visit a typical New England village during the first fifty years of the republic.

The Nashoba Valley & the Johnny Appleseed Trail

A hilly region that's served Bostonians as an easy escape for well over a century, the Nashoba Valley hasn't changed much since the Alcott family set up a commune

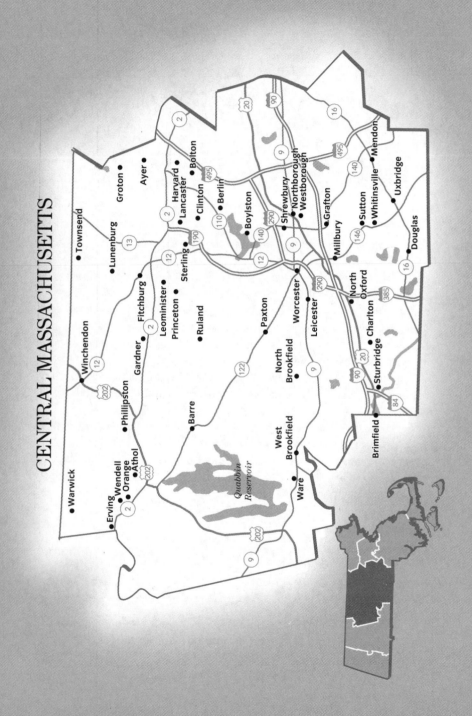

CENTRAL MASSACHUSETTS

TopPicks in Central Massachusetts

- **Old Sturbridge Village,** Sturbridge

- **Quabbin Reservoir and Park,** Ware

- **Fruitlands,** Harvard

- **Worcester Museums** (Worcester Art Museum and the Ecotarium)

- Farm fun on the **Johnny Appleseed Trail**

- **Southwick's Zoo,** Mendon

in Harvard with other transcendentalists in 1843. The **Johnny Appleseed Visitor Center,** 1000 Route 2 Westbound (between exits 34 and 35), Lancaster, MA 01523 (978-534-2302; appleseed.org), and the **North Central Massachusetts Chamber of Commerce,** 860 South St.; Fitchburg, MA 01420 (978-353-7600; northcentral-mass.com), offer maps and brochures on area sights and attractions.

Bolton, Fitchburg, Harvard & Lunenburg

Drawbridge Puppet Theater (ages 10 and under)

1335 Massachusetts Ave. (Route 2A), Lunenburg; (978) 582-1578; drawbridge puppets.com. Shows are Sat and Sun at 10 a.m. and noon. Periodically there is also a Fri night concert series, a **free** magic show every month, and a story-teller once a month (see the website). During the summer there is an additional performance on Wed at 11 a.m. Fee: $6 per person. **Free** parking.

Each 1-hour marionette, puppet, or shadow puppet show has original songs, skits, and special effects with a tour backstage. Coming in costume is encouraged! Special performances, private performances (with a demonstration of the art of "mastering the strings"), puppet workshops, and field trips showcasing puppet and marionette shows for any occasion. *TIP:* Make your reservations in advance; there are only 48 seats in the theater!

Fitchburg Art Museum (ages 8 and up)

25 Merriam Pkwy., Fitchburg; (978) 345-4207; fitchburgartmuseum.org. Open Wed through Fri noon to 4 p.m., Sat and Sun 11 a.m. to 5 p.m. Closed Mon and Tues and most major holidays. Admission: $9 for adults, $5 for seniors and students, free for children 12 and under.

The focus is on American and European Art and local contemporary New England artists. There's also a minor collection of classical art and antiquities from Greece, Rome, Asia, Africa, and South America. Big hits are the permanent family-friendly interactive multimedia Egyptian exhibit and the world-class photography collection. There is a new Learning Lounge Educational Center to help kids study the creative process. Family workshops are scheduled throughout the year.

Fruitlands (all ages)

102 Prospect Hill Rd., Harvard; (978) 456-3924; fruitlands.org. Open from mid-Apr through early Nov, 10 a.m. to 4 p.m. Mon, Wed, Thurs, and Fri; 10 a.m. to 5 p.m. weekends and holidays. The winter season runs from Nov to Apr. The Art Gallery, Museum Store, and the Wayside Visitor Center are open weekends only from noon to 5 p.m. (The historic buildings are not heated so are closed for the winter). There are interpreters in each building to answer questions. Admission: $12 for adults, $10 for seniors and students, $5 for children age 5 through 13, free for age 4 and under; $6 to visit the grounds only. The grounds are open to museum ticket holders for picnics. The Fruitlands Museum Cafe is open Mon through Sat (closed Tues) for lunch from 11:30 a.m. to 2:30 p.m. and for Sun brunch from 11 a.m. to 2 p.m.

Fruitlands Museum, a 210-acre property, includes four museum buildings. The setting provides stunning views of the Nashua River Valley and, in the far distance, of mountains in southern New Hampshire. The Fruitlands Farmhouse (open for visitation) is dedicated to the memory of the transcendentalists, many of whom spent seven months of 1843 in the farmhouse at the bottom of the hill. The transcendentalists believed that people could experience God through nature. Their beliefs led them to develop a unique "back-to-nature" lifestyle, very unusual during their time. They tried living in a communal building on a farm where they could be as self-sufficient as possible. Among them were the Alcott family (Louisa May, her three sisters, and her parents). The group gave its communal home the hopeful name of Fruitlands in the expectation that they would live off the "fruits of the land." Unfortunately they were unable to farm as much sustenance as they had hoped. It seems that they were more interested in philosophizing than farming. Their refusal to use animal labor because they didn't wish to exploit them also made farming the land extremely difficult. For this reason and others, the experiment was unsuccessful and the Alcott family left Harvard and went back to Concord. Not all the group members left. Joseph Palmer stayed and began Freelands, another commune. In 1910 Clara Endicott Sears purchased the property, which had become run-down. She restored the farmhouse and opened it as a museum in honor of the Alcotts and their friends Ralph Waldo Emerson and Henry David Thoreau. The building houses mementos of the group.

Also found on the property are the Shaker Office, the Art Gallery, and the Native American Gallery. The Shaker Office opened to the public in 1922 as the first Shaker Museum in the world. This building was the office for the Harvard Shakers and was built in 1794. It is set up with a series of exhibits about the Harvard Shakers. The Shakers were a celibate religious group who tried to live out "heaven on earth" following the motto "hands to work, hearts to God." Exhibits depict the many industries of the Shaker communities (look for the Sisters' Work Room, full of looms and spinning wheels) and illustrate how business was conducted between the Shakers and the outside world. The Art Gallery houses portraits by primitive folk artists (Fruitlands has one of the largest collections of vernacular portraiture in the US) and landscape paintings, with a sizable collection of paintings from the Hudson River School of Painters along with rotating exhibits. The Native American Collection holds Thoreau's rock and mineral collection and interesting artifacts of the Native Americans who once lived in the area, as well as materials from across North America.

Nature trails (used for cross-country skiing in the winter), the Williard Farm Archaeological Site, the Museum Store, and the **Fruitlands Museum Cafe** (serving light lunches in a gracious setting), round out your day at the museum. Watch for the summer concert series, the Harvest Festival in Sept., and the Winterfest weekends with sledding and winter programs.

TIP: Transportation is available upon request for help getting up the hill. The terrain can be uneven, so wear walking shoes.

Nashoba Valley Winery and Orchards (all ages)

100 Wattaquadoc Hill Rd., Bolton; (978) 779-5521 or (978) 779-9816 (J's Restaurant reservation line); nashobawinery.com. Open year-round 10 a.m. to 5 p.m. (Fri and Sat until 6 p.m.) except Thanksgiving, Christmas, New Year's Day, and July 4; 45-minute weekend tours are given Sat and Sun, 11 a.m. to 5 p.m. (last tour at 4 p.m.). Tours include a glass and six tastings ($10 for adults, free for children under 21). Tastings (21 and up) are $6 for 5 tastings and a complimentary tasting glass from 10 a.m. to 4:30 p.m. daily. Great gift shop full of gourmet specialties and premium Nashoba wine, beer, and spirits.

Pick berries during the summer into the early fall, peaches in midsummer, apples throughout the fall (named the best place to pick apples by the *Boston Parents' Paper*), and be sure to bring a picnic. In the winter it's a nice place to cross-country ski (bring your own equipment). Regardless of the season, you can take a tour of the winery, winner of national and international wine competitions. **J's Restaurant** ($–$$$) on the premises is open Wed through Sat for lunch and dinner, and Sun for brunch (a family favorite is the annual Mother's Day or Father's Day brunch). Festivals and events are held throughout the year. Check the website for the schedule.

Nashua River Rail Trail (all ages)

Parking areas to access the trail can be found in Ayer (60 spaces, access to the Boston and Fitchburg commuter rail, and nonflush public toilets), Groton (12 spaces), or Dunstable (10 spaces). For more information, visit mass.gov/eea/agencies/dcr/massparks/region-central/nashua-river-rail-trail.html or call (978) 597-8802. Free.

The 10-foot-wide Nashua River Rail Trail travels 11 miles through four towns (Ayer, Groton, Pepperell, and Dunstable) along a defunct railroad bed of the Hollis Branch of the Boston and Maine Railroad (thus the name rail trail). In 1982 the last freight train serviced the area, and the state eventually bought the property and repurposed it for local recreation. It's very picturesque for bikers, hikers, cross-country skiers, and equestrians. A slice of the real New England can be found here, particularly on a sunny, crisp autumn day. Directions to the trailheads:

- Ayer: Take Route 2 to exit 38B, and then take Route 111 north to the Ayer Rotary. Take Route 2A off the rotary and follow to Ayer Center. Turn right after Ayer Center, and take the first right onto Groton Street to the parking area on the right.

- Groton: Take Route 495 to exit 31, then Route 119 west for 7 miles to Groton Center. Take a left at Station Avenue to the parking lot beside the trail.

The Rat **Pack**

The **River Rat Race** (mid-Apr) from Athol to Orange started as a bet in 1963 among friends as to whether the Millers River was navigable for canoeists (dams and rapids were problems). The bet escalated into a 6-mile race on March 21, 1964, and today the best canoeists in North America take the challenge to be crowned the King River Rat. The affair starts with a pancake breakfast, a River Rat Parade, and a carnival leading to the River Rat Race, with a field of more than 340 canoeists. A new element is a 5K race for those who prefer land. For more information, contact the **Athol Lions Club,** PO Box 1000, Athol, MA 01331; (978) 249-9038; riverratrace.com.

- Dunstable: Take Route 3 to exit 35, then Route 113 west through Dunstable Center. Take a right onto Hollis Street to the New Hampshire line. Parking is on the left.
- Pepperell: Take Route 113 to Pepperell Center off of Route 119.

Wachusett Mountain Ski Area (all ages)

499 Mountain Rd., Princeton; (978) 464-2300 or (800) SKI-1234 (ski conditions); wachusett.com. Skiing from late Nov to early Apr. Open daily for day and night skiing and snow tubing on the weekends. Call for schedule and rates.
Full snowmaking coverage makes this a fun family ski mountain, the highest mountain in eastern Massachusetts (east of the Connecticut River). Features day and night skiing, 8 lifts (including the 3 high-speed detachable quads, the only ones in the state), and 22 trails on 110 acres of terrain. Wachusett Mountain, in partnership with the MBTA (Massachusetts Bay Transit Authority), will have a weekend ski train service (wachusett.com/default.aspx?tabid=66) to Fitchburg from Boston and then a shuttle to Wachusett. This is one of the only ski areas in the country to offer this (contact Wachusett Mountain for further information). During the off-season you can hike and picnic here, or take the auto road to reach the summit, Wachusett Mountain State Reservation. Two Hollywood movies have filmed at Wachusett Mountain ski area: *Shallow Hal* and *The Legend of Lucy Keyes.* Wachusett Mountain Ski Area is open in the fall for festivals and outings. The annual Kidsfest, held in late Sept, is extremely popular.

Farm Fun

For information on every farm in the state, fruit and vegetable seasons, and farmers' market locations and dates, visit mass.gov/massgrown.

- **Berlin Orchards,** 310 Sawyer Hill Rd., Berlin; (978) 838-2400; berlin orchards.com. Apple picking, hayrides, farm animals, picnicking, farm tours, and Family Festivals. Open late Aug through Oct.

- **Bolton Spring Farm,** 159 Main St., Bolton; (978) 779-2898; bolton springfarm.com. Apples, apple and pumpkin picking, and hayrides.

- **Breezy Gardens,** 1872 Main St., Route 9, Leicester; (508) 892-9201; breezygardens.com. Open springtime through autumn; green-houses, corn maze, and gardens. Hayrides in the fall.

- **Brookfield Orchards,** 12 Lincoln Rd., North Brookfield; (508) 867-6858; brookfieldorchardsonline.com. Apples, apple picking, fall wagon rides, harvest festivals, and country store.

- **A Clear View Farm,** 4 Kendall Rd., Sterling; (978) 422-6442; clear viewfarmstand.com. Home of the true story of "Mary Had a Little Lamb." Hayrides and pick-your-own apples and berries.

- **Davis Farmland, Children's Discovery Farm, and the Mega Maze,** 145 Redstone Hill, Sterling; (978) 422-MOOO; davisfarmland .com. Children's farm and museum, apple orchard and pumpkin patch, three-story zip-line thrill ride, sleepovers, and the largest collection of endangered livestock in the US. Corn maze (Mega Maze hot line: 978-422-8888). Fun for all!

- **Fay Mountain Farm,** 12 Cemetery Rd., Charlton; (617) 981-2051; faymountainfarm.com. Pick your own fruit, festivals, open to the public from sunrise to sunset, trails, picnic area, and pond.

- **George Hill Orchard,** 582 George Hill Rd., South Lancaster; (978) 365-4331 or (800) 699-4331; yourfavoritefarm.com. Pick-your-own farm. Seasonal live music, hay and pony rides.

- **Hollow Brook Farms,** 47 Hollow Rd., Brimfield; (413) 245-9325; hollowbrookfarms.com. Cut your own Christmas tree, cross-country skiing, hay and sleigh rides.

- **Keown Orchards,** 9 McClellan Rd., Sutton; (508) 865-6706; keown orchards.com. Pick your own pumpkins and apples (over 50 varieties, ripening at different times), hayrides, and a farm store.

- **Olde Nourse Farm,** 70 Nourse St., Westborough; (508) 366-2644; oldenoursefarmgourmet.com. Pick your own berries in season.

- **Red Apple Farm,** 455 Highland Ave., Phillipston; (978) 249-6763 or (800) 628-4851; redapplefarm.com. "Pick your own, Dig your own" apples, blueberries, raspberries, pumpkins, or potatoes; farm animals, hayrides, and picnic pavilion.

- **Sholan Farms,** 1125 Pleasant St., Leominister; (978) 840-3276; sholanfarms.com. Panoramic views of Boston. Pick your own apples and pumpkins. Festivals and hayrides. Free Twilight Hikes monthly.

- **Sleighbell Christmas Tree Farm and Gift Barn,** 130 Whittins Rd., Sutton; (508) 234-6953; sleighbelltreefarm.com. Choose-and-cut Christmas tree farm. Holiday gifts, wreaths, and more.

- **Stowe Farm Orchards,** 15 Stowe Rd., Millbury; (508) 865-9860; stowefarm.com. Pick your own apples and pumpkins. Panning for gems, rock-climbing wall, hayrides, Aerial Adventures Ropes Course.

- **Tougas Family Farm,** 234 Ball St., Northboro; (508) 393-6470 or (508) 393-6406; tougasfarm.com. Pick your own fruits, petting zoo, playground, wagon rides, prearranged cider pressing, bakery (featuring homemade donuts), store, and ice-cream stand.

- **West End Creamery,** 481 Purgatory Rd., Whitinsville; (508) 234-2022; westendcreamery.com. Ice-cream stand with views of Swan Pond, corn maze. Adventure Farm and miniature golf.

Harnessing the **Huskies**

For dog-sledding tours and lessons, contact **Northern Exposure Outfitters and Equipment,** 52 Log Hill Rd., Brookfield; (508) 525-5776 or (508) 867-4396; ne-outfitters.com.

Wachusett Mountain State Reservation (all ages)

345 Mountain Rd., Princeton; (978) 464-2987; mass.gov/eea/agencies/dcr/mass parks/region-central/wachusett-mountain-state-reservation.html. The visitor center is open daily 9 a.m. to 5 p.m. in season. The auto road is open from 9 a.m. to sunset. There is a $2 fee to drive the auto road to the summit.

Take the auto road to the highest point in Massachusetts east of the Berkshires, with spectacular views of Boston, the western Massachusetts Berkshires, the New Hampshire mountains, hawk migrations, and the autumn foliage spectacle. Within the 3,000-acre reservation, there are 17 miles of hiking trails (including 3.9 miles of the Midstate Trail, which runs from Ashburnham to the Rhode Island border) used in the winter for cross-country skiing. Wachusett Mountain has the largest known area of old-growth forest east of the Connecticut River in Massachusetts, with trees dating over 350 years old. **Warning:** Hunting is allowed at various times during the year. Check with the visitor center before you hike.

Other Things to See & Do

Animal Adventures, 33 Sugar Rd., Bolton; (978) 779-8988; animaladventures.net. Behind-the-scenes zoo and rescue facility. Open Tues through Sat 10 a.m. to 5 p.m. and Sun noon to 5 p.m.

Erving State Forest, Laurel Lake Recreational Area, 122 Long Pond Rd., Warwick; (978) 544-3939; mass.gov/eea/agencies/dcr/massparks/region-central/erving-state-forest. Scenic area loaded with water-based activities (boating and canoeing, swimming, and fishing). Trails for mountain biking, horseback riding, hiking, and cross-country skiing. Great place for a picnic. There is a $5 parking fee from Memorial Day to Labor Day.

Ft. Devens Museum, 94 Jackson Rd., third floor, Devens; (978) 772-1286; fortdevens museum.org. The museum tells the story of the men and women who worked, trained, and lived at Ft. Devens.

Gallery of African Art, 62 High St., Clinton; (978) 368-0227; galleryofafricanart.org. Large collection from the African continent representative of more than 32 tribes and their art.

Great Wolf Lodge New England, 150 Royal Plaza Dr., Fitchburg; greatwolf.com/newengland. Opening spring of 2014, 68,000-square-foot indoor water park in a very family-oriented lodge with spacious rooms and family suites.

Jumptown, 31 C St., Orange Airport (southside), Orange; (978) 544-5321 or (800) 890-JUMP; jumptown.com. Accelerated fall or tandem? Hmmm?! Minimum age is 18, but great viewing and picnicking spots for those who don't participate. Seasonal.

Lancaster Golf Center, 438 Old Union Turnpike (exit 34 off Route 2), Lancaster; (978) 537-8922; lancastergolfcenter.com. Miniature golf, ice cream, 9-hole par 3 "links" course, 9 batting cages, and bank basketball (hoopsters proceed through 18 stations, scoring points by making bank shots off a wild assortment of angled, curved, and unconventionally configured backboards).

Nashoba Paddler Rentals, 398 West Main St., Route 225 (at the Nashua River), Groton; (978) 448-8699; nashobapaddler.com. Open daily in summer and weekends in the spring and fall for paddles on the Nashua River. Hourly and daily rentals.

Museum of Russian Icons, 203 Union St., Clinton; (978) 598-5000; museumof russianicons.org. More than 500 Russian icons spanning six centuries.

Reed Homestead, 72 Main St (Route 119), Townsend; (978) 597-2106; townsend historicalsociety.org. Depiction of everyday life of five generations of the Reed family in the 1800s.

Top Fun Aviation Toy Museum, 21 Prichard St., Fitchburg; (978) 297-4337; top funaviation.com. Open weekends year-round. Admission fee. More than 2,000 toy airplanes, games, and puzzles from 1928 to the present. Fine tin toys from Germany, Japan, Hungary, and the US. An on-the-wall airport covers an entire wall and gives you a feeling of what it's like to be flying overhead and looking down to the earth below.

Wallace Civic Center and Planetarium, Fitchburg State University, 1000 John Fitch Hwy., Fitchburg; (978) 665-4938; fscfalcons.com. Two ice rinks, plus concerts.

Winchendon Historical Society, 151 Front St., Winchendon; (978) 297-2142; winchendonhistoricalsociety.com. Murdock-Whitney house museum, a 22-room mansion with a diverse collection.

Where to Eat

Blue Moon Diner, 102 Main St., Gardner; (978) 632-4333; bluemoondinergardner ma.com. Open 6 a.m. to 2 p.m. Mon through Fri and 6 a.m. to 1 p.m. on weekends. Breakfast served all day plus down-home lunches. $

Cornerstones Restaurant, 616 Central St., Leominster; (978) 537-1991; corner stonesleominster.com. From burgers to pasta, poultry to seafood and meats. Vegetarian entrees and a kids' menu. Serving lunch and dinner. $–$$

Freight House Antiques and Lunch Counter, 60 E. Main St. (Route 2, the Mohawk Trail), Erving; (413) 422-2828. Amusing shop full of antiques and oddities with a delightful lunch counter serving breakfast, salads, sandwiches, and desserts. $

The 1761 Old Mill, 89 State Rd. East (exit 25 off of Route 2 to Route 2A East), Westminster; (978) 874-5941; 1761oldmill.com. Former sawmill. Standard New England fare—hearty, filling, and delicious. Children's menu. $–$$

Slattery's Restaurant, 106 Lunenburg St., Fitchburg; (978) 342-8880; slatterys restaurant.com. Charming restaurant, extensive menu with kids' specialties. $–$$

Where to Stay

Chocksett Inn, 59 Laurelwood Rd., Sterling; (978) 422-3355 or (800) 331-7829; chocksettinn.com. Junction of I-190 and Route 12. Traditional New England inn with 29 rooms. Guest laundry, workout room, **Chocksett Restaurant** with fireplace, open to the public ($–$$). Full continental breakfast comes with your room. $–$$

Friendly Crossways Hostel and Retreat Center, 247 Littleton County Rd., Harvard; (978) 456-9386 or (978) 456-3649; friendlycrossways.com. The oldest continuously operating privately owned hostel in the US, this stayover offers family rooms, dorm rooms, or private rooms. Linens are included as well as kitchen privileges. $

Wachusett Village Inn, 9 Village Inn Rd., Westminster; (978) 874-2000 or (800) 342-1905 (reservations); wachusettvillageinn.com. Great location, restaurant (the **Black Diamond II Restaurant,** $–$$) with a children's menu, and an outdoor pool. $–$$$

Greater Worcester & the Blackstone Valley

The second-largest city in Massachusetts as well as New England, Worcester loses a lot of tourists to Boston, but it has managed to build a busy cultural life for itself with several good museums. The **Worcester Convention and Visitor's Bureau,** 30 Elm St., Worcester, MA 01609 (508-755-7400; centralmass .org), can provide you with information and maps. Other helpful organizations are Destination Worcester, 446 Main St., Suite 200, Worcester, MA 01608-2368 (508-735-1550; destinationworcester.org); the Worcester Regional Chamber of Commerce, 446 Main St., Suite 200, Worcester, MA 01608 (508-753-2924; worcesterchamber.org); and the City of Worcester, 44 Front St., Suite 530, Worcester, MA 01608 (508-799-1400; worcestermass.org). Meandering south is the Blackstone Valley, designated a National Heritage Corridor, with several formerly company-owned mill towns representative of the Industrial Revolution. It's a picturesque area with many recreational opportunities. Contact the **Blackstone Valley Chamber of Commerce** for more information on the area at (508) 234-9090 or visit their website at blackstonerivervalley.com/attractions.

Worcester

Douglas State Forest and Wallum Lake (all ages)

107 Wallum Lake Rd., Route 16, Douglas; (508) 476-7872; mass.gov/eea/agencies/dcr/massparks/region-central/douglas-state-forest.html. Open daily dawn to dusk; building and restrooms open Memorial Day to Labor Day, then 9 a.m. to 3 p.m. Labor Day to Columbus Day. Parking is $5 per car for state residents during summer. (Directions: I-90, exit 10, Route 395 south, Route 16 east for 5 miles, follow the signs.) Douglas State Forest is an enormous state forest—nearly 5,900 acres—with an abundance of picnic sites and Wallum Lake, a huge lake straddling Massachusetts and Rhode Island. Wallum Lake is a magnet for boating, fishing for stocked trout, and swimming. The beach has a bathhouse and lifeguards. Activities include hiking, mountain biking, horseback riding, snowmobiling, cross-country skiing, hunting, and snowshoeing on miles of trails. **The Midstate Trail,** a 95-mile hiking trail that extends from Central Massachusetts (near the border of

TopEvents in Central Massachusetts

January–September

- **Fire and Ice,** Jan, Old Sturbridge Village, Sturbridge; (508) 347-3362; osv.org

- **Antique Sleigh Rally,** Feb, Old Sturbridge Village, Sturbridge; (508) 347-3362; osv.org

- **Flora in Winter,** end of Jan, Worcester Art Museum, Worcester; (508) 799-4406; worcesterart.org

- **Washington's Birthday Celebration,** Feb, Old Sturbridge Village, Sturbridge; (508) 347-3362; osv.org

- **Central Massachusetts Flower Show,** Feb/Mar, DCU Centrum, Worcester; (800) 533-0229; centralmaflowershow.com

- **Green Day Celebration,** St. Patrick's Day, Wachusett Mountain, Princeton; (978) 464-2300; wachusett.com

- **Earth Day,** Apr, EcoTarium, Worcester; (508) 929-2700; ecotarium.org

- **Maple Days,** Mar, Old Sturbridge Village, Sturbridge; (508) 347-3362; osv.org

- **Lake Quinsigamond Regattas,** Mar through May, Lake Quinsigamond, Quinsigamond State Park, Worcester; qra.org

- **Athol to Orange River Rat Race,** Apr, Athol; (978) 249-9038; riverratrace.com

- **All American River Race,** last Sun of Apr, Sturbridge; (508) 347-9636; angelfire.com/ma3/sturbridgelions/lionscanoerace.pdf

- **Brimfield Flea Market,** May, July, and Sept, Brimfield Common, Brimfield; (413) 283-6149 or (413) 283-2418; brimfieldshow.com or qhma.com

- **Yankee Engine Steam Show,** mid-June, Orange Municipal Airport, Orange; (978) 249-3849; northquabbinchamber.com

- **Longsjo Classic Bike Race,** June, Fitchburg; (978) 345-1577; community-builders.net/2013/06/14/volunteer-for-fitchburgs-longsjo-classic-bike-race

- **Independence Day Celebration** and evening fireworks, July 4, Old Sturbridge Village, Sturbridge; (508) 347-3362; osv.org

- **Fire and Ice** (Fire Engines and Ice Cream), July, Old Sturbridge Village, Sturbridge; (508) 347-3362; osv.org

- **Red-Coats and Rebels Reenactment,** Aug, Old Sturbridge Village, Sturbridge; (508) 347-3362; osv.org

- **Bolton Fair at the Lancaster Fairgrounds,** Aug, 318 Seven Bridge Rd., Lancaster; (978) 365-7206; boltonfair.org

- **Spencer Fair,** Labor Day weekend, 48 Smithville Rd., Spencer; (508) 885-5814; thespencerfair.com

- **Earth Awareness Day,** Aug, Southwick Zoo, Mendon, (508) 883-9182; southwickzoo.com

- **Blackstone River Valley Greenway Challenge,** Sept, Blackstone River Valley; (401) 762-0250; greenwaychallenge.org

- **Early 19th Century Agricultural Fair,** Sept, Old Sturbridge Village, Sturbridge; (508) 347-3362; osv.org

- **Wachusett Mountain Annual Kidsfest,** late Sept, Princeton; (978) 464-2300; wachusett.com

- **Music Fest,** late Sept, Wachusett Mountain, Princeton; (978) 464-2300; wachusett.com

- **Fright Night in the Maze,** Oct, Davis Farmland, Children's Discovery Farm and Megamaze, Sterling; (978) 422-MOOO; davisfarmland.com

Rhode Island) to just west of Mt. Watatic in northern Massachusetts, runs for 7.8 miles through the forest.

EcoTarium (all ages)

222 Harrington Way, Worcester; (508) 929-2700; ecotarium.org. Open year-round, Tues through Sat 10 a.m. to 5 p.m., Sun noon to 5 p.m. Closed New Year's Day, Easter, Thanksgiving, and Christmas. Admission: $14 for adults, $8 for children 2 to 18, free for under age 2. Planetarium programs $5 per person, Explorers Express Train $3 per person. The Tree Canopy Walkway (open seasonally) is an additional fee of $10 (see schedule online). Parking is free.

The EcoTarium (formerly the New England Science Center) is focused on inspiring a passion for science and nature. An $18 million expansion and renovation plan created trails, an outdoor observation walkway, and an overhaul to the existing building's architecture. The Nature Trail traverses the property and rounds the two existing ponds, the Water Pavilion, and the Pier, giving access to more than 50 acres of meadow and woodland habitats. For a 12-minute overview tour of the property, sign up for the Explorers Express Train, a small-scale 1860s steam engine and train. (**Note:** Tall adults may be a bit uncomfortable!) The Tree Canopy Walkway allows you to study and inspect the leaf line of the trees. The walkway, suspended approximately 40 feet above the ground, allows you to observe the habitat of birds, insects, and wildlife. The outdoor exhibits include the very popular river otters, red fox, and several bird enclosures (a bald eagle, a barred owl, a great horned owl, a barn owl, hawks, and a turkey vulture). The EcoTarium also has a porcupine, skunks, and rat snakes in their outdoor Animal Corner. Inside the three-story building are several good interactive environmental exhibits (including their celebrated "The Arctic Next Door: Mount Washington," a wonderful hands-on exhibit that allows visitors to explore the extreme weather and climate on New England's highest peak), a huge natural-history collection, three large aquariums, and a planetarium show (the planetarium schedule is subject to change; call ahead). A great group activity for

Center of **Attention!**

For those who like to be in the middle of things, the geographic center of the state of Massachusetts is the town of Rutland, 12 miles northwest of Worcester.

More Than a **Mouthful**

The Nipmuc's name for Webster Lake (off Routes 16 and 193, Webster) is Lake Chargoggagoggmanchauggagoggchaubunagungamaugg. Not surprisingly, this is the longest geographic name in the US. Rough translation: I fish on my side of the lake, you fish on yours, and no one fishes in between. The road atlas tends to shorten it to Lake Chaubunagungamaug because of lack of space!

field trips or scouting groups is the Tree Climbing Expedition, which includes a training session, supervision of a guide, and the use of harnesses, helmets, and climbing gear for up to 10 people for $300.

John H. Chaffee Blackstone River Valley National Heritage Corridor (all ages)

There are 3 visitor centers in Massachusetts with information on the corridor: at River Bend Farm, located in the Blackstone River and Canal Heritage State Park, 287 Oak St., Uxbridge, (508) 278-7604 (open daily year-round 10 a.m. to 4 p.m.); at the Worcester Historical Museum, 30 Elm St., Worcester, (508) 753-8278 (open Tues through Sat 10 a.m. to 4 p.m.); and at Broad Meadow Brook Wildlife Sanctuary/Mass Audobon, 414 Massasoit Rd., Worcester, (508) 753-6087 (open Tues through Sat 10 a.m. to 4 p.m.). The website for the corridor is blackstonevalley corridor.org or nps.gov/blac/planyourvisit/events.

The **Blackstone River Valley National Heritage Corridor** covers communities from Worcester, Massachusetts, to Providence, Rhode Island. The winding river in the Blackstone Valley gave birth to hydropower that fueled most of the region's mills during the Industrial Revolution. This area is rich with history and leisure pastimes; the area's mills, villages, and canals help to reveal the story of the Industrial Revolution. Contact the visitor centers for a listing of museums and sites and a full schedule of events. Highlights include Waters Farm (watersfarm .com) in Sutton, which has preserved farm life from the 1800s; Lookout Rock in Northbridge, with wonderful vistas of the Blackstone Valley River; and the West Hill Dam and Park in Uxbridge for outdoor leisure, including swimming, fishing, biking, hiking, and riding. Recreational opportunities abound including hayrides, canal boat rides, historic sites and natural areas, canoeing, cross-country skiing, and ice skating. Ask for the auto-route tour map.

Purgatory Chasm State Reservation (all ages)

198 Purgatory Rd., Sutton; (508) 234-3733; mass.gov/eea/agencies/dcr/massparks/
region-central/purgatory-chasm-state-reservation.html. Open daily sunrise to sunset. Purgatory Chasm is closed in the winter because of the danger from snow
and ice, but the park is open. (Directions: I-90 to exit 10A Millbury, Route 146
south to exit 6, at the end of the ramp take a right onto Purgatory Road, Sutton,
follow the signs.) Pay and display parking $2.

The deep chasm is a dramatic sight and a nice spot to hike spring through fall,
but in the summer the cool, damp air is especially pleasant. A marked path leads
down the series of ravines that form the chasm. There are numerous picnic
spots in the reservation, as well as a playground with a merry-go-round, swings,
and a play structure to entertain the kids. *Caution:* This path is steep in spots
and isn't appropriate for children under 16 unless they are experienced hikers. In
lieu of the chasm, there is a a short, easy marked path through the woods that's
more appropriate for younger children (the Spring Path). It is advisable not to
hike the chasm during inclement weather because the rocks and the slopes are
extremely slippery.

Southwick's Zoo (12 and under)

2 Southwick St. (follow signs off Route 16), Mendon; (508) 883-9182 or
(800) 258-9182; southwickszoo.com. Open daily mid-Apr to mid-Oct
10 a.m. to 5 p.m. Admission: $22 for adults, $17 for children 3 to
12 and seniors over age 62, free for children under 3. Free
parking.

If the kids are into animals, they'll love a visit to Southwick's
Zoo, where they're likely to see giraffes, peacocks, cheetahs,
alligators, and more than a hundred other species of animals
on 200 acres—the largest zoo in New England and the
only one to have chimpanzees. There's a petting zoo
and a deer forest where you can approach the deer
and buy food to feed them (50 cents). Most sky-
rides travel through half of a park and return.
At Southwick's Zoo the Skyfari is triangular,
making the overview much more comprehensive;
you never go over the same habitat twice. Kids can take
rides on ponies (new stables), trains, kiddie rides, and camels
(all the rides cost an extra fee). During the summer there are

educational shows every day ranging from bird talks to the "Peacock Party," with trained peacocks that do tricks. Changes and improvements are ongoing; new habitats have been created for the sloths, the cheetahs, the giraffes, the hyenas, and the siamang (a type of ape). The Earth Discovery Center has informative presentations by Earth Limited. A plethora of dining opportunities and picnic areas are scattered throughout the park.

Worcester Art Museum (all ages)

55 Salisbury St., Worcester; (508) 799-4406; worcesterart.org. Open year-round, Wed through Fri and Sun 11 a.m. to 5 p.m., third Thurs 11 a.m. to 8 p.m., Sat 10 a.m. to 5 p.m.; closed major holidays, Mon, and Tues. Admission: $14 for adults, $12 for seniors and students, $6 for children 4 to 17. Free admission on the first Sat of the month from 10 a.m. to noon. The museum offers tours and daily activities for visitors; check the website.

Nearly every period of art is featured in this excellent medium-size city museum with a collection that spans over 51 centuries of history. Highlights include a gallery of mid-20th-century Contemporary art; a 6th-century floor mosaic in the stately Renaissance Court area; a 12th-century Romanesque Chalet called the Chapter House that was moved, stone by stone, from France; Asian galleries featuring an 11-headed, early 10th-century Japanese sculpture; and an extensive collection of Pre-Columbian Art in various media, including gold and ceramic. The museum has a fine representative collection of European painters (more than 478 paintings with a concentration on works of Italian, British, and French origin) and American painters (featuring Colonial paintings, American Impressionists, watercolors, and miniatures on ivory). In the spring of 2014, the John Woodman Higgins collection of medieval arms and armor (including ancient objects from Greek and Roman times) was integrated into the museum's collection; displayed on two floors, it encompasses over 4,000 square feet, allowing the entire collection to be showcased. Be sure to visit the Museum Gift Shop (open during gallery hours) and the Museum Cafe (open Wed through Sat 11:30 a.m. to 2 p.m.), which serves light snacks, lunches, and has a kids' menu. A garden cafe is open during the summer months in the courtyard.

Other Things to See & Do

Breezy Picnic Grounds Waterslides, 520 Northwest Main St., Douglas; (508) 476-2664 or (888) 821-6222; breezysummer.com. Admission fee. Three 300-foot waterslides and picnic grounds on a clear, inviting lake. Popular swimming hole. Restrooms on property.

Broad Meadow Brook Wildlife Sanctuary, 414 Massasoit Rd., Worcester; (508) 753-6087; massaudubon.org. Trails open daily dawn to dusk. Visitor center, open Tues to Sat 9 a.m. to 4 p.m., provides information on the Blackstone River Valley National Heritage Corridor. Largest urban wildlife sanctuary in New England.

Clara Barton Birthplace, 68 Clara Barton Rd., North Oxford; (508) 987-2056, ext. 2013; clarabartonbirthplace.org. Home of America's most famous nurse and founder of the American Red Cross. Admission fee. Check website for hours and seasons of operation.

DCU Center, 50 Foster St., Worcester; (508) 755-6800; dcucentre.com. National and international musical acts, home of the Worcester Sharks of the AHL, as well as family shows. Buy tickets at the box office, or call Ticketmaster at (800) 745-3000.

Hanover Theatre of the Performing Art, 2 Southbridge St., Worcester; (877) 571-SHOW; thehanovertheatre.org. Theater, music, and family entertainment.

Mechanics Hall, 321 Main St., Worcester; (508) 752-5608; mechanicshall.org. Elegant pre–Civil War concert hall with superb acoustics.

Tower Hill Botanic Garden, 11 French Dr., Boylston; (508) 869-6111; towerhillbg .org. Open year-round; call for schedule. Distinctive 132-acre horticultural collection featuring a lawn garden with trees and shrubs, wildlife, and cottage garden, a secret garden with perfumed undergrowth, a systematic garden, an apple orchard, and an orangerie filled in winter with blooming flora. Views of Mt. Wachusetts. Twigs Cafe ($).

Vertical World Adventures, 19 Brigham Rd., Paxton; (508) 344-6776; verticalworld adventures.com. Professionally guided outfitted adventure company. Hiking, rock climbing, mountaineering, and ice climbing. Trips for schools and scouting groups.

Willard House and Clock Museum, 11 Willard St., North Grafton; (508) 839-3500; willardhouse.org. One-hour guided tour offered, seasonal hours, check the schedule. Admission: $10 for adults, $6 for children 6 to 12, free for children under 6. Historic house and clock museum containing paintings, fine arts, and furniture.

Worcester Historical Museum, 30 Elm St., Worcester; (508) 753-8278; worcester history.org. History and exhibits on Worcester.

Worcester Sharks of the AHL, 50 Foster St., Worcester; (508) 929-0500; sharks ahl.com. Preseason starts in Sept; season is Oct through Apr. San Jose Sharks farm team. Hockey games played at the DCU Convention Center.

Worcester Tornadoes, 303 Main St. (office), Worcester; (508) 792-2288; canam league.com/teams/worcester.php. Canadian American minor league baseball. Home field is Fitton Field (located at 1 College St.), a 3,000-seat park at the College of the Holy Cross.

Where to Eat

Barre Mill Restaurant, 90 Main St., Route 32, South Barre; (978) 355-2987; barre mill.com. Open Wed through Sun for dinner and Sun for lunch. Winner of Best Chowder Award. Children's menu. $$

Flying Rhino Cafe and Watering Hole, 278 Shrewsbury St., Worcester; (508) 757-1450; flyingrhinocafe.com. Follow the trail to mouthwatering food! Daily specials, kids' menu. $–$$$

Hebert Candies Mansion, 575 Hartford Turnpike (Route 20), Shrewsbury; (508) 845-8051; hebertcandies.com. Headquarters of Hebert Candies, America's first roadside candy store; watch chocolates being made. Great chocolates (free samples) and make-your-own sundae bar. Children's workshops and events. $

Maxwell Silverman's Toolhouse, 25 Union St. (Lincoln Sq.), Worcester; (508) 755-1200; maxwellmaxine.com. Restored toolhouse factory building; steak and seafood specialties. $–$$$

The Old Timer Restaurant and Tap Room, 155 Church St., Clinton; (978) 365-5980; oldtimerrestaurant.com. This restaurant (ca. 1929) has been a Clinton institution. Live musical entertainment many nights (see schedule). The Sunday afternoon buffet from Sept to June is quite popular. The big honor here is to have your hat retired above the bar (but a very kid-friendly place). $–$$

Webster House, 1 Webster St. (Webster Sq.), Worcester; (508) 757-7208; webster houseweb.com. Family friendly; Greek specialties, homemade pies. Worcester landmark. $–$$

Where to Stay

Beechwood Hotel, 363 Plantation St., Worcester; (508) 754-5789 or (800) 344-2589; beechwoodhotel.com. Boutique hotel of 73 rooms (some with fireplaces or skylights). **Ceres Bistro** is a fine-dining farm-to-table restaurant with a casual vibe ($–$$$). Complimentary continental breakfast. $$–$$$$

Rose Cottage, 24 Worcester St., West Boylston; (508) 835-4034; therosecottage-ma .com. Close to Worcester-area attractions, 1850 Gothic Revival with views of the Wachusetts Reservoir. Rooms have private baths, and there are 2 executive apartments with kitchens for weekly rentals. Homemade breakfasts (except for the executive apartments). $-$$

Quabbin Reservoir & the Greater Sturbridge Area

Quabbin, which means "place of many waters," lives up to its name. The Quabbin Reservoir covers more than 39 square miles (181 miles of shoreline), with 120,000 acres of state-owned watershed land surrounding it. Scenic hikes and trails are especially magnificent in the autumn. Another draw to this area is Old Sturbridge Village, one of the best outdoor living history museum/villages in the country. Contact the **Sturbridge Area Tourist Association,** 380 Main St., Sturbridge, MA 01566 (800-628-8379; sturbridgetownships.com), for more information.

Quabbin Reservoir and Park (all ages)

485 Ware Rd., entrance on Route 9 between Ware and Belchertown; (413) 323-7221; mass.gov/eea/agencies/dcr/massparks/region-central/quabbin-reservoir .html. The reservation is open daily dawn to dusk. Visitor center open year-round 8:30 a.m. to 4:30 p.m. Mon through Fri, and 8:30 a.m. to 4:30 p.m. Sat and Sun from Nov through mid-Mar, changing to 9 a.m. to 5 p.m. during Daylight Savings Time. Free, except for a charge for renting a boat to go fishing (you can fish for free on the shore) and the $6 charge for parking at the 3 boat-launch areas. *Note:* **The west entrance now only accesses the visitor center and the administration building. Only foot or bike traffic is allowed across to both the Winsor Dam and the Goodnough Dike because of security restrictions.**

Fun Fact

When full, Quabbin Reservoir holds 412 billion gallons of water and can safely supply 158 million gallons per day to the city of Boston.

Quabbin Reservoir and Park is a protected watershed of the Quabbin Reservoir, which supplies water to 2.4 million residents of Massachusetts (40 percent of Massachusetts residents). The man-made watershed lands also provide wilderness, wildlife, forest, research, historical, and recreational resources. The visitor center, located at Winsor Dam, provides information about the many hiking trails on the 87-square-mile reservation (the Park) and a few exhibits about the reservoir's construction. The reservoir's design was begun in 1927; the towns of Dana, Prescott, Greenwich, and Enfield were "discontinued," which means that the state bought the land from the residents and then flooded the land after they vacated (for more information on the discontinued towns, visit the Swift River Historical Society Museum, 40 Elm St., New Salem; 978-544-6882; foquabbin.org/srvhs). Before creating Quabbin Reservoir, the land was completely cleared of all edifices, structures, and graves. In all, over 7,600 graves were moved, the majority of which were interred at the Quabbin Park Cemetery in Ware. Enfield Lookout, up a winding road after you cross the dam, overlooks a spectacular view of the reservoir and the hills that were once the town of Enfield. A good, though hilly, walk begins across the road from the lookout (pick up maps at the visitor center). Fishing and boating (for fishing purposes only) are at designated areas. No dogs, swimming, camping or fires, off-road vehicles, sliding on dams, or cross-country skiing. *TIP:* Go to the east or middle entrances for vehicle access to Quabbin Reservoir and Park.

Old Sturbridge Village   (all ages)

1 Old Sturbridge Village Rd., Sturbridge; (508) 347-3362 or (800) SEE-1830; osv .org. Open year-round. Hours change seasonally; check the website for up-to-date information. Admission (good for a second day within 10 days): $24 for adults, $8 for kids 3 to 17, free for children 2 and under.

Worth at least one full day's visit for any family, the village re-creates the daily life of a rural early 19th-century community, with its farms, fields, shops, houses, and outlying mill areas. Beginning in the 1940s, more than forty buildings from all over New England were carefully dismantled and transported here, then painstakingly reassembled and furnished in period style. The period portrayed by the village is particularly significant because it was a time when New Englanders' lives were transformed by the rise of commerce and manufacturing, improvements in agriculture and transportation, emigration and growing urbanization, and the political and social changes of a prospering young country. Younger children will enjoy seeing the costumed interpreters who set the scene, as well as the animals, the unpaved streets, and the interesting simple tools and machines that the interpreters use. An authentic reproduction of a Concord Stage Coach gives rides around the common for an extra fee. Weekends in winter you can be transported by sleigh, or try your skills at sledding or ice skating (weather permitting).

Kidstory caters to kids ages 3 to 10. This interactive area allows the children to try on the settlers' garb and dress of the early 1800s, pretend to cook over a hearth stove, and reenact the life of a student or a schoolmarm in a period school room. Other highlights include a farm, an onslaught of games and puzzles, and an extensive collection of story books. Older kids will enjoy the interaction with the interpreters, who welcome questions and participation in many activities such as sheep shearing, spinning, weaving, gardening, fireplace cooking, tinsmithing, watercolor painting, and candle making. A jam-packed typical day's offering could include a lineup of an old-fashioned baseball game with the villagers, a tug-of-war, a hoops race, milking a cow, and trying your hand at fishing. This is all above and beyond the ongoing demonstrations and the interpreted talks in the historical village buildings. Special events occur all year; call for a schedule since daily events are always changing.

TIP: The Red Coats and Rebels Reenactment is the largest reenactment in New England, with nearly 1,000 participants in a mock battle. This is one of the most popular summer events at the village.

Note: Advance registration is required for fee-based activities. Wear comfortable shoes; the property is large. Bring a stroller for younger children, although you'll have to leave it outside many of the buildings. The village is accessible for visitors with disabilities (more than half of the buildings are wheelchair accessible), and sign-language interpreters are available by prior arrangement.

Letterboxing 101 (aka Geocaching)

To encourage kids to go on a family hike or outing, make it a treasure hunt for a letterbox! Letterboxes are waterproof (usually plastic) cases hidden by a letterboxer and containing a stamp, a stamp pad, and some sort of journal. You affix your own personal stamp to designate your discovery and use their stamp on your own scrapbook. You'll find clues to track down concealed letterboxes on the Internet. For more information on letterboxing and how to start your adventure, visit letterboxing.org, atlasquest.com, or geocaching .com. The Trustees of Reservations have a similar program at their properties throughout the state that they call **Quest Detective** that is geared toward kids (thetrustees.org/things-to-do/special-events/questdetective/).

The Salem Cross Inn Farm and Restaurant (all ages) 🏛 🏇 🍴
260 West Main St. (Route 9), West Brookfield; (508) 867-2345; salemcrossinn.com. Restaurant is open year-round. Seasonal schedule; check their website for up-to-date information on dates and hours. Children's menu. $–$$$

Voted "Best New England Dining for 2013" by *Yankee Magazine,* the Salem Cross Inn is a perennial favorite. Listed in the National Register of Historic Places, the Salem Cross Inn is named for the hex mark on the front door latch that was placed there to fend off witchcraft when the building was erected in 1720. It was built by a grandson of Peregrine White, the only male baby born on the *Mayflower* while in Plymouth Harbor. The 600-acre property is a working farm. In winter sleigh rides are offered (weather permitting) with the Fireplace Feasts. Hayrides are offered with the Drover Roasts in the warmer months, and hiking is allowed. The dining room menu changes with the season. During the winter, roasts are cooked on a roasting jack (the only one remaining in the country), and breads are baked in an original beehive oven. Outdoor grilling takes place in the summer months at the Hex Bar Tavern. Special Family Days throughout the year; call for dates.

TopEvents in Central Massachusetts

October–December

- **BBQ Fest,** Oct, Wachusett Mountain, Princeton; (978) 464-2300; wachusett.com

- **Apple Fest,** late Oct, Wachusett Mountain, Princeton; (978) 464-2300; wachusett.com

- **Taste of the Maze II,** mid-Oct, Nashoba Valley Winery; Bolton; (978) 779-5521; nashobawinery.com

- **Annual North Quabbin Garlic and Arts Festival,** Oct, 60 Chestnut Hill Rd., Orange; (978) 544-9023; garlicandarts.org

- **Great Pumpkin Fest,** Oct, Ecotarium, Worcester; (508) 929-2700 or (508) 929-2703 (tickets); ecotarium.org

- **Annual Harvest Fest and Scarecrow Contest,** Oct, Sturbridge; (508) 347-3313; publickhouse.com

- **Moo Moo Halloween Party,** Oct, Ecotarium, Worcester; (508) 929-2700; ecotarium.org. Buy tickets at (508) 929-2703.

- **Taste of the Maze,** Oct, Nashoba Valley Winery, Bolton; (978) 779-5521; nashobawinery.com

- **Blue Grass and Brew,** late Oct, Nashoba Valley Winery, Bolton; (978) 779-5521; nashobawinery.com

- **Thanksgiving Festival at Red Apple Farm,** Nov, Phillipston; (978) 249-6763 or (978) 534-2302; redapplefarm.com/annual-thanksgiving-harvest-festival

- **Thanksgiving at Olde Sturbridge Village,** Nov, Old Sturbridge Village, Sturbridge; (508) 347-3362; osv.org

- **Holidays at WAM,** Thanksgiving to New Year's, Worcester Art Museum, Worcester; (508) 799-4406; worcesterart.org

- **Chain of Lights Holiday Celebration,** Dec, Worcester County; (508) 753-2920; worcester.org

- **Polar Express,** mid-Dec, Wachusett Mountain, Princeton; (978) 464-2300; wachusett.com

- **Christmas by Candlelight,** Dec, Old Sturbridge Village, Sturbridge; (508) 347-3362; osv.org

- **Christmas Journey,** Dec, Ecotarium, Worcester; (508) 929-2700; ecotarium.org. Buy tickets at (508) 929-2703.

- **Annual New Year's Eve Celebration,** Dec 31, Wachusett Mountain, Princeton; (978) 464-2300; wachusett.com

- **First Night Worcester,** Dec 31, downtown Worcester; (508) 799-4909; firstnightworcester.org

Other Things to See & Do

Aerial Adventures, North Brookfield; (508) 867-9000; aerialadventuresusa.com. Balloon rides and powered parachute instruction give a bird's-eye view of the panorama below.

Norcross Wildlife Sanctuary, 30 Peck Rd., Monson/Wales; (413) 267-9654; norcrossws.org. Trails open Apr through Nov, weather permitting. Two natural-history museums and 8,000 acres (6,000 of which are on private land) of rare wildflowers and plants. The public is welcome on 2 miles of trails that crisscross the 100 acres that can be accessed by the public (a miniaturized version of the greater sanctuary). Don't miss the formal gardens, the orchard plantings, and the open spaces. Family education programs. Picnic area. No dogs allowed. **Free.**

Rock House Reservation, Route 9, West Brookfield; (413) 532-1631; thetrustees .org. Glaciation created the rock refuge inhabited by wintering Indian tribes. The hiking trail is not suitable for young children because of the terrain changes. Scenic.

Stageloft Repertory Theater, 450A Main St., Sturbridge; (508) 347-9005; stage loft.com. Musicals, dramas, murder mysteries, and comedies. Semiprofessional.

White's Landing, 7 Fiskdale Rd. (Route 148), Brookfield; (508) 867-5561; whites landing.com. Boat rentals of canoes and kayaks, historic 1-hour river cruise.

Where to Eat

Cedar Street Restaurant, 12 Cedar St., Sturbridge; (508) 347-5800; cedarstreet grille.com. Gourmet food in a contemporary metropolitan setting. Order small plates for tastes of a variety of dishes tapas-style. Kid-friendly options. $$–$$$

Oxhead Tavern at the Sturbridge Host, 366 Main St., Sturbridge; (508) 347-7393; sturbridgehost.com. Historic building overlooking a lake with typical New England fare. Open for lunch and dinner. $–$$$

Publick House Restaurant, Route 131, 277 Main St. (on the common), Sturbridge; (508) 347-3313; publickhouse.com. Two dining rooms in a time-honored setting; the Historic Tap Room is more traditional and the Ebenezer Tavern is more casual. Each room has a fireplace and shares the same menu and pricing. New England cooking: thick chops, pot roast, lobster pie, and Indian pudding for dessert. Open for all three meals, kids' menu, bake shop. $–$$$

Avellino's and the Duck, 502 Main St. (in the Whistling Swan building), Fiskdale; (508) 347-2321; avellinorestaurant.com (for Avellino's) and theducksturbridge.com (for the Duck Restaurant). The **Avellino Restaurant,** a Diner's Choice winner, is on the first floor and serves traditional Italian fare. Food demo seminars called "Cooking with Rico" (the chef) are held monthly. The **Duck Restaurant** is upstairs and is more laid-back in a barnlike setting. Both have kids' menus and use local purveyors to source their food. $–$$$

Where to Stay

Nathan Goodale House B&B, 11 Warren Rd., Brimfield; (413) 245-9228; brimfield .org. Wonderful location near the center of Brimfield. Beautiful Victorian home. No small children or pets. $–$$

Old Sturbridge Inn & Reeder Family Lodges, 1 Old Sturbridge Rd. (Route 20), Sturbridge; (508) 347-5056 or (800) 733-1830; osv.org/inn. Newly reopened in June of 2013.Wight House (on the National Register of Historic Places) with 10 traditional-style rooms, or a 29-unit modern lodging. Packages include discounted admission to Old Sturbridge Village. Pool for the kids. **Free** breakfast and parking. $–$$

Publick House Properties, Route 131 (on the Common), 277 Main St., Sturbridge; (508) 347-3313 or (800) 782-5425; publickhouse.com. Large complex of accommodations consisting of the **1771 Publick House Historic Inn** (17 rooms), the modern **Country Motor Lodge** (92 rooms), and the **Chamberlain House,** with 6 suite accommodations. All guests have access to the pool and playground at the Publick House. $–$$

Yankee Cricket Bed and Breakfast, 106 Five Bridge Rd., Brimfield; (413) 245-0030; yankeecricket.com. Hand-painted muraled breakfast room, a keeping room with a hearth, outdoor deck overlooking the woods, rooms with private bath. Full breakfast. Kids 12 and up. $$

The North Shore, Cape Ann, and the Merrimack Valley

The ragged coastline of the North Shore begins in the shipyards on Boston's north edges. As the crow flies, it stretches for 30 miles up and around the fist of Cape Ann, in and out of Ipswich Bay, and along to the New Hampshire border. Along the way are the historic towns of Saugus, Lynn, Marblehead, Salem, Gloucester, Rockport, Ipswich, and Newburyport. Families flock to the museums of old Salem to hear the dark tales of the country's early history, retold here on-site and in chilling detail. Enchanting Marblehead's narrow streets and dollhouse-like buildings stand in stark contrast to the workaday fishing villages of Gloucester and Rockport. Beautiful beaches and state parks bring families to Ipswich, Salisbury, Gloucester, Manchester-by-the-Sea, Newburyport, and Topsfield. Mill towns such as Lowell and Lynn, which were on the cutting edge of the Industrial Revolution, are now sites of learning and history. For further information, contact the **North of Boston Convention and Visitors Bureau,** exit 60, Route 95, Salisbury (978-465-6555; northofboston.org), the **Greater Merrimack Valley Convention and Visitors Bureau,** 9 Central St., Suite 201, Lowell, MA 01852 (978-459-6150 or 800-215-9805; merrimackvalley .org), or the **Essex National Heritage Area,** 221 Essex St., Salem (978-740-0444; essexheritage.org. or coastal byway.org).

Saugus

Saugus's main commercial street is Route 1, which divides the town into two parts. On either side of the highway are two interesting tourism sites, the Saugus Ironworks and the Breakheart Reservation. Saugus was settled in 1630, and the first successful ironworks in the country was established here. The Breakheart

TopPicks for the North Shore, Cape Ann, and the Merrimack Valley

- **Parker River National Wildlife Refuge** and **Plum Island,** Newburyport

- **Crane Beach,** Ipswich

- **Salem Maritime National Historic Site** and the **Peabody Essex Museum,** Salem

- **Marblehead Harbor,** especially during Race Week

- **Lowell National Historical Park** and the **American Textile History Museum,** Lowell

- **Bearskin Neck,** Rockport

- **Salem** and all its various sites during **Haunted Happenings**

Reservation is a 600-acre oasis straddling the communities of Saugus and Wakefield. For more information, contact the **Saugus Chamber of Commerce,** 58 Essex St., MEG Building, Saugus; (781) 233-8407; sauguschamber.com.

Breakheart Reservation (all ages)

177 Forest St., Saugus; (781) 233-0834; mass.gov/eea/agencies/dcr/massparks/ region-north/breakheart-reservation.html. Open dawn to dusk year-round. Free. Breakheart is busy year-round. The property includes forestland with a variety of hiking trails, two freshwater lakes, playgrounds, and picnicking shelters with stoves. Pearce Lake, framed by Eagle Rock, is a great spot for a cooling splash on a hot summer's day or to try your hand at catching a big one (catch-and-release programs at both Pearce and Silver Lakes). The beach at Pearce Lake is lifeguarded in season (July 4 to Labor Day) and wheelchair accessible. An extensive trail system encourages hiking, mountain biking, cross-country skiing, snowshoeing, and wildlife viewing with views of Boston, southern New Hampshire, and into the heart of Massachusetts. Annual events include Maple Sugarin', a First-Day Hike, and birding tours. Reservations for special events are required, and a small fee may be charged. For schools and nonprofit groups,

THE NORTH SHORE, CAPE ANN, AND THE MERRIMACK VALLEY

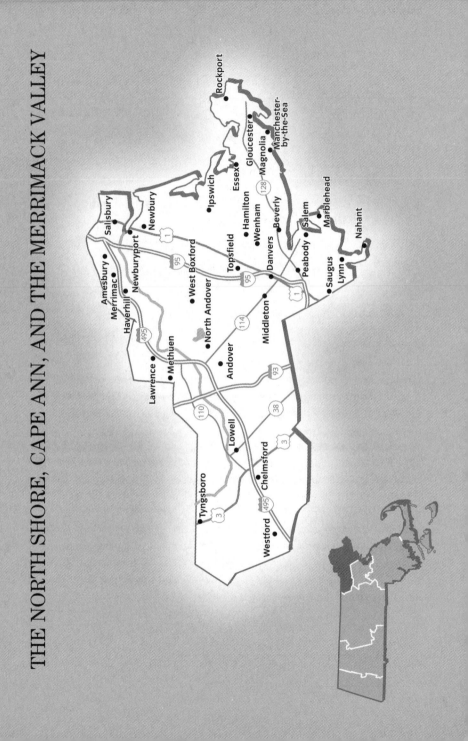

there is **Camp Nihan Environmental Educational Camp** on the Breakheart Reservation property (131 Walnut St., Saugus), with overnight facilities. For more information, call (781) 231-1203. Adjacent to Breakheart is the **Kasabuski Ice Skating Arena** (781-231-4183), which can be paired with a visit to the reservation.

Saugus Ironworks National Historic Site (all ages)

244 Central St., Saugus; (781) 233-0050; nps.gov/sair. Directions: From Route 1 take the Walnut Street exit and follow the National Historic Site signs. Open Apr through Oct, 9 a.m. to 5 p.m. daily. Check the website for tour times and schedules. Free.

The Saugus Ironworks is the birthplace of the ironmaking industry in the colonies. The Iron Works House, one of the last 17th-century buildings in Saugus, was saved and restored in 1915 by Wallace Nutting, an authority on colonial American buildings and furniture and a founder of the colonial revitalist movement. Archaeological digs unearthed the remains of the ironworks, and in 1954 reconstruction of the site was completed. The ironworks has five functioning waterwheels. There are four sets of bellows, a 500-pound water-powered hammer, and a rolling and slitting mill. Park guides run the machinery, but the waterwheels operate only from May through Oct. Blacksmiths demonstrate their skills during special events. Educational programs for kids are offered. Don't forget to visit the interpretive museum.

Where to Eat

Kelly's Roast Beef, 595 Broadway St., Saugus; (781) 233-5000; kellysroastbeef .com. Family owned and operated since 1951. The kids will love the oversize fish tank. Known for its famous rare roast beef overstuffed sandwiches with sauce and fried onion rings. Gluten-free options. $

Kowloon, 948 Broadway, Route 1 North, Saugus; (781) 233-0077; kowloonrestaurant .com. Front entrance guarded by a huge carved tiki. Specialties include Thai, Polynesian, Cantonese, and Szechuan food and sushi. House band Fri and Sat in the main dining room. Kowloon Comedy performs upstairs. $–$$$

Prince Restaurant and Giggles Comedy Club, 517 Broadway, Route 1, Saugus; (781) 233-9950; princepizzeria.com. Pizza and pasta under the leaning tower. Kids' menu. Giggles Comedy Club entertains on weekends. $–$$

Lynn & Nahant

Once part of the same township, Lynn and Nahant evolved into two separate entities. Lynn is an urban center, while Nahant has retained its charm as a small seaside village. A popular seacoast haven for the wealthy in the 1800s, Nahant is connected to Lynn by a causeway. Lynn's earliest settlers were shoemakers by trade, giving birth to a city that in its heyday would earn an international reputation for shoe production.

Lynn Museum (all ages)

590 Washington St., Lynn; (781) 581-6200; lynnmuseum.org. **Check the website for hours and days that they are open. Admission: $5 for adults, free for students.** The Lynn Museum and Historical Society was founded in 1897 to preserve and chronicle Lynn's evolution from an early settlement to a strong manufacturing presence. Wind your way through the interactive displays depicting Lynn's history, its industries, and its citizens. Youth and adult educational programming. The Research Library on Lynn History (soon to be digitized) is run by the Lynn Historical Society and is open by appointment.

Lynn Shore Reservation / Nahant Beach (all ages)

1 Causeway St. (Nahant Causeway), Nahant; (617) 727-1368 or (781) 485-2803; mass.gov/eea/agencies/dcr/massparks/region-north/lynn-shore-and-nahant-beach-reservation.html. **Main parking lot opens dawn to dusk, end of June to the end of Sept. Side parking lots accessible year-round. Parking fee at Long Beach May through Sept 8 a.m. to 5 p.m.**
Nahant Beach, also known as Long Beach, is a crescent of pure white sand lifeguarded until 6 p.m. in season. There are swings, ball fields, racquetball and

Raiders of **the Lost Rock**

The notorious pirate Thomas Veal is said to be buried with his treasure in Dungeon Rock in Lynn Woods. As the legend goes, Veal was trapped in the cave while examining his treasure when an earthquake struck, bringing down boulders and burying him with his booty for eternity. Children dream of uncovering the treasure!

tennis courts, showers and toilets, and a playground near the Lynn end of the beach. The beach promenade (aka Lynn Shore Reservation) goes from **King's Beach** on the Lynn/Nahant line past **Lynn Beach** to Swampscott, about a 2-mile walk. The reservation and beach are available year-round for walking, jogging, and biking. Boats can be launched at Lynn Harbor Marina.

Lynn Woods Reservation (all ages)

106 Penney Brook Rd., main entrance is accessed from Walnut Street, Lynn; (781) 477-7123; ci.lynn.ma.us/citydepartments_lynnwoods; or (781) 593-7773 (friends of Lynn Woods); flw.org. Open dawn to dusk. Download maps from the Internet before your arrival; limited supply at the park headquarters. Call the Program Information hotline for information on tours and special events at (781) 477-7094. Free.

Lynn Woods is the second-largest municipal park in the Greater Boston area, covering 2,200 acres in Lynn, Lynnfield, and Saugus. Three scenic ponds are used as town reservoirs for Lynn, so there is no swimming or boating here, but they are a pretty background seen from some of the hiking trails. A favorite hike for kids is the Jackson Path trail leading to Dungeon Rocks. There's a cave here that you can enter Tues through Sat, May 1 to Oct 31, from 9 a.m. to 2:30 p.m. (subject to change; call for the schedule). For a special treat, a guide, costumed as a pirate, will take the children to the bowels of the cave before Halloween (check the website for the Pirate Festival). Other fun trails lead to the stone tower on Burrill Hill, the rose garden, and the steel tower on Mount Gilead. Thirty miles of scenic trails offer many pleasurable distractions. Pick from mountain biking, horseback riding, and cross-country skiing depending on the season. There's also a playground. Landscape architect Frederick Law Olmsted consulted here and advised that Lynn Woods be left a rugged forest environment; thus, the park is not wheelchair- or stroller-friendly. Lynn Woods Reservation is a very safe park, and the trails are well marked so it's hard to get lost.

Woman of **Valor**

Mary Baker Eddy, a resident of Lynn from 1875 to 1882 (8 Broad St., Lynn; 800-277-8943, ext. 100), was honored in the National Women's Hall of Fame as the only American woman to found a world religion. The Christian Science Church, which she founded, advocates healing through prayer.

Other Things to See & Do

Lynn Auditorium, 3 City Hall Sq., Lynn; (781) 581-2971; lynnauditorium.com. Cultural and event venue holding over 2,100 people.

North Shore Navigators, Fraser Field, 365 Western Ave., Lynn; (781) 595-9400; nsnavs.com. Member of the Future's Collegiate Baseball League. Tickets are $6 for adults and $5 for kids, and $1 will buy you a hot dog! Fireworks at every Fri night home game.

Where to Eat

Porthole Restaurant, 98 the Lynnway, Lynn; (781) 595-7733; portholerestaurant .com. Nautical theme (the waitstaff wear sailor-like attire). Nice ocean view. Signature dish is Baby Haddock Roman. Children's menu. $–$$

Tides Restaurant and Bar, 2B Wilson Rd., Nahant Beach, Nahant; (781) 593-7500; tidesnahant.com. Open year-round for lunch and dinner. This restaurant has great views of Nahant Beach and the Lynn/Boston skyline. Varied kids' menu; standard menu runs from sandwiches, pizza, and pasta to seafood. High chairs. $–$$

Marblehead

In the picturesque harbor town of Marblehead, the streets are so narrow and many of the buildings so small that the town resembles a scaled-down model, but it's a real place where real people live. Walk the twisting streets, eat seafood while you watch the boats, see a historic painting, and immerse yourself in one of the best-preserved seaside villages in Massachusetts.

When you arrive in Marblehead, visit the **Marblehead Chamber of Commerce** at 62 Pleasant St. (781-631-2868; visitmarblehead.com) or go to the chamber's information booth on Route 114, corner of Pleasant and Spring Streets (781-639-8469; marbleheadchamber.org), to pick up a copy of the self-guided walking-tour brochure and to ask questions about the day's activities. The booth is open daily, noon to 4 p.m. midweek and 10 a.m. to 5 p.m. weekends from Memorial Day through Columbus Day. *TIP:* An audio walking tour of Marblehead can be downloaded from your computer at visitmarblehead.com.

Abbot Hall and the Waterfront Parks and Sights
(all ages)

188 Washington St., Marblehead; (781) 631-0528. Abbott Hall (the town hall) has seasonal hours; call to check the hours. **Free.**

Abbot Hall, which still operates as the town hall, is the prime tourist destination in Marblehead. Enter through the main entrance and walk through the lobby and then into the room on your left. You'll be confronted by an enormous painting (9 by 12 feet) of the original *Spirit of '76* by Archibald Willard, given to the town in 1876 by General John Devereux, whose son was the model for the drummer boy. After you've seen the painting, follow the walking tour through Marblehead's spindly streets, ending up by the water. Watch the boats from **Clark Landing** (at the end of State Street) or from **Crocker Park** (11 Front St. off State Street). If you want to have a picnic lunch, there are two excellent sites to choose from: **Fort Sewall**, 11 Fort Sewall Ln., at the end of Front Street, and **Chandler Hovey Park**, 6 Lighthouse Ln., at the end of Follett Street on the eastern end of Marblehead Neck, overlooking the pyramidal skeletal **Marblehead Lighthouse** (1835) and the harbor.

Hide and **Seek**

Militia weapons were stored in **Marblehead Powder House** in 1775, when the British occupied Boston. Today, the Powder House on Green Street stands as one of the few powder houses left in the US.

Jeremiah Lee Mansion and J.O.J. Frost Folk Art Gallery
(ages 6 and up)

170 Washington St., Marblehead; (781) 631-1768; marbleheadmuseum.org/
properties/lee-mansion. The Jeremiah Lee Mansion is open June 1 through Oct,
Tues through Sat 10 a.m. to 4 p.m. The J.O.J. Frost Folk Art Gallery is open year-
round Tues through Fri 10 a.m. to 4 p.m. and Sat 10 a.m. to 4 p.m. June through
Oct. Admission: $5 for nonmembers at the mansion, free at the Frost Folk Art
Gallery.

Tour this outstanding example of Georgian architecture and craftsmanship,
with original hand-painted wallpaper dating from 1771. There's a collection of
19th-century children's furniture and toys scattered throughout the mansion.
Be sure to come on a sunny day to explore the Lee Mansion Gardens, lovingly
maintained and restored by the Marblehead Garden Club as a series of themed
rooms. Across the road from the Lee home is the J.O.J. Frost Folk Art Gallery,
which has a painting and a model depicting life in Marblehead from a seafarer's
point of view.

Other Things to See & Do

Crowninshield Island (formerly named Brown Island), Beacon Street to Dolliber
Cove (see the website for directions), Marblehead; (978) 526-8687; thetrustees.org.
Free admission. Open year-round sunrise to sunset. This island off the coast of
Marblehead is owned by the Trustees of Reservations. The idyllic setting is great for
nature walks, birding, picnicking, swimming, and fishing. To reach the island, you can
walk across during low tide or go by boat. **Warning:** Check the tide schedule, or
you'll get caught on the island. Arrive 1 hour prior to dead low tide, and leave 1 hour
after dead low tide. Free.

Brace for **the Race**

The America's Cup Title was held for three consecutive years in
Marblehead in the 1880s. While it may not be the America's Cup,
Race Week in Marblehead is big doings nowadays, with competi-
tors from around the globe. Race week is held the last week in July.
Call the Boston Yacht Club at (781) 631-3100 or go to mheadrace.org
for details.

Special Times

Sandwiched around the Fourth of July holiday, the **Marblehead Festival of the Arts** (781-639-ARTS; marbleheadfestival.org) is the big kickoff to summer. There is an arts competition for all ages, food, street performances, derbies, and competitions sponsored by area organizations. Parking for some events can be scarce, particularly in Old Town Marblehead.

Devereaux Beach, 155 Ocean Ave., Marblehead. Small beach with picnic tables. Lifeguards, parking fee, and restrooms in season, 2 pavilions with grills. Lime Rickey's Restaurant ($).

Marblehead Model Yacht Club, mmyc.us. Races are held every Sun at 10 a.m. at Redd's Pond, 1 Pond St., from the end of Mar through mid-Oct. Regattas are held four to five times a year. For information, call the Commodore at (978) 828-9765.

Marblehead Toy Shop, 46 Atlantic Ave., Marblehead; (781) 631-9900. Unique and educational toys and gifts.

Where to Eat

The Barnacle, 141 Front St., Marblehead; (781) 631-4236; thebarnaclerestaurant .com. Lunch and dinner. Great chowder and harbor views. Outdoor dining. Casual. $–$$$

Caffe Italia, 10 School St., Marblehead; (781) 631-5700; caffeitaliarestaurant.com. Popular with families. Authentic Italian. $–$$

The Driftwood, 63 Front St., Marblehead; (781) 631-1145. Serving breakfast until 2 p.m. Lots of local color, attracting fishermen, the yachting set, families, and visitors. $

Lime Rickey's Beach Food, 105 Ocean Ave., Devereux Beach, Marblehead; (781) 631-5463; limerickeys.com. Open end of Apr through Sept. Deck and beach dining, with ocean views of Marblehead Neck, the harbor, and the Atlantic. Inside dining on chillier days. Lunch and dinner. Serving sandwiches, seafood, chicken, and beef. Caribbean themed. Wheelchair accessible. $–$$

Amazing
Massachusetts Facts

- The town of Marblehead lays claim to being the birthplace of the American Navy.
- The Wenham Tea House is the oldest teahouse in America.
- The Myopia Polo Field is the oldest polo field in the country (created in 1888) and is the oldest polo club in America.
- The American Textile History Museum in Lowell is the world's largest textile museum.

The Landing, 81 Front St., Marblehead; (781) 631-1878 or (781) 639-1266; thelanding restaurant.com. Lunch and dinner every day. Upscale menu, lots of fresh seafood, loads of specials. Kids' menu. Dine inside or outside on the deck overlooking the harbor. $–$$$

Palmers Restaurant and Tavern, Marblehead; (781) 476-2076; warwick-place .com/Palmers. Dine in the restaurant or watch a movie at the adjoining Warwick Place Cinema and order from a Palmers menu. Great fun for the whole family. $–$$$

Where to Stay

Harbor Light Inn, 58 Washington St., Marblehead; (781) 631-2186; harborlightinn .com. A jewel of an inn with 21 spacious rooms with private bath, family suites, pool, near major sights. Children over 12 welcome. $$–$$$$

A Lady Winette Cottage B&B, 3 Corinthian Ln., Marblehead; (781) 631-8579; aladywinettecottage.com. Great location near the Corinthian Yacht Club overlooking Marblehead Harbor. Choice of two delightful rooms: one with a deck view of the water, the other with a garden view. Children over 5 welcome. $$

The Marblehead Inn, 264 Pleasant St., Marblehead; (781) 639-9999 or (800) 399-5843; marbleheadinn.com. Ten suites with private bath; great for nonsmoking families. Rates include continental breakfast. $$–$$$

Seagull Inn, 106 Harbor Ave., Marblehead; (781) 631-1893; seagullinn.com. Three suites with private bath, walking distance to beach, kayaks, swings, and bicycles. Ruth grinds her own grain for her freshly baked breakfast breads. $$–$$$

Salem

Salem makes the most of its reputation as the location of the infamous Salem witch trials during the 17th century. But there's a lot more to it than this sad and rather gruesome period: A top-notch waterfront area, a world-class museum, and a historic house with a secret stairway are among the highlights of Salem that have nothing to do with witches or trials.

When you arrive in Salem, go to the **Salem Chamber of Commerce** (265 Essex St., Suite 101; 978-744-0004; salem-chamber.org) for free self-guided tour maps and information about the day's activities, or **Destination Salem** (Office of Tourism and Events), 43 Washington St., Salem, MA 01970; (978) 744-3663 or (877) SALEM-MA; salem.org or hauntedhappenings.org. Another place for information on Salem and Essex County is the **National Park Service Regional Visitor Center,** 2 New Liberty St. (at the corner of New Liberty and Essex Streets, Salem; 978-740-1650; nps.gov/sama). The National Park Service Visitor Center offers two fine films that give you a flavor of the area. The 27-minute film *Where Past Is Present* is a great introduction to the history of Salem and Essex County before you go exploring (free). The 40-minute film *Salem Witch Hunt; Examine the Evidence* ($5 for adults, $3 for seniors and kids) is based on the latest research on the witchcraft trials and is extremely thought provoking. Brochures on area attractions are also available. The Salem Trolley tours conveniently start their route at the visitor center. In October an extra information booth is set up

Friendship Renewed

The Salem Maritime National Historic Site is most proud of the *Friendship*, a replica of a 1797 ship built in Salem and owned by Waitt and Pierce. Be sure to pick up a copy of the Junior Ranger Program booklet at the National Park Service Visitor Center, 2 New Liberty St., Salem. Upon completion of the booklet you are awarded a Junior Ranger badge!

How Salem **Got Its Name**

To smooth over conflict between groups of settlers on the Naumkeag Peninsula (near present-day Pioneer Village), the area was renamed Salem, from the Hebrew word *shalom*, or peace.

on the corner of Essex Street and Washington Street to handle the crowd that descends upon the city for **Haunted Happenings** (Salem considers itself the Halloween capital of the world, and tourists do indeed come from all over the globe). Parking can be a challenge; for up-to-date information, go to parkingin-salem.com or HauntedHappenings.org and click on "parking" under the "arrive" icon, or search @GetthruOctober on Twitter.

Cry Innocent (all ages)

Old Town Hall, 32 Derby Sq., Essex Street, Salem; (978) 867-4767; cryinnocent salem.com. Performances summer, fall, and the month of Oct. Admission: $12 for adults, $8 for children 6 to 12.
You are the jury at the trial of Bridget Bishop, the first person hanged for witch-craft in 1692. Buy your tickets early. Bridget is arrested 15 minutes prior to the show by the Almy's clock on Essex Street. The 45-minute performance is interactive and historical in content, written by a professor of English at Gordon College, and done in period costume and the native vernacular of the time.

House of the Seven Gables, aka the Turner Ingersol Mansion and properties (all ages)

115 Derby St., corner of Turner Street, Salem; (978) 744-0991; 7gables.org. Open daily 10 a.m. to 5 p.m., and to 7 p.m. July through Oct. Closed Thanksgiving, Christmas, and the first 2 weeks of Jan. Guided tour admission for the House of Seven Gables: $12.50 for adults, $11.50 for seniors, $7.50 for children 5 to 12, free for children 4 and under. Self-guided tour of Nathaniel Hawthorne's birth-place mid-Apr through Halloween.
A fun place to visit, even for people who aren't familiar with Nathaniel Hawthorne's book *The House of the Seven Gables*. Three underlying themes will be emphasized during your tour: the House of the Seven Gables architecture, the maritime history of Salem, and Nathaniel Hawthorne. Walk through the house (which has under-gone a lot of restoration) to see the secret staircase hidden along the chimney,

which winds up through a wall (this may be all that the younger kids will remember about the house), and the low-beamed attic. Hawthorne's birthplace is on the property; it's furnished with period furniture, and the guides know a lot about the family and their times. Younger ones will especially enjoy the Counting House, whose interior was converted into a nautical-themed space called Kids Cove with hands-on activities for creative play. The dress-up area (in period costume) is a real hit, as are looking through a telescope to spot the Friendship at the National Maritime Historic Site, and sniffing spices typical of those gotten in trade. Take a stroll through the Colonial Restoration Garden and take in the beautiful waterfront. During October be sure to see one of the theater performances, *Spirits of the Gables* or *The Legacy of the Hanging Judge*. Tickets and reservations are required.

New England Pirate Museum (all ages)

274 Derby St., Salem; (978) 741-2800; piratemuseum.com. Open May through Oct, 10 a.m. to 5 p.m. and weekends in Apr and Nov. Extended hours during Haunted Happenings. Admission: $9 for adults, $8 for seniors, $7 for children 4 to 13, free for children under 4. A combination ticket with the Witch Dungeon Museum and the Witch History Museum can be purchased.

With the ever-soaring popularity of the movie series *Pirates of the Caribbean* (the fifth in the series is scheduled for release in 2016*),* hunker down to the New England Pirate Museum to view our local swashbucklers! Buried treasure and pirates are actually part of the North Shore's history. This attraction has it all— it's educational, historical, and fun for kids (what kid isn't interested in pirates, pirate maps, and buried treasure?) who enjoy learning about the local looters such as Blackbeard and Captain Kidd. It takes about 30 minutes to view all of the museum's displays.

For Your Amusement

At the tip of land that juts into Salem Bay can be found **Salem Willows Park** (Fort Avenue, Salem; salemwillowspark.com), a fine destination for an afternoon of picnicking and outdoor activities. The views are good—Beverly's harbor on one side, the south coast of Cape Ann on the other. There's a small amusement park with arcades, a nice merry-go-round, and a pier for fishing and taking a cruise on the *Mahi-Mahi* (800-992-6244; mahicruises.com).

Very **Bewitching**

Laurie Cabot, the "Official Witch of Salem," opened the first witch shop in America in 1970. Governor Michael Dukakis of Massachusetts in a 1977 proclamation decreed that Laurie was the "Official Witch of Salem." The title was to honor her work with special-needs children. Keeping up with our technological age, Laurie, an octogenarian, has reinvented herself with an online store (theofficialwitch shoppe.net) where one can procure witchcraft supplies for spells and rituals.

Peabody Essex Museum (all ages)

161 Essex St., East India Square, Salem; (978) 745-9500 or (866) 745-1876; pem
.org. Open daily 10 a.m. to 5 p.m., open every third Thurs of every month until
9:30 p.m. Closed Mon except holidays. Admission: $18 for adults, free for children up to 16; senior and student discounts; includes admittance to the galleries,
house tours (sign up early, numbers are limited), and library. There is a $5 surcharge to enter Yin Yu Tang's Chinese House within the museum.

One of the fastest-growing museums in the country, the Peabody Essex Museum
is the second-largest art museum in New England and has the third-largest collection. Described by the *New York Times* as a "cross-cultural marvel with world-class
collections of art, architecture, and culture dating back to 1799," the collection of
items gathered by Salem sea captains on their round-the-world voyages is varied
and diverse. The museum has already been recognized in the past for the quality
of its collection in Asian export, American decorative, maritime, and oceanic art.

With the addition of 250,000 square feet of new and renovated galleries and
public spaces (the new wing was designed by Moshe Safdie), the Peabody Essex
Museum can now showcase a larger range of its collection, including African,
Korean, and Indian art; photography (with some of the earliest photographs ever
created); architecture and design; and contemporary Native American art. One
of the highlights of your visit will be a Chinese merchant's 200-year-old house
(the **Yin Yu Tang Chinese House**) from the Anhui province reassembled on
the museum's campus. Stay tuned for a slated expansion in 2019 that will add
175,000 square feet to the museum. Historic homes representing three centuries in Salem are included in the admission price.

The original court documents from the Salem witchcraft trials are part of the collection at **Phillips Library.** The Art & Nature Center just reopened; geared toward children and families to make connections between the natural world and creativity. There is the Atrium Cafe for a quick snack in the new addition, as well as the established **Garden Museum Restaurant,** which is open seasonally late spring through early fall.

Salem Historical Tours: Haunted Footsteps Ghost Tour

(ages 8 and up)

8 Central St., second floor, Salem; (978) 745-0666; salemhistoricaltours.com. Open nightly Apr through Oct 31. Price: $14 for adults, $8 for children 6 to 14. Not suggested for children under six. Reservations suggested.

Salem Historical Tours offers five different tours with topics ranging from the general history of Salem to the old burying grounds, the architecture of Salem, witchcraft, and the ever popular Haunted Footsteps Ghost Tour, which includes many of the aforementioned topics. Under the cover of night, the Haunted Footsteps Ghost Tour is a historically based 1.5-hour walking tour geared to older unflappable kids and their families. Some of the topics covered are sites of documented hauntings, the witchcraft hysteria of the 1600s, colonial murder, and 400 years of the city's history. The guides are in capes and carry lanterns, adding to the spooky atmosphere.

Salem Maritime National Historic Site (all ages)

193 Derby St., Salem; (978) 740-1660; nps.gov/sama. Open daily year-round, 9 a.m. to 5 p.m., for tours of the historic buildings and the *Friendship;* closed Thanksgiving, Christmas, and New Year's Day. The grounds, trails, and outdoor exhibits are open daily round-the-clock. Free, but tours require a reservation by calling (978) 740-1650. Check the website for the tour schedule.

When the nation was young, Salem was a major seaport exchanging goods with the Pacific Rim countries. A 9-acre site located on the waterfront and run by the National Park Service, the Salem Maritime National Historic Site encompasses the **Custom House** (where Nathaniel Hawthorne worked), the **Derby House** (the oldest brick house in Salem), and the **Narbonne House,** built in 1675, which was occupied by descendents of the same family for over 200 years, among other historic buildings, as well as a replica of a three-masted square-rigged vessel, the ***Friendship,*** commissioned in 2003. Start your tour at the National Park Service Visitor Center (2 New Liberty St., Salem). Sign up for one of the two

Things That Go Bump in the Night . . .
Tours of Salem (If You Dare)!

- **13 Ghosts Walking Tour,** 131 Essex St., Salem; (978) 744-0013; salems13ghosts.com

- **Candlelit Ghostly & Graveyard Walking Tours,** 282–288 Derby St., Salem; (978) 740-2929; salemwaxmuseum.com/WalkingTours .html

- **Hocus Pocus Tours,** 1 East India Sq., Museum Place Mall, Salem; (781) 248-2031; hocuspocustours.com

- **Paranormal Salem,** meets at the Witch Trials Memorial (98 Liberty St.), Salem; (978) 494-HUNT; paranormalsalem.com

- **Salem Historical Tours,** 8 Central St., Salem: (978) 745-0666; salem historicaltours.com

- **Salem Night Tours,** 127 Essex St., Salem; (978) 741-1170; salem ghosttours.com

- **The 3-D Salem Time Machine,** 131 Essex St., Salem; (978) 744- 0013; salems13ghosts.com

- **The Salem Witch Walk,** 125 Essex St., Salem; (978) 666-0884; witchwalk.com

- **Spellbound Tours,** 2 New Liberty St. (in front of the National Park Service Visi- tor Center), Salem; (978) 740-1876; spell boundtours.com

tours: the Custom House and the *Friendship* or the Elias Derby mansion and the Narbonne House. The weights and measures at the Custom House are especially fascinating to kids. They'll also enjoy watching demonstrations of the intricate skills required in shipbuilding. Special programming and demonstrations are given by park rangers; call for a schedule.

Salem Pioneer Village 1630 (all ages)

Located in Forest River Park, Salem; (978) 744-8815; pioneervillagesalem.org. Directions: Take Lafayette Street to West Street; enter Forest River Park. See the website for hours of operation. Admission: $6 adults, $4 for children. *Note:* Buy your tickets at the Witch House, 310½ Essex St., Salem.

Want to see how the settlers lived in one of the first enclaves of the Massachusetts Bay Colony? Pioneer Village, the first living-history museum in this country, is the re-created 17th-century fishing village bordering Salem Harbor in Salem's **Forest River Park.** This area was originally referred to as Naumkeag, or "fishing place," by local tribes. Thatched-roof cottages, dugouts, wigwams, a sawmill, a Blacksmith's Shop, and a re-created Governor's House await you. Guides dressed in period New England pioneer costumes demonstrate culinary skills of the time using authentic recipes. Hands-on activities allow kids to test their skills at bundling wool, primers and horn books, and period songs and games. Medicinal herbs and spices typically used in colonial times are on view in the garden.

Salem Trolley Tours (all ages)

8 Central St. (office), Salem; (978) 744-5469; salemtrolley.com. Open from Apr through Oct, 10 a.m. to 5 p.m. (call for the off-season schedule, weather permitting). Price: $15 for adults, $5 for children 6 to 14, free for children under 6.

If you'd rather let someone else do the driving (and that's not a bad idea in busy Salem), the trolley tours are a good deal. The trolley covers 7 miles with 13 stops that include the major sights and attractions of Salem. You can get on and off all day long. Tours start hourly at the **National Park Service Regional Visitor Center,** 2 New Liberty St., Salem. Special tours are offered in Oct during Haunted Happenings (the Tales and Tombstones Trolley Tour and the Ghost and Legends Trolley) and for the December Holiday Show. Ask Salem Trolley about their combination tickets.

Salem Wax Museum of Witches and Seafarers
(ages 6 and up)

288 Derby St., Salem; (978) 740-2929; salemwaxmuseum.com. Open daily, check
the website for variable hours of operation. Admission: $8 for adults, $6 for ages
6 to 13, free for ages 5 and under. Ask about the combination ticket for Salem
Witch Village called the Hysteria Pass or the Fun Pass (not available in Oct).

Featuring 50 wax figures of life-size witches, the museum puts the witch stories in the context of Salem's 17th-century life as a major maritime seaport on
this self-guided tour, and it's not nearly as scary as the Salem Witch Museum.
The museum was voted the number-one Haunted House in Salem during the
Haunted Happenings for its **Frankenstein Laboratory Tour.**

Salem Witch Museum (ages 7 and up)

19 N. Washington Sq., Salem; (978) 744-1692 or (800) 544-1692; salemwitch
museum.com. Open daily 10 a.m. to 5 p.m.; July and Aug, 10 a.m. to 7 p.m. Closed
Thanksgiving, Christmas, and New Year's Day. Extended hours during Haunted
Happenings. Admission: $9.50 for adults; $6.50 for children 6 to 14.

Can't keep the kids away from the witch stories? Head for the 30-minute multimedia presentation about the witchcraft hysteria that gripped 17th-century
Salem. The show is a bit scary and disturbing, and it is definitely not appropriate
for kids under 7. The exhibit—Witches: Evolving Perceptions—looks at the different meanings and interpretations of the word "witch" over time, the practice of
witchcraft today, and the phenomenon of witch-hunting.

Salem Witch Village (ages 6 and up)

282 Derby St., Salem; (978) 740-9229; salemwitchvillage.net. Open year-round,
check the website for the schedule. Extended hours during Haunted Happenings.
Admission: $7 for adults, $5 for children, free for ages 5 and under. Ask about
the combination ticket for the Salem Wax Museum of Witches and Seafarers.

Traces the history of witchcraft from the ancient world through medieval Europe
to modern-day America. The guides are all practicing witches. Burning incense
permeates the museum and can be headache inducing. Even though the displays can be trite at times, the guides are interesting and informative. A ritual
circle with a live spell-casting is intriguing in the **Within the Witching Hour** presentation. The only way to describe the experience is "All you wanted to know
about witchcraft but were afraid to ask." Call for a schedule of workshops. If you
visit during Halloween (the Celtic New Year), be sure to ask for the Hysteria Pass

Amazing
Salem Facts

- Salem was the birthplace of author Nathaniel Hawthorne.
- Ye Olde Pepper Candy Companie of Salem (122 Derby St.) is the oldest candy company in the US.
- The Salem Maritime National Historic Site was the first place designated as a National Historic Site.
- Pioneer Village was the first outdoor museum in America.
- The first elephant to set foot in this country disembarked in Salem in the late 1700s.
- The written ballot was used for the first time in 1629.
- Salem resident William Driver nicknamed the flag "Old Glory."
- The films *Hocus Pocus* and *Bewitched* were filmed here.
- Elias Derby became the first millionaire in America (his home is part of the Salem Maritime National Historic Site).
- The telephone was first demonstrated at Lyceum Hall by Alexander Graham Bell.
- Monopoly was produced and sold by Salem toy and game company Parker Brothers.
- The Peabody Essex Museum is the oldest continuously operating museum (since 1799) in the country.
- The McIntire Historic District has more than 300 historic buildings.

ticket with the Salem Wax Museum of Witches and Seafarers. *Caution:* Displays can be scary for little ones.

Winter Island Maritime Park   (all ages)

50 Winter Island Rd., Salem; (978) 745-9430; salemweb.com/winterisland. Open daily May through Oct, 8 a.m. to 7 p.m. (later for campers). Admission: $10 per car for nonresidents midweek, $15 weekends and holidays. Fee for campsites and boat launch. Camp store on premises.

Owned by the city of Salem, this hidden gem features the remains of Historic Fort Pickering and a working lighthouse, **Fort Pickering Lighthouse.** Unique to most city parks, there is camping here, with 58 RV and tent sites, a lifeguarded beach, a picnic area, a shower house, and a heated function hall. Bring your boat (there is a boat launch) and cruise around Salem Harbor. If you wish to leave your vehicle, the Salem Trolley services the park in the summer. Call for the schedule.

Witch Dungeon Museum (ages 6 and up)

16 Lynde St., Salem; (978) 741-3570; witchdungeon.com. Open Apr through Nov 30, 10 a.m. to 5 p.m. Extended hours during Haunted Happenings. Admission: $9 for adults, $8 for seniors, $7 for children ages 4 to 13, and free for children under 4. Combination ticket available with the New England Pirate Museum and the Witch History Museum.

A highly acclaimed live reenactment of the witch trial of either Elizabeth Proctor or Sarah Good, based on court documents, by professional actors, leads to a bone-chilling conclusion. A guided tour of a re-created dungeon completes this thought-provoking experience.

Beware the **Haunted Houses of Salem**

- 3-D Haunted House, 131 Essex St.
- Count Orlok's Nightmare Gallery, 285 Derby St.
- Frankenstein's Laboratory, 288 Derby St.
- Graveyard Tour, 288 Derby St.
- Haunted Witch Village, 282 Derby St.
- Nightmare Factory, Museum Place Mall

Cut 'em off **at the Pass**

Contact **Destination Salem,** 54 Turner St., Salem (978-744-3663 or
978-741-3252; salemweb.com or salem.org), to find out about special
savings. Ask about combination passes during **Haunted Happenings** in Oct (hauntedhappenings.org). The **Discover Salem Passport**
(not valid in Oct) includes the House of Seven Gables, the Peabody
Essex Museum, the Salem Trolley (in season), and the Salem Witch
Museum (discoversalempassport.com) and must be purchased
online.

Witch History Museum (ages 6 and up)

197 Essex St., Salem; (978) 741-7770; witchhistorymuseum.com. Open Apr
through end of Nov, 10 a.m. to 5 p.m. (last tour is at 5 p.m.). Extended hours during Haunted Happenings. Prices: $9 for adults, $7 for children 4 to 13.
Witch trial stories are told through a historically accurate presentation. Guided
tours through 15 life-size scenes give you the background of the witch persecutions locally and in New England. The tour takes about 20 minutes.

The Witch House, aka The Corwin House
(ages 6 and up)

310 Essex St.; Salem; (978) 744-8815; salemweb.com/witchhouse. Open year-round, with extended summer hours. Guided tours ($10.25 for an adult, $6.25
for a child) and self-guided tours ($8.25 for an adult, $4.25 for a child) depending
upon the season.
The Witch House is a house museum; the only home in Salem still standing that
has direct ties to the witch trials of 1692. This is the original home of Judge Jonathan Corwin, judge at the Salem witch trials. Period furniture is on display. During Oct actors tell ghost stories every evening.

Other Things to See & Do

Gallows Hill Museum/Theatre, 7 Lynde St., Salem; (978) 825-0222; gallowshill
salem.com. Myths and legends surrounding Gallows Hill. Open to the public in Oct,
groups with prior arrangement Apr through Nov.

Harbor Sweets, 85 Leavitt St., Salem; (978) 745-7648 or (800) 243-2115; harbor sweets.com. Take a tour to see how delicious, preservative-free chocolates are made. **Free** samples.

Historic New England's Phillips House, 34 Chestnut St., Salem; (617) 227-3956; historicnewengland.org/historic-properties/homes/phillips-house. View artifacts gathered from worldwide travels in the main house and the collection of carriages and automobiles housed in the carriage house.

Pickering Wharf, Wharf Street (off Derby Street), Salem. Funky shops and restaurants on the harbor near sights and attractions.

Salem Ferry, Blaney Street off Derby, Salem; (978) 741-0220; salemferry.com. Seasonal service May through Oct to Long Wharf (near the Marriott Hotel and the Christopher Columbus Park) in Boston. Check the website for the schedule; onboard concierge to help you plan your day. Special sailings from Hingham to Salem during Haunted Happenings.

Salem Food Tours, Pickering Wharf, Salem; (978) 594-8811; salemfoodtours.com or northshorefoodtours.com. Guided walking culinary, history of the Spice Trade, and cultural tours of Salem. Tastings at local restaurants and shops. Reservations required. Children over age 8 please, $54 per person. Chartered daylong tours for larger groups (up to 30 people). Tastings at farms, shops, and restaurants located on the North Shore. Call for pricing.

Salem Haunted Magic Show, Hawthorne Hotel, 18 Washington Sq., Salem; (888) 830-0038; thesalemmagicshow.com. Ninety-minute interactive magic show in Oct.

Salem Kayak Learning Center, 50 Winter Island Rd., Salem; (978) 270-8170 or (617) 304-2426; kayaksalem.com. Rental of boats and equipment.

Salem Museum, Old Salem Town Hall, 32 Derby Sq., Salem; (978) 744-0007; the salemmuseum.org. Informative exhibits about Salem's legacy and its people. Open daily mid-June to the end of Oct, noon to 5 p.m. **Free.**

Salem Strolls, 20 Pleasant St., Salem; (978) 741-1154; salemstrolls.com. Architectural gems are pointed out by knowledgeable tour guides on your walk.

Salem Theatre Company, 90 Lafayette St., Salem; (978) 790-8546; salemtheatre .com. Quality theater in an intimate setting (50 seats).

Salem Witch Trials Memorial, Liberty Street between Charter and Derby Streets, Salem. Thought-provoking, award-winning memorial dedicated to human rights and tolerance.

The Sea Shuttle, Salem Willows Park Pier, 157 Fort Ave., Salem; (888) 400-0601; sea-shuttle.com. Shuttle boat to Great Misery Island (in Salem Sound). Hike the Trustees of Reservations property half a mile from West Beach coastline, Beverly.

Schooner Fame, Pickering Wharf Marina, Salem; (978) 729-7600; schoonerfame .com. Reproduction of an 1812 schooner. Two-hour tour. Open May through Oct; check schedule. Summer camps teach you the ropes.

Witch City Segway, 283 Derby St., Salem; (781) 626-4000; witchcitysegway.com. Audio narrated tours by "wranglers" (tour guides) of Salem by Segway.

Ye Olde Pepper Candy Companie, 122 Derby St., Salem; (978) 745-2744 or (866) 526-2376; peppercandy.net. America's oldest candy company (since 1806), this is the home of the infamous Salem Gibraltar and the Black Jack candy. Candies are manufactured on the premises.

Where to Eat

Bella Verona, 107 Essex St., Salem; (978) 825-9911; bellaverona.com. Italian specialties of the Verona region served up with pride and care. Winner of the 2013 Best of the Northshore by *Northshore Magazine* for Italian restaurants. Serving dinner. $–$$

Capt.'s Waterfront Grill, 94 Wharf St., Pickering Wharf, Salem; (978) 741-0555; capts.com. Lunch and dinner, Sunday brunch. Views of Salem Harbor and Salem Maritime National Historic Site. Seafood specialties in a fun atmosphere; children's menu. $–$$$

Flying Saucer Pizza, 118 Washington St., Salem; (978) 594-8189; flyingsaucerpizza company.com. Open daily 11 a.m. to 11 p.m. Aliens and sci-fi portraits framed on the wall in retro decor. Gourmet vegetarian, vegan, gluten-free, and dessert pizza options plus standard meat pizzas. Wine and beer. $

In a Pig's Eye, 148 Derby St., Salem; (978) 741-4436; inapigseye.com. Open for lunch and dinner. The restaurant's slogan—"Dine up, Dress down"—pretty much sums up its philosophy. Casual fare; don't miss Mexican night on Mon and Tues. $–$$

Melita Fiore Patisserie, 83 Washington St., Salem; (978) 594-8747; melitafiore .com. Cupcakes, macaroons, cookies, tarts, croissants, and homemade hot chocolate in a French cafe atmosphere. $

Reds, 15 Central St., Salem; (978) 745-3527; redssandwichshop.com. Very popular with locals as well as tourists. Reasonable prices and large portions. Voted Salem's best breakfast by the *Salem Evening News* but serves lunch too. $–$$

Victoria Station, 86 Wharf St., Pickering Wharf, Salem; (978) 745-3400; victoria stationsalem.com. Waterfront dining, indoors or outside on the patio, salad bar, meat and seafood dishes, gluten-free menu. $–$$$

Where to Stay

Amelia Payson Guest House, 16 Winter St., Salem; (978) 744-8304; ameliapayson house.com. Closed in winter. A small bed-and-breakfast with three rooms, all with private bath. Period antiques. Children over 14 please. Complimentary continental breakfast. $$–$$$

The Clipper Ship Inn, 40 Bridge St., Route 1A, Salem; (978) 745-8022; clippership inn.com. Sixty-room motel with annex. Budget-, pet-, and children-friendly. Wheelchair accessible. $–$$$

Hawthorne Hotel, 18 Washington Sq. West, Salem; (978) 744-4080 or (800) 729-7829; hawthornehotel.com. Designated a Historic Hotel of America, the 89-room Hawthorne has great charm and class. Restaurant serves breakfast, lunch, and dinner. $$–$$$$

Henry Derby House, 47 Summer St., Salem; (978) 745-1080; henryderbyhouse .com. Warm and friendly with 3 cozy rooms. Antique and traditional furnishings. Ghostly hauntings of the house have been reported; the house is on one of the haunted walking tours. Surprisingly, kids of all ages are welcome! Expanded continental breakfast. $$–$$$

Salem Inn, 7 Summer St., Salem; (978) 741-0680 or (800) 446-2995 (outside Massachusetts); saleminnma.com. European-style inn; great location. Some rooms have canopy beds, fireplaces, and Jacuzzis. Suites available with kitchenettes. Complimentary continental breakfast. $$–$$$

Salem Waterfront Hotel, 225 Derby St., Salem; (978) 740-8788 or (888) 337-2536; salemwaterfronthotel.com. Great location on the harbor. Minutes from major sites

Literature with **Salem as a Setting**

Children's Books
Carry On, Mr. Bowditch by Jean Lee Latham
Early Thunder by Jean Fritz

Teen and Adult Books
The House of the Seven Gables by Nathaniel Hawthorne
The Crucible by Arthur Miller
The Scarlet Letter by Nathaniel Hawthorne

and a host of restaurants. Swimming pool for kids. Winner of 2013 Best of Northshore Hotels by *Northshore Magazine*. $$–$$$$

Peabody

Home to New England's first mall, the Northshore Shopping Center (now the Northshore Mall), Peabody was a rural farm community that saw huge development in tract homes in the 1950s to supplement the growing demand for affordable homes for families using the GI Bill after World War II. Once known as the Leather City because of all the tanneries within the city limits, the leather industry is now defunct and others have taken its place.

Brooksby Farm and Felton Junior House

(all ages)

Felton Street, Peabody; (978) 531-1631 or (978) 531-7456; essexheritage.org. Open year-round 9 a.m. to 5 p.m., but the farm stand is seasonal (June through Dec).
A municipally owned farm since 1976, Brooksby is a fun place to visit at almost any time of the year. Pick your own strawberries in June; blueberries, peaches, and raspberries in July and Aug; and apples in late summer and fall. Cut flowers in summer, or choose that special Christmas tree in Dec. The barn is home to goats, a llama, sheep, pigs, chickens, a rooster, geese, and ducks. Feeding the animals is allowed. Brooksby offers hayrides (by reservation only) that seat 25 to 30 people, a great idea for a kid's party. Cross-country skiing is available for **free.** However, there is a small charge for equipment rental ($10 for adults, $7 for teens, and $5 for younger children) and lessons ($15). Call (978) 536-7132 to

Peabody **Festival**

The **International Festival,** which takes place the third Sun in Sept, celebrates the diversity of the city, with ethnic food, dance, and cultural events. Call (978) 532-3000 for more information.

reserve your 90-minute lesson. The trails can also be used for snowshoeing and hiking. A farm store sells produce from the farm and related products. For a special family treat, go apple picking in season during the weekend and get a **free** hayride to the orchard!

Owned by the Peabody Historical Society, the **Felton House** is fully furnished with period furniture from the 1600s. On-site are the **Smith Barn** and the **Fire Museum,** which includes Peabody Engine #3. For more information and tours, call the **Peabody Historical Society** at (978) 531-0805 or visit peabody historical.org.

Other Things to See & Do

General Gideon Foster House, 35 Washington St., Peabody; (978) 531-0805; peabodyhistorical.org. Three hundred years of history.

Elizabeth Cassidy Art Museum & Peabody Art Association Gallery, Osborne-Salata House, 33 Washington St., Peabody; (978) 531-0805; peabodyhistorical .org. Furniture, china, and fine and decorative arts on view. Extended hours during special exhibits.

George Peabody House Museum and the Peabody Leather Workers Museum, 205 Washington St., Peabody; (978) 531-0355. George Peabody's birthplace and museum honoring his work as a financier and a famous philanthropist here and in the UK. Peabody was considered the "Leather Capital of the World," as documented in the Peabody Leather Workers Museum.

Where to Eat

Family Fare, 474 Lowell St., Peabody; (978) 536-9049; familyfarepeabody.com. Great Italian and Greek food in a casual atmosphere. Attentive, friendly service. $$

Sea Witch Restaurant and Oyster Bar, 203 Newbury St. (Route 1 N), Peabody; (978) 535-6057. Fresh seafood served in a laid-back, rustic atmosphere. Featured on *Phantom Gourmet.* $–$$$

Su Chang's, 373 Lowell St., Peabody; (978) 531-3366; suchangspeabody.com. Upper-end Chinese food specializing in Cantonese and Mandarin ethnic dishes. Lovely decor. $–$$$

Where to Stay

Marriott Hotel, 8 Centennial Dr., Peabody; (978) 977-9700; marriott.com. Nicely appointed rooms; pool. Great daily brunches with special pricing for children. $–$$$$

Danvers & Middleton

Danvers, once part of Salem, was known as Olde Salem Village and played a major role in the witchcraft hysteria during colonial times. Abutting Danvers is the town of Middleton, which has seen much growth and booming housing development in the last half of the the 20th century.

Endicott Park (under 10 for the playground)

57 Forest St., Danvers; (978) 774-6518; endicottpark.com. Open daily 9 a.m. to sundown. Admission: $1 for residents on weekends and holidays, $3 for nonresidents, free during midweek. Groups of 20 or more must have a permit.

This 165-acre park is owned by the town of Danvers. Attractions include a barn with farm animals and the Larry Crowley Visitor Center Carriage House, where monthly nature presentations are held; trails for hiking, cross-country skiing, or snowshoeing; a pond with a fishing platform (Goodno Pond); playing fields; and picnic tables. A state-of-the-art playground (the Kidstown Playground) is a big attraction for kids. Also on the grounds are **Glen Magna** and the **Derby Tea House,** owned by the **Danvers Historical Society** (978-774-9165; glenmagna farms.org).

Rebecca Nurse Homestead (ages 5 and up)

149 Pine St., Danvers; (978) 774-8799; rebeccanurse.org. Open mid-Apr to mid-June Fri through Sun 10 a.m. to 2 p.m.; mid-June to Labor Day, Fri through Sun 10 a.m. to 3 p.m.; Sept and Oct, Sat and Sun 10 a.m. to 3 p.m. Closed on national

holidays. **Open the rest of the year by appointment only. Owned and operated by the Danvers Alarm List Company. Admission: $7 for adults, $4 for ages 6 to 16, free for kids under 6.**

If you're fascinated by tales of the Salem witch trials, you'll enjoy the original salt-box homestead of the Nurse family. In 1692 the matriarch, Rebecca Nurse, was accused of practicing witchcraft. Her accusers were a group of rebellious teen-age girls who were having fits of hysteria and naming Rebecca as one of their tormentors. Rebecca was executed in July 1692, and her remains were brought back to the family plot and buried in an unmarked grave. The property includes the original Nurse homestead, with 17th- and 18th-century period furnishings; a reproduction of the **Olde Salem Village Meeting House** (featuring a multimedia presentation); the family cemetery, with a monument to Rebecca bearing a poem by John Greenleaf Whittier; and a gift shop.

Witch Hysteria Monument (all ages)

176 Hobart St., Danvers. Open year-round. Free.

Erected 300 years after the witchcraft hysteria of 1692, this monument stands in solemn testimony to the memory of the 25 innocent people who lost their lives. It's located on town land, across from the original site of the Olde Salem Village Meeting House, where many of the accused were questioned.

Other Things to See & Do

Coco Key Water Resort at the Doubletree, 50 Ferncroft Rd., Danvers; (978) 646-1062 OR (978) 777-2500; cocokeyboston.com. Largest indoor water park in

Special Time

The **Danvers Family Festival** (starting the weekend prior to and ending the weekend after the Fourth of July) features road races, dog shows, a bike rodeo, the Fireman's Muster, Endicott Park Day, Irish Night, a golf tournament, various band concerts, Oldies Night, and, of course, the requisite Fourth of July fireworks. Check out the website at danversfamilyfestival.com. The hotline for the festival is (978) 777-0001, ext. 4.

Massachusetts, covering just under 2 acres (65,000 square feet) with 4 big water-slides, a lazy river, and an indoor and outdoor spa with TVs everywhere to watch as you float by! Birthday party packages. **Warning:** This attraction is for deep pockets and may be cost prohibitive. Purchase tickets online only—they will not sell tickets at the door.

Plains Park Skateboard Park, 57 Conant St., Danvers. Open dawn to dusk in season. A great place for children to practice their moves. Structures include a pyramid, a spine, the Bench, the fun box, a half-pipe, a flat pyramid, steel rails, and a cement rail edge.

Where to Eat

Daily Harvest, 103 High St., Danvers; (978) 777-4123; dailyharvestcafe.com. Great sandwiches, soups, and salads in a cozy setting. Fresh and organic ingredients. $

Danversport Grille and Bistro, 161 Elliott St., Danvers; (978) 774-8620; danversport.com. Lovely landscaped outdoor summer dining patio, indoors when the weather changes. Save room for Gilda, the swan-shaped cream puff ice-cream dessert. Surf-and-turf specialties. $–$$$

Hardcover Restaurant, 15 Newbury St., Route 1 N, Danvers; (978) 774-1223; thehardcover.com. Huge salad bar, fresh bread, and cheese blocks. Variety of seating area in a library-like setting. Dinner only. $–$$$

New Brothers Deli, 31 Maple St., Danvers; (978) 750-0100; newbrothersdanvers.com. Cafeteria-style home cooking. Greek specialties. Open for breakfast, lunch, and dinner. $

Nine Elm American Bistro, 9 Elm St., Danvers: (978) 774-9436; 9elm.com. Small intimate restaurant with great specials, everything is prepared to order. Dinner only. Gluten-free choices. $–$$$

Where to Stay

Danvers Courtyard by Marriott, 275 Independence Way, Danvers; (978) 777-8630; marriott.com. A 122-room hotel located near the Liberty Tree Mall. Seasonal outdoor pool. $$–$$$

Top Ice-Cream Spots

- **Cherry Hill Farm,** 210 Conant St., Danvers; (978) 774-0519; cherry farmcreamery.com. Homemade ice cream—huge portions and a long list of flavors. For adults, there's the **Sun 'n' Air Driving Range** (978-774-8180; sunairgolf.com) behind the ice-cream stand to work off those excess pounds from the ice cream you just consumed. Open year-round for ice cream; seasonal golf.

- **Goodies,** 46 Maple St., Danvers; (978) 762-4663; goodies-icecream .com. Gorge on the huge portions in this '50s-hip ice-cream parlor. Step up to the counter and take a spin on the stool, or sit in a booth—you decide. More than fifty flavors of ice cream served! Limited lunch menu.

- **Putnam Pantry Ice Cream and Candies,** 225 Newbury St., Route 1 North, just after the Route 62/Danvers exit, Danvers; (978) 774-2383; putnampantry.com. Opened in 1951, the big attraction is the make-your-own sundae bar (all the toppings and candies are made on the premises). Extremely popular with groups is the Battle of Bunker Hill (the owner is a direct descendant of General Israel Putnam, of "Don't fire until you see the whites of their eyes" fame), with seventeen scoops of ice cream, for $17.75. Indoor seating is reminiscent of ice-cream parlor decor of the 1940s and 1950s.

- **Richardson's Ice Cream and Golf Country,** Route 114, 156 South Main St., Middleton; (978) 774-5450 (ice cream) or (978) 774-4476 (golf); richardsonsicecream.com. Homemade ice cream (since 1952). driving range, miniature golf courses, and batting cages. *TIP:* Richardson's is very popular with locals, and there can be extremely long lines at peak times.

Topsfield

A rural town with agricultural roots, Topsfield is home to the Topsfield Fair, which groans with the expanded influx of thousands of people during fair week. A beautiful bedroom community ribboned with fieldstone walls, verdant green forest and fields, and large estates, it has retained much of its small-town character.

Bradley Palmer State Park (all ages)

40 Asbury St., Topsfield; (978) 887-5931; mass.gov/eea/agencies/dcr/massparks/region-north/bradley-palmer-state-park.html. Park open year-round sunrise to sunset; free. Parking for wading pool is $5; accessible in summer only.

Bradley Palmer, a successful attorney and friend of presidents and kings, bequeathed his mansion (the **Willowdale Estate,** rented for private functions) and grounds to the state of Massachusetts for public use. An extensive trail system is used for hiking, horseback riding, mountain biking, snowmobiling, cross-country skiing, and snowshoeing. The Ipswich River winds through the north end of the property, giving access for canoeing (rentals available at Foote Brothers in Ipswich, see listing) and fishing. It's also a great spot to teach a child to ride a bike since there is a large stretch of flat paved road. A real treat for the under-10 set is the wading pool, open from Father's Day to Labor Day. The centerpiece of the lifeguarded pool is a mushroom-shaped structure with water cascading over it.

Ipswich River Wildlife Sanctuary (all ages)

87 Perkins Row, Topsfield; (978) 887-9264; massaudubon.org. Open year-round Tues through Sun, dawn to dusk, and Mon holidays. Admission: $4 for adults, $3 for seniors and children 3 to 12. Free for children under 3.

The sanctuary has 10 miles of trails on 2,400 acres of land that are protected by the Massachusetts Audubon Society. Start your visit at the information center, where you can pick up a trail map. For families, the best trail leads to the Rockery Pond, a pile of enormous boulders. Continue around the pond (look for ducks, turtles, and frogs), then around the marsh, from which you can look over the wetlands of Topsfield and Ipswich. In late May or early June, the rhododendrons around the pond are breathtakingly memorable and pulsating with color. **Note:** Don't bring your dog—this is a wildlife sanctuary. *Do* bring bug repellent, especially during the spring.

It's a Family **Af-Fair**

Topsfield Fair, Topsfield Fairgrounds, Route 1 North/exit 50 off
Route 95, 207 Boston St., Topsfield; (978) 887-5000; topsfieldfair.org.
Admission: $11 weekdays, $15 weekends and holidays. Free for
children under 8. Parking $10 per vehicle. The Topsfield Fair, held
on the Topsfield Fairgrounds, is the oldest continuously operating
county agricultural fair in the US. Held every Oct the 10 days preced-
ing Columbus Day, the fair features exhibit halls, a flower show, livestock shows, a petting zoo, a vegetable show (with the New England
Giant Pumpkin contest), pig races, various arena shows, and a horse
and ox pull. There are lots of food concessions and a midway. Local
and national talent perform at the grandstand and five smaller stages.
In the past there have been fireworks the Fri night of opening and a
figure-eight race and a demolition derby on the final evening.

Topsfield Fairgrounds (all ages)

**Route 1 North (exit 50 off Route 95), 207 Boston St., Topsfield; (978) 887-5000;
topsfieldfair.org.**
The 83-acre fairground is home to the Topsfield Fair, an agricultural fair held every
Oct. In addition to the Topsfield Fair, numerous off-season events take place here.
Some of the more popular kid-oriented events held throughout the summer are
dog shows, the 4-H Horse Show, the Fresian Horse Show, a big-top three-ring
traveling circus, craft fairs, and the Gem and Mineral Show. Prices and schedule
vary according to event; call the Topsfield Fairgrounds for more information.

Hamilton & Wenham

Hamilton is home to the Myopia Hunt Club and the horsey set. Lots of open land
and rolling fields give this town a more pastoral feeling than neighboring Wenham. As you drive down Route 1A in Hamilton, you will encounter **Patton Park,**
named after native son George S. Patton, with its World War II M4 Sherman tank,
a centerpiece of this town park. Neighboring Wenham is a quieter New England
town, framed by its white-churched village and dotted with older sprawling
homes set among woodlands.

Appleton Farms and Appleton Farm Grass Rides
(all ages)

Appleton Farms, 219 County Rd., Ipswich. Appleton Farm Grass Rides are at the intersection of Cutler Road and Highland Street, Ipswich; (978) 356-5728, ext. 10; thetrustees.org. Open year-round 8 a.m. to sunset. Suggested donation: $3. Additional fee for tours and programs.

Appleton Farms is one of the oldest continuously operating farms in the US. Tours can range from a farmstead tour of the property to a viewing of cows during milking (check the website for the schedule). A dairy store on the premises sells their farm products, and there is a pick-your-own flower field and children's garden. A new series called **Appleton Cooks** teaches culinary skill with guest chefs and artisan bakers. The **Appleton Grass Rides** are a series of trails used for hiking, nature study, cross-country skiing, and snowshoeing. Due to the fragile nature of the trail, horseback riding is no longer allowed. For those who enjoy birding, rare grassland birds can be observed on the Great Pasture. Allow 2 to 3 hours for your visit.

TIP: Trails aren't marked in order to keep them true to their original state (although they have way-finding signs scattered about). Pay attention to your surroundings as it's easy to lose one's way.

Myopia Hunt Club and Polo Fields (all ages)

435 Bay Rd., Route 1A, Hamilton; (978) 468-1019; myopiapolo.org. Polo season begins the last Sun in May and continues until the last Sun in Sept. Matches begin at 3 p.m.; gates open at 1:30 p.m. Admission: $10 per person, 12 and under free.

Polo has always been referred to as the sport of kings, but these days the sport is accessible to all willing to pay the gate fee! The grace, beauty, and athleticism of both horse and rider are mesmerizing—and it's an easy sport for even the wee ones to watch and understand. Need an activity that involves the little ones when they get antsy? During halftime spectators are asked to help prepare the field for the next half by stomping on the divots that have been dislodged by the racing polo ponies. Bring a blanket and a picnic to spread out under the trees, and watch that the little ones don't run out into the field during play.

Wenham Museum (all ages)

132 Main St., Wenham; (978) 468-2377; wenhammuseum.org. Open year-round Tues through Sun, 10 a.m. to 4 p.m. Closed Mon and open most major holidays. Admission: $8 for adults, $6 for children 1 to 18.

Founded by the Wenham Village Improvement Society in 1922, the Wenham Museum, a hidden treasure, is a family-friendly museum of childhood and New England life. The museum's mission is to protect, preserve, and interpret the artifacts of childhood, domestic life, and the history and culture of Boston's North Shore. The Wenham Museum is a social history museum that consists of world-renowned dolls, vintage dollhouses, and antique toy collections; the **Clafflin Gerrish Richards House** (one of the earliest dwellings on the North Shore and on the National Register of Historic Places); a model-train gallery; costume and textile galleries; a historic photography collection made with glass-plate negatives (more than 3,000 photographs are in the collection); and the Family Discovery Gallery, a room set aside for children's hands-on discovery. The Wenham Museum is often called "the train museum" because of its extensive collection of classic model trains, with more than 10 working train layouts that operate by the push of a button. Throughout the year the museum offers 16 changing exhibits and educational and school programming that not only celebrates childhood but connects generations while honoring the local heritage. Children love to have their birthday parties here (by prior arrangement only), coupled with a visit to the Wenham Tea House for dessert.

Wenham Tea House (all ages)

4 Monument St., Route 1A, Wenham; (978) 468-1398; wenhamteahouse.com. Open Tues through Sat 8 a.m. to 5 p.m. for breakfast, lunch, and afternoon tea, Sat and Sun 8 a.m. to 2 p.m. for brunch, and Fri 5 to 9 p.m. for dinner.

Operated by Henry's Fine Foods, the teahouse has a restaurant, a gourmet shop, a gift shop, a baby shop, and an adult clothing store. It's best known for its luncheon menu and afternoon tea. The teahouse is planning on expanding by building an outdoor patio for summertime dining.

Beverly

Beverly, birthplace of George Washington's Navy, is a coastal community that is home to both Endicott College and the Montserrat School of Art. The downtown has many fine restaurants and draws diners from all over the region.

Amazing
Massachusetts Facts

Hospital Point Lighthouse Station (Bay View Avenue) was named for a smallpox hospital on the site. The lighthouse is square in shape, unlike most lighthouses, which are cylindrical.

Lynch Park (all ages)

55 Ober St., Beverly; (978) 921-6067; bevrec.com. Open year-round from 8 a.m. to 8 p.m. in the winter, until 10 p.m. in the summer. Parking for nonresidents is $5 weekdays, $15 weekends and holidays from Memorial Day to Labor Day.

On a windy spring day, Lynch Park is a great spot for kite flying. Once part of the Evans estate (President Taft once summered here), it is now the number-one setting of choice for many bridal pictures and weddings that take place in the park's beautiful rose garden built in the foundation of Taft's cottage overlooking the ocean. Children will delight in the extensive play structure, swings, and band shell (with summer concerts). The two small lifeguarded beaches tend to be rocky, but there's a small snack bar and kayak rentals (**Kayak Learning Center,** 800-94-KAYAK). The annual Beverly Homecoming weeklong festival (end of July to first week in Aug) is centered in Lynch Park.

Misery Islands (all ages)

Salem Bay, 0.5 mile from West Beach, Beverly; (978) 526-8687; thetrustees.org. If arriving by private boat, the price is $5 for adults, $3 for children 12 and under during the summer season, free for the rest of the year.

According to local lore, the islands got their moniker from shipbuilder Robert Moulton, who was shipwrecked and stranded there for three frigid days during a December storm in the 1600s while harvesting timber. Nowadays, they're a great spot for fishing, picnicking, swimming, hiking, and bird sightings. Great views, particularly of Manchester-by-the-Sea. Great Misery and Little Misery are accessible by watercraft. Little Misery Island can also be reached from Great Misery by wading through shallow water at low tide. *TIP:* The **Sea Shuttle** (888-400-0601; sea-shuttle.com), launching from Salem Willows Park Pier, 157 Fort Ave., Salem, will get you to Great Misery Island even if you don't have access to a private boat.

Children's Theater

- **Acting Out,** 56 Island St., Lawrence; (978) 807-1191; actingout theater.com

- **Firehouse Theater,** 1 Market Sq., Newburyport; (978) 462-7336; fire house.org

- **Gloucester Stage Company,** 267 East Main St., Gloucester; (978) 281-4433 (box office) or (978) 281-4099; gloucesterstage.com

- **Marblehead Little Theater,** 12 School St., Marblehead; (781) 631-9697; mltlive.org

- **Neverland Theatre,** 200 East Lothrop St., Beverly; (978) 500-8832; neverlandtheatre.com

- **Summer Theatre at Salem State,** 352 Lafayette St., Salem; (978) 542-7890; salemstate.edu/arts

- **Theater-in-the Open** at Maudsley State Park, Newburyport; (978) 465-2572; theaterintheopen.org

Other Things to See & Do

Bookshop of Beverly Farms, 40 West St., Beverly Farms; (978) 927-2122; book shopof beverlyfarms.com. Old-fashioned bookstore. Extremely helpful and knowledgeable staff.

Cabot House, 117 Cabot St., Beverly; (978) 922-1186; beverlyhistory.org. Price: $5 for adults, free for children under 16. Current home of the Beverly Historical Society. Former home of John Cabot, one of the most prominent families in Beverly. Antique furnishings, social histories, nautical and military exhibits. Other 17th-century historical homes owned by the society are the Balch House at 448 Cabot St. ($5 admission) and the Hale Farm at 39 Hale St (**free**).

Larcom Theatre, 13 Wallis St., Beverly; (978) 922-6313 or (617) 531-1257; larcom theatre.com. Musical performances, comedians.

Long Hill Sedgwick Gardens, 572 Essex St., Beverly; (978) 921-1944; thetrustees
.org. Five acres of rare and beautiful plantings dotted with ponds and highlighted with
structures and statues. Managed by the Trustees of Reservations. **Free.**

North Shore Music Theatre, 62 Dunham Rd., Beverly; (978) 232-7200; nsmt.org.
Musicals, concerts, and children's shows.

Where to Eat

Beverly Depot and Saloon, 10 Park St., Beverly; (978) 927-5402; barnsiderrestaurants
.com. Waiters dressed in engineers' uniforms serve your meal in noisy but festive
surroundings. Still used as a train stop by the MBTA (be careful walking across the
railroad track to get to this restaurant). An extensive salad bar and a variety of breads
come with every meal. If it's your birthday, notify the waiter and you'll get a price
break and a special cake. $$–$$$

EJ Cabots, 282 Cabot St., Beverly; (978) 969-3792; ejcabots.com. A cozy spot for
a casual dinner. Fresh seafood, daily specials, locally sourced ingredients, and kid
friendly. Artwork on the walls supports the Global Deed Foundation's work with tal-
ented, motivated, and underserved youth. Full roster of entertainment from local
bands on weekend nights. $–$$

Cygnet, 24 West St., Beverly; (978) 922-9221; cygnetrestaurant.com. Open for lunch
Mon through Fri and dinner daily. Designer-decorated interior. Great menu, inviting
atmosphere. $–$$$

Depot Diner, 23 Enon St., Beverly; (978) 922-6200; depotdiner.com. Open 6 a.m.
to 3 p.m. Creative omelets, pancakes, waffles, and French toast. Favorites are the
banana pancakes (the bananas are caramelized first) and the hot oatmeal, which is
baked with cinnamon and tastes like dessert. Great lunch choices as well. $

Soma, 256 Cabot St., Beverly; (978) 524-0033; somabeverly.com. Fusion of different
ethnic specialties. $–$$$

Where to Stay

Beverly Garden Suites, 5 Lakeview Ave., Route 1A, Beverly; (978) 922-7535; beverly
gardensuites.com. Suites with kitchenettes; perfect for families. Complimentary in-
room continental breakfast. $–$$

The Wylie Inn and Conference Center, 295 Hale St., Beverly; (866) 333-0859; wyliecenter.com. Located on the campus of Endicott College, which straddles the Atlantic Ocean, the relatively new and well-appointed inn is a testing ground for hospitality students. $–$$$

Cape Ann Region

The towns in this region include Manchester-by-the-Sea, Magnolia, Gloucester, Rockport, and Essex. A great resource for information and brochures is the **Cape Ann Chamber of Commerce and Visitor Center,** 33 Commercial St., Gloucester, MA 01930 (978-283-1601; capeannchamber.com or capeannvacation.com). The Cape Ann area has a breathtaking coastline. An extremely pleasant way to meander along is by hooking up with Route 127 (Route 133 to Essex). For those more interested in getting there at a less leisurely pace, use Route 128.

Manchester-by-the-Sea

Over 12 miles of shoreline grace Manchester-by-the-Sea and the town is probably best known for its stunningly scenic Singing Beach. Many harbors dot the shoreline but the most picturesque is **Tuck's Point** (take Harbor Street off Route 127, at the end of Harbor, take a left onto Tuck's Point Road and follow it to Tuck's Point), with a very small beach, swings, a picnic pavilion, bathrooms, and a roomy covered gazebo on the dock.

Boston Lobsters Tennis Team (all ages)

Manchester Athletic Club (MAC), 8 Atwater Ave., Manchester-by-the-Sea; (877) 617-LOBS or (978) 526-8900; bostonlobsters.net. All home matches are outdoors at the Manchester Athletic Club or in case of inclement weather, the match will take place at the MAC's indoor courts. See the website for the full schedule and pricing (discount for USTA members). Tickets go on sale usually in Nov (regular admission, box seats, and a VIP section with tables and wait service).
A member of the New England Franchise of the Mylan World Team Tennis (WTT) Pro League, the Boston Lobsters, a 2013 Eastern Conference semifinalist, are exciting to watch. The Manchester Athletic Club venue is intimate enough that

you can see your favorite players such as John Isner, Venus and Serena Williams, Martina Navratilova, Martina Hingis, Lindsay Davenport, Anna Kournikova, and James Blake up close—to the enjoyment of thousands of regional North Shore fans. There is plenty of parking adjacent to the court. Since the doors open 2 hours prior to the match, arrive early to avoid the crowds. There are food stands and shopping on-site under the tent and a very festive atmosphere. At every match children are encouraged to meet the players and get autographs. If you have a devoted tennis fan in your family, there are plenty of volunteer opportunities for both adults and children.

Singing Beach (all ages)

119 Beach St., Manchester-by-the-Sea; (978) 526-7276 (summer) or (978) 526-2019 (Parks and Recreation office); manchester.ma.us/pages/manchesterma_recreation/ singingbeach. $5 walk-on fee Memorial Day through Labor Day Fri, Sat, Sun and holidays.

Manchester-by-the-Sea is home to one of the prettiest beaches on the North Shore: Singing Beach, a curving strip of sand that "sings" when you walk on it. Day-trippers from Boston take the train from North Station to the Manchester (Manchester-by-the Sea) stop and walk the mile (a pleasant walk) to the beach. Between Memorial Day and Labor Day, beachside parking is strictly limited to residents only (there will be 20 designated non-resident parking spaces from Oct through Apr), so you'll have to drop the family at the beach, then drive back into town to park in one of the designated areas. At the beach you'll find a snack stand, restrooms, and changing rooms. On the way there, you'll pass **Crosby's Market** (3 Summer St.; 978-526-4444; crosbysmarkets.com), a grocery store that's perfectly located for last-minute picnic fixings, and there's a good ice-cream shop (**Captain Dusty's,** 60 Beach St.; 978-526-1663) right next door, too, for post-beach snacking. Directions: Take Route 128 North from Boston, toward Gloucester. Take exit 15 (School Street) to the end. At the center of town, take a left through the village and follow Beach Street to the end.

Other Things to See & Do

Hiking spots with views

Agassiz Rock, School Street North toward Essex (exit 15 off of Route 128), Manchester-by-the-Sea; (978) 526-8687; thetrustees.org. Owned by the Trustees of Reservations. **Free.**

Coolidge Reservation, Summer Street (Route 127 North), Manchester-by-the-Sea; (978) 526-8687; thetrustees.org. Views of the Atlantic and Magnolia Beach. Owned by the Trustees of Reservations. **Free.**

Where to Eat

Beach Street Cafe, 35 Beach St., Manchester-by-the-Sea; (978) 526-8049; bscafe online.com. Reasonable prices, great location. Breakfast and lunch specials. $–$$

The Landing at 7 Central, 7 Central St., Manchester-by-the-Sea; (978) 526-7494; .thelandingat7central.com. Traditional New England fare, cozy and comfortable. Kids' menu. $–$$

Where to Stay

Old Corner Inn, 2 Harbor St. (off Route 127), Manchester-by-the-Sea; (978) 526-4996 or (800) 830-4996; theoldcornerinn.com. Open May through Dec. Gracious Victorian, former summer home of Danish ambassador. Rates include continental breakfast. $–$$

Gloucester & Magnolia

Gloucester is a grittier seaside village that's well known for its expert fishermen. Most members of the family will recognize the often-reproduced **Fisherman's Statue,** near the drawbridge. The statue, called *The Man at the Wheel,* was commissioned in 1923 to celebrate the town's 300th anniversary. Drive along the Harbor Loop to see the workings of a busy harbor. **The Gloucester Visitor Center,** located at 9 Hough St. (in Stagefort Park), Gloucester (978-281-8865), is open Memorial Day through Labor Day. Another source of in-depth information on Gloucester is **Discover Gloucester,** with an excellent website, discover gloucester.com, or call them at (978) 290-9723. Ask them about the Sea It All

The Lighthouses of Gloucester

- **Annisquam Lighthouse:** built in 1801, Lighthouse Road
- **Eastern Point Lighthouse:** built in 1832, Eastern Point Boulevard
- **Thatcher's Island Twin Lighthouses:** originally built in 1789, seen from Gloucester (off the coast of Rockport)
- **Ten Pound Island Lighthouse:** built in 1821, Gloucester Harbor

Passport and the trail map for the free Gloucester Harborwalk. Magnolia is a village of Gloucester that is filled with grand estates, panoramic ocean views, and the well-heeled; located just north of Manchester-by-the-Sea.

Good Harbor Beach (all ages)

99 Thatcher Rd., Route 127A, Gloucester; (978) 281-9785; gloucesterma.com/good-harbor-beach.cfm. Open from sunrise to sunset. Parking is $25 weekends and holidays, $20 midweek (arrive early or you may not get a spot), and $10 off the daily rate after 3 p.m.

Good Harbor is the most popular swimming beach in Gloucester, and deservedly so. The beach's long white stretch of sand overlooks the Atlantic. Facilities include a small snack stand, showers, and toilets. No dogs allowed. *TIP:* Arrive early; the beach is full by 8:30 a.m.

Hammond Castle Museum (all ages)

80 Hesperus Ave., Magnolia; (978) 283-7673 or (978) 283-2080; hammondcastle .org. Visit the website for the schedule; closed during the winter. Admission: $10 for adults, $9 for seniors and students, $8 for children ages 6 to 12, **free** for children under 6. Special events are held throughout the year. Programs for student groups.

Built in 1926 by John Hays Hammond, an inventor, Hammond Castle Museum is an odd combination of the very old—bits of medieval French houses are built right into the building's walls—and the modern, for its day. The eight-story, 8,600-pipe organ is the largest organ in a private home in the country. Most tours include a short demonstration of the organ, which is now played by a computer. There are lots of other sights here, from a huge 15th-century fireplace to a glass-enclosed courtyard to a swimming pool that Hammond regularly dove into from his bedroom window.

Stage Fort Park (all ages)

1 Hough Ave. (off of Western Avenue), Route 127, Gloucester; (978) 281-8865. Open year-round dawn to dusk. Visitor center open Memorial Day through Columbus Day 9 a.m. to 6 p.m. Parking fee $10 per car midweek, $15 weekends.
The settlers found life too harsh at this location and eventually moved to the Naumkeag Peninsula. Ironically, this area is now a serene location for picnicking, grilling, hiking, listening to summer concerts, and storytelling at the bandstand, or enjoying the 2 beaches (Half Moon and Cressey's Beach) and the playground. Lovely harbor views.

This Town Has Gone to the Dogs

Dogtown, lying within both the town of Rockport and the city of Gloucester, is considered by many to be a mystical place. It got its name from the wild dogs that inhabited this area in the 1700s. A century later Roger Babson (of Babson College fame) bought the land. Inspirational messages are cut in stone by stonecutters who were hired by Babson. Your children may be startled to round a bend of the Babson Boulder trail and come upon a boulder that proclaims "Courage," "Get a Job," or "Industry." Dogtown is a nice area for blueberry picking, walking, mountain biking, and cross-country skiing. *It is very easy to get lost,* so bring a handheld GPS or pick up a map at the **Cape Ann Chamber of Commerce and Visitor Center,** at 33 Commercial St. (978-283-1601). **Walk the Words** (walkthewords .com) is a tour of Dogtown that requires 3 miles of moderate walking (not recommended for the very young or less mobile) and can be booked by calling (978) 546-8122. Directions to Dogtown: Take Route 128 north to Route 127 Annisquam. Turn right onto Reynard Street, follow to the end, and turn left onto Cherry Street. On the right is an ill-kept road with a small sign that reads Dogtown Commons.

Recommended **Reading**

A great companion book before boarding the *Thomas E. Lannon* is **Schooner** by Pat Lowery Collins. This beautifully illustrated children's book describes the building process of the schooner as seen from the point of view of a young boy.

Schooner *Thomas E. Lannon* (all ages)

Seven Seas Wharf at the Gloucester House Restaurant, 63 Rear Rogers St. (Route 127), Gloucester; (978) 281-6634; schooner.org. Operates May through Columbus Day; call for a schedule. Tickets cost $40 for adults, $35 for seniors, $27.50 for children 16 and under. In July and Aug kids sail free at 10 a.m. with an adult on Sat (1 kid per adult).

Sail on a 65-foot schooner past fabulous beaches, estates, lighthouses, and islands. Special themed cruises with panache include lobster bakes, sunset cruises, music, and private charters. The vessel is named after a Gloucester fisherman originally from Newfoundland named Thomas E. Lannon.

Wingaersheek Beach (all ages)

232 Atlantic St. (off Route 133), Gloucester; (978) 281-9785; gloucesterma.com/ Wingaersheek-Beach.cfm. Open dawn to dusk. Parking is $25 weekends and holidays, $20 midweek, and $10 off the daily rate after 3 p.m. Arrive very early; the parking lot fills up quickly.

Wingaersheek is a sandy ocean beach that's an especially good destination for families with young children. They love climbing on the smooth rocks and dunes that line the shoreline and wading in the shallow water. Facilities include a concession stand, showers, and toilets. No dogs allowed. Directions: From Route 128, take exit 13.

Other Things to See & Do

Annisquam Arts Children's Summer Studio, 63 Bennett St., Gloucester; (978) 290-2107; annisquamarts.com. Ages 6 to 14, multisensory studio environment.

Beauport, Sleeper McCann House (ages 10 and up), 75 Eastern Point Blvd., Gloucester; (978) 283-0800; historicnewengland.org. Open the end of May through

Whale Watching and Deep-Sea Fishing

All of these whale-watching tours feature naturalists onboard and/or a touch tank. All are connected to research institutions. Sightings can include humpbacks, fin whales, and dolphins in the waters of Stellwagen Bank, a major whale feeding ground in the Atlantic. Remember to bring warm clothing (even on a hot sunny day), sunscreen, and a camera or video camera, and wear comfortable rubber-soled shoes.

- **7 Seas Whale Watch,** Seven Seas Wharf, 63 Rogers St. (Route 127), Gloucester; (978) 283-1776 or (888) 283-1776; 7seaswhale watch.com. Three generations of sea captains; featured in *National Geographic*, the *Travelers Show* on the Discovery Channel, and voted Best in New England 2012 by *Yankee Magazine*. Harbor sightseeing tours can be arranged.

- **Cape Ann Whale Watch,** Rose's Wharf, 415 Main St., Gloucester; (978) 283-5110 or (800) 877-5110; caww.com or seethewhales .com. The *Hurricane II* claims to be the largest and fastest whale-watching ship north of Boston. More than thirty-five years of experience (1979) ; area's best sighting record for humpbacks (2000-2013). The Ultimate Whale Watch is on a four-passenger vessel with a private captain for $500. Coastal fishing adventures, fireworks cruises during the Harbor Fireworks Festival, and private charters.

- **Captain Bill's Whale Watch and Deep Sea Fishing,** 24 Harbor Loop (near Capt. Carlo's Restaurant), Gloucester; (978) 283-6995 or (800) 33-WHALE; captbillandsons.com. All trips are narrated by the Whale Center of New England (which is right next door). Information collected helped Stellwagen Bank to be declared a national marine sanctuary. Private charters around Cape Ann.

- **Yankee Whale Watch and Deep Sea Fishing,** 121 East Main St., Gloucester; (978) 283-0313 or (800) 942-5464; yankeefleet.com. Noted by *Charter Fishing* magazine as the best deep-sea fishing in New England. Private cruises, overnight trips, and fishing.

mid-Oct. Call for schedule and prices. Whimsical summer home decorated with American and European finds by American designer Henry Davis Sleeper. Admission fee.

Cape Ann Museum, 27 Pleasant St., Gloucester; (978) 283-0455. Reopening summer of 2014, 12 galleries highlighting local history and culture plus 2 antique houses.

Cape Pond Ice, 104 Commercial St., Fort Point Wharf, Gloucester; (978) 283-0174; capepondice.com. Forty-five-minute tour includes ice house, wharf, and the history of the industry and their role in *The Perfect Storm*. Admission: Adults $10, children 7 to 12 $8, under 7 **free.** Check the website for tour times.

Discovery Adventures, 1077 Washington St., Lanesville; (978) 283-3320; disco adventures.com. Sea kayaking, stand-up paddle boarding, and snorkeling adventures around Cape Ann.

Harbor Tours, 66 Harbor Loop off of Rogers St., Gloucester; (978) 283-1979; capeannharbortours.com. Narrated harbor and lighthouse tours; learn about lobstering techniques firsthand. The only water tour that completely circles Cape Ann. Hop on, hop off water shuttle to local attractions. Get your tickets at the Yellow Booth across from Walgreens or reserve online.

Maritime Gloucester, 23 Harbor Loop, Gloucester; (978) 281-0470; maritime gloucester.org. Open Memorial Day through Oct. Working historic waterfront (see vessels repaired and boats constructed) and explore the marine environment of Cape Ann. Exhibits on the fishing history of Gloucester, commercial diving, outdoor aquarium with a touch tank, and films.

Ravenswood Park, Route 127, 481 Western Ave., Gloucester; (978) 526-8687; thetrustees.org. Owned by the Trustees of Reservations, a 600-acre park with cross-country skiing, snowshoeing, and hiking trails. Cape Ann Discovery Center in Ravenswood Park offers many hands-on activities. Picnicking is allowed. **Free.**

Rocky Neck, East Main Street, Gloucester; rockyneckartcolony.org. Oldest working art colony in America, with many eateries, art galleries, and artist studios. **Free.**

Ryan and Wood Distillery Tours, 15 Great Republic Dr., Gloucester; (978) 281-2282; ryanandwood.com. Check the website for tour times. Free hour-long tour of distillery producing vodka, gin, rum, and rye whiskey.

Sargent House Museum, 49 Middle St., Gloucester; (978) 281-2432; sargenthouse .org. Home of sea merchants, patriots, and community leaders. Original works of the famous portrait painter John Singer Sargent, a descendant.

Schooner *Ardelle*, 23 Harbor Loop (Maritime Gloucester), Gloucester; (978) 290-7168; schoonerardelle.com. Guided tour on a locally built schooner in authentic detail. Seasonal.

Where to Eat

Halibut Point Restaurant and Pub, 289 Main St., Gloucester; (978) 281-1900; halibutpoint.com. Open year-round. Good chowder that attracts lots of locals. $–$$

Lobsta Land, 84 Causeway St., Route 128 (exit 12), Gloucester; (978) 281-0415; lobstalandrestaurant.com. The freshest fish overlooking the Gloucester marshland. Voted by Boston Magazine the Best of Boston 2012 for its lobsta' rolls North of Boston. Nice family restaurant, children's specials. $–$$

Madfish Grille, 77 Rocky Neck Ave., Gloucester; (978) 281-4554; madfishgrille.com. Great views of the harbor. People pull their boats up, dock, and eat. Hats off to their creative cooking! Seasonal. $–$$$

Mile Marker One Restaurant, located at Cape Ann's Marina Resort, 75 Essex Ave. (Route 133), Gloucester; (978) 283-2122; milemarkerone.com/index.htm. Open 7 days a week for breakfast, lunch, and dinner. Views of the Annisquam River. Boaters can pull right up to the dock (free dockage). Seafood, fish, pastas, meat dishes, burgers, and sandwiches . . . a little something for everyone. $–$$$

The Rudder, 73 Rocky Neck Ave., Gloucester; (978) 283-7967; rudderrestaurant .com. Lunch and dinner served daily, spring through fall. A family-run restaurant whose fun-loving owners often provide unorthodox entertainment along with their excellent food. Outdoor seating overlooking Smith Cove. Seasonal. $$–$$$

Seaport Grille, 6 Rowe Sq., Gloucester; (978) 989-9799; cruiseportgloucester.com/ seaportgrille. A local favorite. Outdoor deck overlooking Gloucester Harbor. Extensive menu. Kids love to watch the commercial fishing boats and the cruise ships. $–$$$

Where to Stay

Cape Ann Motor Inn, 33 Rockport Rd. Gloucester; (978) 281-2900 or (800) 464-VIEW; capeannmotorinn.com. Thirty-one beachfront units overlooking Long Beach with views of Thatcher Island. $–$$$

Good Harbor Beach Inn, Salt Island Road, Gloucester; (978) 283-1489 or 87-SEA-SHELL; goodharborbeachinn.com. Seasonal. Great location across from Good Harbor

St. Peter's Fiesta

St. Peter's Fiesta (held the last weekend in June) features a variety of events including fireworks, races, and parades. The big attraction is the colorful "blessing of the fleet." Most events occur at the waterfront or in downtown Gloucester. Check out the website at stpeters fiesta.org.

Beach. Wonderful views; family-style. Book early—it's hard to get a room because of so much repeat business. $–$$

Harborview Inn, 71 Western Ave., Gloucester; (978) 283-2277 or (800) 299-6696; harborviewinn.com. Six rooms with private baths, most with views of the harbor. Open year-round. Rates include continental breakfast. $–$$$

Inn at Babson Court, 55 Western Ave., Gloucester; (978) 281-4469; babsoncourt .com. Across from the Old Man and the Wheel famous statue; 3 suites of rooms with ocean views and en suite bathrooms, 18th-century manor house. Children of all ages welcome. Free continental breakfast with a basket of muffins delivered to your door in the a.m. $–$$

Samarkand Guest House, 1 Harbor Rd., Gloucester; (978) 283-3757; samarkand inn.com. Family-oriented bed-and-breakfast across from the beach, in operation since 1966. Open year-round. $–$$

Rockport

The quaint seaside charm of Rockport, with the perfect blend of tranquillity and the arts, has attracted visitors and artists for more than a century, and it is an extremely popular summertime destination for day-trippers and travelers alike. Start your day with a visit to Front Beach or walk to the Point at Bearskin Neck (you can hop in and out of the distinctive shops along the way), or explore Halibut Point State Park or the Paper House. At night the Shalin Liu Performance Center is the place to be. For more information, contact the **Gloucester/ Rockport Chamber of Commerce,** 33 Commercial St., Gloucester, MA 01930; (978) 238-1601 or (978) 546-9372; rockportusa.com.

Bearskin Neck (all ages)

Corner of Dock Square and South Road.
Browse in seaside shops, restaurants, and art galleries. Don't forget to admire Motif #1 (one of the most admired scenes and painted innumerable times), a coastal shack hung with buoys.

Halibut Point State Park and Reservation (all ages)

16 Gott Ave., Rockport; (978) 546-2997; mass.gov/eea/agencies/dcr/massparks/ region-north/halibut-point-state-park.html or thetrustees.org. Open daily year-round, sunrise to sunset. Parking is $2 Memorial Day to Labor Day.
Halibut Point is a lovely place for walking and picnicking by the sea. It's not a sandy beach, though; the shore here is rocky, and kids should be encouraged to keep their shoes on to avoid cutting their feet on rocks or shells. The rocks are also particularly slippery at low tide and every year, someone falls and breaks his or her arm; so do be careful! Take a 20-minute walk around the old quarry (hang on to the kids' hands), then play in the tidal pools. Bring windbreakers and warm clothes—it's usually windy—and keep an eye out for poison ivy. If open, stop by the visitor center housed inside a former World War II Fire Control Tower, with displays on quarrying and Cape Ann's historic granite industry, local geology, and native and military history.

The Paper House (all ages)

Off Route 127, 52 Pigeon Hill St., Rockport; (978) 546-2629; paperhouserockport .com. Open daily Apr through Oct, 10 a.m. to 5 p.m. Admission $2 for adults and $1 for children ages 6 to 14.
Worth a stop—amazingly, everything in the house, from the walls to the furnishings, is made of newspaper, a twenty-year project by Elis Stenman as a leisure-time hobby. Directions: Follow Route 127 in Rockport to Pigeon Cove. After the Yankee Clipper Inn, take the second left onto Curtis Street and another left onto Pigeon Hill Street to number 52 on your right.

Other Things to See & Do

Cape Ann Foodie Tours, Rockport; (617) 902-8291; capeannfoodietours.com. Taste the sweets and see the sights of Rockport.

Jettywalk Arts, 36 Bearskin Neck, Rockport; (781) 462-8340. More than 30 artists are represented in this cool art gallery with something for everyone!

Northshore Kayak Outdoor Center, 9 Tuna Wharf, Rockport; (978) 546-5050; northshorekayak.com. Tours; rentals of kayaks, bicycles, pedal boats, and stand-up paddle boards; instructions; and overnights.

Shalin Liu Performance Center, 37 Main St., Rockport; (978) 546-7391; rcmf.org. Acoustically perfect performance hall. Home of the Rockport Chamber Music Festival; jazz, pop, and world music; films; and lectures. Stunning backdrop view of the ocean through floor-to-ceiling windows during performances.

Where to Eat

Greenery Cafe and Restaurant, 15 Dock Sq., Rockport; (978) 546-9593; greenery-restaurant.com. Serving breakfast, lunch, and dinner spring, summer, and fall. Delightful view of harbor. Salads, pasta, and seafood. $–$$$

My Place by the Sea Restaurant, 68 Bearskin Neck, Rockport; (978) 546-9667; myplacebythesea.com. Open Wed through Mon. Magnificent panoramic view of Rockport coastline; indoor and outdoor dining. Kathy, the chef, is highly acclaimed for her creative dishes. A North Shore favorite in a picture-perfect setting; recognized as one of the top eight restaurants in New England. $$–$$$$

Where to Stay

Addison Choate Inn, 49 Broadway, Rockport; (978) 546-7543 or (800) 245-7543; addisonchoateinn.com. Listed on the National Historic Register. Charming bed-and-breakfast, 6 rooms with private bath, minutes away from the heart of Rockport. Full buffet breakfast; kids over 12 please. $$

Emerson Inn by the Sea, 1 Cathedral Ave., Pigeon Cove, Rockport; (978) 546-6321 or (800) 964-5550; emersoninnbythesea.com. Lovely grounds, traditional New England inn, and a fine restaurant, the Grand Cafe. Children are welcome but you must bring your own pack 'n play. Full hot breakfast in season. $–$$$$

Peg Leg Inn, 1 King St. (Corner of King and Beach), Rockport; (978) 546-2352 or (800) 346-2352; thepegleginn.com. Close to shops, restaurants, art galleries, and across the street from Front Beach. The inn incorporates a series of lovely colonial-era houses overlooking the beach, bay, and ocean. Extra charge for children. $$–$$$

Seven South Street Inn B&B, 7 South St., Rockport; (978) 546-6708 or (888) 284-2730; sevensouthstreetinn.com. Gracious inn, elegantly furnished; outdoor pool; bicycles and helmets provided (adult-size) for your riding pleasure; four-course breakfast. Children over 10 please. $–$$

Essex

Essex is threaded by the tidal-based Essex River and its related marshland, eventually merging with the Annisquam River as they flow out to sea. Retaining its rural flavor and shipbuilding heritage, Essex is also a mecca for antiquing.

Essex Shipbuilding Museum (all ages)

66 Main St./Route 133W, Essex; (978) 768-7541; essexshipbuildingmuseum.org. Open June through Oct, Wed through Sun 10 a.m. to 5 p.m.; Nov through June, Sat and Sun 10 a.m. to 5 p.m.; and by appointment year-round. Guided tour admission: $10 for adults, $5 for kids 6 to 18, free for kids under 6. Gift shop. Reminiscent of the days when more two-masted wooden ships came from Essex than from anywhere else in the world, this excellent museum not only shows you how the ships were built but also gives you the context you need to understand the significance of the industry to the area. The Essex Shipbuilding Museum also houses one of the best maritime collections in the region. Tours include video presentations and hands-on activities for the younger set. Real tools allow kids to try their hand at shipbuilding. A shipbuilding yard is located in the rear of the museum.

Recommended **Reading**

Children's books by Daisy Nell with Cape Ann as the setting: *Rocky at the Dockside* takes place in Gloucester and *Stowaway Mouse* is set in Essex.

White Elephant (all ages)

32 Main St., Essex; (978) 768-6901; whiteelephantshop.com. Open daily year-round Mon through Sat 10 a.m. to 5 p.m., Sun noon to 5 p.m., closed major holidays. The White Elephant Outlet Shop is 1 mile north of the main shop; 101 John Wise Ave. in Essex (everything is at least half off).

Essex is known as an antiques-lover's haven. One of the more interesting shops is the White Elephant, next door to the Shipbuilding Museum. The stock (from Northshore Estates) turns over often due to fair pricing and the one-of-a-kind nature of the goods, but in the past it has included collections of wooden teeth, old train sets, and wasp-waisted dresses from a hundred years ago.

Essex River Cruises and Charters (all ages)

Essex Marina, 35 Dodge St., Essex; (978) 768-6981 or (800) RIVER-06; essexcruises .com. Open May through Oct. Pricing: $25 for adults, $10 for children 4 to 12, 3 and under free. Charters and clambakes a specialty. Call for a schedule (seasonal).

The 90-minute narrated tour cruise on the *Essex River Queen* takes you past beaches, marshes, "old money" estates, and shipbuilding yards. Be sure to bring binoculars to view the many varieties of birds that are found in the marshlands. This is a relaxing and informative tour from a different perspective. Temperatures on the water can fluctuate, so bring a jacket.

Other Things to See & Do

Agawam Boat Charters, 21 Pickering St. (office), Essex; (978) 768-1114; agawam boatcharters.com. Beaches, fishing, island tours, and trips. Seasonal.

Cogswell Grant, 60 Spring St., Essex; (978) 768-3632; historicnewengland.org/ historic-properties/homes/cogswells-grant. Home of Bertram and Nina Little. Collection of American Decorative Art, especially folk art paintings arranged just as the family left them.

Essex River Basin Adventures, 1 Main St., Essex; (978) 768-ERBA; erba.com. Longest-running sea kayak adventure company in Massachusetts. Kayak tours, lessons, and camp. Seasonal.

Stavros Reservation, Island Road (off Route 133), Essex; (978) 526-8687; thetrust ees.org. Sweeping views; easy hiking, picnicking, and bird watching. Free.

Where to Eat

Periwinkles, 74 Main St. (Route 133), Essex; (978) 768-6320; periwinklesrestaurant
.com. Great spot overlooking a picturesque tidal river. Eat outside on the deck during
warm weather. $–$$

Woodman's, 121 Main St. / Route 133, Essex; (978) 768-6057 or (800) 649-1773;
woodmans.com. According to the Woodman family, this is where the first clam was
breaded and fried (in 1916). In the summer there is always a line, maybe because
Forbes FYI Magazine called it the Best Seafood in America. $–$$$

North of Cape Ann

The North Shore continues up the coast to the border of New Hampshire. Main
access roads are Routes I-95 and I-495. Slower going is Route 133 from Ipswich,
connecting to Route 1A toward Newburyport. Nature has blessed Ipswich with
marshland vistas as well as pristine beaches. Crane Beach, a barrier beach with
sweeping white sands, is the town's crown jewel, managed by the Trustees
of Reservations. **Sandy Point State Reservation** at the tip of Plum Island
(accessesed through the Parker River National Wildlife Refuge in Newburyport)
is actually owned by both the town of Ipswich as well as by the state of Massa-
chusetts (mass.gov/eea/agencies/dcr/massparks/region-north/sandy-point-state-
reservation.html). **The Ipswich Visitor Information Center** (inside the Hall
Haskell House), 36 South Main St., Route 1A (978-356-8540; ipswichvisitorcenter
.org), is open Memorial Day weekend to Columbus Day.

Ipswich

Castle Hill (all ages)

**290 Argilla Rd., Ipswich; (978) 356-4351; thetrustees.org or craneestate.org.
Admission fee for grounds and seasonal tours; check the website for rates.
Restrictions apply sometimes due to special-event rentals (such as weddings).**
This is the former home of the Crane family (for whom Crane Beach is named)
now owned and managed by the Trustees of Reservations, a private land trust
whose holdings include many other properties listed in this book. The beautiful

old mansion is the summer home to an excellent performing arts series on Thurs nights (reserve early; tickets sometimes sell out). Audiences sit on the broad lawn to hear the music. There are other seasonal activities as well.

Crane Beach (all ages)

310 Argilla Rd., Ipswich; (978) 356-4354 (beach office) or (978) 356-4351; the trustees.org. Open daily 8 a.m. to sunset year-round. From Memorial Day to Labor Day, the parking fee is $25 per car weekends, $15 midweek, and the admission is reduced by half after 3 p.m. Golf cart beach transport is available for mobility-challenged individuals.

Crane Beach is a long, clean beach that's great for swimming, picnicking, and walking. During the summer season lifeguards are on duty and the bathhouse and snack bar are open. There are several pleasant, easy walks to take from the beach. My family's favorite is a 5-mile Bay Trail nature walk (trail map available) that leads you through the dunes, red maple swamp, pitch pine forest, and heathlands of woolly hudsonia and cranberry bog. Crane Beach is home to more than 200 species of resident and migratory birds, white-tailed deer, red squirrels, red fox, eastern coyote, and opossum. ***Caution:*** Greenbug season lasts for about two weeks in midsummer and can be quite annoying. Horses and dogs are allowed Oct through Mar with a permit. Directions: From Route 1A south of Ipswich, take Route 133 East. Turn left onto Northgate Road. At the end of this road, turn right onto Argilla Road, which ends at the beach.

Crane Wildlife Refuge (all ages)

Reached by private boat only. South of Crane Beach in the middle of the Essex Bay estuary, Ipswich; (978) 356-4351. Check the summer schedule on thetrustees .org. Check the website for pricing.

Tour Choate and Long Islands by foot on the 2-mile trail to the summit. View wildlife, flora, and fauna on this deserted island. Very scenic and chosen for the filming of the 1995 movie *The Crucible* with Winona Ryder. Every year there is a Choate Island Day in the fall dedicated to non–boat owners with transportation to the island for a fee.

Foote Brothers Canoe Rental (ages 3 and up)

Willowdale Dam, 230 Topsfield Rd., Ipswich; (978) 356-9771; footebrotherscanoes
.com. Open Apr through Oct, summer hours 8 a.m. to 6 p.m. Price: $22 to $47 per
canoe midweek, $37 to $47 per canoe weekends and holidays, depending on the
trip that you take. Foote Brothers now has kayak rentals ranging from $22 to $42
per day.

Quietly stroke by the Ipswich River Wildlife Sanctuary or Bradley Palmer State
Park as you meander the Ipswich River's 30 navigable miles. In business for more
than fifty years, Foote Brothers provides canoes, kayaks, and advice for families
who enjoy paddling on a calm river..Shuttle trips for longer journeys; overnight
trips can be arranged.

Russell Orchards (all ages)

143 Argilla Rd., Ipswich; (978) 356-5366; russellorchardsma.com. Open daily from
mid-May through the end of Oct 9 a.m. to 6 p.m. and closing at 5 p.m. in Nov.

More than an orchard, Russell Orchards has a playground, animals in the barnyard that are accustomed to being petted, and hayrides during the fall. In season, pick your own strawberries, cherries, blackberries, blueberries, raspberries,
and apples. Don't leave without buying a few of the delicious homemade dough-
nuts or a bottle of their vintage fruit wine or hard cider.

Wolf Hollow (all ages)

114 Essex Rd., Route 133, Ipswich; (978) 356-0216; wolfhollowipswich.org. Open
to the public on weekends only, year-round; check the website for hours of operation. Weekdays by appointment. Admission: $7.50 for adults, $5 for children ages
3 to 17.

Wolf Hollow is a wild-animal refuge and educational facility dedicated to the
preservation of the gray wolf and to teach people about wolves in the wild. The
wolves' interactions parallel human family units.

Where to Eat

The Clam Box of Ipswich, 246 High St. (Route 1A), Ipswich; (978) 356-9707; ipswich
ma.com/clambox. Open seasonally. Local icon since 1935 shaped like a clam box;
known for its burgers, clams, fries, and scallops. $–$$$

Ithaki, 25 Hammett St., Ipswich; (978) 356-0099; ithakicuisine.com. Greek Mediter-
ranean cuisine. Open for lunch and dinner. Closed Mon. $–$$$

White Farms Ice Cream, 326 High St., Ipswich; (978) 356-2633; whitefarms-ice cream.com. Winner of the top 25 in *Best of Boston* for all New England and the Boston City Search Award for best ice cream. Known for creative ice-cream flavors like Outrageous, Key Lime Pie, Reverse Chip, and Caramel Cow. $

Where to Stay

Inn at Castle Hill, 280 Argilla Rd., Ipswich; (978) 412-2555; theinnatcastlehill.com. One of two Trustees of Reservations bed-and-breakfasts. Money earned helps to preserve and maintain the site. Open Apr through Dec. Luxurious appointments. Views of Crane Beach and the Essex River estuaries. Full breakfast included. $$$–$$$$

Ipswich Inn, 2 East St., Ipswich; (978) 356-2431; ipswichbedandbreakfast.com. Gracious 8-room inn (rates include breakfast). Open to public for breakfast. $$

Newburyport & Newbury

Newburyport is a quaint seaside town imbued with a sense of history and charm. Imposing homes of the Federalist style line the major streets into the downtown area, signaling the wealth of a bygone era when Newburyport was a center of commerce and trade. Major fortunes were made in Newburyport due to its maritime industry. In a revitalized rebirth, the community became a popular tourist destination in the 1970s. Plum Island, which is partly in Newbury and partly in Newburyport is a great location for family recreation. Both Plum Island and the Parker River Wildlife Refuge (which is on Plum Island) are terrific places for family swimming at the beach, hiking the dunes and marshland, and biking. To obtain your *Official Guide to Newburyport,* contact **The Greater Newburyport Chamber of Commerce and Industry,** 38R Merrimac St., Newburyport, MA 01950; (978) 462-6680; newburyportchamber.org.

Maudslay State Park (all ages)

74 Curzon's Mill Rd., Newburyport; (978) 465-7223 mass.gov/eea/agencies/dcr/ massparks/region-north/maudslay-state-park.html. Open year-round dawn to sunset, $2 parking fee.

When the mansion of this 480-acre estate was taken down in the 1950s, the landscaped grounds became a state park. It's a great place on a spring or summer afternoon—picnic spots abound, and there are lots of walking trails through

Outdoor Performances at Maudslay State Park

Maudslay Arts Center at Maudslay State Park, 95 Curzon's Mill Rd., Newburyport; (978) 857-0677 or (978) 499-0050; maudslay artscenter.org. Light classical symphony, dance and jazz performances outdoors or in the MAC Concert Barn. Call for tickets for July through Aug performances. Bring a picnic; sit on the patio or on the lawn (bring a blanket).

Theater-in the-Open at Maudslay State Park, 74 Curzon's Mill Rd., Newburyport; (978) 465-2572; theaterintheopen.org. Check the website for details on showtimes, dates, and price structure. The productions are free but parking is $2. Outdoor theatrical performances since 1980. Shows range from children's performances, Shakespearean comedies and dramas, Greek tragedies, puppetry, and a Haunted Trail at Halloween.

formal gardens, rolling meadows, woods, and an enormous stand of mountain laurel. The most breathtaking shrubs on the property are the azaleas and the rhododendrons that bloom in May and June. In summer attend a performance at the Maudslay Arts Center or the Theater in the Open. Other popular forms of recreation here include biking, horseback riding, and cross-country skiing.

Parker River National Wildlife Refuge (all ages)

6 Plum Island Turnpike, Newburyport, Plum Island; (978) 465-5753; fws.gov/refuge/parker_river. During the plovers' nesting season (early Apr through June), the first parking lot is open and the rest of the beach is usually closed. July is limited; Aug through Mar the beach is open. Otherwise open daily year-round, dawn to dusk. Parking is $5 per car and $2 for bicycles and pedestrians. A refuge pass good for the entire season costs $20.

Covering about two-thirds of Plum Island, the wildlife refuge is a favorite destination for Boston-area families. The refuge is operated by the US Fish and Wildlife Service; it is one of the very few natural barrier beach, dune, and salt marsh complexes left on the coast of New England. Along with the abundant wildlife on view here in its natural habitat, the great attraction of Plum Island (which is what the locals call it) is the beach. Those who are in the know arrive at the refuge very early (before 8:30 a.m. on weekends in the summer), since only a limited number of parking spots are available because of the high demand. Several observation towers are well used by birders in March and April and during the fall, the peak migration periods for ducks and other waterfowl. The views are always good, and there are always birds to see—300 or so species live in the area. The 6-mile-long beach is nearly always deserted. Because of the strong undertow, it's not a good place for families with young children; also, there are no lifeguards. At the extreme end is Sandy Point State Reservation (mass.gov/eea/agencies/dcr/massparks/region-north/sandy-point-state-reservation.html) and Sandy Point (which is owned by the state of Massachusetts), a more placid place for a swim. **Note:** Don't bring pets; do bring bug spray to deter the pesky greenheads in July and early Aug.

Other Things to See & Do

Coffin House, 14 High Rd., Newbury; (978) 462-2634; historicnewengland.org. Home built by the early settlers.

Cushing House Museum, 98 High St., Newburyport; (978) 462-2681; newburyhist .org. Open mid-May through Oct. Call for hours and fees. Depicts the history of the city and rural life through paintings, photos, furnishings, textiles, documents, and decorative arts.

Custom House Maritime Museum, 25 Water St., Newburyport; (978) 462-8681; thechmm.org. Maritime history collection of Newburyport and the Merrimack River valley.

Great Marsh

The North Shore's Great Marsh (greatmarsh.org) stretches from Gloucester in Cape Ann to just below the New Hampshire border in Salisbury. It's a birders paradise with sightings of breeding and migratory birds that depend upon this ecosystem of beach, marsh, estuary, and three tidal rivers.

Biking Shops

Biking shops for rentals in the area include:

Ipswich Cycle, 5 Brown Sq., Ipswich; (978) 356-4500; ipswichcycle
.com

Riverside Cycles, 50 Water St. (Tannery Building), Newburyport;
(978) 465-5566; riversidecycle.com

Merrimac Street Shops, Newburyport. Browsing the quaint shops of Newburyport is a pleasant pastime.

Newburyport's Whale Watch, Hilton's Dock, 54 Merrimac St., Newburyport;
(978) 499-0832 or (800) 848-1111; newburyportwhalewatch.com. Whale watches,
birding trips, dinner cruises, charters. Will do school talks with an inflatable 55-foot fin
whale. Naturalist onboard.

Spencer-Pierce-Little Farm, 5 Little's Ln., Newbury; (978) 462-2634; historicnew
england.org. Prominent local family's 230-acre 17th-century farmhouse and grounds.
Learn about life on a farm through interactive activities. Farm animals on view. Call for
full schedule of events.

Yankee Clipper, on the Boardwalk, Waterfront Promenade Park, Newburyport;
(603) 682-2293; harbortours.com. Open daily Memorial Day to Labor Day. Historical
and colorful tours of Newburyport and its waters; specializing in harbor and sunset
cruises.

Where to Eat

The Black Cow, 54 Rear Merrimac St., Newburyport; (978) 499-8811; blackcow
restaurants.com. Water views of the Merrimack; outdoor deck seating. Daily and
nightly specials and kids' menu. $–$$$

The Grog Restaurant, 13 Middle St., Newburyport; (978) 465-8008; thegrog.com.
Newburyport's oldest historical restaurant, pub-like atmosphere. Best of Boston, Sun-
day brunch. $–$$

Michael's Harborside, 92 Merrimac St. (1 Tournament Wharf), Newburyport; (978)
462-7785; michaelsharborside.com. On the water overlooking the harbor. Specializing

in seafood. Winner of the Best of Boston kids' dining by *Northshore Magazine*. Splashdown kids-only events. $–$$$

10 Center Restaurant, 10 Center St., Newburyport; (978) 462-6652; tencenter street.com. Traditional dining room and a pub. Fireplaces in some of the rooms; lighter fare in the pub. $–$$$

Newburyport Rear Range Lighthouse, 61½ Water St., Newburyport; (800) 727-BEAM; lighthousepreservation.org. Dine at the top of a lighthouse. Very, very expensive, but fun for familes or for a romantic evening. Part of the tab is tax deductible since it goes to charity. Advance reservations required. $$$$+++

Where to Stay

Clark Currier Inn, 45 Green St., Newburyport; (978) 465-8363; clarkcurrierinn.com. Open year-round. Classic 1803 Federal building, 9 rooms, not far from the main shopping area of Newburyport. Request a family-style room; though they're all large, not all bedrooms are appropriate for children (must be 10 or over). There's a comfortable lounge/TV room and a backyard garden and gazebo. Includes a deluxe continental breakfast and afternoon tea. $–$$

Garrison Inn, 11 Brown Sq., Newburyport; (978) 499-8500; garrisoninn.com. Boutique hotel with 24 lushly appointed rooms, bedroom lofts, working fireplaces, and exposed brick walls, all found at this National Historical Landmark. Children of any age are welcome. Complimentary continental breakfast. $$–$$$$

Yakity-Yak, **Let's Kayak!**

Kayaking tours of the salt marshes around Plum Island and the Newburyport area can be arranged by:

Joppa Flats Education Center, 1 Plum Island Turnpike (near Ocean Avenue), Newburyport; (978) 462-9998; massaudubon.org

Plum Island Kayak Tours, 92 Merrimac St., Unit 101B, Newburyport; (978) 462-5510; plumislandkayak.com

TopEvents for the North Shore, Cape Ann, and the Merrimack Valley

January–August

- **Winter Fest,** Feb, downtown Lowell; (978) 469-6150; lowellwinter fest.org

- **Cape Ann Birding Weekend,** first weekend in Feb, (978) 283-1601; capeannchamber.org

- **New England Music Awards,** Feb, 50 Merrimack St. (Lowell Auditorium), Lowell; (978) 459-6150; nemusicawards.com

- **Newburyport Literary Festival,** Apr, Newburyport; (978) 465-1257; newburyportliteraryfestival.org

- **Strawberry Festival,** June, Russell Orchards, 143 Argilla Rd., Ipswich; (978) 356-5366; russellorchards.com

- **Sand and Sea Festival,** late June, Salisbury; beachfests.org

- **Theater in the Open,** June through Sept, 74 Curzon's Mill Rd., Newburyport; (978) 465-2572; theaterintheopen.org

- **Semana Hispana,** mid-June, Lawrence; (978) 686-0900 or (978) 620-3250; merrimackvalleychamber.org

- **St. Peter's Fiesta,** late June, Gloucester; (978) 283-1601; stpeters fiesta.org

- **Danvers Family Festival,** end of June/early July, Danvers; (978) 777-0001, ext. 4; danversfamilyfestival.com

- **Lowell Summer Music Series,** Memorial Day to Labor Day, Boardinghouse Park, Lowell; (978) 275-1829 or (978) 970-5000; lowell summermusic.org or nps.gov/lowe

- **Salem Celebrates the Fourth,** July 4, Salem; (978) 744-3663 or (877) SALEMMA; salem.org

- **Marblehead Festival of the Arts,** July, Marblehead; (781) 639-ARTS; marbleheadfestival.org

- **Salem Maritime Festival and Heritage Days,** end of July, Derby Wharf, Salem; (978) 740-1650; nps.gov/sama

- **Thursday Night Picnic Concert Series,** summer, Crane Estate, Ipswich; (978) 921-1944; thetrustees.org

- **Yankee Homecoming,** last Sat in July (weeklong), Newburyport; (978) 462-6680; yankeehomecoming.com

- **Marblehead Race Week,** late July, Marblehead; (781) 631-3100; mheadrace.org

- **Lowell Folk Festival,** late July, Lowell; (978) 970-4257; lowellfolk festival.org

- **Gloucester Waterfront Festival,** Aug, Gloucester; (978) 283-1601; castleberryfairs.com

- **Newburyport Chamber Music Festival,** Aug, Newburyport; (978) 463-9776; newburyportchambermusic.org

- **Gloucester Blues Festival,** Aug, Stage Fort Park, Gloucester; (978) 325-0705; gloucesterbluesfestival.com

- **Festival by the Sea,** Aug, Masconomo Park, Manchester-by-the Sea; (978) 283-1601; capeannvacations.com

- **Southeast Asian Water Festival,** late Aug, Lowell; (978) 970-4257 or (978) 970-4040; lowellwaterfestival.org

- **Schooner Festival,** Labor Day weekend, Gloucester Harbor; (978) 283-1601; capeannvacations.com/schooner

- **Trails and Sails,** late Sept, Essex County; (978) 740-0444; trailsand sails.org or essexheritage.org

- **International Festival,** Sept, Peabody Square, Peabody; (978) 532-3000 or (978) 538-5704; peabodyinternationalfestival.com

- **Banjo and Fiddle Contest,** Sept, Lowell; (978) 970-5000; nps.gov/lowe or lowellsummermusic.org

- **Appleton Farms Family Farm Day,** autumn, Ipswich; (978) 356-5728; thetrustees.org

Amesbury, Merrimac & Salisbury

In its heyday of the 1940s and 1950s, Salisbury was a magnet for wholesome fun. The beachside arcades and rides were a popular draw for locals. Falling into disrepair and suffering disinterest by merrymakers (not unlike Coney Island and the Atlantic City Boardwalk), the area is trying to reinvent itself. The neighboring towns of Merrimac and Amesbury separated from Salisbury centuries ago and are sluiced through by the Merrimack River.

Amesbury Sports Park (ages 4 and up)

12 South Hunt Rd. (exit 54 off Route 495), Amesbury; (978) 388-5788; amesbury sportspark.net. Open Christmas through mid-Mar for tubing. Call for price and schedule; extended hours during vacation periods. Price based on day of week and time of day.

Formerly owned by Boston Bruins player Brad Park, this is a great place for winter tubing fun. The park has 1 rope tow and 1 conveyor belt to handle the crowds and to give you a boost up the hill. There are 13 different runs at various levels; children ages 4 to 7 must be accompanied by an adult. Young children are required to wear helmets (ages 4 through 7; bring your own or rent one for $3). There is a snack bar and the Corner Kick Pub. Groups are welcome (group discounts are given), so keep that in mind if you decide to visit during peak times. The Sports Park does snowmaking to ensure snow coverage on the hill.

The Sports Park is now offering summer tubing on Neveplast lanes, which you can do fully clothed (although there is some misting involved!); a Zorb ball—the first in North America—a sphere inside another sphere where you are strapped in a seven-point harness and rolled down the hill head over heels; a Water Zorb with no harness, fitting up to 3 people with 5 gallons of water as you're sloshed and bounced down the hill. Crazy new fun things are arriving all the time. Lacrosse, soccer, and rugby camps train kids. ***Warning:*** Call ahead for summer activities at Amesbury Sports Park as they are considering changing or eliminating the summer programs.

Salisbury Beach State Reservation and
Camping Area   (all ages)

Beach Road to Reservation Road, off Route 1A, Salisbury; (978) 462-4481; mass
.gov/eea/agencies/dcr/massparks/region-north/salisbury-beach-state-reservation
.html. Salisbury Beach State Reservation is open year-round and charges a $9
parking fee for cars Memorial Day to Columbus Day.

Close to the border of Massachusetts and New Hampshire, Salisbury Beach State
Reservation, on 520 acres, abuts both the Atlantic Ocean and the mouth of the
Merrimack River. A long stretch of unspoiled, sandy beach is lifeguarded for
safe swimming in season. Beautiful vistas abound, and it's a haven for boating
and fishing. Other facilities include a playground, picnic area, boat launch, and a
concession stand. Restrooms and shower facilities are available near the campground area. The 484 campground sites (call Reserve America, 877-422-6762)
have a limited number of trailer and RV hookups available. Look for harbor seals
on the rocks in the fall and winter months.

Other Things to See & Do

Lowell's Boat Shop, 459 Main St., Point Shore, Amesbury; (978) 834-0050; lowells
boatshop.com. The country's oldest continuous boatbuilding business, birthplace of
the fishing dory. On the National Register of Historic Places and a National Historic
Landmark. Nonprofit working museum and part of the Essex Heritage Trail.

Salisbury Beach Center, Ocean Front and Broadway Streets, Salisbury. Video
games, amusement rides, arcades, restaurants, and snack shops. Kid heaven.

Where to Eat

Hodgies, 71 Haverhill Rd., Amesbury; (978) 388-1211; hodgies.com. Homemade ice
cream, big scoops. $

Sea Glass Restaurant, 4 Oceanfront, North Salisbury; (978) 642-5800; seaglass
oceanside.com. Named a green restaurant for its sustainable practices, modern chic
interior, ocean views. $$–$$$

Greater Lowell and the Merrimack Valley

The Merrimack River winds through the valley, flowing past large cities like Lowell and Haverhill, once large mill towns, and small, picturesque, ramblin' towns like Westford and "The Andovers." The major highway connecting the region is I-495, paralleling the state line of New Hampshire just 10 to 15 miles north of the highway. For further information, contact the **Greater Merrimack Valley Convention and Visitors Bureau,** 40 French St., Lowell, MA 01852; (978) 459-6150 or (800) 215-9805; merrimackvalley.org.

Haverhill

Once a leader in tanneries and the manufacturing of shoes, Haverhill earned the nickname "Queen Slipper City." Haverhill, with an enviable location off of major highways, now has seven technological parks. The downtown has seen a resurgence in chic eateries, the visual arts, and a thriving music scene. Don't miss the new **Bradford Rail Trail,** a 1.3-mile trail along the Merrimack River used for jogging, biking, and strolling. For further information on Haverhill, contact the **Greater Haverhill Chamber of Commerce,** 88 Merrimack St., Haverhill, MA 01830; (978) 373-5663; creativehaverhill.org.

Bradford Ski Area (ages 3 and up)

60 South Cross Rd. (off Salem Street), Haverhill; (978) 373-0071 or (866) 644-SNOW (snow info line); skibradford.com. Open mid-Dec to end of Mar, Mon through Sat 8:30 a.m. to 10 p.m., Sun 8:30 a.m. to 4:30 p.m. Call for prices and specials.

A great place to break a child into the sport of skiing or snowboarding (oops, no pun intended!), Bradford, with a 250-foot vertical drop, is a family-oriented hill with total coverage by snowmaking equipment. Bradford has 15 trails accessed by 3 triple chairs, 2 rope tows, 3 novice carpet conveyors, and 1 T-bar. The night skiing is well lit (100 percent). For the snowboard enthusiast there is a terrain park, and skiers are allowed too. Facilities include a lodge, equipment rentals, a snack bar, and a ski school.

Other Things to See & Do

Chunky's Cinema Pub, 371 Lowell Ave., Haverhill; (978) 374-2200; chunkys.com. Combine dinner and a movie. Leather reclining Lincoln Town Car seats. Order food and drink before and during the show.

John Greenleaf Whittier Birthplace, 305 Whittier Rd., Haverhill; (978) 373-3979; johngreenleafwhittier.com. Open mid-Apr through Oct. Home of famous poet, abolitionist, and Quaker John Greenleaf Whittier. The Haverhill Public Library has a comprehensive collection of material about Whittier, his work, books, letters, and manuscripts. You may also be interested in visiting his Amesbury home (whittierhome .org).

Winnekenni Castle, 347 Kenoza Ave. (Castle Road), Haverhill; (978) 521-1686; winnekenni.com. Lovely recreational setting on 700 acres laced with trails and water features, a notorious Haunted House during Halloween, performances, and fairs.

Andover / North Andover / Lawrence

The towns of Andover and North Andover are referred to as "The Andovers" by the locals. The Andovers are blessed with many recreational opportunities, historic homes, and two stellar boarding schools: Phillips Academy and Brooks School. Lawrence, in its heyday was a hub of manufacturing and mills powered by the Merrimack River. Many immigrants from diverse nationalities settled here and worked in the local factories.

Things to See & Do

Addison Gallery of American Art, 180 Main St. (Phillips Academy), Andover; (978) 749-4015; addisongallery.org. World-class collection of American art.

Lawrence Heritage State Park and Lawrence Visitor Center, 1 Jackson St., Lawrence; (978) 794-1655; mass.gov/eea/agencies/dcr/massparks/region-north/lawrence-heritage-state-park.html. The visitor center, a restored boarding house, has exhibits on the Industrial Revolution and the role that the city of Lawrence played in it. Walk along the canals and the park.

Out and About in **"The Andovers"**

- **Harold Parker State Forest,** 1951 Turnpike Rd., North Andover; (978) 686-3391; mass.gov/eea/agencies/dcr/massparks/region-north/harold-parker-state-forest.html. State forest covering Middleton, Andover, North Andover, and North Reading. Hiking, biking, fishing, horseback riding, nature study, picnicking, swimming, camping, and interpretive programs.

- **Stevens-Coolidge Place and Gardens,** 139 Andover St., North Andover; (978) 682-3580; thetrustees.org. Historic house/museum of diplomat John Gardner Coolidge and his wife, Helen Stevens Coolidge. Set on 95 acres, the estate includes magnificent gardens. Trustees of Reservations property. Admission fees for house and/or garden. Seasonal.

- **Ward Reservation,** 65 Prospect Rd., Andover; (978) 682-3580; the trustees.org. Nice trails on 694 acres used for cross-country skiing, snowshoeing, hiking, and horseback riding. The highest point in Essex County overlooks the Solstice Stones. The Solstice Stones are arranged like a compass, and the spring and fall equinoxes and the summer and winter solstices are all aligned. Open dawn to dusk; allow 2 hours for your visit. Trustees of Reservations property. Free.

- **Weir Hill,** 62 Stevens St., North Andover; (978) 682-3580; thetrustees.org. Activities include hiking, cross-country skiing, picnicking, and horseback riding. Great views of Lake Cochichewick. Trustees of Reservations property. Admission is free.

Lowell

The main tourist attraction of the Merrimack Valley is Lowell, the country's first planned industrial city, in whose enormous brick mills the world's first mass-produced cotton cloth originated. Stop by the **Greater Merrimack Convention and Visitors Bureau** at 9 Central St. (978-459-6150 or 800-443-3332; lowell.org or merrimackvalley.org) for area information.

American Textile History Museum (all ages)

491 Dutton St., Lowell; (978) 441-0400; athm.org. Open Wed through Sun 10 a.m. to 5 p.m. Closed Mon, Tues, Thanksgiving, Christmas, and New Year's Day. Admission: $8 for adults, $6 for children ages 6 to 16, free for children under 6. Please call ahead to verify hours and admission (free Super Saturdays sprinkled throughout the year).

History comes alive at the American Textile History Museum, with 300 years of clothing and textile history. The museum, located in a historic mill building, is interactive and fun and will amaze children with exhibits from the Industrial Revolution to the present. Displays tell the story from early linen processes all the way to carbon fiber, biomimicry (which takes a process in nature like water resistance and creates a textile mimicking that quality), and nanotechnology. Interesting displays include a carbon-free bicycle, space gloves used by NASA, environmental textiles, a hall of clothing from the 1700s to the early 1900s, and 2 galleries with rotating exhibits. A Textile Learning Center has hands-on stuff; playing with gears, weaving a loom, creating with arts and crafts, and educational programs throughout the year.

Lowell National Historical Park (all ages)

Visitor center at Market Mills, 246 Market St., Lowell; (978) 970-5000; nps.gov/lowe. Free parking for the visitor center is located at 304 Dutton St. Check the website for seasonal hours of operation for the visitor center, the Boott Cotton Mills, and the Patrick J Mogan Cultural Center. Admission for the Boott Cotton Mills and the Patrick J. Mogan Cultural Center: $6 for adults, $4 for seniors, $3 for children ages 6 to 16, free for children under 6. The visitor center is free. TIP: There are some free admission days spread throughout the year, check the fee-free days on the Park's website.

Lowell National Historic Park provides excellent presentations and tours that bring Lowell's heyday to life, in some cases, deafeningly so. Lowell was named for Francis Cabot Lowell, the man who came up with the idea (and much of the money) for a planned industrial community. He also had the idea, highly radical in its time, of employing women, who made up the majority of the workforce. Kirk Boott headed up the group of people who planned, financed,

Lots of **Locks**

Another highlight of a family trip to Lowell is the boat ride through the city's intricate canal-and-lock system. Reservations for these tours are strongly recommended; you wouldn't want to arrive in Lowell to find out that your family won't fit onto any boats that day. Tours leave from the Lowell National Historical Park Visitor Center (978-970-5000). The fee is $8 for adults, $6 for children 6 to 16, free for children 5 and under.

and built Lowell. The largest of the cotton mills was named for him, and today the **Boott Cotton Mills Museum** is the star of Lowell. Restored in 1992, the museum re-creates the work environment that the "mill girls" experienced; complete with eighty-eight looms in full operation. Earplugs are available for tourists, but there was no such thing for the workers, who spent about 72 hours a week here, on their feet, without the benefit of ventilation, and earning a weekly wage of $2.25. History comes to life here in more ways than one; be sure to listen to the recorded stories of some of the workers who ran the mills. The Mill Girls and Immigrants Exhibit at the Patrick J. Mogan Cultural Center depicts how the mill girls lived as well as the different ethnic groups that worked at the mills. On Saturday the visitor center hosts the program **Your City Saturday,** which is tailored to families with kids under the age of 10 with lots of projects and interactive play.

Other Things to See & Do

Lowell Memorial Auditorium, 50 East Merrimack St., Lowell; (978) 454-2299; lowellauditorium.com. Seats 2,800. Host to concerts, comedy, musicals, dance, and sporting events.

Lowell Spinners, Edward A. LeLacheur Park, 450 Aiken St. (UMass/Lowell Campus), Lowell; (978) 459-2255 or (978) 459-1702 (box office); lowellspinners.com. Farm league team of the Red Sox playing in a new, 4,700-seat stadium.

Merrimack Repertory Theatre, 50 East Merrimack St., Liberty Hall, Lowell; (978) 454-3926; mrt.org. Contemporary plays and new works. Season runs Sept through May with seven productions.

New England Quilt Museum, 18 Shattuck St., Lowell; (978) 452-4207; nequilt museum.org. A fiber arts museum. Constantly changing exhibits (limited hanging time before the quilts start to stretch). Children's story hour. Aug Quilt Festival.

Tsongas Center, 300 Martin Luther King Jr. Way (on UMass/Lowell's campus), Lowell; (978) 934-5761; tsongascenter.com. Ice hockey and concerts.

Whistler House Museum of Art, 243 Worthen St., Lowell; (978) 452-7641; whistler house.org. Open Wed through Sat 11 a.m. to 4 p.m. Birthplace of artist James McNeill

Farm Favorites

The following is a list of area farms that have pick-your-own fruits and flowers, picnic areas, food stands, hayrides, sleigh rides, batting cages, corn mazes, minigolf, farm animal viewing, or a combination of any of the above:

- **Brooksby Farm,** 38 Felton St., Peabody; (978) 531-1631; essex heritage.org
- **Cider Hill Farms,** 45 Fern Ave. (Route 150), Amesbury; (978) 388-5525; ciderhill.com
- **Green Meadows Farm,** 656 Asbury St., South Hamilton; (978) 468-2277; gmfarm.com
- **Ingaldsby Farms,** 14 Washington St., West Boxford; (978) 352-2813; farmfresh.org/food/farm.php?farm=1358
- **Kimball Farms,** 780 East Broadway, Haverhill; (978) 521-3990 or (866) 965-5262; kimballfarmcornmaze.com
- **Richardson Farms Inc.,** 156 South Main St. (Route 114), Middleton; (978) 774-4476 (golf) or (978) 774-5450; richardsonsicecream.com
- **Smolak Farms,** 315 South Bradford St., North Andover; (978) 682-6332; smolakfarms.com
- **Tendercrop Farm,** 108 High Rd. (Route 1A), Newbury; (978) 462-6972; tendercropfarms.com

TopEvents for the North Shore,
Cape Ann, and the Merrimack Valley

October–December

- **Essex Clamfest,** Oct, Memorial Park, Essex; (978) 283-1601; cape annvacations.com

- **Choate Island Day,** Oct, Crane Wildlife Refuge, Aug; (978) 356-4351; thetrustees.org

- **Salem's Haunted Happenings,** Oct, Salem; (978) 744-3663 or (877) SALEM-MA; hauntedhappenings.org

- **Spirits of the Gables,** Oct, House of the Seven Gables, Salem; (978) 744-0991; 7gables.org

- **Rockport Harvest Festival,** mid-Oct, Rockport; (978) 546-6575 or (978) 283-1601; rockportusa.com

- **Lowell Open Studios,** Oct, downtown Lowell; (978) 459-6150; culture iscool.org/lowell-open-studios

- **Topsfield Fair,** Oct, Topsfield Fairgrounds, Topsfield; (978) 887-5000; topsfieldfair.org

- **Dungeon Rock Pirate Day,** Oct, Lynn Woods Reservation, Lynn; (781) 477-7123; flw.org

- **Apple and Wine Festival,** early Nov, Russell Orchards, Ipswich; (978) 356-5366; russellorchards.com

- **Festival of Trees,** late Nov to early Dec, 13 Branch St., Methuen; (978) 685-8878; methuenfestivaloftrees.com

- **City of Lights Parade,** Sat after Thanksgiving, downtown Lowell; (978) 446-7162 or (978) 459-6150; lowellma.gov or lowell.org/Pages/CityofLights

- **Christmas on Cape Ann,** Dec, Rockport, Gloucester, Manchester, and Essex; (978) 283-1601; capeannvacations.com

- **Holiday Lights,** Dec, 79 Powers Rd., Westford; (978) 692-3033; ski nashoba.com

- **Christmas Walk,** early Dec, downtown Marblehead; (781) 631-2868; marbleheadchamber.org
- **The Greening of the Great House,** Dec, the Crane Estate, Ipswich; (978) 356-4351; thecraneestate.org

Whistler, known for his painting *Whistler's Mother*. Paintings and prints from the 19th and 20th centuries.

Where to Eat

The Club Diner, 145 Dutton St., Lowell; (978) 452-1679. Serving breakfast until 2 p.m. in this remnant of a bygone era. $

Cobblestones, 91 Dutton St., Lowell; (978) 970-2282; cobblestonesoflowell.com. Historic building downtown, friendly service and architecturally interesting dining room. Unusual menu. $–$$$$

Fuse Bistro, 45 Palmer St., Lowell; (978) 323-0424; fuse-bistro.com. Organic, farm-fresh food served in an old firehouse building. $–$$

New Olympia Restaurant, 453 Market St., Lowell; (978) 452-8092 or (978) 459-7652; newolympia.com. Greek food. Try the roast lamb sandwich. Open for lunch and dinner. Children's menu. $–$$$

The Old Court, 29 Central St., Lowell; (978) 452-0100; oldcourtirishpub.com. Irish American food + Irish music = a fun atmosphere! Ask them about their kid-friendly offerings. $

Ricardo's Cafe Trattoria, 110 Gorham St., Lowell; (978) 453-2777; ricardoscafe trattoria.com. Open Tues through Sat for dinner. Ricardo has tried to model his restaurant after the small, welcoming trattorias of Italy. Delicious Italian food. $–$$$

Where to Stay

UMass Lowell Inn and Conference Center, 50 Warren St., Lowell; (978) 934-6920; acc-umlinnandconferencecenter.com. Offers 231 guest rooms near all major attractions. $–$$$

Lowell **Festivals**

- **Winterfest** (Feb), downtown Lowell at Arcand and Tsongas Road. Human dogsled competition, laser show, all-you-can-eat chocolate festival, and soup competition. For more information, call (978) 459-6150 or visit lowell.org or lowellwinterfest.org

- **New England Music Awards,** Feb, 50 Merrimack St. (Lowell Auditorium) Lowell; (978) 459-6150; nemusicawards.com. The New England Music Awards recognizes musical talent in all genres and categories from the region.

- **Lowell Folk Festival** (last full weekend in July). Largest free folk festival in the country; ethnic food, music, and dance. Call (978) 970-4257, (978) 458-6150, or (978) 970-5000 for more information. You can find them at lowellfolkfestival.org.

- **Southeast Asian Water Festival** (third Sat in Aug). Native Cambodian dancing and music at Sampas Pavilion. Call (978) 970-4257 or (978) 459-6150 or visit lowellwaterfestival.org.

- **Banjo and Fiddle Contest** (Sept). Premier East Coast competition at Boardinghouse Park. Call (978) 970-5000, (978) 275-1705, or (978) 458-6150, or visit nps.gov/lowe or lowellsummermusic.org for more information.

Chelmsford, Tyngsboro & Westford

Westford separated from neighboring Chelmsford centuries ago to form its own municipality. Westford is a town of many low-lying hills, apple-growing farms, numerous lakes, and many historic districts. Chelmsford, too, had agricultural roots as well as lumber and quarry production (the quarries are still mined today) but now is a bedroom community for the Greater Lowell region. Tyngsboro, once officially part of Chelmsford, is a more rural community with many streams, lakes, and ponds.

Butterfly Place (all ages)

120 Tyngsboro Rd., Westford; (978) 392-0955; butterflyplace-ma.com. Open daily from mid-Feb through Halloween, visit the website for schedule. Admission: $12 for adults, $8 for children 3 to 12, free for children under 3.

The Butterfly Place is a highly unusual farm where hundreds of butterflies flutter above and through flowering plants and weeds in an enormous solar dome. It's fun to see how many different kinds of butterflies you can identify (the butterflies are native to this part of the country as well as from all over the globe). An introductory video explains the life cycle of the butterfly with small exhibits showcasing the different stages on display. Guides do a show-and-tell and answer any questions. There's a pleasant outdoor picnic spot too. Allow at least an hour to enjoy the Butterfly Place and keep in mind that the temperature is kept fairly warm inside the museum for the comfort of the butterflys so dress accordingly. Birthday party packages can be arranged. **Note:** No tickets are sold a half hour prior to closing. **Warning:** If Westford schools are closed, call ahead to see if the Butterfly Place is open.

Nashoba Valley (all ages)

79 Powers Rd., Westford; (978) 692-3033; skinashoba.com. Open late Nov through mid-Mar, 9 a.m. to 10 p.m. daily (weekends from 8:30 a.m.) for skiing and snow-tubing; call for snowtubing hours and rates or check the website.

Offering 9 lifts (3 triple chairs) and 17 trails. Facilities include a lodge, restaurant, and bar. Packages available. Special events are held throughout the year. A highlight is the Halloween Celebration, with four scary attractions: Castle Morbid, 3-D Keepers Crypt, Nightmare Mansion, and Witches Woods Haunted Hayride. The Holiday Lights festival held the end of Nov through mid-Dec (Fri through Sun) draws a big crowd to *oooh* and *ahhh*.

Where to Eat

Fishbones, 34 Central Sq., Chelmsford; (978) 250-0101; fishbonesofchelmsford.com. Restaurant and fish market in a central location. $$–$$$

Kimball Farm, 400 Littleton Rd., Westford; (978) 486-3891; kimballfarm.com. Home-made products make this a mecca for ice-cream aficionados! Charming building with a country store gift shop and a small cafe. Miniature golf, bumper boats, and a 9-hole golf range. $

Where to Stay

Pine Needles B&B, 148 Depot Rd., Westford; (978) 399-0199; pineneedlesbb.com. Three guest rooms in a woodsy setting; friendly hosts. Full breakfast. $

Radisson Hotel and Suites Chelmsford, 10 Independence Dr., Chelmsford; (978) 256-0800; radisson.com/chelmsford-hotel-ma. Five minutes from the historic heart of Lowell; indoor pool and fitness center. $–$$$

Stonehedge Inn, 160 Pawtucket Blvd., Tyngsboro; (978) 649-4400; stonehedge innandspa.com. Luxurious European-style manor with 30 rooms in French country decor—some with fireplaces. Indoor pool and spa. The Left Bank Restaurant has superb cuisine and wine list, plus a children's menu ($-$$$$). $$–$$$$

Greater Boston

C hock-full of history, New England's largest city seems to have a significant site on every corner. Tourism has always been part of life in busy Boston, and residents don't mind sharing their beautiful city with visitors. They appreciate the smallness of the downtown area as much as you will. What's more, many of the older areas of the North End, Beacon Hill, and the Back Bay are surprisingly compact and therefore walkable for parents and kids alike. Before you arrive, contact the **Greater Boston Convention and Visitors Bureau,** 2 Copley Place, Suite 105, Boston, MA 02116 (617-536-4100 or 888-SEE-BOSTON; bostonusa.com) for maps or brochures.

Avoid restricting your journey solely to the sites along the well-trafficked red line of the Freedom Trail (thefreedomtrail.org). Kids will also enjoy the museums of Boston, especially the Museum of Science and the Children's Museum, as well as the New England Aquarium. Don't miss the bronze statues of Mrs. Mallard and her brood (the heroes of *Make Way for Ducklings*) near the pond in the Public Garden. And be sure to take a day or two to explore the nearby towns of Cambridge, Charlestown, Lexington, and Concord.

SOME PRACTICAL INFORMATION

Accommodations

Boston is an expensive place to stay. If you won't be staying with friends, plan ahead to get the best prices. The hotels listed in this chapter offer family packages throughout the year, but you must reserve ahead of time. An alternative is Bed & Breakfast Agency of Boston (47 Commercial Wharf, Boston; 617-720-3540 or 800-248-9262; boston-bnbagency.com), which maintains an extensive list of bed-and-breakfast accommodations and vacation rentals around the city. They'll

Be in the Know . . .
Boston Nicknames

Beantown, the Cradle of Liberty, the Hub (as in the Hub of the Universe), the City of Champions, B-town, and Red Sox Nation.

match your requirements and price range with an appropriate room, suite, efficiency, or apartment in both Boston and Cambridge. Rates are $149 to $280, double occupancy; kids stay free. Packages include special weekly and monthly rates. Many of the Bed & Breakfast Agency of Boston's inventory allow pets.

Medical

Inn-House Doctor, 212 Carnegie Row, Norwood, MA 02062 (mailing address); (617) 859-1776; inn-housedoctor.com. Payment: cash. It's no fun getting sick while you're on vacation, but lucky for you, these dedicated doctors make house calls within 1 hour and come to more than one hundred hotels in the Boston area 24 hours a day. Staff includes general practitioners, pediatricians, and dentists who are affiliated with area hospitals. The doctors do take medical insurance, but you will need to pay out of pocket and submit the bill for reimbursement with your medical health insurance provider upon your return home (their services are covered by most insurance plans).

Parking in Boston

Parking places are hard to come by in Boston. You'll enjoy your visit more if you leave the car in a parking garage and rely on public transportation, such as the MBTA (aka the "T"), and tour buses to get around.

REDUCED-RATE TICKETS

BosTix Ticket Booths offer half-price, in-person, day-of-performance tickets for theatrical, dance, and musical events. There are two locations in Boston—Copley Square and next to Faneuil Hall—both credit card (except for Discover Card) and cash are acceptable forms of payment. To reach BosTix, call (617) 262-8632 (ext. 229 for customer service), visit artsboston.org or visit bostix.org/page/onsale_today. The Faneuil Hall kiosk is open 10 a.m. to 6 p.m. Tues through Sat, and Sun from 11 a.m. to 4 p.m. (closed Mon, Patriots' Day, Memorial Day, Thanksgiving, and Christmas). The Copley Square Booth has the same hours,

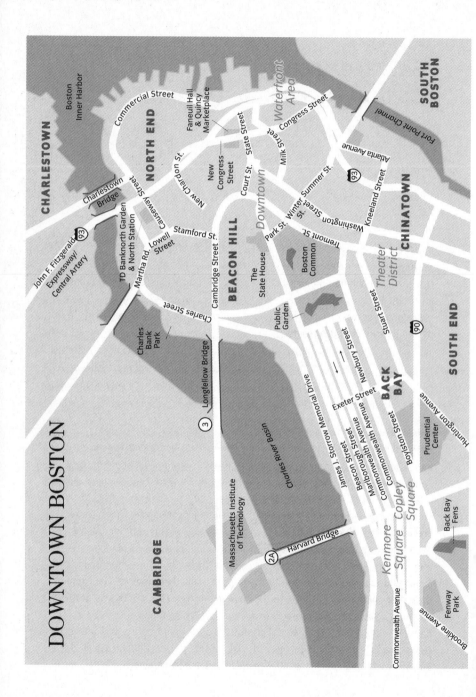

DOWNTOWN BOSTON

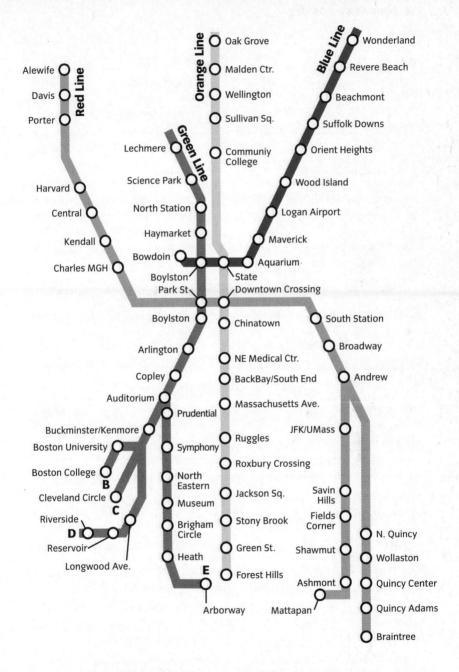

BOSTON AREA SUBWAY MAP

TopPicks in Greater Boston

- **The Museum of Science Campus** (the Science Museum, the Omni Theater, the Hayden Planetarium, and the Laser Light Show), Cambridge

- **Children's Museum**

- **Duckling Statues** and **Swan Boat** ride at the Public Garden

- **New England Aquarium**

- **Charlestown Navy Yard** (Constitution Museum, the USS *Cassin Young*, and the USS *Constitution*), Charlestown

- **Boston sporting events** (Red Sox, Celtics, or Bruins games)

- **Museum of Fine Arts**

- **Boston Harbor Islands National Park and Recreation Area**

- **Drumlin Farm,** South Lincoln

- **Minute Man National Historical Park,** Lexington and Concord

- **Discovery Museums,** Acton

- **The Prudential Skywalk Observatory**

except they are open seasonally Mon as well. The half-price tickets go on sale after 10 a.m. the day of the show (Sun at 11 a.m.). *TIP:* You can check online after 7 p.m. the night prior to see the following day's availability.

TOURS

Beantown Trolley Tours (all ages)

16 Charles St. South at the Transportation Building, Boston; (617) 720-6342 or (800) 343-1328; brushhilltours.com. Prices are $35 for adults, $33 for seniors and students, $15 for children 3 to 11, and free for children under 3. The trolley runs from 9:30 a.m. to 4:30 p.m.; winter schedule Nov through Feb.

An alternative to driving, the trolleys make 17 stops around the city, which will include most of the sites your family will want to see. A learning historical adventure loaded with fun, Beantown Trolley Tours are a local family-owned business that promises you "a wicked good time." Get on and off the trolley throughout the day; the entire narrated tour with about 125 points of interest takes just under 2 hours. The trolleys are open-air in the summer and heated in the winter. Tickets are sold onboard as well as at outlets around the city. *(Note:* Most of the locations accept credit cards; otherwise it's cash only.) Also included in the price of the ticket is a 45-minute harbor cruise from the New England Aquarium May through late fall, weather permitting, or a **free** entrance to the Mapparium at the Mary Baker Eddy Library.

Cityview Trolley Tour (all ages)

Board at any of their 9 stops. Buy your tickets at the Boston Common Visitor Information Kiosk (Park Street MBTA Station), the New England Aquarium Plaza, Quincy Market, North or South Station, Boston; (617) 363-7899; cityviewtrolleys .com. Daily starting at 9:30 a.m. in season Apr through Nov, weekends only Dec to Mar. Tickets: $38 for adults, $36 for students and seniors, $14 for children 3 to 12, under 3 free. There are also discounts and specials online. Price includes a free 45-minute historic Boston Harbor cruise, seasonally offered May to Oct. Each trolley tour has a different spin on visiting Boston, and Cityview Trolley is no exception. Cityview's hook is that it's not a time-waster; they don't stop at area hotels as others do, instead concentrating on all the historic sites that you want to see with a special focus on the Freedom Trail. This is a great choice for people with a limited visiting schedule. The tour takes approximately 1 hour.

The Duck Tour (all ages)

4 Copley Place, Suite 4155, Boston (buy your tickets online or at the booth in the Prudential Center, the New England Aquarium Duck ticket booth, or the Museum of Science); (617) 267-3825 or (617) 450-0068 for group reservations or (800) 226-7442; bostonducktours.com. Offered daily Mar through Nov from 9 a.m. to 1 hour before sunset. Tours leave every half hour from the Huntington Avenue side of the Prudential Center, the New England Aquarium, or in front of the Museum of Science. Prices (not including the Massachusetts Convention Center surcharge): $34.99 for adults, $28.99 for seniors and students, $23.99 for ages 3 to 11, and $10.50 for children under 3. There is an abbreviated seasonal tour with lower pricing. This tour can fit 36 people on a duck, and it's a real quacker! This 80-minute land-and-sea tour is offered on a "duck," an amphibious World War II craft that travels both on land and in the Charles River. The rain-or-shine tour is lots of fun, and you will get many friendly stares as you wind your way through the streets of Boston (possibly because the driver will have you quacking!). Once on the Charles River, the driver/narrator will ask for volunteers to pilot the duck. Children find this to be the best part of the tour. This tour also is the one that seems to be the biggest hit with kids, and it's the original Boston Duck Tour. **Note:** A limited number of tickets are released 30 days prior but sell out quickly; purchase at the ticket counter or online (bostonducktours.com); there are no exchanges or refunds. *TIP:* Be there a half hour prior to boarding.

On Location Tours Boston   (all ages)

Meet at the Boston Common Visitor Center, 139 Tremont St., Boston; (617) 379-6770 or (866) 982-2114; onlocationtours.com. The Boston TV and Movie Sites Bus Tour is $38 for adults and $22 for kids 6 through 9, under 6 are free. Tours are offered Mar through Dec weekends, call for the schedule. The Boston Movie Mile Walking Tour (weekends spring through fall) is $22 for adults and $14 for children 6 to 9, 5 and under free.

No, it's not a Hollywood soundstage set, but your tour will take you behind the scenes to see local filming locations for some of your favorite movies and television shows. See where scenes and backdrops were filmed for movies such as *The Departed, Good Will Hunting, Legally Blonde, Mystic River, Knight and Day, 21, Fever Pitch, Gone Baby Gone, and The Town,* and for some of the most popular television shows, including *Ally McBeal, Boston Legal,* and *Cheers.* Choose between the 90-minute Boston Movie Mile Walking Tour or sit in comfort for the 3-hour, 40-plus-sites bus tour. Insider dirt, tidbits, and dish help make either tour memorable.

Super Tours   (all ages)

100 Terminal St., Charlestown (617) 742-1440 or (877) 34-DUCKS; bostonsuper tours.com. Offered year-round. Prices vary depending on the tour chosen (however, the premium price ticket is a great value); check the website schedule for hours of operation.

This company offers an upper-deck high-riding trolley that allows you to see above the traffic and more of the city itself. It's a bit longer than the other city tours (about 2.5 hours), with 21 stops that you can get on and off at all day long, with unlimited reboarding through Boston and Cambridge. Included in your premium price ticket is a Boston Harbor Super Duck Splash tour, the only duck in Boston Harbor (in season) and a choice of four options to area museums or a Charles River cruise after you have finished your trolley tour. They also offer Evening Tours.

Boston Common & Beacon Hill

The best place to begin a Boston visit is at the corner of the Boston Common and Park Street. The **Boston Common Information Booth** is a few yards from here. At the booth you can collect free maps, brochures, and information about sightseeing tours. The central stop of the T (subway), Park Street, is also right here.

Boston Common is the beginning of the **Emerald Necklace,** the largest continuous green space through an urban center in the US. The park system was designed by Frederick Law Olmsted in 1895 (among other acclaimed projects, Olmsted also designed New York's Central Park). From Boston Common the Necklace stretches through the Public Garden to the Commonwealth Avenue Mall, the Back Bay Fens, through the Muddy River area, to Olmsted Park, Jamaica Park, and Jamaica Pond, and on to the Arnold Arboretum and Arborway before ending at the city's largest green space, Franklin Park. Sail, row, or fish at Jamaica Pond, bike and hike through any of the parks, play golf or visit the zoo at Franklin Park, or hear concerts; there's usually something going on at one of the parks along the Necklace. For daily updates, call the **Parks and Recreation Activities Eventline** (617-635-4505; cityofboston.gov/parks and click on the city calendar option) or call the **Mayors Office of Arts, Tourism and Special Events** at (617) 635-3911; cityofboston.gov/ARTS.

At the foot of Beacon Hill is the **Charles River Reservation** (617-727-1051; mass.gov/eea/ agencies/dcr/massparks/region-boston/ charles-river-reservation or mass.gov/ dcr/hatch-events.html [click on the "For Visitors" tab]), which fronts on the Charles River. The centerpiece is the **Hatch Shell** on the Esplanade (not far from the Arthur Fiedler Bridge), a clamshell-shaped stage for free outdoor summertime concerts, ballets, performances, and films (Free Friday Family Flicks during the summer). Behind the Hatch Shell is a playground, a public outdoor pool with views of the

Holiday Happenings at the Hatch, or
I'm a Yankee Doodle Dandy!

The explosive event that is the cornerstone to celebrating the Fourth of July in Boston is the Boston Pops concert at the **Hatch Shell**. The *1812 Overture* is always the finale—building to a crescendo—with the city's church bells sounding and cannons being fired, all signaling the start of a fabulous Fourth of July fireworks show. With a backdrop of more than a half a million people in attendance, seated in front of the stage, on Storrow Drive (the road is closed to vehicle traffic), or moored on the Charles River, this is the signature event of the summer that you don't want to miss! Good old-fashioned patriotic fun; bring a picnic and arrive *many* hours before the concert begins.

Charles, lots of tennis courts and playing fields, and the **Community Boating Facility** (open to the public for lessons or rentals in season of sailboats and kayaks; 617-523-1038; community-boating.org or sailcbi.org). A unique way to tour the Charles River is with **Gondola di Venezia,** which departs from the Esplanade in front of the Hatch Shell Fri through Sun mid-May through mid-Oct. Tours can fit up to six passengers, and they are private, by reservation only at (617) 876-2800, (800) 979-3370, or bostongondolas.com. Lacing through the reservation is a multipurpose path used for strolling, jogging, biking, or in-line skating. Keep heads up so the children won't be mowed down!

Black Heritage Trail (all ages)
Boston; (617) 742-5415; nps.gov/boaf or maah.org. Tours meet at the Shaw Memorial across from the State House. Please call or visit the website for information and tour reservations. This walking tour is **free.**

The Museum of Afro-American History and the National Park Service operate the Black Heritage Trail. The trail, covering just over 1.5 miles, is a 1.5-hour walking tour of Beacon Hill–area buildings that are important to local and national black history. Along with the African Meeting House, sites include the Hayden House, an important stop along the Underground Railroad; the Charles Street Meeting House, where abolitionists Frederick Douglass and Sojourner Truth preached against slavery; and the monument to Robert Gould Shaw and the Fifty-fourth Regiment, which commemorates the first black division of the Union army during the Civil War. **Note:** Most of the sites on the Black Heritage Trail are private homes not open to the public except for the Abiel Smith School and the African Meeting House.

Boston Common, a Freedom Trail Site (all ages) 🏛 🏕

Bordered by Beacon Street, Charles Street, Tremont Street, and Park Street (where the visitor information center is located); thefreedomtrail.org. Open all day, every day. Free.

On a nice day, a visit to Boston Common is worth a few hours. Tell the kids to imagine what it was like when Boston residents used this "common" area to graze their cattle, then discuss what it may have been like to live here when British soldiers used the Common as a training ground before the Revolutionary War. Nowadays, the Frog Pond is a big attraction year-round. On a hot summer's day, it's a great place for a cool dip. In the winter you can glide along on the ice

Black Heritage Trail Sites, Boston

- Site 1: Robert Gould Shaw and the Fifty-fourth Regiment Memorial, Park and Beacon Streets
- Site 2: George Middleton House, 5–7 Pinckney St.
- Site 3: The Phillips School, Anderson and Pinckney Streets
- Site 4: John J. Smith House, 86 Pinckney St.
- Site 5: Charles Street Meeting House, Mt. Vernon and Charles Streets
- Site 6: Lewis Hayden House, 66 Phillips St.
- Site 7: Coburn's Gaming House, 2 Phillips St.
- Sites 8–12: Smith Court Residences, 46 Joy St.
- Site 13: Abiel Smith School, 46 Joy St.
- Site 14: African Meeting House, 8 Smith Ct.

once the weather dips. Forgot your skates? Don't worry, rentals are available for a nominal fee. The Boston Common Frog Pond Foundation (617-635-2120; bostoncommonfrogpond.org) works in conjunction with the City of Boston Parks and Recreation and runs the **Frog Pond** and skate rentals, the carousel, and the Frog Pond Cafe. At noon on any weekday, regardless of the weather, you're likely to share the park with many of the people who work in downtown offices. Bring a picnic lunch, or watch a softball game. A summer concert series attracts name talent and is popular with older kids, teens, and students. Charles Street separates the Public Garden from Boston Common.

Louisburg Square (all ages)

Between Pinckney and Mt. Vernon Streets on Beacon Hill, Boston. Free.
The stately and distinguished Greek Revival homes overlooking Boston's Louisburg Square in Beacon Hill mirror the wealth of its elite citizens both past and present. A site of interest to *Little Women* fans: Louisa May Alcott and her family lived at number 10 after her success with *Little Women* (long before Louisa's literary success, the Alcott family also lived at 20 Pinckney St.). Swedish Nightingale Jenny Lind, who toured with P. T. Barnum's circus, was married at number 14 Louisburg Sq. *Make Way for Ducklings* fans will remember the book's superb overhead view of the square. Former Senator John Forbes Kerry has a residence on the square (#19 Louisburg Sq.)—but don't get too close or you will risk arrest as his residence is protected by the Secret Service now that he is Secretary of State! Nearby is the House of Odd Windows, 24 Pinckney St., whose facade boasts a wide variety of unusually shaped windows.

Massachusetts State House, a Freedom Trail Site
(all ages)

24 Beacon St. (corner of Park and Beacon Streets), Boston; (617) 727-3676; sec .state.ma.us/trs. State House hours are Mon through Fri, 9 a.m. to 5 p.m.; tours Mon through Fri, 10 a.m. to 4 p.m. (last tour is at 3:30 p.m.). Closed weekends, Thanksgiving, Christmas Day, New Year's Day, and other state and national holidays. Free.
Just up the hill from the Park Street end of the Common is the impressive gold-domed State House, built in 1798 on John Hancock's pasture. The original part of the building, which was designed by Charles Bulfinch, is in the neoclassical or Federal style. Along with the legislative chambers, the state capitol holds a collection of flags, costumes, and other remnants of the state's history. Don't

forget to ask for the handout and map that explain the function and location of the different rooms in the State House, and for the booklet *The Ladybug Story*, which clearly explains to children how a bill becomes law by using an example of schoolchildren who wanted the ladybug to be the official bug of Massachusetts. Walk up by the statue of General Hooker and turn around to see a terrific view of the Common and the tops of the taller buildings of the Financial District. In front of the State House is a fine statue of John F. Kennedy (the sculptor seems to have captured him in midstride as he left Boston for the US Senate, where he served before his presidency). Of the many JFK monuments scattered around Boston and New England, this is the most human.

Museum of African American History (all ages)

46 Joy St. on Beacon Hill, Boston; (617) 725-0022, ext. 222 (Welcome Center) or (617) 742-5415 (connects to the Museum of Afro-American History and the National Park Service Black Heritage Trail); maah.org. Open 10 a.m. to 4 p.m. Mon through Sat; hourly guided tours start at 11 a.m. Admission: $5 for adults, $3 for ages 13 to 17, free for ages 12 and under.

The crown jewels of the Boston campus museum are the **African Meeting House** and the **Abiel Smith School.** The African Meeting House is the oldest standing African American church in the country built by free blacks and is a Boston African American National Historical Site. Boston has a long history of abolitionism (Frederick Douglass spoke here); just after the revolution, Massachusetts

Duck, Duck, Duck, Not Goose!

Friends of the Public Garden (friendsofthepublicgarden.org) and the **Boston Parks and Recreation** (617-635-4505; cityofboston.gov/parks/emerald/public_garden.asp) runs a **Ducklings Day,** an annual parade held on Mother's Day at the Boston Common that reenacts the *Make Way for Ducklings* tale by Robert McCloskey. Kids and dogs come dressed up as their favorite character and follow the ducklings' route from the Boston Common to the Public Garden led by the Harvard Band. Once assembled in the Garden they are greeted and addressed by the mayor of Boston and actors read the beloved story. Call for exact times (recently the registration was at 10 a.m. and the parade started at noon).

declared itself one of the first free states, with full citizenry extended to black residents. Before and during the Civil War, this was the headquarters of the Underground Railroad, which helped many escaped slaves leave the South and find new homes and livelihoods in the North. The Abiel Smith School was the first public school in the nation for black children. The museum galleries and exhibits and the Museum Store are also found here. A great educational program called the Underground Railroad Overnight Adventure allows older school groups an overnight stay at the museum and a flashlight tour of the Underground Railroad sites on Beacon Hill by reservation only.

Public Garden (all ages)

Bordered by Beacon Street, Arlington Street, Boylston Street, and Charles Street, Boston. For general information, contact Friends of the Public Garden at (617) 723-8144; friendsofthepublicgarden.org or cityofboston.gov/parks/emerald/ public_garden.asp. Open year-round. Free.

The Public Garden, founded in 1837, is the first public botanical garden in the country and encompasses 24 acres of planted landscape. Walk toward the corner of Charles and Beacon Streets. Here the kids will find the bronze sculptures of Mrs. Mallard and her brood. Ask the kids to name the ducks (the first one is Jack, followed by Kack, Lack, Mack, Nack, Ouack, Pack, and Quack). Next, head for the lagoon, where your family may well see real-life cousins of the Mallard family!

The **Swan Boat** ride is a must; (617) 522-1966 or (617) 733-2009 (general information); swanboats.com. The boats are on the lagoon daily from mid-Apr through mid-Sept, open 10 a.m. to 5 p.m. in the summer, to 4 p.m. in the spring and fall, weather permitting. The fare is $3 for adults, $1.50 for children 2 to 15; free for children under 2. It's a short 15 minutes or so—and people-powered; a boatswain pedals the boat from his or her perch behind a wooden swan. Remember not to feed the birds!

Before or after your ride, be sure to check out the impressive statue of George Washington astride his horse at the Commonwealth Avenue entrance to the Public Garden. The beautiful shrubbery, trees, and plantings, along with the picturesque bridge over the swan pond, attract many budding artists. For an audio tour of the Public Garden (narrated by Henry Lee), downloadable to your iPod, visit friendsofthepublicgarden.org.

Other Things to See & Do

Otis House Museum, 141 Cambridge St., Boston; (617) 227-3956; historicnew england.org. Open year-round Wed through Sun 11 a.m. to 4:30 p.m. (last tour). Admission: $8 per adult, $4 for students (free for Boston residents). Headquarters of Historic New England. Period home of the prominent Otis family, built by Charles Bulfinch (architect of the Massachusetts State House).

The Red Wagon, 69 Charles St., Boston; (617) 523-9402; theredwagon.com. Designer kid labels at budget prices, books, and toys.

Where to Eat

Bakery Panificio, 144 Charles St., Boston; (617) 227-4340; panificioboston.com. Open for breakfast, lunch, and dinner. Quaint cafe with a dozen small tables and a counter looking out on bustling Charles Street. Unusual baked breads, pastries, and sandwiches, and delicious entrees. $–$$

Bull & Finch Pub (Cheers), 84 Beacon St., Boston; (617) 227-9605; cheersboston .com. Open daily, 11 a.m. to last call at midnight. The bar in the television show *Cheers* was modeled after the Bull & Finch. There's a souvenir gallery selling *Cheers* paraphernalia. Upstairs is the Hampshire House, housing the library, which has a Sunday brunch and special events to commemorate major holidays. $

The Hungry I, 71½ Charles St., Boston; (617) 227-3524; hungryiboston.com. Duck your head upon entering the doorway (there is an Ouch sign that serves as a warning). Eat alfresco on a Beacon Hill private patio or dine inside in a charmingly elegant atmosphere. *Note:* No high chairs, but the chef will cook special meals to accommodate children. $–$$$$

Where to Stay

Beacon Hill Bed & Breakfast, 27 Brimmer St., Boston; (617) 523-7376; beaconhill bandb.com. This brick row house overlooking the Charles River has 2 large bedrooms with nonworking fireplaces and private baths. There are cots and sofa beds but no cribs. Rates include a full breakfast. Parking, which is not included in your room rate, is in a nearby garage. For ease of movement, there is a trolley stop and the MBTA nearby. $$$

Beacon Hill Inn and Bistro, 25 Charles St., Boston; (617) 723-7575; beaconhill hotel.com. Intimate 13-room inn close to the MBTA, local attractions, and restaurants; winner of *Boston Magazine*'s Best of Boston Hotel Award for their impeccable service and lovely interiors. Children welcome. Award-winning restaurant (the Beacon Hill Bistro). $$–$$$$

Downtown & Financial District

If your family is hungry for information about the city, or if you'd like to join a free 90-minute guided tour of highlights of the Freedom Trail, walk over to the **National Historical Park Visitor Center,** 0 Faneuil Sq., Faneuil Hall Boston, MA 02109 (617-242-5642; nps.gov/bost), within Faneuil Hall on the first floor. You'll find maps, books, and helpful staff. The small bookstore has an excellent collection of reasonably priced books about lesser-known people and events in Boston and New England history.

Boston by Little Feet (ages 3 and up)

8 Faneuil Hall Marketplace, third floor, Boston; (617) 367-2345; bostonbyfoot .org/tours/Boston_By_Little_Feet. Tours are offered from May through Oct (check their website for a detailed list of tours and times and to book). Children must be accompanied by an adult.

Covering part of the Freedom Trail as well as other sites that are of particular interest to kids, Boston by Little Feet (operated by Boston by Foot) is a family-oriented, 1-hour tour of the downtown area that gives kids a great introduction to Boston's history and architecture. Other kid and teen favorites are: Reinventing Boston: A City Engineered, a 90-minute tour that focuses on the underground utilities, the way the city has grown down as well as up; the "Big Dig," the depression of the central artery into Boston, the largest and most expensive construction project in the country; the Dark Side of Boston, geared toward older children and teens, focuses on crime, disease, and disasters; and the Heart of the Freedom Trail, a 90-minute, more in-depth tour of the Freedom Trail and local sites.

Freedom Trail (all ages)

Pick up a map of the trail at the National Historical Park Visitor Center, 0 Faneuil Sq., Faneuil Hall, Boston (617-242-5642) or at either of these Charlestown Freedom Trail sites: the Bunker Hill Monument, 0 Monument Sq. (the National Park Museum is at 43 Monument Sq.), or at the Charlestown Navy Yard; (617) 242-5601; cityofboston.gov/freedomtrail. Only 3 of the sites charge a fee: the Old State House, the Old South Meeting House, and the Paul Revere House. A fee is sometimes charged at the Charlestown Navy Yard for the Constitution Museum (the fee is currently being underwritten by an anonymous donor); the *USS Constitution* and the *USS Cassin Young* tours are free. From spring through Nov there are 12 free 60-minute guided tours a day by park rangers. *Yankee Magazine* in 2012 named it the best free tour in Boston. Free year-round talks are offered at Faneuil Hall every half hour and the Bunker Hill Monument on the hour.

The Freedom Trail, a 2.5-mile walking tour of the city's colonial and revolutionary landmarks, begins or ends at either the Boston Common or the Bunker Hill Monument. Only three of the sites are owned by the federal government; the rest are owned and operated by the city of Boston, by the state of Massachusetts, or are privately owned. The Freedom Trail is easy to follow; just look for the red line on the sidewalk. If your children are young, the walk as a whole may be too long; instead, you may wish to visit just a few of the landmarks.

Freedom Trail Foundation (all ages)

99 Chauncy St., Suite 401 (office address), Boston; (617) 357-8300; thefreedomtrail .org. Purchase your tickets online (adults $12, kids 6 to 12 are $6.50, under 6 free) or in person at the Boston Common Visitor Center (an additional service charge is tacked on if you pay in person).

Founded in 1958, Boston's iconic Freedom Trail is a 2.5-mile red-brick or painted path leading to 16 of America's most historic sites. The foundation offers self-guided audio tours ($15 online) or 90-minute guided walking tours of the

Beantown for Beginners

Sing a Song of People by Lois Lenski and Giles Larouche has Boston as its background and gives a good overview as an introduction to Beantown for the children.

Freedom Trail Sites

- Boston Common
- State House
- Park Street Church
- Granary Burying Ground
- King's Chapel and Burying Ground
- Franklin statue and site of the first public school
- Old Corner Bookstore
- Old South Meeting House
- Old State House
- Boston Massacre site
- Faneuil Hall
- Paul Revere House
- Old North Church
- Copp's Hill Burying Ground
- *USS Constitution* at the Charlestown Navy Yard
- Bunker Hill Monument
- Battle of Bunker Hill Museum

Freedom Trail that begin in Boston Common. The guides, dressed in Colonial garb, are professional actors and historians who portray a lesser known historical figure (a B-lister!) from the American Revolution that they have researched in order to give you a tour of Boston and the events that led up to the revolution from the point of view of their characters. Families will love the "Pirates and Patriots" tour, the "African-American Patriots" tour, or the "Walk into History" tour.

Granary Burying Ground, a Freedom Trail Site (all ages)

Next to the Park Street Church on Tremont Street, near the corner of Tremont and Park, Boston; cityofboston.gov/freedomtrail. Open all year. Free.
The Granary Burying Ground is the final resting place of Paul Revere, John Hancock, Samuel Adams, and the five victims of the Boston Massacre. No rubbings, please.

Old South Meeting House, a Freedom Trail Site

(all ages)

310 Washington St., corner of Washington and Milk Streets, Boston; (617) 482-6439; oldsouthmeetinghouse.org. Open daily, year-round, from Apr through Oct,

9:30 a.m. to 5 p.m., and from Nov through Mar, 10 a.m. to 4 p.m. Admission: $6 for adults, $5 for seniors and students, $1 for children to age 18. Ask about the Freedom Trail combo ticket with the Paul Revere House and the Old State House for further savings ($13 for adults, $2 for kids up to age 18). Buy the Revolution Brewing ticket for the Old South Meeting House and the Boston Tea Party Ships and Museum online at trustedtours.com/store/boston-tea-party-ships-museum-and-old-south-meeting-house-package.aspx for tremendous savings ($26.95 adults and $14.50 kids ages 4 to 12).

The Old South Meeting House began its life in 1729 as a church but quickly became a gathering place for political and revolutionary meetings, earning the reputation as a hotbed of activity. The band of colonists who participated in the Boston Tea Party in 1773 dressed as "Indians" here before they sneaked down to the harbor. Today the meetinghouse serves as a museum of the colonial and revolutionary period, with highlights of public speeches that paved the way to our freedom of speech and a re-creation of events during this period, a good gift shop, and an interesting map model of Boston. A scavenger hunt guides the kids through the exhibits (pick it up at the front desk). Incidentally, Old South still has a political life: During campaign years politicians often use it as a venue for announcing their candidacies as well as other speaking engagements. Concerts, lectures, walking tours, and special events are held throughout the year. *TIP:* In December an annual Reenactment of the Boston Tea Party starts here, winding its way down to Boston Harbor—buy your tickets early!

King's Chapel and
Burying Ground

King's Chapel is the oldest burying ground in the city (1630). People of note buried here are Mary Chilton, the first woman to step off the *Mayflower*; John Winthrop, the first governor of Massachusetts; and William Dawes, who rode to warn the colonists that the British were coming.

Amazing
Massachusetts Facts

- Massachusetts has the oldest active constitution in the world. It was drafted in 1780.
- Massachusetts is one of only four commonwealths that are states (the others being Kentucky, Virginia, and Pennsylvania).
- In the first federal census (1790), Massachusetts was the only state in the Union to have no slaves.
- There are 351 cities and towns in Massachusetts.
- The first American public library was founded in Boston.
- Harvard, founded in 1636, was the first college in the nation, but the campus buildings date from the early 18th century.

Old State House and the Boston Massacre Site, a Freedom Trail Site (all ages)

206 Washington St. (corner of Washington and State Streets), Boston; (617) 720-1713; bostonhistory.org. Open daily 9 a.m. to 5 p.m. (last tourists are encouraged to be here by 4 p.m.) and to 6 p.m. in July and Aug (last tourists at 5 p.m.); closed Christmas, New Year's Day, the first week in Feb, and Thanksgiving. Admission: $10 for adults, $8.50 for seniors and students, and free for children under 18. The brick Old State House, built in 1713, is the oldest surviving public building in Boston and the second-oldest public building in America. Historians consider the Old State House and the Boston Massacre Site the birthplace of the American Revolution. It manages to hold its own against the glass skyscrapers that surround it. Kids enjoy looking at the lion and unicorn on the building's gables. When the building was erected, it was the seat of the British government in the colonies, and these symbols of the Crown indicated that fact. The current lion and unicorn aren't the originals; when the Declaration of Independence was read from the building's rooftop in July 1776, Bostonians removed these symbols of the Crown and burned them (the lion and unicorn weren't replaced until recently). In front of the building (Congress and State Streets) is a star inside a ring of cobblestones, marking the site of the Boston Massacre. On March 5, 1770, a frightened group of British soldiers fired into a crowd of colonists

who had gathered to protest recent crackdowns on customs duties and taxes. Though it was hardly a massacre, five people were killed on this spot, including a former slave, Crispus Attucks. Thereafter Sam Adams used the incident as a rallying point in his frequent speeches against the British to incite revolution—the American Revolution! An interesting exhibit, "Hands-On History," is designed for children and their parents to interactively learn about the history of the Old State House.

Where to Eat

Fajitas & 'Ritas, 25 West St., Boston; (617) 426-1222; fajitasandritas.com. A good place for an informal Tex-Mex lunch or dinner. Features make-your-own fajitas, as well as chili. $

The 21st Amendment, 150 Bowdoin St., Boston; (617) 227-7100; 21stboston.com. JFK wrote speeches in the back of this historic pub (family-friendly during the day and known as a watering hole for locals at night). Informal pub menu. $–$$

Where to Stay

Omni Parker House, 60 School St., Boston; (617) 227-8600 or (800) 843-6664; omni hotels.com. An old hotel in a great location; everything, including the Common, is within a few minutes' walk from the front door. The executive suites are perfect for families; ask about the Omni kids program, where a backpack with crayons and a coloring book are provided, and milk and cookies are sent to the room. $$–$$$

Quincy Marketplace, Government Center & TD Garden

Since its rebirth in the 1970s, Quincy Marketplace has been a mecca for both locals and tourists. Upscale shops, historic buildings, street performers, and a wide variety of restaurants add to the intrigue. Nearby, Government Center, with its tall, modern buildings, adds architectural interest to the landscape. Don't miss the **free** Wednesday Night Concert Series at City Hall Plaza in the summer (celebrateboston.com).

Faneuil Hall, a Freedom Trail Site (all ages)

Merchants Row, 0 Faneuil Hall, Boston; (617) 242-5642 (National Park Service Visitor Center); nps.gov/bost/historyculture/fh.htm. Open daily 9 a.m. to 5 p.m. (closed on Thanksgiving, Christmas, and New Year's Day), unless an event is scheduled, but the visitor center on the first floor is open until 6 p.m. Talks are on the hour and the half hour starting at 9:30 a.m., and the last talk is given at 4:30 p.m. Free.

Faneuil Hall is a historic site, a pedestrian zone, the entry to a massive shopping area, and a food market. An old market building, Faneuil Hall itself was the site of many pre–Revolutionary War meetings, which is why it's called the "cradle of liberty." National Park Service guides give a 20-minute historic talk about the history of the hall. Later in history, social reformers such as Frederick Douglass and William Lloyd Garrison spoke here, piggybacking on the liberty and freedom theme. Tell the kids to look for the gold-plated grasshopper weathervane atop the building. Made in 1742, the grasshopper has become one of Boston's symbols.

Faneuil Hall Marketplace, aka Quincy Market
(all ages)

Between State and Congress Streets, Boston; (617) 523-1300; faneuilhallmarket place.com. Open Mon through Sat 10 a.m. to 9 p.m., Sun 10 a.m. to 6 p.m.; closed Thanksgiving Day and Christmas. Free.

Beyond Faneuil Hall is copper-domed Quincy Market, in the center, and the North and South Market buildings on either side. The granite Greek Revival building has lived a long life as a marketplace. When it was built in 1826, the east portico was right on the edge of the harbor. The brick North and South Market buildings were built in subsequent years to accommodate the growing needs of the city's meat and produce wholesalers. In the 1970s the city hired an architectural firm to restore the buildings and their surrounding cobblestone streets into an area that would be suitable for a pedestrian shopping area. Obviously, the project was a success; many tourists now come to Boston just to see the marketplace, and many locals come here to eat lunch and people-watch. The Quincy Market building itself is mostly devoted to take-out food vendors who sell everything from frozen yogurt to overstuffed deli sandwiches to pizza-by-the-slice to raw shellfish. Once you and your family have purchased your meal, head toward the large center area called the Rotunda, which is full of tables, chairs, and benches. The North and South Market buildings hold shops and restaurants, from the kitschy to the upscale. Outdoors, regardless of the temperature, you're likely to see several street musicians, jugglers, mimes, and other performers. It's a fun place to spend an afternoon.

Government Center and City Hall Plaza (all ages)

1 City Hall Sq., between Congress and Cambridge Streets, Boston; (617) 635-3911 (office of special events) or (617) 635-4505 (Wed night concerts and movies by the Parks Department); cityofboston.gov/arts. Free.

This is the home of the mayor of Boston and the location of several state and federal offices. It's also a great place to eat lunch on the steps or to listen to a nighttime concert sponsored by the city of Boston. The summer concert series, Wednesday Evenings on the Plaza, features musical happenings on Wed. Call for more information and a schedule of events.

Sports Museum of New England (all ages)

150 Causeway St. (GPS address), 100 Legends Way, levels 5 and 6 at the TD Garden, Boston; (617) 624-1234 (recorded info) or (617) 624-1235; sportsmuseum.org. Open 10 a.m. to 4 p.m. daily. Closed major holidays and special event days; check the website before you go. Admission: $10 for adults, $5 for seniors and children 10 to 18, free for children under 10.

The museum has two floors of New England sports memorabilia, covering the Boston Red Sox, Boston Bruins, Boston Celtics, New England Patriots, Boston Marathon, New England Revolution, and a variety of other amateur and professional sports. Special exhibits have featured old ballparks and women's Olympic hockey and basketball. The most satisfied visitors are kids who follow the Red Sox, Celtics, or Bruins, but enthusiastic sports fans will probably enjoy looking at the collections of memorabilia, such as century-old baseball spikes and the

Sporting around Town

Hey, sports fans—to reach the **Boston Celtics Basketball Team,** call (617) 523-6050 or visit nba.com/celtics. Preseason begins in Oct, and the regular season is from Nov to Apr. To reach the **Boston Bruins Hockey Team,** call (617) 624-1900 or (617) 624-2327 for tickets or visit bruins.nhl.com. The preseason is in Sept, and the season begins in Oct and ends in Apr. *Note:* Playoffs could extend the season.

life-size carved statues of Boston idols Larry Bird, Carl Yastrzemski, Bobby Orr, Ted Williams, and Harry Agganis. Budget some time to watch several of the videos of big-game highlights. **Note:** If you come on the morning of a night game, you might be able to peek in and get a behind-the-scenes look at the teams practicing. *TIP:* Behind-the-scenes tours are done during the off-season after the playoffs of the Celtics or Bruins (if they qualify) until Labor Day.

TD Garden (all ages)
100 Legend Way (150 Causeway St. GPS address), Boston; (617) 624-1000 (recorded event line) or (617) 624-1050 (administrative offices); tdgarden.com. Open year-round; check the schedule of events and games.
The Boston Celtics and Boston Bruins play at the TD Garden, site of the venerable Boston Garden. Call Ticketmaster (800-745-3000; ticketmaster.com) for concert tickets and for Celtics and Bruins tickets. The Ice Capades are an annual favorite, as are other ice-show extravaganzas, family shows, and other sporting events. World-renowned concerts and performers for the preteen and teen set and up are also held here. The TD Garden is a 19,600-seat arena.

Other Things to See & Do

Colonial Lantern Tours, Building 8, Faneuil Marketplace; (774) 454-8122; lantern tours.com. Ninety-minute candlelit tours of Boston; take the Ghost Tour based on actual events or the Boston History Tour starting at Faneuil Hall and ending up in Boston Public Garden at the Liberty Tree.

The Leonard P. Zakim Bunker Hill Bridge, leonardpzakimbunkerhillbridge.org. I-93 upper and lower decks, crossing the Charles River from Charlestown to Boston. Named in memory of civil rights leader and activist Lenny Zakim. Widest cable-stayed bridge in the world.

New England Holocaust Memorial, Carmen Park, Congress Street near Faneuil Hall; (617) 457-8755; nehm.org. Open all day, every day; free. Designed by architect Stanley Stitowitz, six glass towers commemorate the deaths of 6 million Jews during World War II. Guided tours by a child of a survivor or a Holocaust educator can be arranged for groups. **Free.**

Where to Eat

Durgin Park, 340 Faneuil Hall Marketplace, Boston; (617) 227-2038; arkrestaurants .com/durgin_park. Extremely noisy, bustling place that has had customers coming back for almost two centuries. Real down-home New England fare—the original comfort food. $–$$

Ye Olde Union Oyster House, 41 Union St., Boston; (617) 227-2750; unionoyster house.com. Open daily for lunch and dinner. Billing itself as "America's Oldest Restaurant." Delicious New England regional cooking from land and sea. Slightly overpriced but conveniently located, and a local icon. $–$$$$

Where to Stay

XV Beacon, 15 Beacon St., Boston; (617) 670-1500 or (877) XVBeacon; xvbeacon .com. Boutique hotel welcoming children. Upon arrival, refreshments are served, followed by dessert in your room. Monogrammed kid-size robes and slippers, bubblegum-scented bath salts, Wii consoles, kids' menu, and room service are just some of the amenties offered for the wee ones. Ask about their family packages. Gourmet delicacies at the Mooo Restaurant. $$$–$$$$

The Millennium Bostonian, 26 North St. (at Faneuil Hall Marketplace), Boston; (617) 523-3600 or (866) 866-8086; millenniumhotels.com. Luxurious hotel across from Faneuil Hall Marketplace. $$–$$$$

North End

The North End is an Italian neighborhood with excellent restaurants, terrific cafes, and fun festivals on most summer weekends (particularly the Feast of Saint Anthony in Aug), as well as several of Boston's most famous historic sites, which is appropriate since it's the oldest surviving neighborhood in the city. It's an easy walk from Quincy Market (parking is tough to find on the narrow streets of the North End).

Copps Hill Burial Ground, a Freedom Trail Site (all ages)
45 Hull St. (near Old North Church), Boston; ci.boston.ma.us/freedomtrail/ coppshill.asp. Open daily 9 a.m. to 5 p.m. for self-guided tours. Free.
Copps Hill Burial Ground, Boston's second-oldest cemetery, has views of the

waterfront—Charlestown, the Navy Yard, the USS *Constitution,* and the Boston
Harbor. Buried here are Robert Newman, the sexton who hung the lantern at
Old North Church ("one if by land, two if by sea") warning the patriots the night
before the Lexington and Concord battle, and Shem Drowne, the fabricator of
Faneuil Hall's grasshopper weathervane. Enter from Hull Street, pause, and look
across the street at the narrowest house in Boston (9 feet, 6 inches wide), at 44
Hull St.

Old North Church, a Freedom Trail Site (all ages)

**193 Salem St., Boston; (617) 523-6676 or (617) 523-4848 (gift shop); oldnorth.com.
Check the website for hours and for Sun services schedule. Free, but a donation is appreciated.**

In 1775 Robert Newman, the church's sexton, hung two lanterns from the belfry
to alert Paul Revere and his compatriots of the British troops' departure from
Boston, by boat, on their way to Lexington and Concord to capture Samuel
Adams and John Hancock. This is the city's oldest church that is still standing.
Behind-the-scenes 30-minute guided tours of the Bell Ringing Chamber where
a young Revere worked as a bell ringer, and the Crypt where fallen American
Revolutionary soldiers are interred. Pricing: $6 for adults and $4 for ages 11 and
under. Across the street is **Paul Revere Mall,** with the famous statue of Revere.

Paul Revere's House, a Freedom Trail Site (all ages)

**19 North Sq., Boston; (617) 523-2338 or (617) 523-1676; paulreverehouse.org.
Open daily from Apr 15 through Oct 31, 9:30 a.m. to 5:15 p.m.; daily from November 1 through April 14, 9:30 a.m. to 4:15 p.m. (closed Mon Jan through Mar,
Thanksgiving Day, Christmas Day, and New Year's Day). Admission: $3.50 for
adults, $3 for seniors and students with ID, $1 for children 5 to 18, free for
children 4 and under. For extra savings, ask about the Freedom Trail combo ticket
with the Old South Meeting House and the Old State House for further savings
($13 for adults, $2 for kids up to age 18) either online or at the Old State House or
at the Old Meeting House.**

The oldest house in downtown Boston. Revere left from here to make his famous
ride. The Paul Revere House is a great place for kids to get an up-close view of
domestic life during this period. Owned and operated by the Paul Revere Memorial Association, opened to the public in 1908.

A great introduction to Boston
for the little ones

Larry Gets Lost in Boston by John Skewes and Michael Mullin (illustrated by John Skewes) is a delightful introduction to Beantown for children. Searching the city for his lost dog Larry, Pete visits Boston's highlights. The book is chock-full of vivid and bright illustrations for the younger set.

Other Things to See & Do

Boston by Segway, 420 Commercial St., Boston; (866) 611-9838; bostonbysegway .com. Narrated by audio device, 1- or 2-hour tours of the city highlights by Segway; your adventure will be captured and you will take home a USB chronicling your trip.

Where to Eat

Most Boston families think of the North End as one big restaurant. There's something for everyone here, from thin-crust pizza to fresh seafood to family-style Italian restaurants with large tables and friendly waitstaff.

Bova's, 134 Salem St., Boston; (617) 523-5601; northendboston.com/bovabakery. Many North Enders say that Bova's is the best Italian bakery in town. Another reason why locals like it: It's open 24 hours a day for baked goods, pizza, and subs. North Enders refer to Bova's as the Beacon in the Night. $

Caffe Vittoria, 290–296 Hanover St., Boston; (617) 227-7606; vittoriacaffe.com. Open daily 7 a.m. to midnight. The decor is way over the top—faux marble tables, gilded mirrors, and garish murals of Italian seascapes—and that's all part of the scene. While the kids enjoy gelato, adults can savor espresso or cappuccino at this North End coffee shop. $

Massimino's Cucina Italiana, 207 Endicott St., Boston; (617) 523-5959; massiminos boston.com. Open daily. Somewhat difficult to find but worth it! Known for traditional cooking and reasonable prices; 13 different chicken dishes on the menu. $–$$

Mike's Pastry, 300 Hanover St., Boston; (617) 742-3050; mikespastry.com. Another North End institution. The kids will marvel at the selection of pastries and cookies. $–$$

Pizzeria Regina, 11½ Thatcher St., Boston; (617) 227-0765; pizzeriaregina.com. Open Sun through Thurs 11 a.m. to 11:30 p.m., Fri and Sat 11 a.m. to midnight. At the original Pizzeria Regina (open since 1926), you'll find high-backed booths, no-nonsense service, pitchers of soft drinks, and delicious thin-crust pizza. You may encounter a line when you get here, since there are no reservations. It's worth the wait. $–$$

Ristorante Lucia, 415 Hanover St., Boston; (617) 367-2353; luciaristorante.com. Open for lunch and dinner. Open the intricately inlaid parquet doors under the canopy to an Old World decor featuring marble everywhere and a hand-painted mural center-piece. Attentive service. $–$$$

Ristorante Villa-Francesca, 150 Richmond St., Boston; (617) 367-2948; ristorante villafrancesca.com. Open daily for lunch and dinner. Inviting restaurant; the front windows lift up on warm summer days to bring the street life closer. $$–$$$$

Where to Stay ⊖

A Golden Slipper, Lewis Wharf, Boston; (781) 545-2845; bostonsbedandbreakfast afloat.com. A Catalina Chris Craft Cruiser, a 40-foot yacht is your berth for the night. Two private staterooms with bath, continental breakfast served in the morning. $$$–$$$$

Seaport & the Waterfront Area

The waterfront area can boast of a high concentration of kid-friendly museums and attractions. The New England Aquarium is one of the most progressive in the country; in Seaport the Museum Wharf features the Children's Museum and the Boston Tea Party Ships and Museum. The Rose Kennedy Greenway threads its way along the waterfront. If time allows, be sure to take in a whale watch or cruise to one of the Boston Harbor Islands maintained by the National Park Service. The World Trade Center is a venue for major trade shows in the Seaport section of Boston.

Boston Children's Museum (ages infant to 10)

308 Congress St., Museum Wharf, Boston; (617) 426-6500; bostonchildrens museum.org. Open daily 10 a.m. to 5 p.m., Fri extended hours until 9 p.m.; closed New Year's morning, Thanksgiving, and Christmas. Admission: $14 for everyone 1 and up, free for tots 12 months or younger. Fri night special: Admission is $1 per person from 5 to 9 p.m. year-round. Children younger than 16 must be accompanied by an adult at all times.

Families shouldn't miss the Children's Museum, which turned 100 in 2013, Boston's first green museum. It's a hands-on romp of a place with exhibits such as Playspace, a toddlers-only play area (under 3, please), and the ever-popular three-story climbing structure called the New Balance Climb, a vertical maze that stretches from the first floor to the third (don't let the little ones in here; you won't be able to fit yourself inside to get them out if they get stuck). The old standards include Bubbles, part of the Science Playground, where kids learn about science through bubble play; the Japanese House, an authentic Japanese silk merchant's house given as a gift from Kyoto, Japan, to its sister city of Boston; Johnny's Workbench, for a taste of creating and exploring with tools; and Kidpower inspires kids to eat healthier and be more active so that they can (literally) climb the Kidpower walls or light up an interactive dance floor. Other exhibits include Arthur's World (based on the books by Mark Brown), where children can be on television with Arthur, play in Arthur's backyard sleepover, see the Elmwood Library, and visit his classroom. Peep's World, adapted from the PBS show *Peep and the Big Wide World,* has hands-on exhibits based on science and nature. Outside is the Smith Family Waterfront Park and the Children's Nature Trail (the plants are still maturing—like the kids!). Ask at the front desk about family-oriented activities and new traveling exhibits. To save money, you can bring your own lunch and eat in the first-floor lunchroom or outside by the Milk Bottle. Au Bon Pain has a kids' menu if you don't want to drag your lunch around with you.

Boston Harbor Islands (all ages)

The Boston Harbor Islands National Recreation Area includes 34 islands and peninsulas spread over 50 square miles of bays, harbors, and rivers within the Greater Boston Harbor basin. The Massachusetts Department of Conservation and Recreation (DCR, Mass Parks) is one of 12 managing partners (along with the National Park Service) and owns and manages more than half of the islands in the park. For visitor information, visit the partnership website at bostonharborislands.org. The

National Park Service can be contacted at (617) 223-8666, nps.gov/boha, or call the Massachusetts Department of Recreation and Conservation at (781) 740-1605, ext. 205, or (617) 727-7676; mass.gov/eea/agencies/dcr/massparks/region-south/boston-harbor-islands.html. Check the websites for the hours of operation. To reserve a campsite on Lovell's, Peddock's, Bumpkin, or Grape Island, call (877) 422-6762 for Reserve America. For ferry service from Quincy, contact the MBTA at (617) 222-6999 or (617) 222-3200 (MBTA customer service) or visit their website at mbta.com; for Hingham, Hull, and Boston, contact Boston Best Cruises at (617) 770-0040; bostonsbestcruises.com. The Harbor Islands Visitor Center is on the Rose Kennedy Greenway between Faneuil Hall and the Long Wharf Marriott Hotel.

Close to this urban area is a series of 34 islands, each of which has its own unique flavor. Only eight of these islands are reachable by public ferry; the rest are accessed by private motor craft or car. Six islands are part of a hub-and-spoke system that revolves around the main island, George's Island, with a water shuttle service to the other five:

- George's Island: Visitor center with a 9-minute film on the island, a museum, Fort Warren, restrooms, a snack bar, and a gift shop.
- Lovell's Island: Remains of a fort, an unsupervised beach, hiking, and camping*.
- Spectacle Island: A lifeguarded beach, visitor center, a marina, restrooms, snack bar, gift shop, walking trails, and great harbor vistas.
- Peddock's Island: Remains of an Old Fort, yurt and tent camping*, hiking, bathrooms, a visitor center, and bird watching.
- Bumpkin Island: Ruins of a farmhouse and children's hospital with rustic camping* and bathrooms. Beautiful views of the harbor.
- Grape Island: Varied wildlife, rustic camping*, and bathrooms.

    *Most camping areas have picnic tables and a barbeque grill.

There is also a direct ferry from Long Wharf to Spectacle Island run by **Boston Best Cruises** (617-770-0040; bostonsbestcruises.com), and a direct ferry from the EDIC Pier in South Boston to **Thompson Island** on summer weekends run by the Thompson Island Outward Bound (thompsonisland.org/about-us/public-access). School and youth groups can arrange overnights to **Thompson Island's Outward Bound Program** by contacting (617) 830-5144. A narrated 3-hour tour to the **Boston Light,** the oldest and most historic lighthouse site in the US, on **Little Brewster Island** in Boston Harbor can be arranged by calling (800) 838-3006; brownpaperticket.com/producer/14530.

Boston Tea Party Ships and Museum   (all ages)

300 Congress St., on the Congress Street Bridge, Boston; (617) 338-1773; boston teapartyship.com. Open daily; the first tour of the *Beaver II* and the *Eleanor* (the *Dartmouth* is under construction and will arrive in 2016) is at 10 a.m.; the last tour of the day is at 4 p.m. during the winter. During the summer the last tour of the day is at 5 p.m. Prices are $25 for adults and $15 for children for 1 ship (tours alternate between the ships and after your tour you are free to explore the other ship). Be sure to visit Abigail's Tea Room and the gift shop. Buy the Revolution Brewing combo ticket for the Old South Meeting House and the Boston Tea Party Ships and Museum online at trustedtours.com/store/boston-tea-party-ships-museum-and-old-south-meeting-house-package.aspx for tremendous savings ($26.95 for adults and $14.50 for kids ages 4 through 12), or if you are a Massachusetts resident, register online for the buy-one-get-one-free ticket offer called the Hometown Pass.

Of course, they are not the authentic ships, but they are a good full-size facsimile of the *Beaver* and the *Eleanor* built using the same tools and techniques that would have been used in the18th century. The "colonists" onboard will retell the story that everyone knows: In 1773, to protest the high taxes imposed on tea, 90 Boston revolutionaries gathered at the Old South Meeting House and, accompanied by a large group of sympathizers, made their way to the *Beaver,* the *Dartmouth,* and the *Eleanor.* They slipped aboard and threw the ships' contents—342 chests of tea—into the harbor. Set aside 75 minutes to visit the award-winning multisensory film *Let It Begin Here,* the virtual exhibits, the expanded museum, the restored tea ships, one of two only remaining tea chests (the Robinson half chest) from the Boston Tea Party, and the reenactment of the dumping of the tea into the harbor. *TIP:* In December an annual Reenactment of the Boston Tea Party starts at the Old South Meeting House and winds its way down to the Boston Tea Party Ships. Buy your tickets early!

Christopher Columbus/Waterfront Park   (all ages)

110 Atlantic Ave., across from Quincy Marketplace, Boston; (617) 635-4505; boston harborwalk.com or cityofboston.gov/parks. Open daily.

When the kids need a place to run off some energy, head to Christopher Columbus/Waterfront Park; it's one of the few places in Boston where people can actually relax on the waterfront without having to order something to eat. There's a nice playground (watch the little ones; the crow's nest is inviting, but the climb down is beyond most toddlers' abilities), as well as lots of room to stretch your legs. The rose garden is dedicated to Rose Fitzgerald Kennedy, the late matriarch of the Kennedy clan, who was born near here. **Note:** Along Boston's waterfront area there's no physical barrier to prevent your children from tumbling into the water. Keep a sharp eye out.

Institute of Contemporary Art (all ages)

100 Northern Ave., Boston; (617) 478-3100 (information) or (617) 478-3103 (box office); icaboston.org. Open Tues through Sun 10 a.m. to 5 p.m. with extended hours on Thurs and Fri to 9 p.m. Closed Mon (except for major holidays), July 4, Thanksgiving, Christmas, New Year's. Admission: $15 for adults, free for children 17 and under. Free every Thurs night from 5 to 9 p.m. and free for families the last Sat of every month (up to 2 adults per family accompanied by a child 12 and under).

Cutting-edge architecture (designed by Diller Scofidio Renfro) and breathtaking views will be your first impressions. The institute is melding contemporary visual arts with the contemporary performing arts, film, and media to provide a global perspective on cultures, ideas, and their artistic expression. Temporary exhibits on a variety of themes will augment the museum's permanent contemporary art collection. A 325-seat Performing Arts Center, the Water Cafe Restaurant (617-478-3291), with outdoor seating overlooking Boston Harbor, an education space, and a media resource center have expanded the museum's offerings. Lots of family activities abound (check the ICA's schedule), but the free Play Dates program on the last Sat of each month seems to be the true draw (pun intended) for families!

New England Aquarium (all ages)

1 Central Wharf, Boston; (617) 973-5200 or (617) 973-5206 (reservations); neaq .org. Open Mon through Fri 9 a.m. to 5 p.m. and weekends 9 a.m. to 6 p.m. in winter; Sun through Thurs 9 a.m. to 6 p.m. and Fri and Sat 9 a.m. to 7 p.m. in summer. Closed Thanksgiving, Christmas, and the a.m. of New Year's Day. Admission: $24.95 for adults, $17.95 for children 3 to 11, free for children under 3. Combo tickets are available with IMAX or Whale Watch.

One of Boston's greatest attractions is the New England Aquarium, and rightly so. Penguins, turtles, sea lions, and sharks share the stage with thousands of smaller aquatic animals, all contained in brilliantly designed tanks and pools. Plan to spend at least a couple of hours here, beginning with the harbor seal tank in front of the aquarium.

As you walk in the first set of double doors to the aquarium, turn to your left for the Trust Family Foundation's Shark and Ray Touch Tank (Opened in 2013), the largest touch tank on the East Coast; it looks like a big lagoon. Encourage your children to be gentle when touching these creatures. Kids get a kick out of the penguins, the first thing that you see upon entering the aquarium building. The little blue penguins from Australia aren't babies, they are the smallest penguin species in the world (half the size of the other three species in the exhibit), with a bit of a Napoleon complex. The four-story glass tank (with an ocean tank webcam), wrapped by a spiral ramp with giant viewing windows (which have been extended), is the highlight of the aquarium, replicating a coral reef with 2,000 different animals and 130 species. The coral reef was completely redesigned in 2013 to more closely copy a real coral reef environment, and more protective features were added. The smaller species feel safer and can hide; as a consequence, there is more courting and mating—a recipe for much happier fish! Many kids wonder why the larger fish don't eat the smaller fish in the tank. The answer is that the larger predatory fish are fed first so they don't eat the smaller fish.

Scuba divers go out four to five times per day for feeding, cleaning, and doing medical checks. On some of the descents, the divers wear head-cams attached to their masks and the video pictures are projected onto a giant screen at the top of the tank. The top of the tank has been completely renovated with a glass rail to help viewage. Educators answer children's questions on what they are viewing on the video screen as well as in the tank. The educators are in constant communication with the divers and can relay questions to them. At the Yawkey Coral Reef Center ringing the top of the tank, seven exhibits showcase reef biodiversity, allowing closer inspection of often-overlooked animals such as garden eels (a bizarre snakelike fish that burrows into the sand; dozens of them in a small space look like reeds of grass from afar), pipefish, and flying gunards. There is nothing like being eye to eye with a shark or walking up and down the many levels to follow a sea turtle's movements through the water.

The Orphan **Seal**

After the kids have seen the aquarium and understand the interplay between the sea and the creatures that live in it, I recommend they read *The Orphan Seal* by Fran Hodgkins and Dawn Peterson, a wonderful book for ages 3 and up.

On the third level is the ever-popular Edge of the Sea Tide Pool exhibit, which allows kids of all ages to touch and hold small marine creatures such as sea stars; horseshoe, hermit, and spider crabs; blue mussels; and sea urchins. Don't miss the New Balance Foundation Marine Mammal Center, featuring northern fur seals. Talks are presented about the northern fur seal as well as a demonstration of a training session (on Fri at 12:30 and 2:45 p.m. lucky audience members are chosen to stretch out and exercise with the seals set to music). Two special programs that are about as interactive as it gets are the Meet and Greet with the Harbor Seals or the Northern Fur Seals ($100 for nonmembers per person, ages 9 and up; ages 7 through 9 must be accompanied by a paying adult) and the Behind the Scenes Tour ($16 per person; ages 7 and up holding an admission ticket).

New England Aquarium Whale Watch
(must be at least 3 years old and a minimum of 30 inches tall)
1 Central Wharf; (617) 973-5200 (New England Aquarium general information) or (617) 973-5206 (reservations); neaq.org; (617) 227-4321 (Boston Harbor Cruises), bostonharborcruises.com. Whale watch operates Apr to Nov. Call for schedule since hours and times vary. Price: $47 for adults, $36 for children 3 to 11, $16 for under age 3. Reservations are recommended. Check in 30 minutes prior to departure. Ask about the combo ticket with the New England Aquarium.
The New England Aquarium in partnership with **Boston Harbor Cruises** operates a whale-watching tour on their fleet of high-speed catamarans from Central Wharf to Stellwagen Bank (America's only whale-feeding sanctuary), the prime feeding grounds off the coast of Massachusetts for whales, dolphins, seabirds, and other marine life. The trip is approximately 3.5 hours round-trip. Once at the National Marine Sanctuary, sightings of humpback, finback, minke, pilot, and the endangered right whale are a mind-blowing experience. An alternative for those who aren't keen on being on the water too long is to travel to Provincetown and

make the shorter boat trip from there (see the "Cape Cod" chapter). For boaters, the trip down is lovely; it's a great way to cool off on a hot day while spotting whales and enjoying the harbor, coastline, and ocean. Profits help to support research and conservation scientists at the New England Aquarium. There is a naturalist onboard trained by the New England Aquarium and an education station for the kids. There is a 99 percent sighting rate and more than 100,000 people go on the New England Aquarium Whale Watch annually!

Cruising Boston Harbor

For a short or long trip around the harbor or to nearby coastal towns, try one of these cruise lines: **Boston Harbor Cruises** (1 Long Wharf, next to the Marriott and the New England Aquarium, off Atlantic Avenue and State Street; 617-227-4321; bostonharborcruises .com) offers whale watching, harbor cruises, Provincetown ferries, and **Codzilla,** a 40-minute, wet 'n' wild, zippy, high-geared harbor cruise with pulsating loud music (children will especially love this ride). **Massachusetts Bay Lines** (60 Rowes Wharf; 617-542-8000; massbaylines.com) features sightseeing, harbor tours, and music cruises, as well as audio tours in French, Spanish, and Mandarin Chinese. The **Liberty Fleet of Tall Ships** (67 Long Wharf [ticket office]; dock is at 1 Central Wharf at the New England Aquarium; 617-742-0333; libertyfleet.com) offers passengers the opportunity to participate in sailing the ship by hauling the sails. *TIP:* For all these cruises, bring a lunch and a sweater or jacket; even on warm days the wind can make it chilly out on the open water.

The two popular dinner-cruise lines are **Odyssey Cruises** (60 Rowes Wharf, off Atlantic Avenue; 866-307-2469 or 800-946-7245; odysseycruises.com) and the *Spirit of Boston* (200 Seaport Blvd., the ship is docked at Seaport Trade Center at Commonwealth Pier— the B Street intersection with Seaport Boulevard, across from the Seaport Hotel; 617-748-1450; spiritcruises.com or spiritcitycruises .com). These cruise lines feature dancing, fine food, and a tour of the harbor.

Rose Kennedy Greenway (all ages)

Chinatown Park to the North End Park (or vice-versa), Boston; (617) 292-0020; rosekennedygreenway.org. Open daily, staffed from 7 a.m. to 11 p.m. Free. The Greenway Carousel is $3 a ride, open in season from 11 a.m. to 9 p.m. through Columbus Day and weekends with shortened hours until New Year's Eve.

Named after the matriarch of the Kennedy clan, the Rose Kennedy Greenway is an urban park that wraps around the city's Waterfront district, extending into Chinatown for about 1.5 miles. The Greenway is in a great centralized location near many kid-friendly museums and attractions (the aquarium, harbor cruises, whale watches, the IMAX theater, and the Children's Museum). An oasis in the midst of the city, kids can run freely and play in this series of six parks with features like spouting fountains and canals, gardens and benches, and picnic spots. Don't miss the Mother's Walk with pavers dedicated to moms—maybe it will inspire your family to donate a paver in your honor! The Greenway Carousel at Tiffany & Co. Foundation Grove across from the Faneuil Hall Marketplace is the latest addition to the Greenway. This is the most accessible carousel in all of New England incorporating universal design (there is a spot for a wheelchair on the carousel). Boston schoolchildren created pictures of animals (called characters) that were carved by Newburyport sculptor Jeff Briggs in place of traditional horses. A host of programs and activities are held on the Greenway May through Oct that are free.

Simons IMAX Theater at the New England Aquarium (all ages)

1 Central Wharf, Boston; (617) 973-5200 or (617) 973-5206; neaq.org. Open daily; call for a schedule of showtimes and films. Price: $9.95 for adults, $7.95 for children 3 to 11, free for kids under 3. Special pricing if you buy a double feature. Combo tickets available with the New England Aquarium.

Children always seem to enjoy IMAX theaters, and this IMAX has a giant screen that is taller than a six-story building, the largest movie screen in New England. And what child doesn't like the special effects of a 3-D movie with those funky glasses? The great thing about IMAX is the clarity of the screen and the surround sound. Lots of underwater movies are shown here to allow visitors to see aquatic places and animals that they can't imitate in an aquarium setting.

Water Shuttles and Taxis

- **Boston's Best Cruises** runs daily between Hingham, Hull, Salem, Quincy, Logan Airport, and Long Wharf. Call (617) 222-6999, (617) 222-3200, or (978) 741-0220 (Salem Ferry info) (bostonwatertrans portation.com, bostonsbestcruises.com, or salemferry.com) for detailed departures, schedules, and prices plus information on tours, cruises, and whale watches.

- **Airport Water Taxi and "On Call" City Water Taxis** shuttle between harborside wharves to more than 20 locations around Boston for roughly $10 (one-way) and $17 round-trip per person (higher pricing for Charlestown and the Black Falcon Cruise Ship Terminal); children under 12 are free. Operates daily, 7 a.m. to 10 p.m. (Sun until 8 p.m.); call (617) 422-0392 or visit citywatertaxi .com. Closed Thanksgiving and Christmas. The water taxis are fully covered and heated in the colder months.

- **Rowes Wharf Water Shuttle** travels between Logan Airport and 18 docks, including Rowes Wharf, for $17 round-trip (under 12 free). For information, call (617) 406-8584 or visit rowes wharfwatertransport.com. Sunset cruises, private charters, harbor tours, and tours of the Boston Harbor Islands are also offered. Call (617) 261-6620 or visit bostongreencruises .com. A free bus shuttle (#66) at the airport dock links to the airline terminals. Call (800) 23-LOGAN or check out massport.com/logan. *TIP:* For those who have a layover and wish to tour Boston, the shuttle stores luggage for their water taxi patrons coming from the airport or the cruise ship terminal!

Women of **History**

The Women's Heritage Trail (get maps at Boston Common; bwht
.org) includes the homes of Elizabeth Peabody, founder of the kindergarten movement, and Sarah Hale, the reputed author of "Mary
Had a Little Lamb."

Other Things to See & Do

Bank of America Pavilion, 290 Northern Ave., Boston; (617) 728-1600; livenation
.com. Seasonal (May through Oct) open-air covered venue with extraordinary views of
Boston Harbor. Top performers, from current top pop stars (such as Beck, Daugherty,
Imagine Dragons, One Republic, and the Postal Service) to stars and bands from the
1970s (past performers have been Diana Ross; Chicago; Earth, Wind and Fire; Allman
Brothers; and Meatloaf).

Irish Heritage Trail, begin at Christopher Columbus Park or Fenway Park, Boston;
irishheritage trail.com. Maps are available at the Greater Boston Convention and Visitor Centers at the Boston Common and the Prudential. The Irish Heritage Trail is a
self-guided tour that covers more than 70 sites (20 in downtown Boston, the rest are
scattered around the city).

Where to Eat

Ashburton Cafe, 1 Ashburton Place, Boston; (617) 248-3957; ashburtoncafe.com.
Open 6:30 a.m. to 3:30 p.m. Deli catering to workers in nearby businesses and staff of
the Children's Museum. There are tables inside, but the emphasis is on takeout. $–$$

The Barking Crab, Fort Point Landing, 88 Sleeper St.; (617) 426-CRAB; barkingcrab
.com. Clam shack atmosphere, very casual and laid-back. Children's menu. $$–$$$$

The Chart House, 60 Long Wharf, Boston; (617) 227-1576; chart-house.com.
National chain with great views of Boston Harbor and standard fare of seafood and
grilled meats. $$–$$$$

The Daily Catch, 2 Northern Ave., South Boston; (617) 772-4400; dailycatch.com.
Fresh seafood, lobster fra diavolo, calamari, and squid are house specialties. $$–$$$

The Milk Bottle, Museum Wharf (next to the Children's Museum), 308 Congress St., Boston; (617) 426-6500. Open daily mid-May to Oct, 7 a.m. to 9 p.m. The Milk Bottle snack bar is run by Au Bon Pain and has excellent salads, sandwiches, soup, and, of course, ice cream and frozen yogurt. The bottle on display was donated to the Children's Museum in 1977 by the H. P. Hood Company, a large dairy. It can hold 58,620 gallons of milk. $–$$

South Station, corner of Summer Street and Atlantic Avenue, Boston. South Station has a pleasant food court area and lots of tables. $–$$$

Where to Stay ⊖

Boston Harbor Hotel, 70 Rowes Wharf, Boston; (617) 439-7000, or (800) 752-7077; bhh.com. Prestigious hotel with a good location on the waterfront. Coloring books, cookies and milk, 60-foot lap pool with kids' hours, complimentary movies and DVDs, family-fun packages. During the summer months the hotel hosts the free "Music and Movie Fridays." A large screen is set up by the gazebo on the water side of the hotel near the Rowes Wharf Grill. $$$–$$$$

Harborside Hyatt, 101 Harborside Dr., East Boston (at Logan Airport); (617) 568-1234 or (800) 233-1234; bostonharbor.hyatt.com. The 270-room Harborside, located just beyond Logan Airport, has beautiful views of the Boston harbor and skyline with slightly better pricing than downtown Boston hotels. Water shuttle service is available to nine stops. Fitness Center and a great restaurant (the Harborside Grill) with indoor and patio seating; spectacular views of the Boston waterfront. $$–$$$$

Marriott Long Wharf, 296 State St., Boston; (617) 227-0800; marriott.com/hotels/travel/boslw. A stone's throw from the aquarium and close to Quincy Market and other area attractions. Cookies served every evening; pool, game room, and health club. Family Fun package in the summer. $$–$$$$

Seaport Hotel, 1 Seaport Ln., South Boston; (617) 385-4000 or (877) 732-7678; seaportboston.com. Across from the World Trade Center. Deluxe hotel with pool for kids to soak in. Kids are welcome to pick from a toy chest upon check-in and can borrow children's books and games from the library. $$–$$$$

Chinatown, the Theater District & Downtown Crossing

Indulge your family's senses with Chinatown's foods, smells, and sights; take in a top-notch performance in the Theater District, then head over to Boston's main shopping district, known as **Downtown Crossing.** Wander down the bricked-over section of the busy Washington Street shopping district, a pedestrian zone, past street vendors and performers. You're likely to see a mounted police officer or two. They're accustomed to kids' questions, and the horses are very gentle, but ask first before allowing your kids to pat the horses' noses.

Year-Round Performances That Children Enjoy

Blue Man Group/Charles Playhouse Stage 1 (ages 5 and up), 74 Warrenton St., in the Theater District, Boston; (617) 426-6912 (general information or box office); blueman.com. Schedule varies week to week; call or go online for tickets and schedule (Ticketmaster: 617-982-2787 or (800) 258-3626). Seats are from $70 to $123 per person. It's hard to explain this unusual avant-garde production with a little bit of everything thrown in, except to say that it's an enjoyable treat for the whole family. Children under 5 aren't allowed to attend the show. *Warning:* If you sit in the front rows, be sure to wear the raincoats that are provided.

Shear Madness/Charles Playhouse Stage 2 (ages 5 and up), 74 Warrenton St. in the Theater District, Boston; (617) 426-5225 (general information and box office); shearmadness.com. Call the box office for tickets and schedule or go online. Tickets are $50 per person. Boston's smash comedy whodunit opened in 1980 and is in the *Guinness Book of World Records* as the longest-running play in the history of American theater. The kids will think that it's awesome that the audience votes on the guilty party and thus influences the play's outcome.

Chinatown (all ages)

Between Stuart and Essex Streets, Boston.
Walk through the ornate arch with the four marble Foo dogs into Boston's Chinatown for a gastronomic treat. It's hard to choose from among the many restaurants. If you like to cook Chinese, this area is a great resource for Asian ingredients. Most signs in front of the shops are in both English and Chinese. A great time to expose the kids to a different culture is at the Chinese New Year celebration in late Jan or early Feb.

Where to Eat

Back Deck, Corner of West and Washington Streets, 2 West St., Boston; (617) 670-0320; backdeckboston.com. Grilled burgers and meats just like Dad would serve hot off the grill! Gluten-free and kids' menu available. $–$$

East Ocean City, 25–29 Beach St., Boston; (617) 542-2504; eastoceancity.com. Open daily. One of the best restaurants in Chinatown. Specializes in Cantonese and Hong Kong–style seafood, but everything's good. $–$$

Empire Garden, 690 Washington St., Boston; (617) 482-8898; empiregardenboston .com. Serving breakfast, lunch, and dinner and dim sum Sunday brunch. Housed in an old theater, the Emperor's Garden is highly regarded. $–$$

Jacob Wirth, 31–37 Stuart St., Boston; (617) 338-8586; jacobwirth.com. For an unexpected treat in the Theater District, go to Jacob Wirth, a surprisingly genuine German restaurant that has high ceilings and long tables and features a broad menu with weekly specials. $–$$

Where to Stay

The Langham Boston, 250 Franklin St., Boston; (617) 451-1900 or (800) 543-4300; boston.langhamhotels.com. Offers 318 nicely appointed rooms, a gourmet restaurant, a fitness center, and an indoor pool. The Chocolate Buffet at the Cafe Fleuri is a big hit with the kids (every Sat from 11 a.m. to 3 p.m. Sept to June). The buffet costs $42 for adults, $29 for kids 5 to 12; **free** for kids under 4. The hotel also offers a kids' corner station at the Sunday brunch. Ask about their family packages (subject to availability). $$$–$$$$

Copley Square & the Back Bay

It's hard to imagine now, but until 1857 this part of the city was a smelly tidal flat, fronted by a failed dam, called the Back Bay (Boston itself was actually a peninsula). By the mid-19th century, the city had grown so much that the marshy tidal flats became an advantageous area for expansion, and the landfill operation began. When it ended in 1890, the 450-acre area was crisscrossed with Boston's only grid system, and well over 1,000 new buildings had been built to house more people and businesses. While you're in the Back Bay area, be sure to stroll over to Commonwealth Avenue and cross into the green area called **Commonwealth Mall** that runs from the Public Garden to the **Fenway,** part of Boston's **Emerald Necklace.** You'll see other families here, mostly locals walking their dogs and stretching their legs. As you walk west (away from the Public Garden), note that the eight streets between here and Massachusetts Avenue are named in alphabetical order: Arlington, Berkeley, Clarendon, Dartmouth, Exeter, Fairfield, Gloucester, and Hereford. The **Greater Boston Convention and Visitors Bureau** is located at 2 Copley Place, Suite 105, Boston, MA 02116; (888) SEE-BOSTON or (617) 536-4100; bostonusa.com.

Boston Athletic Association's Boston Marathon Sites
(all ages)

40 Trinity Place, fourth floor (offices). Finish line on Boylston Street just in front of the Boston Public Library and Copley Square; (617) 236-1652; baa.org. Open daily. Free.

This is the most popular viewing spot during the Boston Marathon's 26-mile Hopkinton-to-Boston race; on any day but Patriots' Day, you too can cross the finish line. Runners come from all over the world to compete in this prestigious marathon (in 2012, 26,655 runners entered, 22,485 runners started and 21,616 crossed the finish line!). The Tortoise and the Hare bronze sculptures are in the Copley Square Plaza in front of Trinity Church, a heartbreaking setting for the nonwinners of the race.

Boston Ballet (all ages)

539 Washington St. (the Boston Opera House) is the performance venue for the Boston Ballet; 19 Clarendon St., Boston, is the location of the Boston Ballet offices and ballet classes; (617) 695-6950 (Boston Ballet/Boston Ballet School) or (617) 695-6955 (box office); bostonballet.org.

Pass It On

If you're thinking of doing a lot of touring, the **Boston City Pass** (888-330-5008; citypass.com/boston), good for nine consecutive days beginning the first day you elect to use your City Pass ticket booklet, includes five sites, coupons, and a map for one low price: the Skywalk Observatory, the Museum of Science, the Museum of Fine Arts, the New England Aquarium, and a choice between the Old State House or the Harvard Museum of Natural History. Prices for the Boston City Pass are $54 for adults and $39 for children 3 to 11, a huge savings. Buy online or in person at any of the City Pass attractions.

The **Go Boston Card** allows you up to 53 choices of sightseeing favorites in a larger radius that includes Boston and environs. You can buy it for one day or longer, up to seven days, starting at $52.99 per adult ($37 for kids 3 to 12). The pass includes discounts for shopping and restaurants, a map, and a guidebook. Free cancellation insurance for nonactivated passes. You can also download the pass onto your smartphone or print it at home. Contact Smart Destinations, 85 Merrimack St., second floor, Boston; (800) 887-9103; gobostoncard.com or smartdestinations.com/boston.

The Boston Ballet was the first professional repertory ballet company in New England and has garnered an international reputation as one of the finest ballet companies in North America as well as one of the top ballet companies in the world. The Boston Ballet's version of *The Nutcracker* is the most popular in the country; for the best seats, buy your tickets months in advance. Precurtain talks given by Boston Ballet artists take place 1 hour prior to the performance and deepen children's understanding and appreciation of the ballet. The Conversation with the Artistic Director takes place in the lobby after certain performances. Call the Boston Ballet for a schedule. For Boston Ballet tickets, purchase online at bostonballet.org, or visit the Opera House box office (check the website for the hours).

Beacon of Light

Be in the know and surprise the locals! The colored lights on top of the spire of the old Hancock building at 200 Berkeley St. signal the weather:

- Solid blue = clear view

- Flashing blue = clouds are due

- Solid red = rain ahead

- Flashing red = snow instead (except in summer, when flashing red means the Red Sox game was rained out!)

John Hancock Tower (all ages)
200 Clarendon St., Boston.
The Hancock Tower (although the John Hancock insurance company moved!) is a 62-story rhomboid, an unusual shape for a building and one that makes it change in appearance when you see it from different angles. From Copley Square, it's a sharp, slim jab of reflective glass; from downtown, it's a wide mirror for the older Hancock building next to it. For a professional-looking photo, take a picture with the Trinity Church's reflection on the building. After September 11, 2001, the observatory at the top was closed.

Newbury Street Shops, Art Galleries, and Restaurants (all ages)
Newbury Street from Arlington Street to Massachusetts Avenue, Boston.
Newbury Street is Boston's boutique row. Designers' shops rule the roost here, though there are plenty of other businesses, including art galleries, several excellent secondhand-clothing shops, designer boutiques, and many others. Whether or not you enjoy window shopping, it's also a nice street for walking, since the sidewalks are slightly wider and there are lots of sidewalk cafes that will tempt you to rest for a while over a drink or a light meal.

The Prudential Skywalk Observatory and the Shops at Prudential Center (all ages) 🍴 🛍

Prudential Tower, 50th floor, 800 Boylston St., Boston; (617) 859-0648; skywalk boston.com. The Skywalk Observatory is open 10 a.m. to 10 p.m. daily mid-Mar through the end of Oct, 10 a.m. to 8 p.m. Nov through mid-Mar. Admission: $16 for adults, $11 for children 3 to 11. The last elevator is a half hour prior to closing. Purchase tickets at the kiosk in the Prudential Arcade or at the Skywalk entrance on the 50th floor. *Note:* The Skywalk closes for private events, so call ahead.

The Skywalk Observatory offers a fabulous 360-degree view of Boston. Informative exhibits of Boston's history and facts are on the wall of the observatory. The **Top of the Hub Restaurant and Lounge** (617-536-1775; topofthehub.net) on the 52nd floor is open until 10 p.m. Sun through Thurs, and until 11 p.m. Fri and Sat (closed on Christmas Day). The Lounge is open until 1 a.m. Sun through Wed and 2 a.m. Thurs through Sat. A late-night dining menu is offered in their lounge once the restaurant is closed. The Top of the Hub is a fantastic place for expansive mealtime views of Boston and vicinity. The stores and carts below in the **Shops at Prudential Center** (800-SHOP-PRU; prudentialcenter.com) run the gamut from trendy to "old money" conservative. On Sat evenings in summer, the Shops at Prudential Center hold a Family Film Festival at sundown on the Prudential Center's South Garden with **free** activities at 6 p.m. leading up to the **free** movies (rain dates are the following Wed).

Other Things to See & Do

Boston Public Library, 700 Boylston St., Boston; (617) 536-5400; bpl.org. Offers a variety of events for kids. Past programs have included a kid's cinema, magician performances, and storyteller hours. A teen room offers video gaming, crafts, and ASA college planning. Call or visit their website for a schedule. **Free** tours.

Clarendon Street Playground, Clarendon Street, between Commonwealth and Marlborough Streets, Boston; (617) 247-3961; nabbonline.com/committees/clarendon_street_playground/committees/clarendon_street_playground. Center-of-the-city respite for children.

Gibson House Museum, 137 Beacon St., Boston; (617) 267-6338; thegibsonhouse .org. Open year-round Wed through Sun (tours are at 1, 2, and 3 p.m.); closed on major holidays. Cost: $9 for adults, $3 for children under 12. National Historic Landmark with original Victorian furnishings and artifacts collected by three generations of Gibsons.

Stores at Copley Place, 100 Huntington Ave., Boston; (617) 262-6600; simon.com/ mall/copley-place/stores. Upscale shopping in the heart of Boston.

Where to Eat

Abe and Louie's, 793 Boylston St., Boston; (617) 536-6300; abeandlouies.com. The smartly dressed chic of Boston gather here for great food and conversation. Street- side cafe reigned over by the imposing Prudential Center Complex, as well as indoor dining. Surprisingly welcoming to children. $–$$$$

Cactus Club Restaurant and Bar, 939 Boylston St., Boston; (617) 236-0200; best margaritas.com. Caribbean, Cuban, and Tex-Mex food, outdoor or indoor dining, fun atmosphere, children's menu. $–$$

Emack and Bolio's, 290 Newbury St., Boston; (617) 536-7127; emackandbolios .com. This local chain of ice-cream shops specializes in unusual homemade flavors. $

Hard Rock Cafe, 22-24 Clinton St., Boston; (617) 424-7625; hardrock.com/boston. Open daily for lunch, dinner, and more! A fun place to eat—the burgers are excellent. The souvenir shop sells T-shirts, pins, hats, sweatshirts, and jackets commemorating your visit. $$

Stephanie's, 190 Newbury St., Boston; (617) 236-0990; stephaniesonnewbury.com. Outdoor cafe-style dining (great people-watching location) in season, or choose to dine inside in air-conditioned comfort. Featuring comfort-food classics, pastas, and fragrant dinner entrees. Kids' menu. $$–$$$

Where to Stay

The Back Bay Hilton, 40 Dalton St., Boston; (617) 236-1100 or (800) HILTONS; hilton.com. Offers excellent family packages and promotions subject to availability. Child-friendly features are a heated pool, a free gift for kids 12 and under at check-in, and a kids' menu in the hotel restaurant and through room service. $$–$$$$

Boston Common Hotel and Conference Center, 40 Trinity Place, Boston; (617) 933-7700; bostoncommonhotel.com. Great value in a top-notch location. Small and intimate for a big-city hotel (only 64 rooms), the continental breakfast is complimen- tary. $$–$$$

Boston Park Plaza Hotel, 64 Arlington St., Boston; (617) 426-2000 or (888) 625-5144; bostonparkplaza.com. A grande dame of a hotel. Family package rates are available. $$–$$$$

Copley Square Hotel, 47 Huntington Ave., Boston; (617) 536-9000 or (800) 225-7062; copleysquarehotel.com. Great location across from Copley Place and the Prudential Complex. Reasonable and attractive first-class hotel opened in 1891. Complimentary tea every afternoon. $$–$$$$

Huntington Avenue to the Fenway & Kenmore Square

When your family is ready for another bout of museum-hopping (don't do it all in one day or you'll never have the energy for all the don't-miss exhibits), check out the Christian Science Church Campus, the Museum of Fine Arts, and the Isabella Stewart Gardner Museum. Looking for family entertainment instead? Take the kids to a performance of the Boston Pops at Symphony Hall, a baseball game at Fenway Park, or a play at Wheelock Family Theatre.

Christian Science Church, Mary Baker Eddy Library, and the Mapparium (all ages)

The Christian Science Church is at 210 Massachusetts Ave., Boston; (617) 450-2000; tfccs.com or christianscience.com/church-of-christ-scientist/the-mother-church-in-boston-ma-usa/tour-the-mother-church. The Mother Church has had extensive renovations. Tours of the church are Tues noon to 4 p.m., Wed 1 to 4 p.m., Thurs through Sat noon to 5 p.m., and Sun 11 a.m. to 3 p.m. Free. For concert listings of their world-famous organ, visit the website or call (617) 450-3793. The Mary Baker Eddy Library and the Mapparium are located at 200 Massachusetts Ave., Boston; (617) 450-7224, (888) 222-3711, or (800) 288-7155; marybakereddylibrary.org. The library is open 10 a.m. to 4 p.m. Tues through Sun. The library is free, but if you wish to tour the Mapparium, Quest Gallery, and Monitor Gallery, the price is $6 for adults, $4 for ages 6 to 17, college students, and seniors; free for kids under 6.

The international headquarters of the First Church of Christ, Scientist, has several buildings of architectural note, including the 1894 original American Romanesque edifice and the extension, which make up the Mother Church (with one of the world's largest working pipe organs).The largest privately owned open space in the city, the Christian Science Church's 14-acre plaza incorporates a long reflecting pool (no wading), with a wonderful circular fountain at its eastern end. But your kids should feel free to pull off their shoes and wade in the fountain's sprinkler—that's what it's there for. The plaza is a great place for the kids to work off any excess energy that they haven't lost during the day. When the kids have satisfied themselves with the delights of running around in the plaza and splashing in the fountain, walk through the passageway between the Colonnade building and the church to the bronze-doored Christian Science Publishing Society (where *The Christian Science Monitor* is published) and view the photo gallery.

When you're done, proceed to the Mary Baker Eddy Library, which houses the world-famous stained-glass Mapparium globe. The Mary Baker Eddy Library is dedicated to the power of ideas to inspire individuals and change. The exhibits are on life's deeper meaning. There are many interactive exhibits for children. The Quest Gallery features an adventure game that engages kids to go up a mountain, plan what they would take with them, and challenge them with a variety of choices (the challenges involve courage and joy). Another game includes interacting with colors on a wall to uncover words. Your children will love creating a page of art to make a postcard and displaying it on a big wall. In the Hall of Ideas, a fountain in the middle of the hall bubbles up words as well as water. The words and quotes (more than 800 quotes cycle through) seem to float on the water. After the quote surfaces for about 10 seconds, the words spill over onto the floor and move up a wall onto a screen. The quote is then re-formed, and the source is noted as well as when and where the author lived, before it dissolves. The quotes represent cultures from across the world and 3,000 years of history. Kids love to follow the words on the floor (it is actually a sleight of hand done with mirrors, but don't tell your kids!).

The Mapparium has always been a huge attraction. Originally installed at the Christian Science Publishing Society building, the building has evolved into the library for the society. The 30-foot glass globe (which you can still walk into) is three stories high and is the original art from 1935 showing the map of the world in 3-D as it was then. It looks like stained glass, but it's actually painted glass. There are new light panels that are customized for different shows (*The Big Blue Earth* show is very well liked). The Mapparium always amazes and each guide gives the tour his or her own spin, whether focusing on architecture, the art of stained glass, or geopolitical boundaries.

Fenway Park and the Boston Red Sox (ages 3 and up)

4 Yawkey Way, Boston; (877) 733-7699 (information) or (877) RED-SOX9 (tickets), (617) 482-4SOX (touch-tone), or (617) 226-6000 (executive offices); redsox.com. The ticket office is open from 10 a.m. to 5 p.m. The walk-up ticket sales office near Gate D sells the Fenway Park tours. Ask about discounted family days.

Fenway Park, opened in 1912, is the home of the Boston Red Sox. It is still a great place to take in a ball game. Even after a recent refurbishment, it's still a bit rickety, but its size (smallest in Major League Baseball) and genuine old-time charm make it the best place in the country to watch a game. Since you're never far from the field, there's not a bad seat in the house. Opening day is very popular with Bostonians, many of whom have not stopped smiling since the Curse of the Bambino was finally broken in 2004 and the Red Sox won the World Series for the first time in eighty-six years. The ballpark opens 2 hours before start time; this is an opportunity to try to score signed balls and autographs from the players. Get to the ball park early. There are game-day festive performances on Yawkey Way (you must have a ticket to the game to be admitted) featuring bands, balloon artists, face painters, stilt walkers, and the like.

Fenway Park Tours are offered Mon through Sun year-round 9 a.m. to 5 p.m. (6 p.m. on nongame days) in the summer and 10 a.m. to 5 p.m. in the winter, leaving every hour on the hour. If there is a game, the last tour leaves 3 hours before game time. The tour shows the highlights of the park, including the press box, the Green Monster seats (atop of the deck on the left field wall; great views of the game below), the grandstand seats (the oldest seats in all of baseball), and going up to the Budweiser Roof Deck and seeing the red seat that is 502 feet from home plate (site of the longest home run ever hit in the park courtesy of Ted Williams). Sometimes the tour is granted access to a walk around the playing field and the Club House. For information and pricing, call (617) 226-6666.

Warning: The tour tickets are sold on a first-come, first-served basis and the tours do sell out, especially the last tour on game days.

TIP: Post a scoreboard message for a minimum $50 donation—select games are a minimum $100 donation—the money generated goes to the Red Sox Foundation. Call (617) 226-6377 (deadline is three days in advance) or visit redsoxfoundation.org/scoreboard by 6 p.m. the evening prior to the game; for a marriage proposal only, call (617) 226-6831.

Isabella Stewart Gardner Museum (all ages)

280 The Fenway, Boston; (617) 566-1401 (info) or (617) 278-5156 (box office); gardner museum.org. Open Wed through Mon, 11 a.m. to 5 p.m. and Thurs closing at 9 p.m.; closed on Thanksgiving, Christmas, New Year's Day, Patriots' Day, and July 4. Park at the Museum of Fine Arts garage and lot on Museum Road (there is a parking fee). Admission: $15 for adults, $12 for seniors, $5 for students with ID; free for children under 18. There is a $2 discount at the Museum of Fine Arts if you visit within two days of the Gardner Museum or if you have an EBT card. Or for you Red Sox fans, receive $2 off your ticket price by wearing something "Red Sox." Free for everyone named Isabella, on your birthday, and on Columbus Day. An audio guide on selected pieces is available for $4. Cafe G (tickets to the museum are not required; call 617-566-1088 to make a reservation) and gift shop.
The museum was once the home of Isabella Stewart Gardner, who built Fenway Court to house her personal art collection. A New York native, Gardner shocked Boston with her short-sleeved dresses and her unorthodox habits (local lore has it that she walked her pet lions down Beacon Street on leashes, like poodles; in reality, she never owned lions). Her legacy to her adopted city is this museum with an eclectic collection from all over the world spanning 30 centuries. When Gardner died in 1924, she left the museum in a public trust. The heart of this 1903 Venetian-style palazzo is a glass-ceilinged, four-story courtyard that holds a lovely indoor garden. Every painting, sculpture, and piece of furniture is in the same spot where she chose to place it a century ago. Much of the art collection is from the Italian Renaissance (Titian, Michaelangelo, Raphael, Botticelli) and Dutch 17th-century master period (Rembrandt), but there are several fine late 19th-century pieces too, notably the portrait of Gardner painted by her friend John Singer Sargent, a beautiful small seascape by James McNeill Whistler, and works by French Impressionists Manet and Degas. Despite the grandness of the building and the breathtaking art collection, the staff manages to preserve the museum's origins. Flowers and plants are tastefully placed throughout the museum, and staff members talk of Gardner as if she were still in charge. Art-loving families should budget at least 2 hours to explore the museum. To keep their interest, suggest to the kids that they try to spot the animals in many of the paintings and sculptures, or ask for the *Family Guide* at the information desk.

Field of **Dreams**

Zachary's Ball by Matt Tavares is about Zachary going to see the the Red Sox play at Fenway Park, his first Major League game.

An education studio holds family programs on weekends in the new wing (the museum doubled their size in 2012, but the space is used mostly by staff and not to expand the collection). A concert series is held on Sun from Sept to May and select Thurs evenings; check the website for details.

Jillian's and Lucky Strike Lanes (ages 7 and up)

145 Ipswich (behind Fenway Park), Boston; (617) 437-0300; jilliansboston.com. Open daily to children under 18 until 8 p.m. (all children must be accompanied by an adult). Price: Charges are per game; no cover charge—you pay for what you play. Restaurants on each floor Outdoor dining patio for Tequila Rain and a roof deck for Lucky Strikes bowling.

This 70,000-square-foot "entertainment mecca" includes a giant-screen video wall arcade, foosball, 12 plasma screens, and high-tech bowling (22 lanes). Adult supervision is necessary to play table tennis or use one of the 34 pool tables. Good luck convincing the kids to leave.

Museum of Fine Arts (all ages)

Avenue of the Arts, 465 Huntington Ave., Boston; (617) 267-9300; mfa.org. The entire museum is open daily 10 a.m. to 4:45 p.m., and until 9:45 p.m. on Wed, Thurs, and Fri with free admittance after 4 p.m. on Wed. The museum is closed July 4, New Year's Day, Patriots' Day, Thanksgiving, and Christmas. Free tours (included with the price of admission) are given daily at various times. General admission: $25 for adults, $23 for seniors and students, $10 for children 7 through 17; free for children under 7; free for children under 17 on school days after 3 p.m., weekends, and Boston school holidays. The admission price now includes a second visit within a 10-day period. Extra charge for special exhibits. Call for information. There is a $2 discount at the Isabella Stewart Gardner Museum if you visit within two days of your visit to the MFA.

The Museum of Fine Arts is one of the country's great city museums, holding collections of fine art, antiquities, furniture, silver, and ceramics. Highlights include the Monet collection and the works of Corot, Renoir, Rembrandt, Manet,

Pissarro, Gauguin, and van Gogh; the famous portraits of Samuel Adams and Paul Revere by John Singleton Copley; several excellent portraits by John Singer Sargent (his murals enhance the grand staircase and the rotunda; an entire gallery is dedicated to his portraiture); and mummies, altars, and hieroglyphics in the Egyptian rooms (the classical Egyptian collection is the second largest in the world). Set time aside to see the new Art of the Americas wing, the Contemporary Art Wing with seven new galleries, and the Musical Instrument Gallery with instruments from around the world! Don't try to see the museum without a plan; you'll get lost, and the kids will get bored.

TIP: A good idea is to determine a meeting place before exploring the building. The museum is large and complex, and there is no paging system to find stray parents. When you arrive, go to the Information Center and ask the staff about the day's family-oriented activities (there are usually several). If your family is particularly interested in seeing certain works of art, have a staff member mark the location on a map as well as the shortest way to get there. The museum shop is an excellent source of gifts and souvenirs; allow some time for this. There are plenty of family programs geared to kids during school vacations and other selected dates as well as art classes, a family Art Cart, a toddler storytime, a drawing in the gallery program, family tote bags with sketch pads and colored pencils, art connection cards, and workshops. Check the website or call for details. There are also other public programs, such as concerts and films geared toward all ages.

Symphony Hall (age 5 and up)

301 Massachusetts Ave., Boston; (617) 266-1492 or (888) 266-1200 for the box office; bso.org. The BSO performs Oct through Nov and Jan through Apr. The Boston Pops performs Dec and May through June. Call for schedule, pricing, and free tour information.

Home of the Boston Symphony Orchestra (popularly known as the BSO), Symphony Hall is the most acoustically perfect auditorium in the US. Tours (reservations required) are given as part of the BSO Youth Concert Series, which include instrument demonstrations and tours of Symphony Hall. Plan ahead if you wish to attend. The tickets go on sale each spring for the following fall/spring series and they sell out rather quickly; call the Youth Activities Office at (617) 638-9375. Also check out the Family Concert Series with concerts targeted toward ages 2 to 5 or 3 to 8 and their families with free preconcert activities. You can get same-day discounted tickets for the BSO Tues and Thurs evening performances and the Fri afternoon performance at the rush ticket window: Arrive by 5 p.m. on Tues and Thurs and by 10 a.m. on Fri. To order tickets by phone, call Symphony Charge at (617) 266-1200 or (888) 266-1200; for online orders, check out bso .org. The same musicians play for the Boston Symphony Orchestra (who sometimes have guest conductors) and the **Boston Pops;** the difference is that the Boston Pops plays a more whimsical popular program, from Broadway hits, jazz, Latin, and swing to classical favorites. A highlight of the summer season is the Boston Pops concert on the Esplanade on the Fourth of July. Free behind-the-scenes tours of Symphony Hall during the Symphony's season Wed at 4 p.m. and two Sat a month at 2 p.m. (see website for schedule).

Wheelock Family Theatre (all ages)

200 The Riverway at Wheelock College, Boston; (617) 879-2147 (theater office) or (617) 879-2300 (box office). Box office is open Tues through Fri 10 a.m. to 6 p.m.; wheelockfamilytheatre.org. Productions are Fri at 7:30 p.m., Sat and Sun at 3 p.m.; extended schedule during school breaks and holidays. Price: $20 to $35 per person, depending on seat location. Reservations required.

The 660-seat theater has an excellent reputation for traditional productions and nontraditional casting, featuring multigenerational and multicultural casts. Musicals, classics, dramas, and original plays are offered from Oct through May.

Other Things to See & Do

Charles River Canoe and Kayak Center, 1071 Soldiers Field Rd. (look for the green kiosk), Boston (mailing address: 2401 Commonwealth Ave., Newton, MA 02466); (617) 965-5110; paddleboston.com. One of five locations offering lessons and guided trips on the Charles River and the Atlantic Ocean plus rentals. Kids' camp as well. Call for schedule.

Where to Eat

Museum of Fine Arts Bravo Restaurant, 465 Huntington Ave., Boston; (617) 267-9300; mfa.org. Open Mon through Fri for lunch, dinner Wed through Fri, and weekend brunch. Children's menu. $$$

Petit Robert Bistro, 468 Commonwealth Ave., Kenmore Square, Boston; (617) 375-0699; petitrobertbistro.com. Home-style French bistro food. The French-born chef is highly regarded on both coasts. Outside cafe dining in good weather. Kids' menu. $–$$$

Where to Stay

Hotel Buckminster, 645 Beacon St., Boston; (617) 236-7050 or (800) 727-2825; boston hotelbuckminster.com. No-frill tourist-class hotel in Kenmore Square located near Fenway Park and Boston University. Rooms and multi-bedroom suites for families. Laundry facilities. The Buckminster attracts business travelers, Fenway Park visitors, families, and parents of students. $–$$$$

Hotel Commonwealth, 500 Commonwealth Ave., Boston; (617) 933-5000 or (866) 784-4000; hotelcommonwealth.com. Deluxe hotel. Rooms overlook either Kenmore Square or Fenway Park/Mass Pike. Rooms are spacious and decorated in soothing colors with marble floors in the bathroom. Great location for Fenway Park; family and sports packages are subject to availability. Kids can pick from a cart with small toys or stuffed animals upon check-in. $$$–$$$$

Brookline & Jamaica Plain

Brookline is a separate city in government only; everything else about it is very much part of Boston city life. To the south of Brookline, Jamaica Plain is part of Boston proper.

The Arnold Arboretum (all ages)
125 Arborway, Jamaica Plain; (617) 524-1718; arboretum.harvard.edu. The grounds are open dawn to dusk year-round; the visitor center is open Nov through Mar noon to 4 p.m. and Apr through Oct 10 a.m. to 5 p.m. (closed Wed). Free walking tours and family activities on selected dates. Ask to borrow the kid-friendly discovery backpack!

Harvard University established the 281-acre Arnold Arboretum in 1872, the first in the country. Designed by Frederick Law Olmsted, the arboretum specializes in trees, shrubbery, and vines displayed in a beautiful parklike setting. Two peak visitation times are spring, when everything is in bloom and the air is heady with the aroma of budding trees and plants, and autumn, for the vibrant colors. Passive recreational activities that are allowed on the property are cross-country skiing, snowshoeing (no groomed trails), walking, jogging, and biking (biking on paved paths only). Dogs on a leash are allowed, but you are requested to pick up after them. To keep the arboretum pristine, no picnicking or food is allowed on the grounds. Come prepared with sunscreen in the warm-weather months as well as bug repellent for twilight. Don't miss the tree mob; a conversation with a specialist on little-known plant facts. You are notified about the location and time by mobile device, Facebook, or e-mail; think flash mob!

Franklin Park Zoo (all ages)

1 Franklin Park Rd., Boston; (617) 541-LION; zoonewengland.org. Open Oct through Mar from 10 a.m. to 4 p.m. daily, Apr through Sept from 10 a.m. to 5 p.m. weekdays, 10 a.m. to 6 p.m. weekends and holidays. Last entry half hour prior to closing. Closed Thanksgiving and Christmas. Admission: $18 for adults, $12 for children 2 to 12, free for kids under 2. Admission is kids' price the first Sat of each month from 10 a.m. to noon. Call for directions and parking instructions (parking is free).

The Tropical Rain Forest, the Australian Outback Trail, the Kalahari Kingdom, the 10,000-square-foot playground, the Savanna Exhibit of Giraffes, Serengeti Crossing, and Butterfly Landing (open mid-June through mid-Sept and included in the admission price) are the highlights of the 72-acre Franklin Park Zoo. The 3-acre Rain Forest holds a pygmy hippopotamus, a dwarf crocodile, Baird's tapirs, a giant anteater, ring-tailed lemurs, and many different species of exotic and free-flight birds. The Franklin Farm has a contact area with familiar farm animals. The Aussie Aviary at the Outback Trail is very interactive; walk around the aviary with thousands of brightly colored budgie birds, which are native to Australia. Purchase a seed stick and you can even feed them! At the Serengeti Crossing area, your children can see zebras, ostriches, warthogs, and wildebeests. Special events at the zoo include Zoo Howl (around Halloween), Breakfast with the Animals for Families, plus the Snorin' Roarin' Sleepover program every Fri and Sat night from 7 p.m. to 9 a.m. the next morning ($55 for nonmembers; must be age 6 or older and accompanied by a parent. It includes a nighttime snack, breakfast, and admission to the zoo the next day) for groups and families by reservation. The Franklin Park Zoo is also a great place for a children's birthday party.

Larz Anderson Park and the Larz Anderson Auto Museum (all ages)

15 Newton St., Brookline; (617) 522-6547 (Transportation Museum); larzanderson .org. Open year-round Tues through Sun, 10 a.m. to 4 p.m. Closed Mon and major holidays. Admission: $10 for adults, $5 for seniors and children 6 to 16, free for children 5 and under.

For a pleasant family outing, go to Larz Anderson Park (a 60-acre park in Brookline). Housed in an 1888 carriage house that looks like a castle, the Larz

Anderson Auto Museum boasts an impressive collection of restored antique horse-drawn carriages (rotating exhibits) and classic cars (America's oldest collection). Don't miss the children's activity room with car-related toys. Held most Sundays from May through Oct, the Outdoor Lawn Show includes bicycles, motorcycles, and automobiles of the past, plus food vendors and family activities for an extra charge (check their website for the schedule). Family programs and lectures are found online.

On the rise behind the Auto Museum is a wonderful picnic spot that is also one of the best kite-flying hills in Greater Boston. Off to the left at the bottom of the knoll are soccer fields and a baseball diamond. Next to the playing fields is a great playground with an unusual seesaw made from old telephone poles; don't miss the duck pond with more choice picnicking sites. Kids love feeding the birds while you picnic here!

Other Things to See & Do

Boston's Children's Theatre, Calderwood Pavilion, Boston Center for the Arts, 527 Tremont St., Boston; (617) 424-6634; bostonchildrenstheatre.org. Year-round productions.

Frederick Law Olmsted National Historic Site, 99 Warren St., Brookline; (617) 566-1689; nps.gov/frla/index.htm. Founder of the design and study of landscape architecture.

John F. Kennedy Birthplace National Historic Site, 83 Beals St., Brookline; (617) 566-7937; nps.gov/jofi. The name says it all. Open mid-May through Oct.

Puppet Showplace Theatre, 32 Station St., Brookline; (617) 731-6400; puppetshowplace.org. Puppet workshop held before selected shows. Puppetry for more than 30 years.

Waterworks Museum, 2450 Beacon St., Chestnut Hill; (617) 277-0065; waterworksmuseum.org. History of the Chestnut Hill Reservoir and the pumping station.

Where to Eat

Brookline Family Restaurant, 305 Washington St., Brookline; (617) 277-4466; brooklinefamilyrestaurant.com. Open daily for breakfast, lunch, and dinner. Mixture of Greek and Turkish food. Try the shish kebabs and the homemade desserts. Very affordable. $–$$

J. P. Licks, 659 Centre St., Jamaica Plain; (617) 524-6740; and 311 Harvard St., Brookline; (617) 738-8252; jplicks.com. Open year-round. Great ice cream. $

Rubins Restaurant and Kosher Deli, 500 Harvard St., Brookline; (617) 731-8787; rubinsboston.com. Open Sun through Fri, closed Sat. Best corned beef in B-town, winner of *Boston Magazine*'s Best Deli in 2012. $–$$

Where to Stay

The Beech Tree Inn Bed and Breakfast, 83 Longwood Ave., Brookline; (617) 277-1620; thebeechtreeinn.com. Ten rooms (shared or private bath) on a private tree-lined street. Accepts well-behaved pets and children. $–$$

Samuel Sewall Inn, 143 St. Paul St., Brookline; (617) 713-0123 or (888) 713-2566; samuelsewallinn.com. Fourteen rooms, all with private bath. Great location near Coolidge Corner, Children's Hospital, and Fenway Park. Charmingly restored by interior designer. All children are welcome. Sister property of the Bertram Inn. $–$$$$

Biking in Boston & Cambridge

One of the city's many fine green spaces is the **Charles River Reservation** (for information contact the **Division of Urban Parks and Recreation;** 617-626-1250; mass.gov/eea/agencies/dcr/massparks/region-boston/charles-river-reservation.html), which borders the Charles, in both Boston and Cambridge, from Science Park all the way up to Harvard. A nice riverside bike ride (too long to walk) begins on the Boston side at the Community Boating Facility boathouse, next to Massachusetts General Hospital. (Call **Urban AdvenTours,** 103 Atlantic Ave., Boston; 617-670-0637 or 800-979-3370; urbanadventours.com for family bike rides with guides and rentals available along the Charles River in Boston and Cambridge). Continue along the riverside area called the Esplanade, which runs below Beacon Hill and the Back Bay, past the Hatch Shell. This is where the Boston Pops performs free concerts during the summer (the Fourth of July concert and fireworks program regularly attracts half a million people), and, on summer Fri evenings, it's where free movies are shown (imagine several thousand people gathered on blankets to watch *The Wizard of Oz* outdoors). You'll find several good playgrounds in this area, too. Continue along past the lagoon up to the bridge at Massachusetts Avenue—just to confuse you, this is called the Harvard Bridge (a good spot to view the Head of the Charles Regatta). On the Cambridge side, ride along the Charles between MIT and Harvard. On Sunday from April through October, Memorial Drive is closed to auto traffic between the Western Avenue Bridge and the Eliot Bridge. The drive fills with walkers, strollers, bikers, skateboarders, and in-line skaters.

Cambridge & Somerville

As home to two of the country's most illustrious universities, **Harvard University** and **Massachusetts Institute of Technology** (MIT), bustling Cambridge owes much of its vibrancy to the schools' students, faculty, and staff, who are ruthless judges of food, bookstores, museums, art galleries, fashion, film, and the performing arts. As a result, the cultural life in this relatively small city is as good as that in any other city in America. You'll find enough shopping in and around Harvard Square to satisfy the most demanding teenager, and the range of food will thrill everyone. Don't leave Cambridge without walking through Harvard Square (location of the Discovery Information kiosk) and Harvard Yard (the best place to begin a trip to Cambridge), or without driving along Massachusetts Avenue until you reach MIT. These places give you the essence of the flavor of Cambridge. Step down to the Charles River along Memorial Drive and the graceful Weeks Bridge. You'll see the Radcliffe and Harvard boathouses here, and, if you're lucky, a few oarsmen will carry their sculls out to the river while you're watching. Walk along the river; you'll pass the graceful sycamore trees that line Memorial Drive. Do yourself a favor and leave the car in a garage; parking is nearly impossible to find, and if you're lucky enough to find a spot, you'll have to keep running back to feed quarters into the meter. (Cambridge meter maids have a sixth sense about every meter that runs out, and they are impervious to protests.) For tourist information on Cambridge, contact **Cambridge Visitor's Information,** 4 Brattle St., Cambridge, MA 02138 (617-441-2884 or 800-862-5678; cambridge-usa .org), or the **Cambridge Chamber of Conference,** 859 Massachusetts Ave., Cambridge (617-876-4100; cambridgechamber .org). Somerville, a model city, is shedding its nickname of "Slumerville" by being the best-run city in Massachusetts. A mere 2 miles from Boston proper, Somerville is sliced by the McGrath O'Brien Highway. Developers are now eyeing this small metropolis and building is booming. National companies like Legoland (opening in May 2014) are planting

Ice, Ice Baby!

Cambridge has two great places to show off your spins and double axles:

- **Kendall Square Skating Rink,** 300 Athenaeum St.; (617) 492-0941; skatekendall.com. Seasonal outdoor ice skating in Kendall Square, rentals, skating school, cafe, heated indoor area overlooking the ice. Admission: $5 for adults, $1 for under 13. Skate rentals: $8.50 for adults, $5 for under 13. Holiday on Ice (a free ice show) is held in mid-Dec, with local vendors giving out free small samples.

- **Charles Hotel,** 1 Bennett St.; (617) 864-1200 or (800) 882-1818; charleshotel.com. Seasonal outdoor ice skating in front of the Charles Hotel in Harvard Square, skate rentals, and a snack bar. Admission to the rink: $5 for adults, $3 for children 12 and under. Skate rentals: $5 for adults, $3 for under age 12.

roots at the new Assembly Row at Assembly Square complex. Artists are drawn to Somerville—only New York has more artists per capita. The antithesis of good art is bad art and there is a museum here for that too: the Museum of Bad Art!

Harvard Museum of Natural History and the Peabody Museum of Archaeology & Ethnology (all ages)

Harvard Museum of Natural History, 26 Oxford St., Cambridge; (617) 495-3045; hmnh.harvard.edu. Peabody Museum of Archaeology & Ethnology, 11 Divinity Ave., Cambridge; (617) 496-1027; peabody.harvard.edu. Open daily 9 a.m. to 5 p.m. Closed Thanksgiving, Christmas Eve, Christmas, and New Year's Day. Admission: $12 for adults, $10 for seniors and students, $8 for children 3 to 18, free for children under 3. Free to Massachusetts residents every Sun morning (year-round) from 9:00 am to noon and on Wednesdays from 3:00 to 5:00 pm (Sept through May). One ticket admits you to both museums. Free family educational and engaging programs (kids' classes, clubs, vacation programming, family performances, and family days; check the website).

More than 240,000 visitors underscore the popularity of the **Harvard Museum of Natural History** and the **Peabody Museum of Archeology & Ethnology** with families—no surprise here, the museum was a Nickelodeon Parents' Pick. There are 17 galleries to explore with more than 12,000 specimens including 500 taxidermied animals from all over the world, dinosaur fossils and skeletons, the world-renowned Blaschka Glass Flowers, and the varied and in-depth mineralogical and geological displays of gemstones (the amethysts are ginormous) and meteorites, all of which are highlights of the Natural History Museum.

The Great Mammal Hall, restored to its original 19th-century glory, houses a 15-foot giraffe, bison, and three huge whale skeletons. Ice Age animals like the Mastodon, the 15-foot Giant Sloth and the Glyptodon (a VW-size giant armadillo that lived 10,000 to 15,000 years ago in Texas) draw gasps of wonder from children in the fossil mammal gallery. Encourage the kids to hunt for the world's largest egg of the extinct elephant bird (last seen in the early 18th century). The Kronosaurus skeleton with teeth the size of bananas (a marine reptile 42 feet long and the only mounted skeleton in the world of a Kronosaurus) and the largest freshwater turtle shell in the *Guinness Book of World Records* are in the Romer Hall of Paleontology. Be sure to see the rhino, hippo, elephant, ostrich, and lions restored to stunning lifelike vibrancy and arranged in order of the enormously diverse environments on the African continent in the Africa gallery.

A gallery on Arthropods (anything with a hinged outside skeleton) displays lobsters, butterflies, centipedes, scorpions, and more. There's an exhibit on amber that lets the kids see all the fossilized bugs within the stone using magnification. Arthropods make up 80 percent of all the species on the planet and all the ants in the world combined weigh as much as the entire human race! In the Fishes gallery, the Hammerhead and Mako Sharks are the centerpiece, with two giant sharks hanging from the ceiling, as well as a 700-pound tuna. Amazingly, there are more fish in the sea than amphibians, birds, and mammals combined, some-30,000 species. The Mollusks Exhibit has a "Please Touch" section where one can listen to the sound of the sea in the shells. The New England Forests exhibit is jam-packed with forest wildlife; learn about the past ecosystems, when there were wolves and caribou, listen to the sounds of the forest, and find the tadpoles in the woodland pond.

When you are through exploring the natural-history museum, make your way to the **Peabody Museum of Archaeology & Ethnology,** connected through the third-floor galleries. The focus is on the cultures of Central America as well as North America and the Pacific Islands. There's a lot of information on the Maya culture, and the Hall of the North American Indian has Native American clothing, four Alaskan totem poles (18 feet tall!), dioramas, basketry, and katsinas and changing exhibits on the Penobscot, mural paintings, and Harvard's colonial

Harvard **Art Museums**

The Harvard Art Museums are closed until the fall of 2014. The Sackler, the Fogg, and the Busch Reisinger Museums are in the final phases of renovation and expansion. A new state-of-the-art museum designed by Renzo Piano will house all three museums at the 32 Quincy St. location. The landmark 1927 building will be rehabbed and expanded. Call (617) 495-9400 or visit harvardartmuseums.org/ for updated information.

- **Arthur M. Sackler:** Art of Asia, the Mideast, and India and ancient art. Closed until the fall of 2014.

- **Busch-Reisinger Museum:** Central and northern European art, huge focus on German-speaking countries and cultures. Closed for renovations until the fall of 2014.

- **The Fogg:** French and Italian art. The Fogg also houses the Straus Center for Conservation, which specializes in research and scientific evaluation of art. Closed to the public until the fall of 2014.

history. Free family educational programs, kids' classes, clubs, and vacation learning opportunities are offered to expand kids minds while having fun!

Legoland Discovery Center (up to age 10)

Assembly Row, Assembly Square, Somerville; legolanddiscoverycenter.com/boston. Open Mon through Sat 10 a.m. to 9 p.m., Sunday 11 a.m. to 7 p.m. Price: Adults are $22.50 and children 3 to 12 are $18, free for 2 and under.

Opened in May 2014, the Legoland Discovery Center is the first one of its kind in the state and the only one in New England. Over 40,000 square feet of exciting play space for kids and their families will provide many hours of entertainment and creativity for the wee ones (targeted for toddlers up to age 10). Housed inside the Discovery Center, activities include Legoland master classes on building a structure taught by builders, a LEGO factory tour interactive exhibit demonstrating how LEGO bricks are manufactured, a 4-D cinema, a LEGO Miniland with a diorama of LEGO blocks built in the shape of iconic Boston buildings, large duplex blocks for the beginning builder, a center for building sleek, fast Legoland cars and racing them against other young competitors, LEGO rides, and a cafe.

Let Me **Entertain You**

The street entertainers in Harvard Square are easy on the pocket-book (they depend on tips from the crowd) and diverse. Performing in the wide pedestrian area between Brattle and Mt. Auburn Streets, they offer a range of acts that can be pretty good (tell the kids that this is where singer Tracy Chapman got her start). On a warm afternoon it's nice to sit on the low brick walls, have a snack, and let the street life entertain the family for a while.

Shopping, dining, and an AMC theater are the icing on the cake to attract families to the Assembly Row Complex, luring them from all over New England just as Shopper's World did back in the day (1950s) in Framingham.

MIT Museum (all ages)

265 Massachusetts Ave., Cambridge; (617) 253-4444; web.mit.edu/museum. Open daily 10 a.m. to 5 p.m. year-round. Closed major holidays. Admission: $10 for adults, $5 for students, seniors, and ages 5 to 18; free for children under 5. Free the last Sun of each month Sept through June.

Throughout the year, the museum offers student and family programs as well as workshops. The Sunday we were there, students were racing robots that they had designed and built. The Innovation Gallery has some of the most cutting-edge research at MIT on view. The museum has a fantastic holographic collection from the 1940s to the present, and a robot and artificial intelligence area. Other MIT offerings include:

- **Compton Gallery,** 77 Massachusetts Ave., Building 10, Room 150. Open daily 10 a.m. to 5 p.m. (closed on major holidays). Free. The artwork on display is not part of a permanent collection—instead there are revolving art exhibits in many media and fields including science, technology, architecture and history.

- **Hart Nautical Gallery,** 55 Massachusetts Ave., Building 5. Open daily 10 a.m. to 5 p.m. (closed on major holidays). Free. The Hart is known for its ship model collection, autonomous underwater robots, artifacts, drawings, marine art, the history of ship design and construction, and information on the MIT Ocean Engineering Department.

Mt. Auburn Cemetery (all ages)

580 Mt. Auburn St., Cambridge; (617) 547-7105; mountauburn.org. The main gate is open from 8 a.m. to 5 p.m. seven days a week with extended hours during the summer months. The office is open Mon through Fri 8:30 a.m. to 4:30 p.m., Sat from 8:30 a.m. to 12:30 p.m. Free. Guided tours are offered throughout the year; call for schedule.

Mt. Auburn Cemetery, a National Historic Landmark, may sound like a strange place for a family outing, but when you arrive there, you'll see why so many Cambridge and Boston families (more than 200,000 people visit each year) make this a weekend destination. Its 174 acres are planted with 1,000 varieties of trees, shrubs, flowers, and other plants. This was the first landscaped cemetery in America when it was founded in 1831. The best time to visit is during the spring, when it seems as though every plant is in bloom. Stop at the office at the main gate or at the visitor center for a map or an audio tour ($7), and ask about the day's special activities and horticultural tours. Mt. Auburn Cemetery includes the resting places of Henry Wadsworth Longfellow, Isabella Stewart Gardner, Mary Baker Eddy, Winslow Homer, Arthur Schlesinger, Joyce Chen, and Fanny Farmer. Mt. Auburn Cemetery has been designated as an important birding area by the Massachusetts Audubon Society. Concerts, tours, and lectures are offered. **Note:** No dogs, picnicking, gravestone rubbings, cycling, or in-line skating!

Museum of Science Campus (all ages)

1 Science Park, Boston/Cambridge line; (617) 723-2500; mos.org. *The Museum of Science* **is open from July 5 through Labor Day, Sat through Thurs 9 a.m. to 7 p.m., Fri 9 a.m. to 9 p.m.; between Labor Day and July 4, Sat through Thurs 9 a.m. to 5 p.m., Fri 9 a.m. to 9 p.m. Extended hours during school vacation. The campus is closed on Staff Appreciation Day (in Sept; check in advance), Thanksgiving, and Christmas. Admission to the** *Museum of Science* **is $23 for adults, $21 for seniors, $20 for children 3 to 11; free for children under 3.** *The Mugar Omni Theater* **charges $10 for adults, $9 for seniors, and $8 for children 3 to 11. For a schedule of films at the** *Mugar Omni Theater* **call (617) 723-2500.** *The Hayden Planetarium* **costs $10 for adults, $9 for seniors, and $8 for children. Call (617) 723-2500 for a schedule.** *The Laser Light Show* **is shown at various times throughout the year, since it's in the plantearium; check the schedule at mos.org. Admission to the** *Laser Light Show* **is $10 for adults, $9 for seniors, and $8 for children 3 to 11. Parking is convenient at the attached Museum of Science garage building**

(parking fee). **Many cafes with fare ranging from sandwiches to burgers to pizza are on the main level of the museum.**

The museum campus consists of the Museum of Science, the Mugar Omni Theater, the Hayden Planetarium, and the Laser Show. If you want to see the museum exhibits as well as other attractions, you'll have to buy separate tickets. Buy your Omni tickets early, since it often sells out quickly, especially on winter weekends. It is highly recommended to order your tickets in advance on the web at tickets.mos.org.

Straddling a dam at the mouth of the Charles River, the **Museum of Science** deserves its reputation as a favorite field trip for Boston-area school kids. The museum is enormous, with more than 700 interactive exhibits; bring a stroller if you have toddlers. Young kids may not want to leave the Discovery Center, which was designed (and recently renovated) with them in mind. Other favorite exhibits include the Live Animal Shows; the Butterfly Garden (extra fee); the 3-D Digital Cinema (extra fee); the Theater of Electricity; the dinosaur exhibit, which outlines the latest theory that birds and dinosaurs are closely related; Triceratops Cliff (the colossal fossil), a 65-million-year-old almost complete skeleton discovered in 2004, one of only four in the world; and the Chick Hatchery, where you observe chicks hatching from eggs. The Computer Museum (which is now permanently closed) gave the Museum of Science its virtual fish tank exhibit, the computer club house, and Cahner's Computer Place. The Science Museum continually brings in some blockbuster temporary traveling exhibits such as the Dead Sea Scrolls, Pompeii, and Mammoths and Mastedons. On Fri nights the Gilliland Observatory is open at 8:30 to 10 p.m. in season for stargazing (on the rooftop of the museum), weather permitting, and it's **free!** Museum Overnights are available to large groups and members under prior arrangement.

The Mugar Omni Theater, a five-story theater with the only domed IMAX theater in New England, has stadium seating, digital screens, and surround sound. The 50-minute films are extremely realistic and can cause motion sickness or acrophobia. Tell your kids to close their eyes if something is upsetting to them.

At the **Hayden Plantarium** (recommended for ages 4 and up), your family can relax for your 45-minute introduction to the stars after walking around the museum. Rotating seasonal shows illustrate the cyclic nature of the stars and their relationship to Earth. The Hayden Planetarium is the most technologically advanced theater in New England.

Bookstore-Hopping in Harvard Square

- **Harvard Bookshop,** 1256 Massachusetts Ave., Cambridge; (617) 661-1515; harvard.com

- **Schoenhof's,** 76A Mt. Auburn St., Cambridge; (617) 547-8855; schoenhofs.com. For foreign-language books.

- **The Harvard Coop,** 1400 Massachusetts Ave., Cambridge; (617) 499-2000; store.thecoop.com

- **The World's Only Curious George Store,** 1 John F. Kennedy St., Cambridge; (617) 547-4504; thecuriosugeorgestore.com.

The **Laser Light Show** shares space with the Hayden Planetarium. The Laser Light show is set to rock music. Past shows have been choreographed to synchronize the laser lights with music from Pink Floyd, Queen, and the Beatles.

Other Things to See & Do

Assembly Row at Assembly Square, 300 Grand Union Blvd., Somerville; (617) 684-1511; assemblyrow.com. Fifty premier outlet stores, a hotel, office space, an AMC theater, and Legoland opening in 2014.

Boston Breakers, Dilboy Stadium, 110 Alewife Brook Pkwy., Somerville; (617) 945-1704; bostonbreakerssoccer.com. The oldest women's professional soccer team in the US. Their season runs from mid-Apr to mid-Aug.

Charles River Boat Company, 100 Cambridgeside Galleria Place Cambridge; (617) 621-3001; charlesriverboat.com. Tours from May through Oct. Hour-long tour of the lower Charles River and the major sights found alongside its riverbanks. A Boston Harbor and locks cruise, and the sunset sail are other great choices. Boats depart from across the Royal Sonesta Hotel at the Cambridgeside Galleria at Lechmere Canal Park.

Longfellow National Historic Site, 105 Brattle St., Cambridge; (617) 876-4491; nps.gov/long. Open late May through late Oct. Home of poet Henry Wadsworth

Longfellow while he taught at Harvard and former Revolutionary Headquarters of George Washington.

Minuteman Bikeway Trail, start at Alewife "T" stop in Cambridge; (617) 349-4604; minutemanbikeway.org. A 10.5-mile bike/hike trail from Cambridge through Arlington to Lexington to Bedford.

Museum of Bad Art, the Somerville Theatre, Basement, 55 Davis Sq., Somerville; (781) 444-6757; museumofbadart.org. The name says it all! Other satellite galleries are located in Dedham and Brookline.

Taza Chocolate, 561 Windsor St., Somerville; (617) 284-2231; tazachocolate.com. Taza Chocolate Factory tour.

Where to Shop

Black Ink, 5 Brattle St., Cambridge; (617) 497-1221 or (866) 497-1221; blackink boston.com. Find the perfect gift or unexpected treasure here when you come in to just poke around.

Cambridgeside Galleria, 100 Cambridgeside Place, Cambridge; (617) 621-8666; cambridgesidegalleria.com. Shopping plaza for clothes-hound teens and their families.

The Garment District, 200 Broadway near Kendall Square, Cambridge; (617) 876-5230; garment-district.com. Used consignment and vintage clothing as well as new stuff too. Also houses Boston Costume.

Oona's Experienced Clothing, 1210 Massachusetts Ave., Cambridge; (617) 491-2654; oonasboston.com. One of Cambridge's best vintage and secondhand stores. Mecca for teens.

Where to Eat

Asgard, 350 Massachusetts Ave., Cambridge; (617) 577-9100; classicirish.com. Kids love the stately feel of the place. American and Irish specialties. Children's menu. $

Bartley's Burger Cottage, 1246 Massachusetts Ave., Cambridge; (617) 354-6559; mrbartley.com. Features burgers and other simple fare. Students congregate here for the large helpings and low prices. $

First Printer Restaurant, 15 Dunster St., Cambridge; (617) 497-0900; thefirst printer.com. Lunch and dinner on the site of a 1630s British American print shop. Comfort food and ice cream to go. $–$$$

Full Moon, 344 Huron Ave., Cambridge; (617) 354-6699; fullmoonrestaurant.com. A *Parent's Paper* award-winning choice: great food, children's menu, kids' play space, and special events and lectures on child raising. $–$$

Koreana, 154 Prospect St at Broadway, Cambridge; (617) 576-8661; koreana boston.com. This Korean restaurant has great food. There is a barbecue set in the middle of the table to cook your dinner. Kids love it. $–$$

Red Bones, 55 Chester St. in Somerville; (617) 628-2200; redbonesbbq.com. Real Southern barbecue. Extensive kids' menu for $4.95. $–$$$

Zoe's, 1105 Massachusetts Ave., Cambridge; (617) 495-0055 or (617) 495-0031; zoes cambridge.com. Greek-American retro diner. Their breakfast is unbeatable! $

Where to Stay

Charles Hotel, 1 Bennett St., Cambridge; (617) 864-1200 or (800) 882-1818; charles hotel.com. Great location near Harvard Square; indoor heated lap pool (special children's hours), children's book area in their library, and children's menu. $$–$$$$

Royal Sonesta, 40 Edwin Land Blvd., Cambridge; (617) 806-4200 or (800) SONESTA; sonesta.com/Boston. Across from the Cambridgeside Galleria and near the Museum of Science Campus. Cookies, coloring book and scavenger hunt upon arrival; kids cooking classes. During the summer bicycles can be requested from guest services (no fee charged), and you can sign up for boat rides on the Charles River. Year-round pool. Family packages, subject to availability. $$–$$$$

Charlestown

Charlestown has reinvented itself since the 80's, and the cornerstone has been both the Charlestown Navy Yard (with its crown jewel, the USS *Constitution*) and the Bunker Hill Monument and Museum. The lovely brownstone homes off City Square Park have been snapped up by young professionals and movers-and-shakers. A great source of information on Charlestown is sponsored by the **Charlestown Business Association** at charlestownbusiness.com or charlestown online.net.

Bunker Hill Monument, a Freedom Trail Site   (all ages)

0 Monument Sq.; (617) 242-5641 (for a park ranger); nps.gov/bost. The monument is open daily from 9 a.m. to 6 p.m. in the summer and 5 p.m. in the winter; closed Thanksgiving, Christmas, and New Year's Day. Free.

In the center of Charlestown, the Bunker Hill Monument rises from the spot where, in June 1775, Colonel William Prescott or General Israel Putnam (there is some controversy over who uttered this famous phrase) told his revolutionary militia, "Don't fire 'till you see the whites of their eyes." As most schoolchildren know, the British eventually won the battle but not until they had lost well over 1,000 soldiers to Prescott's forces; the battle was an effective morale booster to the revolutionaries in the early days of the war. Climb the grassy hill, which is actually called Breed's Hill (the Bunker part of the name comes from the farmer that owned the hill), to reach the base of the obelisk-shaped monument. (Be fore-warned: There are 294 winding steps, about a 10-minute climb, not an appropriate ascent for younger kids or for parents who don't want to carry them most of the way.) A park ranger is available for talks on request.

Bunker Hill Museum, a Freedom Trail Site   (all ages)

43 Monument Sq. (across the street from the Bunker Hill Monument), Charlestown; (617) 242-7275; nps.gov/bost. Open from 9 a.m. to 6 p.m. in the summer and until 5 p.m. in the winter. Free.

Down the steps from the Bunker Hill Monument, across from the Massachusetts gate, lies the Battle of Bunker Hill Museum, which opened in June 2007. The museum's permanent collection has good dioramas of the battle, paintings, drawings, maps, pictures, descriptions, in-depth information on the Battle of Bunker Hill and the American Revolution, and a toy soldier display. The second-floor exhibits, hosted by the Charlestown Historical Society, cover the history of Charlestown and the monument. The first floor is a community space for group usage and has public restrooms

The Charlestown Navy Yard and the USS *Constitution*, a Freedom Trail Site   (all ages)

55 Constitution Rd., Charlestown Navy Yard, Charlestown; (617) 242-5601 (visitor center); nps.gov/bost; (617) 242-5670 (USS *Constitution*–Navy); nps.gov/bost/historyculture/usscont.htm; (617) 242-5653 (USS *Cassin Young*); nps.gov/bost/historyculture/usscassinyoung.htm, (617) 426-1812 (*Constitution* Museum); ussconstitutionmuseum.org or nps.gov/bost/navy-yard.htm. The USS *Constitution* is

open in the summer daily from 9 a.m. to 6 p.m., and Thurs through Sun from 10 a.m. to 4 p.m. in the winter (Nov through Mar). (Guided tours are on the hour and half hour; last tour at 3:30 p.m. in the winter and in the summer 5:30 p.m. The top deck is open for a 20-minute self guided tour until 6 p.m. in the summer and until 4 p.m. in the winter.) Free. The USS *Cassin Young* is open from 10 a.m. to 5 p.m. in summer, 10 a.m. to 4 p.m. in winter. Free. The *Constitution* Museum is open mid-Oct through Apr 30 from 10 a.m. to 5 p.m., summer from 9 a.m. to 6 p.m. Free. The Charleston Navy Yard is closed Thanksgiving, Christmas, and New Year's Days. Parking is at the underground garage outside the main gate on Constitution Road (it's a privately operated garage across the street) and you get half-price parking if you get your ticket stamped at the Visitor Center Information Desk or the *Constitution* Museum Information desk.

The Charlestown Navy Yard is an on-site memorial to the thousands of warships that were built here between 1800 and 1974. The highlight is a visit to the USS *Constitution*. "Old Ironsides," as it's known (for its resilience rather than its materials; it's an all-wood ship), began its service in 1797; it's still commissioned, though it leaves the dock only six times a year for a turnaround so that it ages evenly. (It's difficult to obtain tickets to be onboard, but you can watch from shore as the *Constitution* makes its way to South Boston's Castle Island, is saluted by cannon, and turns back to port. Call for a schedule.) The tour of the triple-decked ship, given by navy crew members, runs approximately 25 minutes and is well worth planning for (try to arrive early in the day to avoid being part of a too-large group). *TIP:* You must go through a security check to enter to see Old Ironsides, have ID with you (for international visitors, you need a passport)! To orient you to the Navy Yard, start at the visitor center/bookstore (Building 5). The USS *Constitution* Museum (Building 22) has exhibits dedicated to the history of the ship, with a wonderful 20-minute introductory film, *All Hands on Deck*. Don't miss the wonderful playground at Shipyard Park (beyond the *Constitution* Museum), which features a shiplike climbing structure; and the USS *Cassin Young*, built in 1943 and decommissioned in 1960, representing the ships that were produced at the Charleston Navy Yard. The free 45-minute guided tour

Young at **Heart**

The USS *Constitution* is the heart and soul of the US Navy, and it is the oldest commissioned ship in the world.

below deck is offered four times a day in the summer and three times a day in the winter (the schedule may vary due to budgetary restraints); otherwise, visitation will be restricted to the main deck. *TIP:* On the USS *Cassin Young* you must be at least 4 feet tall in order to clamber up or down various ladders to get beyond the main deck.

Other Things to See & Do

Boston Harborwalk, running 39 miles from the Chelsea Creek to the Neponset River through East Boston, Charlestown, the North End, the downtown waterfront, and on to East Boston and Dorchester; (617) 482-1722; bostonharborwalk.com. Scenic walk eventually totaling 47 miles to enjoy the city's landscape, history, and culture.

Courageous Sailing Center, 197 Eighth St., Pier 4, Charlestown Navy Yard, Charlestown; (617) 242-3821; courageoussailing.org. **Free** sailing program for Boston area kids, from beginners to advanced sailors. Rent a sailboat; lessons offered in July and Aug.

Where to Eat

Figs, 67 Main St., Charlestown; (617) 242-2229; cheftoddenglish.com. An offshoot of Olives, Todd English's first trendy restaurant, Figs is a hip spot that serves creative pizzas and pasta dishes. $$

Navy Yard Bistro and Wine Bar, Sixth Street, Charlestown; (617) 242-0036; navyardbistro.com. Winner of the Best in Boston 2012 by *Boston Magazine.* Cozy and charming with a neighborhood feel. Indoor and outdoor dining. Dinner only. $$-$$$

Where to Stay

Bunker Hill Bed and Breakfast, 80 Elm St., Charlestown; (617) 241-8067; bunkerhillbedandbreakfast.com. Petite Victorian charmer built in 1885. Two bedrooms, antiques, and patio located 2 blocks from the Bunker Hill Monument and close to Boston. Pets and kids welcome. Full breakfast. $$

Dorchester

Columbia Point has the showcase John F. Kennedy Library, the University of Massachusetts Boston campus, and the Commonwealth Museum, with views of the

Boston Harbor and skyline. Close by are the offices of the *Boston Globe* and the Bayside Exposition Site. The area can be somewhat daunting for walking (especially at night); a car is best here.

John F. Kennedy Library and Museum (ages 4 and up)

Columbia Point (next to the University of Massachusetts Campus; take Morrissey Boulevard off I-93 and follow the signs), Boston (Dorchester); (866) JFK-1960 or (617) 514-1600; jfklibrary.org. Open daily from 9 a.m. to 5 p.m.; closed Thanksgiving, Christmas, and New Year's Day. Admission: $14 for adults, $12 for seniors and students with ID, $10 for ages 13 to 17; free for children under 12. Cafe open all day.

The John F. Kennedy Library and Museum is the busiest of all the presidential libraries. The library itself is rarely visited by tourists, however; for most visitors the attraction here is the museum's excellent exhibition program about JFK and his brother Robert, complete with reminiscences taped by several close friends of the Kennedy clan. The self-guided tour starts with a 17-minute film narrated by President Kennedy, the 35th president of the US. The tour then goes to the Democratic National Convention where Kennedy was nominated. The campaign trail is re-created, including the first televised debates between John F. Kennedy and opponent Richard Nixon. Relive election night with coverage by Walter Cronkite and other famous reporters of the '60s. The tour continues with a full-length color film of the Inaugural Address, and then enters the White House with the first family in residence. Other exhibits of interest include press conferences with President Kennedy, coverage of the first manned exploration of space, a treatment on the Cuban Missile Crisis, the famous televised tour of the newly redecorated White House by Jacqueline Bouvier Kennedy, and a mock White House Oval Office with documents and pictures of Kennedy and civil rights leaders of the 1960s. The building itself, designed by I. M. Pei and completed in 1979, remodeled and rededicated in 1993, is an extraordinary sight from the expressway: Its sweeping shape captures JFK's love of the ocean and of sailing.

Other Things to See & Do

Commonwealth Museum, 220 Morrissey Blvd., Columbia Point (between UMass and the Kennedy Library), Dorchester; (617) 727-9268; commonwealthmuseum.org. Open 9 a.m. to 5 p.m. Mon through Fri. After viewing the introductory 12-minute historical film on Massachusetts, visit the historical artifacts and documents. Interactive displays for the kids.

TopEvents in Greater Boston

January–August

- **Chinese New Year,** late Jan or early Feb, Chinatown, Boston; (617) 635-3911, (617) 350-6303, or (617) 635-3485; cityofboston.gov

- **New England Boat Show,** Feb, Boston Convention and Exhibition Center, 415 Summer St., Boston; (800) 225-1577 (New England Boat Show); newenglandboatshow.com

- **New England Flower Show,** Mar, Seaport World Trade Center, Boston; (617) 933-4900 (Massachusetts Horticultural Society); masshort.org/Mass-Hort-at-the-Flower-Show

- **Boston Massacre Reenactment,** Mar, Old State House, Boston; (617) 720-3290; bostonhistory.org

- **Saint Patrick's Day Parade,** Mar, South Boston; (617) 635-3911 or (617) 436-3377; southbostonparade.org or cityofboston.gov/arts

- **Boston Red Sox Opening Day,** Apr, Fenway Park, Boston; (877) RED-SOX9; redsox.mlb.com

- **Boston Marathon,** Patriots' Day (the third Mon in Apr), Hopkinton to Boston; (617) 236-1652; baa.org

- **Paul Revere and Billy Dawes' Ride Reenactment,** Patriots' Day, Lexington; (781) 862-2480 or (978) 369-6993; battleroad.org

- **Battle of Lexington and Concord Reenactment,** Patriots' Day, Lexington; (781) 862-2480; battleroad.org

- **Big Apple Circus,** Apr and May, Boston; (800) 922-3772; bigapple circus.org

- **SoWa Open Market,** Sun in May through mid-Oct 10 a.m. to 4 p.m., 500 Harrison Ave., Boston; sowasundays.com

- **Ducklings Day,** Mother's Day, Boston Public Garden; (617) 723-8144; friendsofthepublicgarden.org

- **Earth Fest,** May, Hatch Shell, Boston; (617) 822-9600; myradio929 .com/earthfest.aspx

- **Lilac Sun,** May, Arnold Arboretum, Jamaica Plain; (617) 524-1718; arboretum.harvard.edu

- **Street Performers Festival,** spring, Faneuil Hall Marketplace, Boston; (617) 523-1300; faneuilhallmarketplace.com

- **Bunker Hill Day,** June 17, Charlestown; (617) 242-5601; nps.gov/bost or charlestownonline.net

- **Scooper Bowl,** June, Boston City Hall Plaza, 1 Cambridge St., Boston; scooperbowl.org

- **Opening Ceremonies for Boston Harborfest,** end of June, Faneuil Hall, Boston; (617) 523-1300; faneuilhallmarketplace.com

- **Harborfest,** end of June/beginning of July, Boston; (617) 227-1528 or (617) 973-8500; bostonharborfest.com

- **Boston Pops Fourth of July Concert,** July 4, Esplanade, Boston; (617) 536-4100 or (617) 266-1492; bostonusa.com; bostonpops.org

- **USS *Constitution* Turnaround,** July 4, Charlestown Navy Yard, Charlestown; (617) 242-5601 (visitor center) or (617) 426-1812 (*Constitution* Museum); ussconstitutionmuseum.org or (617) 536-4100; bostonusa.com

- **Artbeat,** third weekend in July, Davis Square, Somerville; (617) 625-6600, ext. 2985; somervilleartscouncil.org

- **North End's Saint Festivals,** nearly every weekend in June through early Sept, North End; (617) 536-4100 or (617) 635-3911 (mayor's office of cultural affairs); cityofboston.gov, northendboston.com/visiting/feasts, or bostonusa.com

- **Caribbean Carnival Parade,** Aug, Dorchester; (617) 445-2019; bostoncarnival.org

- **Boston Greenfest,** Aug, Boston; (617) 477-4840; bostongreenfest.org

Dorchester Heights Monument, Thomas Park (off of Telegraph St.), Dorchester; (617) 242-5642; nps.gov/bost/historyculture/dohe.htm. Open dawn to dusk. Site of General George Washington's first victory over the British. Admission is **free.**

National Center for Afro-American Artists, 300 Walnut Ave., Roxbury; (617) 442-8614; ncaaa.org. Open 1 to 5 p.m. Tues through Sun. Adults are $5, kids are $4. Exhibits, films, concerts, and tours.

Quincy, Milton & Dedham

Just a few miles south of Boston proper is Quincy, which has the unique claim to fame of being both the birthplace and the burial place of two US presidents: John Adams, the second president, and his son, John Quincy Adams, the sixth president. Milton, a bedroom community of Boston, has the most conserved land (Milton Land Conservation Trust) within 20 miles of Boston.

Adams National Historic Park (ages 5 and up)

1250 Hancock St. (visitor center and start of tour) 135 Adams St. (site of the Old House and the Carriage House), Quincy; (617) 770-1175 (visitor center) or (617) 773-1177 (headquarters); nps.gov/adam. Open daily mid-Apr through mid-Nov 9 a.m. to 5 p.m. Admission: $5 per person; free for children under the age of 16. Note: You can visit the birthplaces only as part of a guided tour, which lasts about 2 hours. A free trolley from the visitor center goes to the birthplaces and the Old House and the back to the visitor center; last tour at 3:15 p.m.

The Adams National Historical Park, run by the National Park Service, is the house and gardens of the Adams family. When John and Abigail Adams moved here in 1787, fifty-six years after the house was built, there were only seven rooms. As their fortune grew, they expanded the house until it had 20 rooms. Of special note here are the library, with its 14,000 volumes in twelve languages,

Children's **Literature**

Why Don't You Get a Horse, Sam Adams by Jean Fritz and Trina Schart Hyman. This is a great introduction for children to the American Patriot Samuel Adams.

and the study, where John Adams died on July 4, 1826, fifty years to the day after the Declaration of Independence was signed. Here also are the small saltbox houses where the two Adams presidents were born (Franklin Street, Quincy).

Adams Presidents' Crypt at the United First Parish Church (all ages)

1306 Hancock St., Quincy; (617) 773-1290 or (617) 773-0062 (tour line); ufpc.org. Tours run from April 19 through November 11, Mon through Fri 11 a.m. to 4 p.m. and Sat and Sun noon to 4 p.m. Suggested fees: $4 per adult; free for children 12 and younger.

This church holds the remains of the two Adams presidents and their wives. The tour includes a visit to the sanctuary, the president's pew (which you can sit in), and their crypt. The building was erected in 1828 during John Q. Adams's presidency. Both Adams presidents were members of the congregation. Annual Presidential Wreath laying ceremonies are on the birthday anniversaries of President John Adams (Oct 30) and President John Quincy Adams (July 11) at noon.

Blue Hills Reservation and Blue Hills Trailside Museum (all ages)

840 Hillside St. (the Reservation), 695 Hillside St. (Headquarters), Milton; (617) 698-1802 (DCR); mass.gov/eea/agencies/dcr/massparks/region-south/blue-hills-reservation.html. The reservation is open dawn to dusk. Parking is free; $3 for a trail map. The Blue Hills Trailside Museum is at 1904 Canton Ave., Route 138, Milton; (617) 333-0690 or (617) 333-0952; massaudubon.org/bluehills. The museum is open Thurs through Sun and Mon holidays 10 a.m. to 5 p.m. Price for the Trailside Museum is $3 for adults and $1.50 for children 2 to 12.

The Blue Hills Reservation and State Park is operated and managed by both the Massachusetts Audubon Society and the Massachusetts Department of Recreation and Conservation (DCR). The Blue Hills Trailside Natural History Museum, operated by the Massachusetts Audubon Society for the DCR, at the foot of Blue Hill, has a collection of live native animals and offers a natural-history program, displays on the park, and a visitor center with trail maps and information on the Blue Hills Reservation.

Blue Hills Reservation, at 7,000 acres, is one of the largest metropolitan parks in the US, with 22 hills. One of the highlights is the Blue Blaze Skyline Trail, which traverses over the tops of many of the hills, affording spectacular views of the countryside, the Boston skyline, the Boston Harbor, and the Atlantic Ocean. It can be done in small sections depending on your family's hiking ability: For those families who are looking for a gentler hike, there are easy loop trails. Houghtons's Pond is considered Boston's busiest freshwater swimming hole, attracting thousands of locals on scorching summer days (which can be a negative if you are looking for solitude). A weather observatory (available to school groups by appointment) is maintained at the summit of the Great Blue Hill and is often cited in forecasts of Boston-area weather. There are ponds for nonmotorized boating (check with the visitor center to find out about the ponds) and fishing activities for those holding a fishing license at Houghton Pond, plus a 36-hole golf course (the Ponkapoag Golf Course in Canton). The trails can be accessed for biking (seasonal) and horseback riding (year-round). Winter activities include cross-country and downhill skiing, ice skating at the DCR rink, and snowshoeing. There are programs such as maple sugaring; ask at the visitor center or visit their website. Blue Hills Reservation has year-round access and activities.

William F. Rogers Blue Hills Ski Area
(aka Blue Hills Ski Area)   (all ages)

4001 Washington St., Route 138 (exit 2B off Route 95), Canton; (781) 828-5070; ski-bluehills.com. Check their website for hours, prices, and start- and end-of-season dates.

Operated by a leasee of the Department of Conservation and Recreation for the Commonwealth of Massachusetts. Ski or board from early morning until late at night. Don't have your own equipment? Want to teach the kids how to ski? Rentals and youth instructional programs (as well as for the parents) are available

Weather or Not?

The **Blue Hill Weather Observatory** has the oldest continuously operating weather observatory in the US. In 1989 the building was declared a National Historic Landmark and is now both a weather museum and a science center observatory. Call (508) 822-0634 for recorded weather forecasts for the Greater Boston Metropolitan Area, the local marine forecasts, or climate information for southern New England. Call (617) 696-1014 (bluehill.org) for the observatory staff, or (617) 696-0562 for a group tour.

here. A former owner poured money into updating the snowmaking capabilities and grooming of the Blue Hills Ski area.

Other Things to See & Do

Fairbanks House, 511 East St., Dedham; (781) 326-1170; fairbankshouse.org. Oldest timber-frame home in the country (lived in by eight generations of the Fairbanks family).

Quincy Quarries Historic Site, Ricciuti Drive, Quincy; (617) 698-1802 or (617) 727-4573; mass.gov/eea/agencies/dcr/massparks/region-boston/name-state-park.html. Open sunrise to sunset. Hike, rock-climb, and picnic. Park rangers run programs here.

USS *Salem CA-139,* 739 Washington St., former Quincy Shipyard, Quincy; (617) 479-7900; uss-salem.org. US Naval Shipbuilding Museum featuring the world's only preserved Heavy Cruiser.

Where to Eat

Grumpy Whites, 211 Sea St., Quincy; (617) 770-2835; grumpywhites.com. Open Sun through Wed 11:30 a.m. to 9 p.m. and Thurs through Sat until 10 p.m. Phantom Gourmet hidden jewel, with delicious comfort food in a low-key atmosphere. Best burgers (served on garlic bread) and lobsta' rolls you've ever had! $–$$$

La Paloma, 195 Newport Ave., Quincy; (617) 773-0512; lapalomarestaurant.com. DeliciousMexican food since the '80's. $–$$

Acton, Burlington, Concord, Lexington & Lincoln

Just a few miles to the northwest of Cambridge are the historic towns of Lexington and Concord. The "shot heard round the world" was fired in Lexington, and the subsequent first battles of the Revolutionary War were fought there and in Concord. During the nation's first century, Concord attracted thinkers and writers such as Nathaniel Hawthorne, Ralph Waldo Emerson, Louisa May Alcott, and Henry David Thoreau, whose homes are now open to the public. Thoreau's beloved Walden Pond is a terrific spot to learn a little about Thoreau or to picnic, sunbathe, and swim. The DeCordova Museum and Sculpture Park in Lincoln is another great picnic spot as well as an innovative contemporary art museum. Waltham is still the home of several industries, although the emphasis now is on high tech. Acton, Framingham, and Natick still manage to maintain open spaces and promote family activities. For more information, contact the **Greater Merrimack Convention and Visitors Bureau** at 9 Central St. (978-459-6150 or 800-443-3332; lowell.org or merrimackvalley.org) or the **Lexington Chamber of Commerce and Visitor Information,** 1875 Massachusetts Ave., Lexington, MA 02420 (781-862-2480 chamber, 781-802-1450 visitor center; lexingtonchamber .org or tourlexington.us), or the **Concord Visitor Center** (run by the **Concord Chamber of Commerce**), 58 Main St., Concord, MA 01742 (978-369-3120; concordchamberofcommerce.org), open daily from the end of Mar through Oct from 10 a.m. to 4 p.m. Guided walking tours are offered Fri through Sun and holiday Mondays, and by appointment. **Freedom's Way National Heritage Area** unites many towns into a link that pushed for liberty in the past and preservation today. Call (978) 772-3654 or visit freedomsway.org for more information.

deCordova Sculpture Park and Museum (all ages)

51 Sandy Pond Rd., Lincoln; (781) 259-8355; decordova.org. Open Memorial Day weekend to Columbus Day weekend daily 10 a.m. to 5 p.m. Winter hours are Wed through Fri 10 a.m. to 4 p.m., Sat and Sun 10 a.m. to 5 p.m. Check the website for holiday closures. Admission to the gallery and Sculpture Park: $14 for adults, free for under 12 years of age. Admission is also free the first Wed of every month for all nongroup visitors. The Sculpture Park welcomes pets and picnicking. Cafe, gift shop and the Hive Summer Camp. *TIP:* **Upon entering ask for the free Family Activity Kit at the front desk.**

Housed in the castlelike brick mansion of a wealthy early 20th-century Boston businessman, the DeCordova Museum is dedicated to promoting appreciation of Contemporary Art by American as well as international artists. An ambitious schedule of exhibitions attracts a large, loyal audience. Outdoors on the museum's beautiful grounds, the Sculpture Park features permanent and temporary sculptures, some of which are musical and most of which will intrigue the kids. Check the museum for a schedule of events. The DeCordova Sculpture Park and Museum also offers drop-in family educational programming including "Artful Play" (geared to ages 2 through 5)

and "Artful Exploration" (geared for children under age 12) to help families engage with the art on view as well as the artists' materials and prophesies.

Drumlin Farm (all ages)

208 South Great Rd., South Lincoln; (781) 259-2200 (Drumlin Farm) or (800) AUDU-BON; massaudubon.org. Nature center open Mar through Oct, Tues through Sun and Mon federal holidays (except Thanksgiving, Christmas, and New Year's Day), 9 a.m. to 5 p.m. Open Nov through Feb, Tues through Sun and Mon federal holidays, 9 a.m. to 4 p.m. The trails are only open when the nature center is open. Admission: $8 for adults, $6 for seniors and children 2 to 12, free for children under 2. Drumlin Farm is a 206-acre magnet for Boston-area families with young children. Across the street is the headquarters of the Massachusetts Audubon Society. Drumlin Farm is a "working farm," which means that the exhibits are built around what you might find on a typical New England farmstead: kitchen gardens, flower gardens, crops, meadows, ponds, and, of course, lots of barnyard animals, including cows, pigs, sheep, goats, and chickens, as well as forest creatures. Don't miss the easy hike to the top of their glacial drumlin (the hill runs parallel to the direction of the glacial flow), one of the highest points in Greater Boston. Excellent kid-oriented demonstrations, discussions, and walks by teacher/naturalist guides are given daily. *Note:* Picnicking is allowed in designated areas only; no dogs allowed. Special programming includes in-season sleigh rides and hayrides for $2 per adult and $1 per child and maple sugaring from mid-Feb through Mar.

Lexington Battle Green/Lexington Visitor Center (all ages)

1875 Massachusetts Ave., Lexington; (781) 862-1450; lexingtonchamber.org. Costumed guides give ongoing tours weekends in the spring and from 9 to 5 p.m. Memorial Day through Oct. Free.

Battle Green is the site of the first battle of the American Revolution on Apr 19, 1775, between the local colonists (the Minutemen, so named because they were ready at a moment's notice) and the British Redcoats. The **Lexington Visitor Center,** across the street from the Minuteman Statue (erected in memory of the valiant men who gave their lives), has a diorama of the battle, a gift shop, and visitor information. Every Patriots' Day (the third Mon in Apr), there is a reenactment of the Battle of Lexington by the Lexington Minute Man Company on the Green at 6 a.m.

Minute Man National Historical Park   (all ages)

**Battle Road, Route 2A, Lexington/Lincoln line and on to Concord; (781) 674-1920
(Minute Man Visitor Center, 250 North Great Rd. in Lincoln); nps.gov/mima. Open
daily from 9 a.m. to 5 p.m. Apr through Oct. Reduced winter hours; call for schedule. Free.**

Minute Man National Historical Park extends along Battle Road from Lexington
to Lincoln to Concord. It was established to commemorate the events that took
place along the winding, hilly road on April 18–19, 1775. Stop at the visitor center on Route 2A for an excellent 25-minute multimedia presentation. The Road to
Revolution, which will orient you to the history and sights of the area. There's a
nice 1-mile walk (follow the markers) to the ruins of the Fiske House, a farmhouse
that was in the midst of the battle area. An interesting (but long) hike is the
5-mile (10 miles round-trip with no shuttle at either end) Battle Road Trail from
Fisk Hill to Meriam's Corner in Concord. Also of interest is an entire restored
colonial neighborhood centered around Hartwell Tavern. Park rangers dressed
like 18th-century colonists offer daily musket-firing demonstrations during the
peak season. Whittemore House behind the Minute Man Visitor Center has arts-
and-crafts events, walking tours, and historical lectures. Bike tours of Battle Road

On the Road to **Liberty**

The **Liberty Ride** (sponsored by the town of Lexington; 781-862-0500,
ext. 206; libertyride.us) runs weekends in Apr and May and daily
Memorial Day through the last Sun in Oct. This 90-minute route covers major Lexington and Concord attractions and is narrated by a
costumed guide—you can get off and on at the sights of your choice.
Tickets are $28 for adults and $12 for students ages 5 to 17; free for
children under age 5. There is free parking behind the Lexington
Historical Society Headquarters at 13 Depot Sq. Departures are at 10
a.m., 11:30 a.m., 1 p.m., and 2:30 p.m.; boarding is at the Lexington
Visitor Center, 1875 Massachusetts Ave., Lexington. To start your Liberty Ride in Concord, boarding is 45 minutes later than the Lexington
schedule at the North Bridge Parking lot on Monument Street in Concord (a half mile from Concord Center on the right). Discounts and
coupons are given onboard.

Path of Glory

The **Minuteman Bikeway Trail** is a fun path to travel from northern **Cambridge through Arlington, Lexington, and Bedford.** It's a 10.5-mile path that begins at the Alewife station in Cambridge (the northernmost stop on the Red Line) and follows some unused railroad tracks, ending in suburban Bedford. For more information about this trail, check out minutemanbikeway.org.

in Minuteman National Park can be arranged by calling Concord Bike Tours at (978) 501-7097. A good book to read before arriving for children ages 4 through 8 is *Sam the Minuteman,* by Nathaniel Benchley and Arnold Lobel.

Old North Bridge/Old North Bridge Visitor Center (all ages) 🏛

Off Monument Street (Old North Bridge) and 174 Liberty St. (visitor center), Concord; (978) 369-6993 or (978) 318-7810; nps.gov/mima/index.htm. Part of the Minute Man National Historical Park.

Begin your trip to Concord at the Old North Bridge. This is the spot where the "shot heard round the world" was fired (actually the first shot ordered by a colonial officer against the King's Army). This is why the Old North Bridge is considered the birthplace of the American Revolution (the first shot that killed a British soldier, the first day, according to the park ranger). The current bridge is actually the fifth reproduction since that historic event. Nearby (a 10-minute walk) is the North Bridge Visitor Center, on Liberty Street. Park rangers answer questions at the center and also offer good presentations at the bridge itself (from late May to early Nov daily; winter by advance request only). The home that Louisa May Alcott grew up in and Nathaniel Hawthorne and Margaret Sidney lived in was called the Wayside and is inside the park boundaries. It is reopening for tours after extensive renovations in the spring of 2015 ($5 per adult; **free** for kids under age 16).

Orchard House (all ages) 🏛

399 Lexington Rd., Concord; (978) 369-4118; louisamayalcott.org. Open from Apr through Oct, Mon through Sat 10 a.m. to 4:30 p.m., Sun 1 to 4:30 p.m.; Nov through Mar, Mon through Fri 11 a.m. to 3 p.m., Sat 10 a.m. to 4:30 p.m., Sun 1 to 4:30 p.m. Closed Jan 1 and 2, Easter, Thanksgiving, and Christmas. Admission:

American **Heritage Houses**

The Lexington Historical Society (781-862-1703; lexingtonhistory.org) operates the following American Heritage Houses. Tickets can be purchased at any of the houses. Price: $7 for adults and $5 for kids ages 6 to 16 (one house); $12 for adults and $8 for kids ages 6 to 16 (three houses); under 6 free.

- **Buckman Tavern,** 1 Bedford St., Lexington; (781) 862-4731. Open daily Apr through the end of Oct, 10 a.m. to 4 p.m. (guided tours every half hour). The gathering spot for the local Minutemen in the wee hours prior to the encounter with the British soldiers on Lexington Green on April 19, 1775.

- **Hancock Clarke House,** 36 Hancock St., Lexington; (781) 861-0928. Open weekends Apr through Memorial Day, daily June through Oct, from 10 a.m. to 4 p.m. (tours hourly). Home of Church of Christ Reverends John Hancock (minister from 1698 to 1752) and Jonas Clarke (minister from 1752 to 1805). John Hancock (Clarke's first cousin by marriage and Reverend Hancock's grandson, as well as the future signer of the Declaration of Independence) and Samuel Adams (member of the Boston Tea Party and the Sons of Liberty and future governor of Massachusetts) were visiting when Paul Revere and William Dawes came to warn them that the British were coming.

- **Munroe Tavern,** 1332 Massachusetts Ave., Lexington; (781) 862-0295. Open weekends Apr through Memorial Day, daily June through Oct, from noon to 4 p.m. (guided tours every hour). The British troops commandeered the tavern and used it as a hospital to treat their troops. The property has beautiful period gardens and a teahouse with light refreshments.

$10 for adults, $8 for seniors and students with ID, $5 for children 6 to 17, free for children under 6. Family rates are available. Guided tours are on the half hour from Apr through Oct, but for other times of year, please call on that day for tour times. *TIP:* Discount coupons are found on the website.

Near the middle of Concord is the home where *Little Women* author Louisa May Alcott lived as an adult. The house is remarkably homey and informal; there are no ropes or fences, and there are enough recognizable items on view to make Alcott's fans feel as though she and her sisters have just left the room (it's where *Little Women* was written and set). Be sure to take the tour here. At certain times there are first-person tours, with a costumed guide portraying a family member or character from one of Alcott's books. Check their website for these programs: Welcome to Our Home Tour, Christmas Program, Morning with the Alcotts, the Wedding Reenactment, and other family activities.

Scottish Rite Masonic Museum and Library, National Heritage Museum (all ages)

33 Marrett Rd. (Route 2A), Lexington; (781) 861-6559; nationalheritagemuseum .org. Open Wed through Sat 10 a.m. to 4:30 p.m. Admission and parking are free (fee for guided tours).

Exhibits on American history and culture with special emphasis on American freemasonry and fraternalism. Revolving exhibits on Americana.

Sleepy Hollow Cemetery (aka Authors' Ridge) (all ages)

148 Bedford St. and Court Lane, Route 62, Concord; (978) 318-3233; concordnet .org./pages/ConcordMA_Cemetery/sleepy. Open dawn to dusk. Free.

Sleepy Hollow Cemetery is on the National Register of Historic Places. The remains of Ralph Waldo Emerson, Henry David Thoreau, Nathaniel Hawthorne, Louisa May Alcott, Daniel Chester French, Ephraim Wales Bull (developer of the Concord grape), and Elizabeth Peabody (founder of the kindergarten movement) among other notables reside here in Author's Ridge.

The Discovery Museums: Children's Discovery Museum
(under age 6) and **Science Discovery Museum** (ages 6 and up)

177 Main St., Acton; (978) 264-4201; discoverymuseums.org. Check the website for seasonal hours. Admission: $11.50 for adults and children (must visit both on the same day). Children under 1 get in free.

The Children's Discovery Museum, housed in an old Victorian home, encourages touch and exploration. A favorite is the Water Discovery exhibit, where kids

Walking Tours

Guided Walking Tours of Concord, sponsored by Concord's Chamber of Commerce, focus on three themes: literary (Concord authors), historical (Concord's history), and the American Revolution (Concord's role). The 2-hour tours run from Apr through Oct, Fri to Sun and holiday Mondays and by appointment. The price is $20 for adults and $5 for kids 12 and under. For more information, contact the Concord Visitor Center, 58 Main St.; (978) 369-3120; concordchamberof commerce.org.

can create huge bubbles and play with water. The train room with Brio trains helps kids enact fantasies of ticket selling and getting on a train to undiscovered places; the Discovery Ship, located in the attic of the Victorian house, is great fun for improvisations.

Interactive exhibits throughout the Science Discovery Museum encourage hands-on experimentation and invention. Children particularly enjoy the Inventor's Workshop woodworking shop. The music room encourages discoveries of things that can be used to make music, such as rubber balls, tuning forks, a music wall, and an air harp, which uses beams of light to make certain sounds. The sea of clouds is a dish with fog in it that helps children understand what a cloud is like. A recording booth in the Sound Area allows children to explore sound effects. Popular with adults and their kids is the thermal-imaging camera showing body temperature and testing insulation efficiency. All of these hands-on activities prove that science can be fun!

These museums are a big hit with inquisitive, playful kids. Ongoing fun and educational entertainment on any given day could include butterfly making, face painting, visits from superheroes, and music performances. Check the schedule.

Walden Pond State Reservation (all ages)

915 Walden St., Route 126, Concord; (978) 369-3254; mass.gov/eea/agencies/dcr/ massparks/region-north/walden-pond-state-reservation.html. Open daily; seasonal hours. Price: $5 parking fee all year.

Walden Pond can be a crowded place, especially when the water is warm enough for swimming. It's best to come here in the off-season; otherwise, it's hard to imagine the peace that Henry David Thoreau found when he lived here alone. His cabin was taken down long ago but there is a replica of the one-room cabin that serves as a simple reminder of the unpretentious man who chose Walden Pond as his home and wrote *On the Duty of Civil Disobedience* and *Walden* (which is credited with the birth of environmentalism). Ungroomed trails for cross-country skiing and snowshoeing in Walden Woods; canoeing, fishing, and kayaking are allowed on Walden Pond. No pets. *TIP:* Call before traveling; if the parking lot is full, you will be turned away.

Other Things to See & Do

Codman Estate, 34 Codman Rd., Lincoln; (781) 227-3956; historicnewengland.org. Open second and fourth Saturdays from June through Oct 15. Tours on the hour, 11 a.m. to 4 p.m. Admission is $5 for adults and $2.50 for students. The Codman Estate spans 200 years of history (and five generations of Codmans), showing different architectural influences of the residing families. Beautiful grounds.

Concord Museum, 200 Lexington Rd. (53 Cambridge Turnpike—GPS address), Concord; (978) 369-9763 or (978) 369-9609 (taped information); concordmuseum.org. Call for revolving schedule. Price: $10 for adults, $5 for children 6 to 18, free for children under 6. Americana mixed with artifacts from the time of the American Revolution to the days of Thoreau. Literary collection.

Great Brook Farm State Park, 984 Lowell St., Carlisle; (978) 369-6312; mass.gov/eea/agencies/dcr/massparks/region-north/great-brook-farm-state.html. A *Yankee Magazine* editors' pick. Holstein dairy cows on a working farm, home to the first robotic milking system. Twenty miles of trails for hiking, biking, cross-country skiing, and horseback. Great ice-cream stand. Parking fee of $2.

Gropius House, 68 Baker Bridge Rd., Lincoln; (781) 259-8098; historicnewengland.org. First home in the US designed by Walter Gropius, father of the Bauhaus school of architecture and a key figure in modern architecture of the 20th century. Admission fee.

Old Manse, 269 Monument St., Concord; (978) 369-3909; thetrustees.org. Trustees of Reservations property, historical site; famous residents were Ralph Waldo Emerson and Nathaniel Hawthorne. Admission fee.

Ralph Waldo Emerson House, 28 Cambridge Turnpike, Concord; (978) 369-2236. Thirty-minute tours mid-Apr to late Oct., Thurs through Sat 10 a.m. to 4:30 p.m., Sun and Mon holidays 1 to 4:30 p.m. Adults $8, $6 for kids 7 to 17, free for age 6 and under. Emerson's home from 1835 to 1882.

River Cruises on the Concord and Sudbury, Concord; (978) 371-1785. River cruise on a pontoon boat with meal service by reservation only.

South Bridge Boat House, 496 Main St./Route 62, Concord; (978) 369-9438. Canoe and rowboat rentals, lunch and dinner service on a pontoon boat.

Thoreau Farm, 341 Virginia Rd., Concord; (978) 451-0300; thoreaufarm.org. Open weekends early May to Oct. Tours are at 11 a.m., 1 p.m., and 3 p.m., and are $6 for adults and $4 for kids. Thoreau's birthplace.

Where to Eat

Bedford Farms Ice Cream, 68 Thoreau St., Concord; (978) 341-0000 and 18 North Rd., Bedford; (781) 275-6501; bedfordfarmsicecream.com. Homemade ice cream is served in a pretty pastoral garden setting. Sundae Party Packages for groups of 50 or more. $

Helen's Cafe, 17 Main St., Concord; (978) 369-9885. Prompt, friendly service, great breakfasts and lunches, lines during peak times. $

Lexx, 1666 Massachusetts Ave., Lexington; (781) 674-2990; lexxrestaurant.com. Global cuisine. Try the aromatic Moroccan stew. Upscale menu for adults, but the old standards are found on the kids' menu. $–$$$

Mario's Italian Restaurant, 1733 Massachusetts Ave., Lexington; (781) 861-1182; marioslexington.com. Family-style restaurant serving pasta and pizza. $

Michael's Restaurant, 208 Fitchburg Turnpike, Concord; (978) 371-1114. Specializing in Italian dishes. $$

Rain Forest Cafe, 75 Middlesex Turnpike at the Burlington Mall, Burlington; (781) 272-7555; wwwrainforestcafe.com. You don't need rain gear to eat here, but there are thunderstorms every 20 minutes, waterfalls, electronic jungle animals, and fish tanks. $–$$

Serafina Restaurant, 195 Sudbury Rd., Concord; (978) 371-9050; serafinaristorante .com. Tuscan-style food in a surprisingly chic interior (exterior is in a small shopping plaza). $–$$$

The Chateau, 43 Middlesex Turnpike, Middlesex Commons Shopping Center, Burlington; chateaurestaurant.com. Part of a chain of Italian restaurants in eastern Massachusetts. Menu features a number of entrees under 600 calories! Kids' menu. $–$$

Where to Stay

Colonial Inn and Restaurant, 48 Monument Sq., Concord; (978) 369-9200; concordscolonialinn.com. On National Register of Historic Hotels; rumored to have one haunted room (room 424), which they don't rent out without the consent of the earthbound client. Close to sights, shopping, and restaurants in charming Concord Center. $$–$$$

The Inn at Hastings Park, 2027 Massachusetts Ave., Lexington; (781) 861-0131; innathastingspark.com. Opening in 2014. Three historic buildings; 22 rooms and suites (many with fireplaces), a very family-friendly property. Artistry on the Green Restaurant with a kids' menu. $$$–$$$$

My Old House Bed and Breakfast, 12 Plainfield St., Lexington; (781) 861-7057; maryvansmyoldhouse.com. The *This Old House* television series filmed an entire season here while renovating and updating this home to a B&B in a lovely Lexington neighborhood. Children and dogs are welcome. Full breakfast. $

North Bridge Inn, 21 Monument St., Concord; (978) 371-0014 or (888) 530-0007; northbridgeinn.com. Six well-appointed suites in a great location near downtown and the local sights. Families feel very welcomed. Full breakfast comes with the room. $$–$$$

Metrowest

MetroWest (metrowestvisitors.org) lies west of Boston and east of Worcester and is the second-largest employment center in Massachusetts. The area is home to museums, wildlife refuges and sanctuaries, state parks, and historical homes. Some of the cities and towns are more rural in character, others are dense with residences, and a few are known as shopping magnets, like those found along Route 9 in Natick and Framingham.

The major corridor circumnavigating Boston is Route 95, while the Mass Turnpike leads to points west of Boston. The communities that are serviced by both Route 95 and the Mass Turnpike grew and developed as a direct result of their proximity to Boston.

Garden in the Woods/New England Wildflower Society (all ages)

180 Hemenway Rd., Framingham; (508) 877-7630; newfs.org or newenglandwild .org. Garden in the Woods is open Tues through Sun and holiday Mondays mid-Apr through Oct, 9 a.m. to 5 p.m., with extended hours Apr through early July, Thurs until 7 p.m. Admission: $12 for adults, $9 for seniors, $6 for children 3 to 17, free for kids under 3.

Largest landscaped collection of native wildflowers, shrubs, ferns, and trees in New England spread over 45 acres. Over 1,500 native plant species, and over 300 endangered or rare species are found at Garden in the Woods. Informal guided tours at 10 a.m. weekdays and at 2 p.m. weekends, free with admission. Largest wildflower selection for sale in New England and the whole Northeast. Outdoor cultural, environmental, and educational programs are sprinkled throughout the year, including nature walks, festivals, family-bonding fun, new family activity area, and birthday parties.

Great Meadows National Wildlife Refuge (all ages)

Headquarters and visitor center at 73 Weir Hill Rd., Sudbury; (978) 443-4661; secondary access to the refuge is at 181 Monson Rd., Concord; fws.gov/refuge/great _meadows. Visitor center open Mon through Fri 8 a.m. to 4 p.m. Trails are open dawn to dusk year-round. Free in Sudbury, however, there is a fee in Concord.

Walking trails for bird watching of migratory birds and diverse wildlife as well as hiking along pools and uplands bordering the Concord and Sudbury Rivers. Boating and hunting are allowed. Environmental and educational programs can be set up for groups. Dogs are not allowed.

Longfellow's Wayside Inn (all ages)

72 Wayside Inn Rd., Sudbury; (978) 443-1776 or (800) 339-1776; wayside.org.

The historic Longfellow's Wayside Inn—a Massachusetts Historic Landmark as well as being on the National Register of Historic Places—is a pleasant place to spend a night. The red clapboard building, the oldest operating inn in the country, was built in 1702, becoming an inn in 1716; Henry Ford bought it and renovated it in the early 1920s. Originally the inn was known as Howe's Tavern (1716–1861). After Henry Wadsworth Longfellow published *Tales of a Wayside Inn* and credited the inn for inspiration, the name was changed in 1897 to Longfellow's Wayside Inn. There are 10 guest rooms, two of them (original to the house) reached by a narrow staircase, all with private bath. The dining room serves all three meals (reservations recommended for dinner). On the Wayside Inn's 120-acre grounds is the Red Stone School, famous as the school that Mary and her little lamb attended; Henry Ford moved the building here from nearby Sterling, Massachusetts, during the 1920s renovation project (the schoolhouse is open daily Fri through Sun, mid-May through mid-Oct, 11:30 a.m. to 5 p.m., weather permitting). Also of interest is the gristmill (built in 1929 on-site), which grinds the meal and flour for corn muffins and wheat rolls. It's open Wed through Sun 9 a.m. to 5 p.m. Apr through Nov. The inn offers Family Fun Days (check website). Our favorite night to dine at the inn is Wednesday, when costumed musicians parade throughout the inn playing the fife and drum (mid-Apr through Sept). Don't miss the Colonial Faire and Muster, held the last Sat of Sept at the Wayside Inn's south field; it features military reenactments, fife and drum demonstrations, exhibits, crafts, and costumed interpreters.

Other Things to See & Do

Assabet River Wildlife Refuge, 680 Hudson Rd., Sudbury; (978) 562-3527; fws .gov/refuge/Assabet_River. Forest and wetlands, 15 miles of hiking and half that for biking. Hunting, fishing, birding, wildlife viewing. Exhibits and educational programs at the visitor center.

Beaver Brook Reservation, Mill Street, Belmont and Waltham; (617) 727-5380; mass.gov/eea/agencies/dcr/massparks/region-boston/beaver-brook-reservation .html. First reservation created by the DCR. A beautiful, natural habitat consisting of 59 acres of ponds, meadows, forest, and marsh (look for the scenic waterfall for a perfect picnic). A great tot play area within the reservation is the **Waverly Oaks Playground,** known for its spraying fountains and pool, climbing structures, and picnic tables.

Broadmoor Wildlife Sanctuary, 280 Eliot St., Natick; (508) 655-2296; mass audobon.org. Nature center with educational programs, 9 miles of trails on 800 acres through fields, forests, and ponds with connecting bridges over brooks and wetlands.

TopEvents in Greater Boston

- **Cambridge Carnival International,** Sept, Central and Kendall Square, Massachusetts Avenue, Cambridge; (617) 863-0476 or (617) 441-2884; cambridgecarnival.org; cambridge-usa.org

- **Boston Arts Festival,** Sept, Christopher Columbus Park, Boston; (617) 635-3911; cityofboston.gov; celebrateboston.com/boston-arts-festival.com

- **Colonial Faire and Muster,** late Sept, Longfellow's Wayside Inn, Sudbury; (978) 443-1776 or (800) 339-1776; wayside.org or sudbury ancients.org

- **Head of the Chares Regatta,** Oct, Charles River, Cambridge/Boston; (617) 868-6200 or (617) 868-5048; hocr.org

- **Three Apples Storytelling Festival,** midautumn, Bedford Center for the Arts, Bedford; (781) 287-0069; threeapples.org

- **Halloween Pet Parade,** mid-Oct, Faneuil Hall Marketplace, Boston; (617) 523-1300; faneuilhallmarketplace.com

- **Battle of the Red Tavern,** last Sat in Oct, Longfellow's Wayside Inn; (978) 443-1776; wayside.org or sudburyminutemen.org

- **Boo at the Zoo,** Oct, Stone Zoo, Stoneham; (781) 438-9517; zoonew england.org

- **Zoo Howl,** Oct, Franklin Park Zoo, Boston; (617) 989-2025; franklin parkzoo.org

- **Ballet Day,** Veteran's Day, Boston Children's Museum, 308 Congress St., Boston; (617) 426-6500; bostonchildrensmuseum.org

- ***The Nutcracker,*** Nov through early Jan, Boston Ballet, Boston; (617) 695-6950; bostonballet.org

- **Christmas Tree Lighting,** late Nov/early Dec, Boston Common, Boston; (617) 635-4505; cityofboston.gov/parks

- **Zoo Lights,** late Nov to end of Dec, Stone Zoo, Stoneham; (781) 438-5100; zoonewengland.org

- **Holiday Lighting Ceremony,** Sat before Thanksgiving, Faneuil Hall, Boston; (617) 523-1300; faneuilhallmarketplace.com

- **Blink,** late Nov to New Year's, Faneuil Hall, Boston; (617) 523-1300; faneuilhallmarketplace.com

- **Black Nativity,** Dec, Blackman Auditorium at Northeastern University, Boston; (617) 442-8614; blacknativity.org

- **Boston Tea Party Reenactment,** Dec, Old South Meeting House to Boston Harbor; (617) 482-6439; oldsouthmeetinghouse .org or osmh1.drupalgardens.com/history/boston-tea-party/ boston-tea-party-annual-reenactment

- **Newbury Street Holiday Stroll,** Dec; (617) 267-2224; newbury streetleague.org

- **First Night,** Dec 31, Boston; (617) 635-3911; firstnightboston.org

Charles River Museum of Industry, 154 Moody St., Waltham; (781) 893-5410; crmi.org. Open Thurs through Sun 10 a.m. to 5 p.m. America's first factory. Explores the textile, watch (the Waltham Watch Company had an international reputation), bicycle, automobile, and tool industries.

Cochituate State Park, 93 Commonwealth Rd., Route 30, Natick; (508) 653-9641; mass.gov/eea/agencies/dcr/massparks/region-north/cochituate-state-park.html. Canoeing and kayak rentals on three large lakes. Fishing and swimming are allowed. Fee $5.

Danforth Museum, 125 Union Ave., Framingham; (508) 620-0050; danforthmuseum .org. Open Wed and Sun noon to 5 p.m., Thurs noon to 8:30 p.m., Fri and Sat 10 a.m. to 5 p.m. Price is $11 for adults, $8 for students, **free** for kids under 12. Featuring American art and a junior gallery for families.

Girl Scout Museum at Cedar Hill, Patriots' Trail Girl Scout Council, 265 Beaver St., Waltham; (781) 893-6113 or (781) 373-4360 (museum); girlscoutseasternmass.org/ aboutus/girl-scout-museum.html. Girl Scout equipment, memorabilia, and uniforms from days past on display.

Gore Place, 52 Gore St., Waltham; (781) 894-2798; goreplace.org. Grounds open year-round dawn to dusk. Check the website for the guided-tour schedule. A historic mansion, farm, and gardens spread over 45 acres. Small animal farm. Admission fee.

Museum of World War II, Natick; (508) 651-7695 (staff) or (508) 651-7696 (to request a visit); museumofworldwarii.com. Private museum with more than 6,000 historical items relating to World War II. Tours by appointment only. **Free.**

Rose Art Museum at Brandeis University, 415 South St., Waltham; (781) 736-3434; brandeis.edu/rose. One of the largest collections of modern and contemporary art from America and Europe in New England. Specializing in art from the last half of the 20th century.

Spellman Museum of Stamps and Postal History, 235 Wellesley St. (at Regis College), Weston; (781) 768-8367; spellman.org. Open Thurs through Sun noon to 5 p.m. Admission: $8 for adults; $3 for children 16 and under with a free pack of stamps given to each child. Two million stamps from all over the world. Features a children's activities center, a museum store, a post office, and a library.

Stonehurst, 100 Robert Treat Paine Dr., Waltham; (781) 314-3290; stonehurst waltham.org. Check the website for the self-guided and guided tour schedule. Shingle-style home designed by H. H. Richardson for the Paine family, with grounds designed by Frederick Law Olmsted. Grounds open daily sunrise to sunset. Fee.

Where to Eat

Firefly's, 350 East Main St., Marlborough; (508) 357-8883; fireflysbbq.com. Old-fashioned Southern BBQ. Winner of more than 20 awards. $–$$

Lizzy's Ice Cream, 367 Moody St., Waltham; (781) 893-6677; lizzysicecream.com. Homemade, award-winning ice cream. $

Longfellow's Wayside Inn, 72 Wayside Inn Rd., Sudbury; (978) 443-1776 or (800) 339-1776; wayside.org. Fine Yankee fare in a historic setting. $–$$$

Solea Restaurant and Tapas Bar, 388 Moody St., Waltham; (781) 894-1805; solea restaurant.com. Open for lunch Thurs through Sun and dinner daily. A communal meal can be had by ordering several hot and cold tapas dishes. Our favorite was the roasted duckling with berry sauce—ummm—mouthwatering! $–$$$

Tatnuck Bookseller Cafe, 18 Lyman St., Westborough; (508) 366-4959; tatnuck .com. Book warehouse store/cool cafe combo. $

Where to Stay

Inn on the Horse Farm, 277 Old Sudbury Rd., Sudbury, (978) 443-7400 or (800) 272-2426; innonthehorsefarm.com. Inn on 9 acres, three horses who love to be fed carrots, pond, and pastures. $$–$$$

Longfellow's Wayside Inn, 72 Wayside Inn Rd., Sudbury; (978) 443-1776 or (800) 339-1776; wayside.org. Small 10-room historic inn on lovely grounds. Full breakfast. $$–$$$

Reading, Stoneham & Winchester

Reading and Stoneham (known as "the Friendly Town") are residential suburban communities less than 12 miles from Boston. Winchester is an affluent bedroom community with a small-town feel about 8 miles from Boston.

Stone Zoo (all ages)

149 Pond St., Stoneham; (781) 438-5100 or (617) 541-LION, ext. 5466; zoonew england.org. Open daily Apr through Sept, 10 a.m. to 5 p.m. (until 6 p.m. week-ends and holidays); Oct through Mar, open 10 a.m. to 4 p.m. daily. Closed Thanks-giving and Christmas Days and for special events. Admission: $9 for adults, $7 for children 2 through 12, free for children under 2. The first Sat of every month, everyone is charged the kids' price!

This 26-acre property is home to a wide variety of animals including the very popular Tennessee black bears (they were rescue animals) and the tree-dwelling white-cheeked Gibbon monkeys who don't usually like temperatures below 40°F (they go indoors!). The Treasure of the Sierra Madre exhibit is home to jaguars, cougars, and coyotes of the Southwest and northern Mexico. The touchable barnyard animals are very friendly and approachable; our favorite is the pygmy zebu from India. The kids will most likely run from exhibit to exhibit—try to keep up! For toddlers there is the Playful Paws Play group; older kids love the zoo camps and the wild adventures education programs.

Other Things to See & Do

Griffin Museum of Photography, 67 Shore Rd., Winchester; (781) 729-1158; griffinmuseum.org. Current, emerging, and well-known photographers' work on display. Photographic art exhibits, lectures, and programs.

Jordan's Furniture's IMAX, 50 Walker's Brook Dr., Reading; (781) 439-6555 or (866) 8-JORDANS, ext. 6800; jordansimaxtheatre.com. IMAX movie theater. Call or visit their website for showtimes and pricing.

Jordan's Furniture's Trapeze School of Boston, 50 Walker's Brook Dr., Reading; (781) 942-7800; boston.trapezeschool.com. "Fly like an eagle" while hooked up to safety equipment. Pricing: 1 swing for $10, 3 for $25. Classes.

South of Boston

More than a million tourists pass through "America's Hometown" each year, and for good reason. The *Mayflower II*, Plymouth Rock, and Plimoth Plantation tell the well-known story of our country's first permanent European settlers vividly, with only minor embellishments. Of the many tourist attractions that are packed into this tiny town, the rock, the ship, and the outdoor museum are by far the most interesting to kids. If you can, try to visit Plymouth during the spring or late fall—Thanksgiving is best, of course—when there are fewer tour buses. Also of keen interest are the cities of New Bedford and Fall River. New Bedford, a whaling capital and a leader in the maritime industry, can count on the New England Whaling Museum and the New Bedford Whaling National Historic Park to relay the significance of the town's ties to the sea and the importance of the fishing industry to present-day New Bedford. Fall River, a prominent mill town that produced textiles that were shipped all over the world, is now home to Battleship Cove. For more information, contact the **Greater Boston Convention and Visitors Bureau,** 2 Copley Place, Suite 105, Boston, MA 02116 (617-536-4100 or 888-SEE-BOSTON; bostonusa.com), the **Plymouth County Convention and Visitors Bureau,** 170 Water St., Suite 24, Plymouth, MA 02360 (508-747-0100 or 800-231-1620; seeplymouth.com), or the **Southeastern Massachusetts Convention and Visitors Bureau,** 794 Purchase St., New Bedford, MA 02742 (508-999-5231; visitsemass.org).

SOUTH OF BOSTON

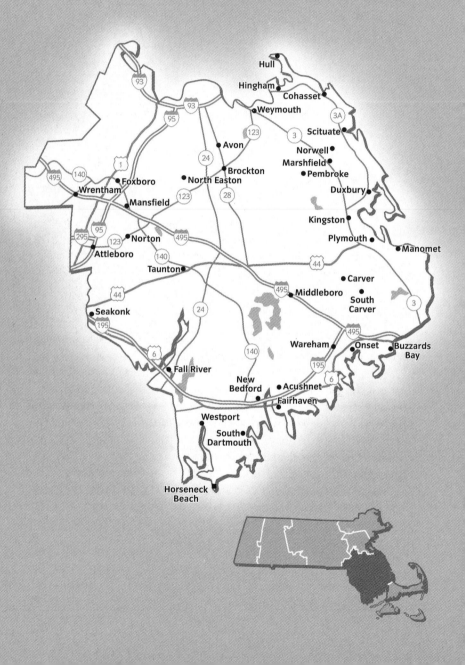

Hingham, Hull & the Upper South Shore

Shaped like an elbow, the west side of Hull has a commanding view of Boston Harbor and the Boston Harbor Islands, as does the neighboring, more high-brow town of Hingham. Wompatuck State Forest and World's End in Hingham (designed by Frederick Law Olmsted) are calming respites after an active week. Lots of activities for families in this area are water-based fun. Explore the North River in Marshfield, sunbath at Nantasket Beach, take a ferry ride to Boston, or paddle an ocean kayak. For information on Nantasket, contact the **Hull-Nantasket Chamber of Commerce** at (781) 925-9980 or hullchamber.com, and discoverhingham.com for **Discover Hingham.**

Nantasket Beach and the Nantasket Beach Reservation (all ages)

205 Nantasket Ave., Hull; (781) 925-9980; hullchamber.org (Hull Chamber of Commerce) or (781) 925-1777; mass.gov/eea/agencies/dcr/massparks/region-south/nantasket-state-park.html (Nantasket Beach Reservation), or (781) 925-0472; paragoncarousel.com (Paragon Carousel). Open year-round; $10 parking fee in season. The Paragon Carousel is open spring and fall Fri through Sun, and daily mid-June through Labor Day. Check the website for hours of operation. It is $2.50 per ride and a book of 10 passes is $20.

TopPicks South of Boston

- **Plimoth Plantation,** Plymouth
- *Mayflower II* and **Plymouth Rock,** Plymouth
- **Duxbury Beach,** Marshfield/Duxbury
- **New Bedford Whaling Museum** and the **Seaman's Bethel,** New Bedford
- **Battleship Cove** and the **Fall River Carousel,** Fall River
- **Horseneck Beach State Reservation,** Westport

Seven miles of clear Atlantic Ocean water and clean, lifeguarded beach (in season, late June to early Sept) will attract your family, as will the Paragon, a vintage carousel (only a hundred still in existence in the US) with 66 hand-turned horses and 2 Roman chariots built in 1928 by the Philadelphia Toboggan Company. Waterfront activities include a lively concert series called the Endless Summer Waterfront Festival in Sept, and the annual Chowderfest held in January. There are bathhouses, a small bandstand, and a concession stand, and the beach area has been restored to its heyday best. Nearby is a bounty of restaurants to choose from within walking distance to the beach.

Wompatuck State Park (all ages)

204 Union St., Off Route 228, Hingham; (781) 749-7160; friendsofwompatuck.org or mass.gov/eea/agencies/dcr/massparks/region-south/wompatuck-state-park .html. Open daily dawn to dusk. Admission to Wompatuck State Park is free.
Wompatuck State Park, named after an Indian chieftain from the colonial period who deeded the land to the settlers, covers some 3,526 acres and offers 262 campsites (some with trailer hookups) and shower facilities (call Reserve America; 877-422-6762; reserveamerica.com for campsite reservations). Biking paths are threaded throughout the park (12 miles of bike trails), and there is a boat ramp for boating fun (flat-bottomed rowboats only). Other popular forms of recreation are cross-country skiing, fishing, horseback riding, and hiking through a system of woodland trails beyond the bike paths. Interpretive programs are offered. Wompatuck State Park is home to Mount Blue Spring, which is a drinkable source of water. Try it—it is refreshing!

World's End Reservation (all ages)

250 Martins Ln., Hingham; (781) 740-6665; thetrustees.org. Open daily 8 a.m. to sunset (open at 7 a.m. weekends). Admission: $6 for adults, free for children 12 and under.
World's End Reservation is managed by the Trustees of Reservations and has breathtaking panoramic views of Hingham, Hull, and the Boston skyline. World's End is one of 34 islands and four peninsulas in the Boston Harbor Islands National Recreational Area (but the trustees own and maintain it). Four drumlins (hills) created by glaciation are found on the 251-acre site laced with 4.5 miles of trails for fairly easy walking, snowshoeing, cross-country skiing, or horseback riding along the rocky coast, verdant meadows, and forests. This is also a birding site, especially during the migration seasons in the spring and fall, and numerous butterflies are attracted to the vegetation here.

Other Things to See & Do

East Coast Hui, 30 Peggotty Beach Rd., Scituate; (617) 548-7988; eastcoasthui.com. Learn to surf.

Hingham Ferry to Boston, (617) 227-4321 (Boston Harbor Cruises); bostonharbor cruises.com (click on "Commuters"). Year-round ferry service.

Hull Lifesaving Museum, 1117 Nantasket Ave., Hull; (781) 925-LIFE; lifesaving museum.org. US lifesaving-station-turned-museum. Educational programming. Admission: $5 for adults, **free** for children 18 and under.

Mary's Boat Livery, 2205 Main St. (Route 3A), Marshfield; (781) 837-2322; marys boatlivery.com. Rent a powerboat and explore the North or South River.

Nantasket Kayak, 48 George Washington Blvd., Steamboat Wharf Marina, Hull (781) 962-4899; nantasketkayaks.com. Kayak and stand-up paddleboards. Rentals and lessons.

South Shore Music Circus, 130 Sohier St., Cohasset; (781) 383-9850; musiccircus .com. Children's summer theater productions and concerts.

South Shore Natural Science Center, 48 Jacobs Ln., Norwell; (781) 659-2559; southshorenaturalsciencecenter.org. Programs for children and their families, nature trails (open sunrise to sunset), and animal exhibits.

Herring Runs

Sites to view the herring returning to their spawning grounds:

- **Herring Run Park,** Route 14, Pembroke
- **Herring Run,** Jackson Sq., Weymouth
- **Island Creek** at Route 3A, Duxbury
- **Jones River** at Elm Street, Kingston
- **Town Brook** at Plimoth Grist Mill, Plymouth

Winslow House, 634 Careswell St., Route 139, Marshfield; (781) 837-5753; winslow house.org. Open mid-May through mid-Oct. Owned by several generations of Winslows (who were public servants or in the military) and Daniel Webster.

Where to Stay & Eat   ⊖ 🍴

Cohasset Harbor Resort, 124 Elm St., Cohasset; (781) 383-6650; cohassetharbor resort.com. Informal, cozy hotel, 50 rooms, newly renovated in spring of 2014, on the harbor, 3 restaurants to satisfy all tastes; the Olde Salt House Restaurant is completely alfresco waterfront dining and Brisa's Tapas is a great option for the little ones with smaller appetites. Indoor pool. Continental breakfast with all rooms. $–$$$

Nantasket Beach Resort, 45 Hull Shore Dr., Nantasket; (781) 925-4500; nantasket beachhotel.com. Great location, steps to the beach, the **Paragon Grill** fine-dining restaurant, bayside fitness, hot tub, and pool. $–$$$

Red Lion Inn, 71 South Main St., Cohasset; (781) 383-1704; redlioninn.propoohd .com. Historical inn (a former stagecoach and Underground Railroad stop), nicely appointed with a restaurant, bar, and pool. $$$

Duxbury

Heading south of Boston during the summer? In their Cape Cod–bound haste, many people miss Duxbury Beach, one of the finest barrier beaches along the Atlantic coast. On your way there, drive or walk across the Powder Point Bridge, the longest wooden bridge on the East Coast. The pedestrian portion of the bridge is wide, allowing room for walkers to pass behind the fishing enthusiasts who gather along the bridge.

Duxbury Beach, aka Blakeman's Public Beach (all ages)   🌊

260 Gurnet Rd., at the end of Route 139 (accessed through the Green Harbor section of Marshfield); (781) 837-3112; duxburybeach.com. Lifeguards are on duty from late May through early Sept 10 a.m. to 4 p.m., weather permitting, but the beach is open from 9 a.m. to 8 p.m. daily. Parking is $15. No dogs are allowed. This 6-mile-long stretch of sand and beach grass is a favorite of locals; voted #1 Beach in *Boston Magazine*. The old-fashioned, full-service bathhouse is a great find for car-bound travelers. Spend the day on the beach, then wash the sand and salt water off the kids (and yourselves) before returning to the car. The beach has

It's **for the Birds!**

Best bird-watching bets are:

- **The Daniel Webster Wildlife Sanctuary,** Winslow Cemetery Road, Marshfield

- **North Hill Marsh Wildlife Sanctuary,** Mayflower Street, Duxbury

- **North River Wildlife Sanctuary,** 2000 Main St., Marshfield

- **World's End Reservation,** 250 Martins Ln., Hingham

a good snack bar, lunchroom, and an outdoor grill restaurant (Blakeman's at Duxbury Beach, open mid-June to Labor Day Tues through Sun from 5 to 8 p.m.).

King Caesar House (ages 8 and up)
120 King Caesar Rd., Duxbury; (781) 934-6106; duxburyhistory.org. Open July through Labor Day, Wed through Sun 1 to 4 p.m. Admission: $5 for adults, $2 for seniors and students, free for children under 6.
This is the Federal-style home of Ezra Weston, a successful shipping magnate of the 19th century. Original wharves are located in Bumpus Park, where Ezra's ship, *The Hope,* was built. The main house has a children's bedroom with a collection of period dolls and toys on view that is fascinating to kids. A knot herb garden and a perennial garden are also on the property.

Other Things to See & Do

Art Complex Museum, 189 Alden St., Duxbury; (781) 934-6634; artcomplex.org. Wed through Sun 1 to 4 p.m. **Free.** Founded by the Weyerhauser family. Contemporary Art, Asian art, Shaker objects, works on paper, and American paintings. The kids will enjoy the tea ceremonies (call for schedule).

Captain Gershom Bradford House, 931 Tremont St., Route 3A, Duxbury; (781) 934-6106; duxburyhistory.org. Open Sun from July to Labor Day from 1 to 4 p.m. Admission: $3 for adults, $1 for seniors and students, free for children under 6. Sea captain's home dating from 1800s; everything within is original to Captain Bradford. Four generations of Bradfords lived here.

John Alden House, 105 Alden St., Duxbury; (781) 934-9092; alden.org. Open Wed through Sat noon to 4 p.m. (the last tour is at 3:30 p.m.) June through Sept. Price: $8 for adults, $5 for kids 3 to 18, **free** for kids under 3. Home of *Mayflower* Pilgrims John and Priscilla Alden.

Myles Standish Monument State Reservation, Crescent St., Duxbury; (508) 747-5360; mass.gov/eea/agencies/dcr/massparks/region-south/myles-standish-monument-state-reservation.html. Myles Standish Monument, perched on a hill with panoramic views, has 125 steps to the top. Walking trails and picnic tables.

Nathaniel Winsor Jr. House, 479 Washington St., Duxbury; (781) 934-6106; duxburyhistory.org. First floor open to the public year-round from 9 a.m. to 4 p.m. weekdays. **Free.** Federal mansion done in period furnishings. Headquarters of the Duxbury Rural and Historical Society.

Amazing
Massachusetts Facts

- America's oldest lighthouse is on Little Brewster Island off the coast of Hull.
- First Parish Church (19 Town Sq., Plymouth) is the oldest continuous ministry in New England.
- Old Ship Church (107 Main St., Hingham) is the oldest wooden church in the US that has been in continuous use.
- The first canal in America was dug in the 1630s by the Pilgrims. It connected Plymouth Bay to Green Harbor in Marshfield.
- The first radio program in the world was broadcast in Marshfield on Christmas Eve 1906.
- The 1794 Court House Museum in Town Square (top of St. Leydon Street) in Plymouth is the oldest wooden courthouse in the country.
- The Forefathers Monument (170 Allerton St.) in Plymouth is the largest solid granite monument in the US. The Myles Standish Monument, Crescent Street, Duxbury, marks the site where his home once stood.

Where to Eat

Farfar's Danish Ice Cream Shop, 272 St. George St., Duxbury; (781) 934-5152; farfarsicecream.com. Delicious ice cream made daily on the premises. $

Milepost Restaurant and Tavern, 581 Tremont St., Duxbury; (781) 934-6801; milepostrestaurant.com. Colonial atmosphere, piano player Fri and Sat nights with traditional New England fare. $$–$$$

Wildflower Cafe, 8 Chestnut St., Duxbury; (781) 934-7814; wildflowercafe.us. Great for breakfast and lunch; corn bread comes with all breakfasts, and lunch features homemade soups. Open for dinner Thurs through Sat nights. $–$$

Where to Stay

Winsor House Inn, 390 Washington St., Duxbury; (781) 934-0991; winsorhouseinn .com. Restaurant and pub on-site. Historic home with 3 rooms and a carriage house suite 1 block from the beach. Children of all ages are welcome. $$–$$$

Plymouth

When you arrive in Plymouth, your first stop should be one of the two excellent tourist information centers. Adjacent to the highway, the **Massachusetts Tourist Information Center** (exit 5 on Route 3 South; 508-746-1150; seeplymouth .com), aka the Plymouth County Convention and Visitors Bureau, carries an excellent selection of books, maps, and brochures. The parking lot is large, and there are clean restrooms and picnic tables. The hard-to-stump staff is happy to answer your questions and point you in the right direction. Open year-round daily from 9 a.m. to 3 p.m. with extended hours to 5 p.m. in the summer for staffed visitor information (the rest area is open 24 hours a day) The **Plymouth Visitor Information Center,** 130 Water St., Plymouth, MA 02361 (508-747-7525 or 800-872-1620; open Apr through Nov 9 a.m. to 5 p.m. with extended hours in the summer), and Destination Plymouth (508-747-7533 or 800-872-1620; seeplymouth.com), at 134 Court St., open Mon through Fri year-round, are near most of the sites your family came to Plymouth to see. The selection of tourist literature at the Plymouth Visitor Information Center is good, the staff is helpful, and the restrooms are conveniently located. Open daily Apr to Nov, 9 a.m. to 5 p.m.; extended hours in the summer and at other busy times.

Colonial Lantern Tours (ages 6 and up)

Different meeting spots depending upon the tour chosen, Plymouth; (774) 454-8126 (reservations); lanterntours.com. Offered from Apr through Nov. Two public tours nightly; reservations recommended. Special themed tours are given at Halloween and Thanksgiving, plus the Christmas Holiday Stroll. Price: $12 for adults, $10 for children 6 to 16, free for children under 6. Buy your tickets online, at the John Carver Inn, or at the visitor center on Water Street.

As you carry your punched-tin lantern through the streets of town, you are given a glimpse of Plymouth past and present. This guided walking tour, given the much coveted AAA rating, covers about a mile circuit about town and lasts for 1.5 hours. Daily tours give the history of the town (the Historic Colonial Lantern Tour) or recount spine-tingling tales of Plymouth (the Ghost and Legends Tour). The owner is a former teacher and educator, so the tours emphasize the history of Plymouth.

Dead of Night Ghost Tours (ages 6 and up)

31 North St., Plymouth; (508) 866-5111 or (508) 277-2371; deadofnightghosttours .com. Open daily year-round in the evening. Prices: $13 for adults and $10 for children 12 and under. Purchase tickets at 31 North St., the Plymouth Visitor Center at 130 Water St., or from the hearse by Plymouth Rock before the tour starts.

Paranormal investigators lead exciting guided tours of discovery, tracking down the ghosts of historical figures. Use of paranormal equipment and devices helps the guides and the group become ghost hunters. You are encouraged to bring your camera to capture your sightings. Four themed tours are offered that give you background on the history and customs of Plymouth. Our family's favorite was the Combo Tour; a 2-hour guided tour uniting their famous Twilight Lantern Ghost Tour with a visit to two haunted historical houses for $20. You can also choose to spend the night in one of the homes for an extra fee. Alas, we did not have the courage!

The Jabez Howland House (all ages)

33 Sandwich St., Plymouth; (508) 746-9590; seeplymouth.org. Open Memorial Day through Columbus Day, then Thanksgiving and Thanksgiving weekend, 10 a.m. to 4:30 p.m., tours every half hour. Admission: $5 for adults, $2 for children 6 to 12, free for children under 6.

The Jabez Howland House is the only surviving house in Plymouth that is known to have been inhabited by *Mayflower* passengers John and Elizabeth Howland.

The tour lasts for a half hour and is extremely informative. Alec Baldwin, Humphrey Bogart, Ralph Waldo Emerson, Henry Wadsworth Longfellow, Dr. Benjamin Spock, Joseph Smith Jr., Henry Cabot Lodge Jr., Franklin Delano Roosevelt, George H. W. Bush, George W. Bush, and Sarah Palin are some of the notable descendents of the Howlands. The Jabez Howland House is on the National Register of Historic Places.

Mayflower Society Museum and Library (all ages)

4 Winslow St., Plymouth; (508) 746-2590 (museum) or (508) 746-3188 (library); the-mayflowersociety.com. The museum is open Fri through Sun from Memorial Day to mid-June, 11 a.m. to 4 p.m.; daily end of Apr through Oct, 11 a.m. to 4 p.m. The library is open year-round Mon through Fri from 10 a.m. to 3:30 p.m. for research, except holidays. Admission for the museum is $5 for adults, $1 for children 6 to 16, and free for children 6 and under and residents of Plymouth. The library charges $5 for nonmembers. *TIP:* Call ahead if the temperature peaks; since there is no air-conditioning, the museum may be closed.

The museum, a beautiful white building with a sweeping double staircase, offers a mother lode of history. The original owner of the house (built in 1754) was Edward Winslow (a great-grandson of the pilgrim Edward Winslow), who fled to Canada (Halifax, Nova Scotia) along with other Tories when the Revolutionary War began. The author and transcendentalist Ralph Waldo Emerson was married in the front parlor in 1835. The Mayflower Society Library, just down the driveway from the museum, is a wonderful resource if you're interested in genealogy. The building is the headquarters of the General Society of Mayflower Descendants, which has extensive archives and libraries of information that are open to the public. Watch for the Pilgrim Progress the first four Fridays in Aug at 6 p.m. and Thanksgiving morning, when a costumed group, representing the Pilgrims who survived the first winter, parade through many historic locales in Plymouth.

Mayflower II (all ages)

State Pier on the Waterfront, across from 74 Water St., Plymouth; (508) 746-1622; plimoth.org. Open end of Mar through the Sun following Thanksgiving 9 a.m. to 5 p.m. Admission: $10 for adults, $7 for children 5 to 12, free for children under 5, free for children 4 and under unless part of a school group. Special rates if you visit two or more sites. The Heritage Pass includes the *Mayflower II*, Plimoth Plantation and the Plimoth Grist Mill for $35 for adults and $21 for children 5 to

Boat Excursions in Plymouth

- **Captain John Whale Watch and Deep Sea Fishing,** 10 Town Wharf; (508) 746-2643 or (800) 242-AHOY; captjohn.com. Floating classroom (in springtime only), with a naturalist and a professional marine biologist onboard with every whale watch. Whale-watch tour price: $47 for adults, $29 for children under 12. Discount coupon on website. Deep-sea fishing prices: $55 for adults and $40 for kids 3 to 12 for a full day; $38 for adults and $30 for kids 3 to 12 for a half day; free for kids under 3. Late-fall fishing trips are $95 per person. Capt. John's will help you clean and bag your fish.

- **Captain Tim Brady and Sons,** 1 Town Wharf; (508) 746-4809; fish chart.com. Sportfishing, deep-sea fishing, or whale-watching tours daily from Apr to Nov on the *Mary Elizabeth.*

- **Pilgrim Belle,** 77 Water St., *Mayflower II* State Pier; (508) 747-3434; pilgrimbellecruises. Seventy-five-minute day cruise from mid-May to Oct or 90-minute sunset cruise of Plymouth Harbor in July and Aug on a Mississippi-style paddlewheeler. Sunday brunches and dinner theme cruises. Prices vary depending on the cruise.

- **Plymouth Cruises aboard Lobster Tales,** 9 Town Wharf (East end of Route 44); (508) 746-5342; plymouthcruises.com. The Lobster excursion gives a harbor tour of historic Plymouth, followed by the hauling of lobster traps and an examination of the catch (crabs,

12. The Combination Ticket gives you access to the *Mayflower II* and Plimoth Plantation for $29.95 for adults and $19 for children 5 to 12. Children 4 or under are free unless booked as a school group. *Note:* Your Combination Ticket may be used at the Plimoth Plantation for two consecutive days and is also good for a third day at the *Mayflower II* within one year of purchase.

Near Plymouth Rock is the *Mayflower II*, a reproduction of the original ship that brought the Pilgrims to Plymouth. The costumed staff knows all sorts of facts

fish, and lobster). Touch tank onboard. Price: $16 for adults, $12 for children under 12. From May through Sept there is a family-oriented ice-cream cruise on Wed and Fri nights. Wine-tasting cruises sail Thurs nights in July and Aug at $55 per person. The Pirate Cruise is recommended for ages 4 to 11. Kids don pirate hats and makeup to role-play the lives of pirates. An enemy pirate vessel has stolen a treasure and your job is to recapture the booty. A celebration ensues after a battle with the enemy and the return of the plunder with buccaneer brew, dancing, music, and singing. Price: $19 per person.

- **Plymouth to Provincetown Express Ferry,** 77 Water St., Mayflower II State Pier; (508) 747-2400; provincetownferry.com. Round-trip pricing $44 adults, $25 for children under 12. One-way is $35 and bikes are $5. Narrated tour of Plymouth Harbor. Leave Plymouth at 10 a.m. and arrive in Provincetown at 11:30 a.m. Leave Provincetown at 4:30 p.m. and arrive in Plymouth at 6 p.m.

- **Plymouth Watersports and Charter Fishing,** 23 Town Wharf Dr.; (508) 747-1577; plymouthwatersport.com. Boat, kayak, flyboard, and Jet Ski rentals. Beach ferry to Plymouth beach and water taxi service. Charter fishing.

- **Plymouth Whale Watching,** 77 Water St., Mayflower II State Pier; (508) 747-3434; plymouthwhalewatching.com. Tickets: Adults are $43 and kids are $25. Original whale-watching company with naturalist onboard.

about the ship, which seems astonishingly small when you think about the 102 people who crowded onto it during its first journey from England to America. Allow approximately 1 hour to see everything including the dockside exhibits. This is a self-guided tour, but there are Pilgrim crew members, and on occasion Wampanoag staff members, to answer your questions.

Pilgrim Hall Museum (all ages)

75 Court St., Plymouth; (508) 746-1620; pilgrimhallmuseum.org. Open daily, Feb through Dec 9:30 a.m. to 4:30 p.m., closed in Jan and on Christmas Day. Admission: $8 for adults, $5 for children 6 to 15 (family rate of $25), under 6 free, and free for residents of Plymouth. Free parking.

The Pilgrim Hall Museum is the oldest continuously operating American museum (in operation since 1824). The museum holds the largest existing collection of Pilgrim possessions, including Myles Standish's sword, John Alden's bible, and William Bradford's chairs. The only known contemporaneous painting (the portrait was painted from a live figure) of a *Mayflower* passenger, Edward Winslow, is here too. Ask at the information desk for the treasure hunt for kids—a little prize is given at the end.

Plimoth Grist Mill and Gift Shop (all ages)

6 Spring Ln., Plymouth; (508) 747-4544; plimoth.org. Admission: Adults are $6 and children 5 to 12 are $4.50. Special rates if you visit two or more sites. The Heritage Pass includes the Plimoth Plantation, the *Mayflower II*, and the Plimoth Grist Mill for $35 for adults and $21 for children 5 to 12. The Combination Ticket visits Plimoth Plantation and the Plimoth Grist Mill for $29.95 for adults and $19 for children 5 to 12. Children 4 and under are free unless part of a school group. *Note:* Your Combination Ticket may be used at the Plimoth Plantation for two consecutive days and is also good for a third day at the Plimoth Grist Mill within one year of purchase.

Idyllic site just a short walk from the waterfront and the *Mayflower II*. Tour the working mill (a reproduction), which demonstrates the corn-grinding methods of the Pilgrims. Call (508) 746-1622, ext. 8242, to check if the mill will be operating on the day of your visit. Pop into the gift shop to purchase cornmeal and sampe (also known as grits), then relax on the deck with a snack while observing the wildlife on Town Brook and the ponds beyond in Brewster Gardens.

Plimoth Plantation (all ages)

Route 3A,137 Warren Ave., Plymouth; (508) 746-1622; plimoth.org. Open mid-Mar through the Sun following Thanksgiving daily, 9 a.m. to 5 p.m. Special events are ongoing in the winter and Feb school vacation. Admission: $25.95 for adults, $15 for children 5 to 12, free for children under 5. Special rates if you visit two or more sites. The Heritage Pass includes the Plimoth Plantation, the *Mayflower II*, and the Plimoth Grist Mill for $35 for adults and $21 for children 5 to 12. The Combination Ticket visits Plimoth Plantation and either the *Mayflower II* or the Plimoth

Grist Mill for $29.95 for adults and $19 for children 5 to 12. Children 4 or under are free unless booked as a school group. *Note:* Your Combination Ticket may be used at the Plimoth Plantation for two consecutive days and is also good for a third day at the *Mayflower II* within one year of purchase. Ask about applicable discounts. The Patuxet Cafe at the Henry Hornblower II Visitor Center features Colonial English and Native Cultures entrees. A museum shop is also in the visitor center. Plimoth Plantation is 3 miles south of the *Mayflower*. Free parking.

One of New England's best living museums is Plimoth Plantation. An introductory 14-minute film (located at the visitor center) created by the History Channel will orient you to the museum. Budget at least half a day to see this remarkable reproduction of a 17th-century English village. It is populated by authentically costumed people who play, convincingly, the parts of the residents. Ask them questions about their clothes, their chores, what they do for fun, what they eat, how they survive without indoor plumbing—whatever comes to mind.

The Wampanoag Homesite, comprising two longhouses and a weetu, is interpreted by native Wampanoag staff in traditional dress. Massasoit, the Wampanoag chief, sent Hobbamock and his family to live near the Pilgrims, teach them to survive, translate and interpret, and keep track of their doings.

At the Craft Center, artisans re-create crafts using the same materials and many of the same tools that were used in the 1600s.

Visitors will find rare and minor breeds of 17th-century bloodlines of farm animals scattered throughout the English Village and the Nye Barn. "Rare breeds" denotes less than 2,000 of the breed exist in the world today and fewer than 200 of the breed live in the US. Petting of the animals is allowed (but from your side of the fence!).

The best day of the year to visit the plantation is Thanksgiving, of course; call ahead for a meal reservation. The gift shop has a large stock of books about Plymouth, the indigenous people of New England, and the Pilgrims' lives and times. Go on the website for the calendar of events and brochures; ask about children's activities at the Family Discovery Center and educational programming. Dining events are themed: Eat Like a Pilgrim with 17th-century manners; A Taste of Two Cultures with a Native and Pilgrim menu; the Wampanoag Social Feast is a traditional native meal; and the 1627 Harvest Dinner with the Pilgrims

Recommended Children's Books
on Plymouth and the Pilgrim Story

The First Thanksgiving by Jean Craighead George, illustrated by Thomas Locker
The Pilgrims of Plimoth written and illustrated by Marcia Sewall
Sarah Morton's Day: A Day in the Life of a Pilgrim Girl by Kate Waters

samples the food, entertainment, and table settings of the day hosted by a Pilgrim interpreter in costume speaking in 17th-century dialect.

Richard Sparrow House (all ages)

42 Summer St., Plymouth; (508) 747-1240; sparrowhouse.com/SparrowMain. Open daily Apr through Christmas Eve 10 a.m. to 5 p.m.; daily Jan through Mar, Thurs through Sat 10 a.m. to 5 p.m. Closed Easter, July 4, Thanksgiving, and Christmas. Admission: $2 for adults, $1 for children.

Built in 1640, the Richard Sparrow House is now Plymouth's oldest surviving wood-frame house. The sparsely furnished house gives visitors a view of early Pilgrim life in an authentic setting.

Plymouth Rock (all ages)

Across from 74 Water St. in Pilgrim Memorial State Park, Plymouth; (508) 747-5360; mass.gov/eea/agencies/dcr/massparks/region-south/pilgrim-memorial-state-park.html. Open year-round dawn to dusk. Free.

As any schoolchild in America can tell you, the first European settlers in Plymouth stepped off the *Mayflower* onto this rock in 1620. Considering its prominence in American history, the size of the rock may disappoint you; it's a rather ordinary-looking boulder. Nevertheless, it's the number-one tourist attraction in Plymouth.

Priscilla Beach Theatre (all ages)

796 Rocky Hill Rd., Manomet; (508) 224-4888; pbtheatre.org. Open June through mid-Sept and weekends the rest of the year.

The Priscilla Beach Theatre (a 200-seat barn theater) is the country's oldest summer-stock playhouse. The theater also runs a performing arts workshop for kids (two-week programs; everything culminates in four performances). Call ahead for show schedules and for more information about the summer workshops.

Other Things to See & Do

Bettyann's Cranberry Harvest Tours, Plymouth Visitor Information Center at the Rotary, Plymouth; (508) 801-2300; cranberrytours.com. One-and-a-half-hour tour of the cranberry bogs and the harvesting of the crop.

1809 Hedge House, 126 Water St., Plymouth; (508) 746-0012; plymouthantiquarian society.org/historic. Open Wed through Sun, June to Aug, 2 to 6 p.m. Museum house from the Federal period filled with decorative art, furnishings, toys, China Trade treasures, paintings, and textiles from the 1800s.

Heliops Helicopter, 226 South Meadow Rd. (mailing address), Plymouth; (781) 934-7079 or (617) 571-6117; heliops.com. Fly out of Plymouth Airport for tours of Boston and the South Shore. Seats four passengers; weight restrictions.

Beaches in Plymouth

- **Nelson Memorial Beach,** 255 Water St. Good swimming, free parking, and a playground.

- **Plymouth Long Beach,** 130 Warren Ave., Route 3A. Lifeguarded beach with snack bar and bathhouse. Parking fee: $15 on weekends, $10 on weekdays.

- **Stephen's Field Park,** 132R Sandwich St. (1 mile south of Plymouth Center), just off Route 3A. Free parking, a small duck pond, a beach, tennis courts, picnic tables, and a playground.

- **Whitehorse Beach,** Taylor Avenue. Lifeguard, no restrooms, free parking.

- **Morton Pond Park,** 35 Summer St. Lifeguards and bathhouse. Walk or bike around the pond. Great for younger kids. One mile from downtown.

Imagination Island, 12 Resnik Rd., Plymouth; (508) 747-7447; imaginationislandusa .com. Open Mon through Sat 10 a.m. to 5 p.m. and Sun 11 a.m. to 5 p.m. **Free** for adults and children under 1. Weekdays $10, weekends, school vacations, and holidays $12. Indoor play center (5,500 square feet) geared for the under-8 set awarded the "Best of the Best" by *Parents* magazine.

Jenney Museum, 48 Summer St., Plymouth; (508) 747-4544; jenneymuseum.org. Historical museum offering walking tours of Plymouth.

Little Shoes, 359 Court St., Plymouth; (508) 747-2226. Good selection of specially priced children's shoes below regular retail.

Mayflower Brewing Company, 12 Resnik Rd., Plymouth; (508) 746-2674; may flowerbrewing.com. Twenty-minute tour of the brewing process on Sat from 11 a.m. to 3 p.m. with a tasting. Tastings (no tours) on Thurs and Fri.

Native Plymouth Tours, Plymouth: (774) 454-7792; nativeplymouthtours.com. Tour of Plymouth given by Native American guides.

Plimoth Cinema at Plimoth Plantation, 77 Water St., Plymouth; (508) 746-1622; pli moth.org. Daily showings of first run independent films at 4:30 p.m. or 7 p.m.

Plymouth Bay Winery, 114 Water St. Rear, Plymouth; (508) 746-2100; plymouth baywinery.com. Tastings of wine made from locally grown native grapes and berries. Reservations encouraged.

Plymouth Memorial Hall, 83 Court St., Plymouth; (508) 830-4087; memorialhall .com Modern, 1,350-seat performing arts center and concert hall. Call for the sched- ule of events.

Plymouth Pilgrims, Forges Field, 83 Jordan Rd., Plymouth; (401) 255-1049; pilgrims baseball.com. The New England Collegiate Baseball League; home games June through Aug at 6:30 p.m.

1749 Spooner House, 27 North St., Plymouth; (508) 746-0012; plymouthantiquarian society.org/historic. Open Thurs to Sat 2 to 6 p.m. June to Aug. Mid-18th-century home occupied by generations of the same family for more than 200 years.

1677 Harlow Old Fort House, 119 Sandwich St., Plymouth; (508) 746-0012; plymouth antiquariansociety.org/historic. Seventeenth-century period Pilgrim home open Thurs 10 a.m. to 3 p.m. June through Aug. Colonial home skills and crafts are represented and interpreted. Admission.

Where to Eat

Cabby Shack, 30 Town Wharf, Plymouth; (508) 746-5354; cabbyshack.com. Fish a specialty (but there is variety on their menu). Open deck seating when weather is accommodating. Entertainment. Little Minnow (kids) menu. $–$$$

Cupcake Charlie's, 6 Town Wharf, Plymouth; (508) 747-9225; cupcakecharlies.com. Try the chocolate raspberry surprise! $

East Bay Grille, 173 Water St., Town Wharf, Plymouth; (508) 746-9751; eastbaygrille .com. Waterfront, views of the harbor. Casual dining. $$–$$$

Lobster Hut, 25 Town Wharf, Plymouth; (508) 746-2270; lobsterhutplymouth.com. Lobster in the rough with great views of the Plymouth Bay breakwater. $–$$

Peaceful Meadows Ice Cream, 170 Water St. (Village Landing Marketplace), Plymouth; (508) 746-2362; peacefulmeadows.com. Other locations in Carver and Middleborough. Homemade ice cream. $

Star of Siam, 589 State Rd., Route 3A, Manomet; (508) 224-3771; starofsiamplymouth .com. An excellent take-out Thai restaurant (with a few tables outside in the summer) in the Manomet area of Plymouth, just a few miles south of Plymouth's Long Beach. $–$$$

Where to Stay

Auberge Gladstone, 1 Vernon St., Plymouth; (508) 830-1890 or (866) 722-1890; aubergegladstone.com. Walking distance to historic downtown (1 block from Plymouth Rock), seasonal harbor views, family rooms, outdoor Jacuzzi. Tasteful and comfortable. A continental option is offered. $–$$

The John Carver Inn, 25 Summer St., Plymouth; (508) 746-7100 or (888) 906-6181; johncarverinn.com. A large hotel/motel in the middle of town, with a themed Pilgrim pool and the Hearth and Kettle Restaurant. $–$$$

Pilgrim Sands, 150 Warren Ave./Route 3A, Plymouth; (508) 747-0900 or (800) 729-SANDS; pilgrimsands.com. On Long Beach, near the Plimoth Plantation. Double rooms or efficiencies; call ahead to request an efficiency apartment. There are two pools—one indoors, one outdoors, plus a private beach. Free continental breakfast. $–$$

Carver, South Carver & Middleborough

Along Route 58 in Carver (and on many back roads in the area as well), your family may see some of the state's cranberry bogs. Half of the country's cranberry crop comes from the marshy, sandy bogs in this area, and cranberries are Massachusetts's number-one agricultural product. When it's harvest time (mid-Sept through early Nov), the farmers use machines to shake the berries from their vines. They corral the berries into large crimson islands, then use enormous vacuum hoses to scoop the harvest into trucks. Middleborough is the cranberry capital of the world, as well as a great place to go antiquing.

Edaville Railroad (under 10)

5 Pine St. (GPS address), Route 58, Carver; (508) 866-8190 or (877) EDAVILLE; edaville.com. Call for schedule and pricing or look on the Edaville Railroad website (*Note:* Only open for special themed events sprinkled throughout the year; pricing changes depending upon the event).

Ellis D. Atwood, whose initials (EDA) gave birth to the name Edaville, built the railroad to run 5 miles into cranberry country to serve his cranberry business in the 1940s. A regional landmark from the 1950s through the 1990s, Edaville has been revived as a vacation destination for families. Don't miss the 2-mile narrow-gauge railroad ride (it takes about 20 minutes) through the cranberry bog, lakes, and countryside. Today Edaville Railroad is a family amusement park with trains, 13 vintage amusement rides, a carousel, a museum, and the Cranberry World Experience filled with classic cars, cranberry harvesting tools and apparatus, and Ellis's Playhouse (an indoor play area). Hungry? There are plenty of venues to fill up at; try K.C.'s Cafe, the Choo-Choo Barbecue, or one of the many snack bars.

Myles Standish State Forest (all ages)

Entrances at 194 Cranberry Rd., South Carver or Long Pond Rd., Plymouth; (508) 866-2526; mass.gov/eea/agencies/dcr/massparks/region-south/myles-standish-state-forest.html. The camping fee of $12 per night for residents ($14 for out of state) includes showers. There is a $5 parking fee to swim at College Pond.

Bike, hike, fish, or swim at Myles Standish State Forest, just a 20-minute drive from Plymouth. The 14,635-acre park was Massachusetts's first state forest when it was created in 1916. There are 13 miles of quiet walking trails, and the highlight of the park is the 15 miles of bike paths and the 35 miles of horseback-riding paths. The forest has more than 20 ponds (College Pond is designated for swimming; the rest are for fishing or for the campsite visitors), and lots of picnic spots in the forests and meadows. There are more than 400 tent/RV sites (no hookups) with restrooms and hot showers, plus fireplaces and picnic tables at each site. Each camping area has its own swimming pond. Our family's favorite is the Curlew Camping Area—it reminds us of lazy summer days à la Huck Finn! For reservations call Reserve America at (877) 422-6762 or book online at reserveamerica.com.

Other Things to See & Do

Middleboro Historical Museum, Jackson Street, Middleborough; (508) 947-1969; middleboroughhistoricalassociation.org. Mr. and Mrs. Tom Thumb of circus fame donated their collection of miniatures. Seven-building complex.

Where to Eat

Dave's Diner, 390 West Grove St., Middleborough; (508) 923-4755; davesdiner.com. A Phantom Gourmet favorite. Dave's Diner brings you back to the nostalgia of the 1950s. Comfort food. $

Little Red Smokehouse, 145 South Main St., Carver; (508) 465-0018; littleredsmokehouse.com. Closest thing to Southern BBQ down-home cookin' in the region. $-$$

Where to Stay

On Cranberry Pond, 43 Fuller St., Middleborough; (508) 946-0768; oncranberrypond.com. Large cape (11,000 square feet) with three ponds on the property on a working cranberry bog. Wintertime fun includes ice fishing, ice skating, snowshoeing, and cross-country skiing on groomed trails. Chickens provide farm-fresh eggs for breakfast (children can go out and collect them). Featured on the *Food Network* and *Martha Stewart* magazines. Ages 7 and above please. $$

TopEvents South of Boston

January–August

- **The Moby Dick Marathon Reading,** early Jan, New Bedford Whaling Museum, New Bedford; (508) 997-0046; whalingmuseum.org

- **Plimoth Farmers' Market,** all year, Plimoth Plantation, Plymouth; (508) 746-1622; plimoth.org

- **Chowderfest,** Jan, Nantasket Beach, Nantasket; (781) 925-9980; hullchamber.com

- **AHA!,** second Thurs of each month; (508) 996-8253, ext. 205; aha newbedford.org

- **Annual New Bedford Half Marathon and Downtown Run,** Mar, New Bedford; (617) 566-7600; newbedfordhalfmarathon.com

- **St. Patrick's Day Parade,** Mar, Scituate; (781) 545-4000; scituate chamber.org/events/st-patricks-day-parade

- **Taste of Southcoast,** May, Pier 3, New Bedford; (508) 990-2777; downtownnb.org

- **Fisherman Memorial,** Memorial Day, Seamen's Bethel, New Bedford; (508) 992-3295; portsociety.org

- **Taunton Riverfront Festival,** early June, Taunton; (508) 821-9347; neighborhoodcorp.org/festival.

- **Strawberry Thanksgiving,** late June, Plimoth Plantation, Plymouth; (508) 746-1622; plimoth.org

- **Day Out with Thomas the Train,** summer, Edaville Railroad, South Carver; (508) 866-8190; edaville.com

- **Colonial Pilgrim Wedding,** summer, Plimoth Plantation, Plymouth; (508) 746-1622; plimoth.org

- **Comcast Center for the Performing Arts,** summer-long concerts, Mansfield; (508) 339-2333; livenation.com/venues/14479/comcast-center

- **New Bedford Folk Festival,** early July, New Bedford; (508) 673-8523; newbedfordsummerfest.com

- **Brockton Fair,** June/July, Brockton Fairgrounds; (508) 586-8000; brocktonfair.com

- **Whaling City Festival,** mid-July, Buttonwood Park, New Bedford; (508) 996-3348 or 508-287-4153; whalingcityfestival.com.

- **'50s Night,** third Thurs in July, downtown New Bedford; (508) 971-6033; destinationnewbedford.org

- **Feast in the Wild,** July, Buttonwood Park Zoo; New Bedford; (508) 991-6178: bpzoo.org

- **Illumination Night,** late July, Onset Harbor; (508) 295-7072; onset village.com

- **Feast of the Blessed Sacrament,** end of July/Aug, New Bedford; (508) 992-6911 or (508) 999-5231; portuguesefeast.com

- **Onset Blues Festival,** Aug, Onset, Buzzards Bay; (508) 295-7072; onsetbluesfestival.com

- **Buzzards Bay Regatta,** Aug, Buzzards Bay, (508) 997-0762 (NewBedford Yacht Club, New Bedford, hosts odd years Regatta) or (508) 748-0540 (Beverly Yacht Club, Marion, hosts even years Regatta); buzzardsbayregatta.com

- **Marshfield Fair,** mid-Aug, 140 Main St., Marshfield Fairgrounds; (781) 834-6629; marshfieldfair.org

- **Plymouth Waterfront Festival,** late Aug, downtown Plymouth; (508) 830-1620; plymouthwaterfrontfestival.com

- **King Richard's Faire,** late Aug–Oct, 235 Main St., Carver; (508) 866-5391 (during the fair) or (952) 238-9915; kingrichardsfaire.net

- **Great Feast Holy Ghost,** end of Aug, Kennedy Park, New Bedford; (508) 324-2028; fallriverma.org

Onset & Wareham

Onset is a charming village that is part of Wareham. Onset Beach enjoys the warm waters that the Cape is known for and is a lovely spot to hear a free musical concert or watch a free film at the bandstand across from the pier on a warm summer evening. If the weather gets too hot, "cool it" at Water Wizz—families have been "just chilling" here for decades! Don't miss the Blues Festival, the Cape Verdean Festival, Illumination Night, or July 4 on the bay. The **Cranberry Regional Visitor Center** (covering the south coast of Massachusetts) is open seasonally on I-195. Contact the Information Center in Wareham, (508) 295-5504; seeplymouth.com/visitor-centers/cranberry-region-visitors-center.

Other Things to See & Do

AD Makepeace, 158 Tihonet Rd., Wareham; (508) 295-1000; admakepeace.com. Cranberry bog tours and events year-round.

Cape Cod Canal Cruises, Onset Pier, Wareham; (508) 295-3883 or (800) 492-8082; hy-linecruises.com. Narrated cruises on the canal and Jazz and Blues Cruises May through Oct, departing from the Onset Town Pier.

Onset Beach, Onset Avenue (Cranberry Highway/Routes 6 and 28 to Onset Avenue), Wareham.

Water Wizz, Route 28, 3031 Cranberry Hwy., Wareham; (508) 295-3255; waterwizz .com. Open June 1 to mid-June on weekends, daily mid-June through Labor Day. Water park with wave pool, tube rides, family pool with lily-pad crossing, lazy river, slides, and children's play area with water sprays and waterfalls. *The Way, Way Back* with Steve Carell was filmed here!

Where to Eat

Stash's Onset Beach, 182 Onset Ave. (at Onset Pier), Onset; (508) 291-7200; stashs onsetbeach.com. The only restaurant on Onset beach; pizza, seafood, Greek and Italian dishes, burgers and hot dogs. Eat outside on the deck at the umbrella-covered tables overlooking the bay. $–$$

The Stonebridge Bistro, 5 East Blvd., Onset; (508) 291-2229; stonebridgebistro .com. Open Wed through Sun for dinner and lunch on the weekends. Views of Onset

Bay, the marina, and the stone bridge. Great food; the chocolate fondue dessert is a big hit with families. $–$$$

Where to Stay

The Inn on Onset Bay, 181 Onset Ave., Onset; (508) 295-1126; innononsetbay.net. Twenty-three-room inn across from the beach. Family-friendly rooms, some with kitchenettes, each with its own bathroom. $–$$

Greater New Bedford (Acushnet, Dartmouth, Fairhaven, New Bedford & Westport)

The entire downtown area of New Bedford seems to be a monument to the city's world-famous whaling days. The **New Bedford National Historical Park,** 33 William St., New Bedford, MA 02740 (508-996-4095; nps.gov/nebe), is a wonderful source of information for the Whaling Museum, the Seaman's Bethel, the Rotch-Jones Duff House and Garden Museum, and the Schooner *Ernestina.* The visitor center is open daily year-round 9 a.m. to 5 p.m. (closed Thanksgiving, Christmas, and New Year's). Be sure to watch the 22-minute vintage orientation film, *The City That Lit the World,* shown on the hour (the film is subject to change). Don't miss the exhibits on the whaling history, the whaling trade, and the people and the ethnic groups who were significant. For information on Greater New Bedford, contact the **Destination New Bedford Visitor Center,** 52 Fisherman's Wharf, Pier 3, New Bedford, MA 02740 (508-979-1745 or 800-508-5353; destinationnewbedford.org or visitsemass.com). Destination New Bedford is open Memorial Day through Labor Day, Mon through Fri 8 a.m. to 4 p.m. and weekends 9 a.m. to 4 p.m.; Mon through Fri 8 a.m. to 4 p.m. the rest of the year.

Buttonwood Park Zoo (under 10)

425 Hawthorn St., New Bedford; (508) 991-6178 or (508) 991-4556; bpzoo.org. Open daily Mar through Sept 9 a.m. to 5 p.m., and Oct through Feb 9 a.m. to 4 p.m. (closed Thanksgiving, Christmas, and New Year's Day). Admission: $8 for

adults and $4 for children 3 to 12, free for children under 3. Special rates for New Bedford residents. Free parking.

The Buttonwood Park Zoo, owned by the city of New Bedford, has been called one of the best small zoos in the country by the Association of Zoos and Aquariums. All of the animals (cougars, black bears, bald eagles, bobcats, among others) are indigenous to Massachusetts (the theme encapsulates the Berkshire Mountains to Buzzards Bay) and represent the diversity of the wildlife in our state (with the exception of the Asian elephant exhibit). A farm area features domestic rare-breed animals; have your children be on the lookout for the Randall Lineback cows and the Suffolk Punch Draft horses. Don't miss the Wildlife Carousel or the Zoo Train (all proceeds benefit educational programming and fun family events). The Buttonwood Zoo is a nice, gentle introduction to animals for young children, and parents like it because the scale is very manageable. Animal encounters can be arranged for closer interaction with the bears, seals, and elephants; help in their feeding, participate in their training, and ask questions of the zookeeper (**Note:** extra fee). The zoo's after-closing's Flashlight Adventures are very popular with groups. You can choose from the Critter Camp-In (a sleepover) or the Twilight Tour. Set aside 1 to 2 hours to take in the zoo, and when you're through with your touring, get a snack in the Bear's Den Cafe and Patio before exploring Buttonwood Park. Buttonwood Park (which contains the zoo) was designed by Frederick Law Olmstead.

Demarest Lloyd State Park (all ages)

Barney's Joy Road, South Dartmouth; (508) 636-3298 (summer phone) or (508) 636-8816 (winter phone); mass.gov/eea/agencies/dcr/massparks/region-south/demarest-lloyd-state-park.org.html. Open from Memorial Day to Labor Day, 8 a.m. to 6 p.m. weekends and 10 a.m. to 6 p.m. weekdays. From Memorial Day through Labor Day, parking is $7 per car. Directions: Take Route 24 south to Route 195 east to the Faunce Corner exit. Turn right onto Faunce Corner Road; cross Route 6 onto Chase Road and follow the signs.

Not far from New Bedford is South Dartmouth and Demarest Lloyd State Park, a beautiful beach with calm water (ideal for families with younger kids), long sandbars, great hiking trails, restroom facilities, and lots of picnic tables in a shady area; it is also a great birding site. Considering how pleasant this beach is, there are surprisingly few people midweek (during the weekends the gates close as soon as the parking lot fills up—usually by 10 a.m.). **Warning:** Watch the kids at low tide; the sandbars drop off suddenly.

Horseneck Beach State Reservation (all ages)

5 John Reed Rd. (Westport Point), Route 88, Westport; (508) 636-8816; mass.gov/ eea/agencies/dcr/massparks/region-south/horseneck-beach-state-reservation.html. From Memorial Day through Labor Day, parking is $8 per car. Directions: Take Route 24 south to Route 195 east to Route 88. To reserve a campsite call Reserve America at (877) 422-6762; reserveamerica.com.

Just to the west of Dartmouth is Westport, a site of another gorgeous beach, Horseneck Beach. Horseneck Beach State Reservation, covering 600 acres, has a 2-mile-long stretch of sand and cobble. It offers a bathhouse, a snack bar, picnic tables, a 100-site campground adjacent to the beach (open mid-May through mid-Oct), hiking, great fishing off the Causeway at Gooseberry, a boat ramp on Gooseberry Island, and good swimming. Horseneck State Beach is a haven for birds and is a prime spot that birders "flock" to (pun intended!). **Warning:** From the refuge area to the camp it is cobbly rock; wear foot protection, i.e., water shoes!

New Bedford Whaling Museum (all ages)

18 Johnny Cake Hill, New Bedford; (508) 997-0046; whalingmuseum.org. Open Apr through Oct daily, 9 a.m. to 5 p.m., every second Thurs of the month until 8 p.m.; Nov through Mar, Tues to Sat 9 a.m. to 4 p.m. and Sun 11 a.m. to 4 p.m., and every second Thurs of the month until 8 p.m.; open holiday Mondays 9 a.m. to 4 p.m. Closed Thanksgiving, Christmas, and New Year's Day. Admission: $14 for adults, $6 for children 6 to 14, free for children 5 and under. Audio tours are free but a license or ID is required.

The New Bedford Whaling Museum is more than 100 years old and global in scope with more than 750,000 objects relating to the whaling industry (the largest on the planet!). Kids are justifiably awed by the tools of the trade: enormous hooks, harpoons, and a 90-foot-long whaling bark that they are welcome to climb on. The scrimshaw collection is remarkable for its quality and depth— among the 2,000 items on display (out of a collection of 5,000 items, the largest scrimshaw assembly in the world) are a sled and a birdcage carved from whalebone. Don't miss the three continuously running films (in a loop) on the *History of Whaling,* a documentary on the fishing industry today in New Bedford and its modern commercial fisheries (New Bedford is the number-one American commercial fishing port in America), and the panorama-shot film that documents a whaling voyage around the world. Each film is about 15 minutes in length and you can view one or all three. The 66-foot skeleton of a blue whale—one of three in the US, and one of six in the world—is an amazing display hanging from the ceiling. An illuminating exhibit, "Conduct Us to Our Hope," showcases the Old Dartmouth region of New Bedford, Westport, Fairhaven, Dartmouth, Acushnet, and its Native American and pre-colonial inhabitants. On the second floor is found the *Lagoda,* an 89-foot half-scale replica of a whaling ship. Walk around the top deck to get the feel of a whaling vessel. Another popular exhibit with the kids is the Forecastle, a fully rigged windless model of the front of a whaling vessel. Children are encouraged to crank the anchor, participate in deck activities, and try out the seamen's bunks in the full-size sleeping quarters. Nearby is a black-and-white film on whaling, which can be somewhat graphic for kids since it shows the harpooning of a whale. The Observation Deck overlooks the entire harbor and has free stationary telescopic binoculars, giving you a closer look at the harbor activity. The annual reading of the classic tale of *Moby Dick* by Herman Melville takes place on Jan 3 (Melville was a crew member on a whaler that departed from New Bedford). The museum tries to incorporate kid-friendly activities and crafts during school holiday and summer vacation periods. The New Bedford Whaling Museum is part of New Bedford's National Historical Park.

Ocean Explorium at New Bedford Seaport (all ages)

1 Compass Place, 174 Union St., New Bedford; (508) 994-5400; oceanexplorium .org. Open Thurs to Sun 10 a.m. to 4 p.m. year-round. Closed most major holidays, refer to their website. Pricing: $8.50 for adults, $6.50 for children 3 to 17, and free for ages 2 and under.

The site focuses on hands-on learning and interactive exhibits on the interrelationship and dependency between humans and the sea. Touch tanks rule here; your child will especially love the Ray and Shark Touch Tank where they can feel the velvet smoothness of the rays, and the Sandy Bottom touch tank with crabs and sea stars. Graphic screens provide information about the species within the tanks. Science on a Sphere is a pretty impressive piece of electronic equipment that projects 3-D images of Earth from outer space via data collected from satellites. The sphere can display past information as well as real-time information depicting environmental issues that affect our planet. Make sure you try out the interactive craft and science experiments at the Explorer Zone. For the younger set, the Discovery Bay Activity Center is geared to toddler-age children up to age 6 and is filled with games, puzzles, and arts and crafts. What makes this museum special is the way that the staff personalizes each guest's experience.

Seaman's Bethel (all ages)

15 Johnny Cake Hill, New Bedford; (508) 992-3295; portsociety.org. Open Memorial Day through Oct daily 10 a.m. to 4 p.m. Donations accepted.

Beth means "house," and *El* means "God" in Hebrew; the translation is thus a house of God or church. The chapel was visited by Herman Melville and described in *Moby Dick*. The chapel is a memorial to those who were lost at sea, with plaques all over the wall. Seamen would come to pray before going out to sea and upon their return to give thanks. The schoolroom on the bottom floor was used to teach the seamen reading, writing, and arithmetic, and to improve their navigational skills. The school was run by the New Bedford Port Society, which was largely composed of Quakers. The Seaman's Bethel is part of New Bedford's National Historical Park.

Other Things to See & Do

Carabiners Indoor Climbing, 328 Park St., New Bedford; (508) 984-0808; carabiners .com. Amazing indoor climbing wall with instruction for all ages and levels.

Captain Leroy's Deep Sea Fishing, 226 Pope's Island, Route 6, New Bedford; (508) 992-8907; captainleroys.com. Fishing and offshore trips.

Cuttyhunk Ferry Company, 66B State Pier, South Bulkhead, New Bedford; (508) 992-0200; cuttyhunkferryco.com. Visit Cuttyhunk (part of the Elizabeth Islands 14 miles off the coast of New Bedford) aboard the M/V *Cuttyhunk* in under an hour. Sightseeing tours.

Fort Taber Park and Fort Taber–Fort Rodman Military Museum, 1000 Rodney French Blvd., New Bedford, (508) 994-3938; forttaber.org. Restored fort and collection of military paraphernalia and artifacts in the museum. Historical reenactments.

Lloyd Center for the Environment, 430 Potomsea Rd., Dartmouth; (508) 990-0505; lloydcenter.org. Five miles of walking trails depicting biodiversity and scenic views, open dawn to dusk. **Free.** Visitor center (call for hours) with animal, endangered species, and long-term coastal conservation and ecosystem exhibits, and hands-on activities. Named one of the 15 most special places by the DEM.

New Bedford Art Museum, 608 Pleasant St., New Bedford; (508) 961-3072; newbedfordartmuseum.org. Vintage bank turned museum. Local, national, and international artists are on display. Contemporary and historic art.

New Bedford Bay Sox, 230 Hathaway Blvd., Paul Walsh Field, New Bedford; (855) BaySox1 or (802) 578-9935; nbbaysox.com. Member of the New England Collegiate Baseball League.

New Bedford Fire Museum, 51 Bedford St., New Bedford; (508) 992-2162; new bedford-ma.gov/fire/museum.html. Restored fire trucks and related exhibits and art in an authentic firehouse. They are trying to transfer to a new agency; it may be closing, so call ahead.

The New Bedford Museum of Glass, 61 Wamsutta St., New Bedford; (508) 984-1666. Collection of more than 7,000 objects spanning 3,000 years of glassmaking.

Osprey Sea Kayak, 489 Old County Rd., Westport; (508) 636-0300; ospreyseakayak .com. Kayak and stand-up paddleboard rentals, guided tours, and youth programs.

Rotch-Jones-Duff House and Garden Museum, 396 County St., New Bedford; (508) 997-1401; rjdmuseum.org. Greek Revival mansion of whaling magnate William Rotch Jr. Formal gardens. Part of New Bedford's National Historical Park.

Schooner Ernestina, New Bedford State Pier, New Bedford; (508) 996-4095 (New Bedford National Historical Park); ernestina.org. The schooner, a National Historic Landmark, was a Grand Banks fisher, Arctic expedition vessel, and a survey and trade ship. Part of New Bedford's National Historical Park.

Seastreak, 49 State Pier, New Bedford; (800) 262-8743; seastreak.com. New Bedford to either Vineyard Haven or Oak Bluffs in Martha's Vineyard, Apr through the end of mid-Oct. Connecting interisland Nantucket service through Hy-Line. Prices one-way to Martha's Vineyard: $40 adults, $20 ages 2 to 12, $7 for bikes.

Watchout Fishing Charter, 306 High Hill Rd., Dartmouth; (508) 998-7965; watchoutfish.com. Captain Ned's Charters for fishing and whale watching.

Whaling City Clippers, New Bedford High School Athletic Field, 230 Hathaway Blvd., New Bedford; (978) 465-3046 (New England Football League) or (508) 971-2066 (owner); whalingcityclippers.com. Greater New Bedford's only semipro football team; part of the New England Football League. Playing July through Oct at 7 p.m. on Sat nights when at home. Children 12 and under are always free, adults are $5.

Whaling City Expeditions, 52 Fisherman's Wharf., New Bedford; (508) 984-4979; whalingcityexpeditions.com. Launch, tours, and cruises.

Zeiterion Theater, 684 Purchase St., New Bedford; (508) 997-5664 (general information) or (508) 994-2900 (box office); zeiterion.org. The Zeiterion, an old vaudevillian theater, has a full schedule of concerts, theater, movies, choirs, and ballets.

Where to Eat

Bittersweet Farm Restaurant and Tavern, 438 Main Rd., Westport; (508) 636-0085; lafrancehospitality.com. Country setting for fine dining halfway between Fall River and New Bedford. $$$

Davy's Locker, 1480 East Rodney French Blvd., New Bedford; (508) 992-7359; davyslockerrestaurant.com. Voted best seafood for 11 consecutive years, good quality, reasonable prices. $–$$$

Fathoms Bar and Grill, 255 Pope's Island, New Bedford, (508) 993-3400; fathoms bar.com. Great food with a view to match. Seafood straight from the dock. $–$$

Freestones City Grill, 41 Williams St., New Bedford; (508) 993-7477; freestonescity grill.com. Housed in a former bank building, cozy and casual. Known for its chock-full lobster rolls, juicy burgers, and cheese fondue. Kids' menu. $–$$

Waterfront Grille, 36 Homers Wharf, New Bedford; (508) 997-7010; waterfrontgrille .com. Only restaurant right on the harbor. Fresh seafood. $$–$$$

Where to Stay

Melville House Bed and Breakfast, 100 Madison St., New Bedford; (508) 990-1566; melvillehouse.net. Built in 1855, the house was home to Herman Melville's sister and Herman would come to stay quite often. This charming colonial, on a quiet street close to sights, features 3 rooms and is an environmentally green bed-and-breakfast. Gourmet, all-natural continental breakfast. $$

Paquachuck Inn, 2056 Main Rd., Westport Point; (508) 636-4398; paquachuck.com. On the National Register of Historic Places; small boat dock available to guests. Nine bedrooms overlook the water. Welcoming well-behaved children and their parents. Buffet breakfast. $$–$$$

Seaport Inn and Marina, 110 Middle St., Fairhaven; (508) 997-1281; seaportinn andmarina.com. Comfortable waterfront hotel and marina. Indoor pool and Jacuzzi. Pet friendly. Complimentary hot breakfast. $–$$

Fall River

Though it's inland from the Atlantic, Fall River sits on Mt. Hope Bay at the mouth of the Taunton River. Fall River is a major seaport, and Battleship Cove is a magnet for those who enjoy touring warships and other vessels. For information on Fall River, contact the **Southeastern Massachusetts Convention and Visitors Bureau,** 794 Purchase St., New Bedford, MA 02742; (508) 999-5231; visitsemass .com. The Fall River Office of Tourism had some fiscal issues and is closed at this time. While in Fall River, check out a restaurant serving delicious Portuguese food, a local specialty.

Battleship Cove (all ages)

Exit 7 off Route 24, 5 Water St., Battleship Cove, Fall River; (508) 678-1905, (800) 533-3194, or (508) 678-1100; battleshipcove.com. Open daily year-round, 9 a.m. to 5 p.m. (closing at 4:30 p.m. late Oct through mid-May); closed Thanksgiving, Christmas, and New Year's Day. Admission: $17 for adults, $10.50 for children 6 to 12, free for children under 6. Free parking.

Today Battleship Cove holds six US Navy warships from the World War II era, including a submarine. The USS *Massachusetts* is the biggest, by far, and probably the most interesting to the kids, who will avail themselves of the opportunity to clamber throughout the ship's nine decks (you don't have to take a tour in order to explore the ship). The *Massachusetts* was moved here in 1965 to stand as a permanent memorial to the more than 18,000 Massachusetts men and women who gave their lives in service during World War II, Vietnam, Korea, Desert Storm, and September 11. Be sure to pick up a brochure when you arrive; it's easy to get lost. Try out the hammocks that served as the sailors' bunks, climb the turrets, and admire the enormous main deck. Next, check out the Soviet-built missile *Corvette, the Hiddensee,* built in 1984 and acquired by Battleship Cove in 1997. Other National Historic Landmark designees at Battleship Cove are the destroyer *Joseph P. Kennedy Jr.,* the submarine *Lionfish,* and PT boats 617 and 796. There is a growing aircraft collection that includes the Cobra Attack Helicopter, the Huey Helicopter, and the T28 trainer plane. For a marvelous history lesson, Battleship Cove offers Nautical Nights, an overnight encampment for organized youth and school groups ($55 to $60 per person depending upon the season). The participants speak to former crew members, get to tour all the ships, have knot-tying and Morse code lessons, eat sailor's grub, and sleep in the sailors' bunks throughout the ships. Since Battleship Cove preserves the world's largest collection of historical naval ships, the experience is educational besides just being fun! Birthday party packages are available as well—how cool is that? *TIP:* Set aside about 4 hours to tour Battleship Cove.

Fall River Carousel (all ages)
5 Water St., Battleship Cove, Fall River; (508) 678-1100, ext. 122; battleshipcove .com/carousel. Open year-round; seasonal hours. Rides are $1 for a single ride and seven for $5.

Battleship Cove is also home to the Fall River Carousel, a restored merry-go-round that was moved here from Dartmouth in the early 1990s. The four dozen horses are hand-carved and hand-painted, made by the Philadelphia Toboggan Company in 1920. Bring a picnic lunch; there's a nice grassy area next to the carousel.

Fall River Historical Society Museum (all ages)
451 Rock St., Fall River; (508) 679-1071; lizzieborden.org. Open May through Oct, Tues through Fri 9 a.m. to 4 p.m. (hourly tours 9 a.m. to 3 p.m.) and weekends June through Sept to 4 p.m. (hourly tours 1 to 4 p.m.). The museum reopens the weekend before Thanksgiving until Dec 31 for a Victorian Holiday Open House (Mon through Fri 9 a.m. to 4 p.m. and weekends from 1 to 4 p.m.). Admission: $8 for adults, $6 for children.

"Lizzie Borden took an axe, gave her mother forty whacks, when she saw what she had done, she gave her father forty-one,"—every girl remembers this jump-rope song. At the Fall River Historical Society, headquartered in a granite mansion, there are more than 10,000 items related to the Lizzie Borden trial, the largest collection in the US and the world. The Lizzie Borden collection is just a small part of this museum, which offers a tour of the former mansion of the Robeson, Remington, and Brayton families, nautical exhibits, paintings, 19th-century decorative arts, and furnishings, as well as 2,000 items of clothing and costumes in a revolving exhibit. Beautiful grounds and gardens with bubbling fountains, gazebos, and terraces can be strolled. Be sure to visit during the Victorian Holiday Open House. The museum is resplendent with holiday decorations and has been featured many times in the magazine *Victorian Homes*. For a special holiday treat, take your family to the Easton Tea Room located next to the museum at 458 High St., during the Victorian Holiday Open House.

TopEvents South of Boston

September–December

- **Endless Summer Waterfront Festival,** Sept, Nantasket Beach, Nantasket; (781) 925-9980; hullchamber.com

- **Apple/Peach Festival,** Sept, 1203 Main St., Acushnet; acushnet.ma.us

- **The Working Waterfront Festival,** end of Sept, Fisherman's Wharf, New Bedford; (508) 993-8894; workingwaterfrontfestival.org

- **Harvest Festival,** Oct, Plimoth Plantation, Plymouth; (508) 746-1622; plimoth.org

- **New Bedford Seaport Chowder Festival,** Oct (Colombus Day weekend), Pier 3, New Bedford; (508) 990-2777; downtownnb.org

- **Plymouth Philharmonic Concerts and Orchestra,** Oct through May; (508) 746-8008 for schedule; plymouthphil.org

- **National Cranberry Festival,** Oct, Edaville Railroad, South Carver; (877) 332-8455; edaville.com

- **Pumpkins Aglow,** Oct, Edaville Railroad, South Carver; (877) 332-8455; edaville.com

- **Boo at the Zoo,** Oct, Buttonwood Park Zoo; New Bedford; (508) 991-6178: bpzoo.org

- **The Haunted Rail Yard,** mid-Oct, Old Colony and Fall River Railroad Museum, Fall River; (508) 674-9340

- **Cranberry Harvest Celebration,** Oct, A D Makepeace Bogs, 158 Tihonet Rd., Wareham; (508) 322-4000; admakepeace.com or cranberries.org/festival/festival

- **Plimoth Plantation's Thanksgiving Celebration,** Nov, Plymouth; (508) 746-1622 (Plimoth Plantation) or (800) USA-1620 (Destination Plymouth); seeplymouth.com or plimoth.org

- **Sampe Festival,** Nov, Plimoth Grist Mill, 6 Spring Ln., Plymouth; (508) 746-1622; plimoth.org

- **America's Hometown Celebration,** Nov, Plymouth; (508) 746-1818; usathanksgiving.com

- **Pilgrim's Progress,** Thanksgiving, Plymouth; (508) 746-2590 (The Mayflower Society) or (800) USA-1620 (Destination Plymouth); the mayflowersociety.com, seeplymouth.com, or visitplymouth.org

- **National Day of Mourning** (Native American point of view), Nov, Cole's Hill, Plymouth; (508) 747-0100 (Plymouth County Convention and Visitors Bureau) or (617) 286-6574 (United American Indians of New England); uaine.org or seeplymouth.com

- **Victorian Christmas,** Nov through Dec, Fall River Historical Society, Fall River; (508) 679-1071; lizzieborden.org

- **La Salette Festival of Lights,** Thanksgiving through early Jan, 947 Park St., Route118, Attleboro; (508) 222-5410; lasalette-shrine.org

- **Christmas Festival of Light,** mid-Nov through Jan. 1 Edaville Railroad, South Carver; (877) EDAVILLE; edaville.com

- **Downtown Holiday Stroll,** Dec, downtown New Bedford; (508) 990-2777; downtownnb.org

- **Holiday ZOObilee,** Dec, Buttonwood Park Zoo; New Bedford; (508) 991-6178: bpzoo.org

- **Christmas at the Plimoth Grist Mill,** Dec, Plymouth; (508) 746-1622; plimoth.org

- **Charles Dickens's *A Christmas Carol* Performance and Dinner,** Dec, Plimoth Plantation, Plymouth; (508) 746-1622; plimoth.org

- **Christmas Parade,** Dec, downtown Fall River; (508) 667-5929; fall river.org

- **Lighting of Taunton Green Christmas Festival,** Dec, Taunton; (508) 821-1000; taunton.ma.gov

- **City Celebrates New Year's Eve,** Dec 31, downtown New Bedford, aha.org or destinationnewbedford.org.

Other Things to See & Do

Children's Museum of Greater Fall River, 441 North Main St., Fall River, (508) 672-0033; cmgfr.org. Highlights include the Circle Room, Dino Dig, World of Water, Lego Room, and All About Colors. $8 for everyone ages 1 and above.

Little Theatre of Fall River, two venues; 340 Prospect St. and Bristol Community College, 777 Ellsbree St., Fall River; (508) 675-1852; littletheatre.net. Performances throughout the year.

Marine Museum at Fall River, 70 Water St., Fall River; (508) 674-3533. *Titanic, Andrea Doria,* and Fall River Line exhibits and artifacts.

Old Colony and Fall River Railroad Museum, across from Battleship Cove, Central and Water Streets, Fall River; (508) 674-9340; ocandfrrailroadmuseum.com. Check the website for the seasonal summer and fall schedule. New England railroad memorabilia and historical displays.

Spindle City Ballet, 288 Plymouth Ave., Fall River; (508) 677-2130 and (508) 536-6073; spindlecityballet.org. Highlighting locally trained classical ballet dancers. *Nutcracker* production every year.

Where to Eat

Clipper Restaurant, 459 South Main St., Fall River; (508) 679-4700. Highly regarded, the Clipper has been on the Travel Channel. Portuguese food. $$–$$$

Jerry Remy's Sports Bar and Grill, 1082 Davol St., Fall River; (508) 676-7369; jerryremys.com. The place for sports fans. Home of the huge video wall (Screen Monsters) to watch the New England teams. American-style food including gluten-free options. Kids' menu. $–$$

Sagres, 181 Columbia St., Fall River; (508) 675-7018; sagres.com. Reopening in May 2014 (extreme fire damage). Highly regarded family restaurant specializing in Portuguese dishes. $–$$

Tipsy Toboggan, 75 Ferry St., Fall River; (508) 567-0550; thetipsytoboggan.com. Roaring fireplace, mountain lodge decor, family seating. Try the chocolate sequoia desert . . . yummy! $–$$$

Trio Cafe, 201 South Main St., Fall River; (508) 679-5781. Extensive and creative menu focusing on Portuguese food. Family owned, friendly and attentive service. $$–$$$

Where to Stay ⊖

Lizzie Borden Bed & Breakfast, 230 Second St. (GPS address), Fall River; (508) 675-7333; lizzie-borden.com. Five-room inn and museum (former home of the infamous Borden family). One-and-a-half- to 2-hour guided tour (the general public gets only an hour tour, so it's a bonus to stay overnight here!), videos, and snacks. $$$

Attleboro & Seekonk

Attleboro, even though geographically it's a Massachusetts city, feels a close connection to Providence both regionally and culturally. The Attleboro Industrial Museum and the Capron Zoo in Attleboro are worth a quick detour. Not only does the Seekonk Speedway have racing cars zooming around the speedway, it also has a popular Sunday flea market May through Oct that you and your family can speed around in!

Things to See & Do

Attleboro Industrial Museum, 42 Union St., Attleboro; (508) 222-3918; industrial museum.com. Call for schedule. **Free.** Artifacts, photos, tools, and machinery related to the industrial history of Attleboro.

Capron Park Zoo, 201 County St., Attleboro; (508) 222-3047 or (774) 203-1840; capronparkzoo.com. Many Asian, African, and American species are represented. Nocturnal building for nighttime animals.

Seekonk Speedway, 1710 Fall River Ave., Seekonk; (508) 336-9959; seekonkspeed way.com. NASCAR track.

Where to Stay ⊖

Hilltop Hotel and Conference Center, 213 Taunton Ave., Seekonk; (508) 336-8700; hhotelseekonk.com. Business-class-style hotel 6 miles from Providence, Rhode Island. New Ten Mile Grille Restaurant opening in late spring of 2014. Cribs. Complimentary continental breakfast. $$

Avon, Brockton, Foxborough, Wrentham & the Tri-Town Area

Foxborough is home to Gillette Stadium, which hosts both the New England Revolution professional soccer team and the New England Patriots NFL professional football team, three-time winner and World Champion of the Super Bowl. If sports aren't your thing, stop by Patriots Place shopping mall in Foxboro or Wrentham Village Premium Outlets in Wrentham for a day of outlet shopping of discounted designer labels. Follow your day of shopping with an evening at the Comcast Center in Mansfield for your evening entertainment.

5 Wits Patriot Place (ages 7 and up)

202 Patriot Place, Foxboro; (508) 698-1600; 5-wits.com. Tues through Thurs 11 a.m. to 8 p.m., Fri and Sat 11 a.m. to 10 p.m., and Sun 11 a.m. to 8 p.m. Price: $18 for adults and $14 for children 12 and under. Snack bar on premises.

Become an adventurer in one of two interactive entertainment experiences: Espionage or 20,000 Leagues. In Espionage, after being briefed on the theft of blueprints of a satellite by an evil corporation, your team must solve puzzles and challenges to save the planet even with a possibility of a mole in your midst. Dodge lasers, crack safes, disarm bombs; every mistake could change the outcome, and the fate of the world rests on your shoulders! In 20,000 Leagues the setting is a museum. Stumbling across Captain Nemo's submarine, the Nautilus, you journey through the vessel by using your wits and senses to solve mental and physical challenges in order to escape. Complete Captain Nemo's experiments and fight a giant squid to get out alive. It takes teamwork to progress from room to room—be prepared for many surprises. This tour has received many accolades (although it can be somewhat frightening for little ones). The group dynamic and the guidance you receive from the tour guides change from show to show.

Gillette Stadium (formerly Foxboro Stadium) (all ages)

1 Patriot Place, Foxborough; (508) 543-0350 (Gillette Stadium), (508) 543-8200 (NE Patriots), or (800) 543-1776 for tickets; patriots.com/gillette-stadium.

Home to both the New England Revolution and the New England Patriots. Venue site for concerts and special events. The stadium opened for the 2002 season. This modern architectural wonder is a complete upgrade over the former

So . . . You Want Your Name Up in Lights?!

The Name in Lights Program at Gillette Stadium buys you a message on the matrix board to mark a special occasion for a fee (a huge hit to commemorate a child's birthday while watching his or her favorite team play). To have a message displayed at a Patriots game, call (508) 543-8200; for a Revolution game, call (877) 438-7387.

stadium, which was torn down after the new state-of-the-art stadium was built. Every seat has a fabulous view.

New England Patriots (all ages)

Gillette Stadium, 1 Patriot Place, Foxborough; (508) 543-8200 or (800) 543-1776 for tickets; patriots.com.

New England's professional NFL football team, three-time winner and World Champion of the Super Bowl. Preseason games are scheduled in August. The football season starts mid-Sept and runs through late Dec, unless they qualify for the playoffs and the Super Bowl. The New England Patriots play in the new Gillette Stadium when at home. To get an insider's sneak peek of the Patriots, attend one of their training camp practices in July for free (check the website for the posted schedule). If you are a die-hard fan, you can purchase signed, worn, and used items from their website (the proceeds go to charity).

New England Revolution (all ages)

Gillette Stadium, 1 Patriot Place, Foxborough; (508) 543-0350 (Gillette Stadium) or (877) GET-REVS for tickets; revolutionsoccer.net.

MLS professional soccer team that has a growing following. The soccer season is from Mar through Oct.

Other Things to See & Do

Brockton Rox, 1 Feinberg Way. Brockton; (508) 559-7000; brocktonrox.com. Professional independent minor league baseball team. The Rox play in Brockton's Campanelli Stadium. *TIP:* Be aware of your surroundings in Brockton.

Comcast Center, 885 S. Main St., Mansfield; (508) 339-2333; ticketmaster.com/venue/8213. A Live Nation–owned amphitheater seating just under 20,000 people with one-third covered seats, one-third open-air seats, and one-third sitting on the lawn. Major concerts are staged here May through the early fall.

Easton's Children's Museum, the Old Fire Station, 9 Sullivan Ave., North Easton; (508) 230-3789; childrensmuseumineaston.org. Hands-on kids' activities and special events.

Fuller Craft Museum, 455 Oak St., Brockton; (508) 588-6000; fullermuseum.org. One of only eight contemporary-craft museums in the US. Located on 22 acres of woodland laced with trails, a sculpture garden, and courtyards on Porter's Pond. Exhibits cover post–World War II to the present. Cafe.

Golf Museum, 300 Arnold Palmer Blvd., Norton; (774) 430-9100; mgalinks.org. Opened in 2002, it traces the history of golf in Massachusetts. **Free.**

Patriot Place, 2 Patriot Place, Foxborough: (508) 203-2100; patriot-place.com. Visit the Hall at Patriot's Place, 5Wits, the Nature Trail and Cranberry Bog, winter ice skating, Showcase Live, the Cinema de Lux, the Renaissance Hotel and Spa, shopping, dining, and more.

Wrentham Village Premium Outlets, 1 Premium Outlets Blvd., Wrentham; (508) 384-0600; premiumoutlets.com. Open Mon through Sat 10 a.m. to 9 p.m., Sun 10 a.m. to 6 p.m. (extended hours on Sun in the summer and holiday periods). Shop till ya drop! Save on designer labels and name brands for the entire family. Outlets specializing in children's clothing include Polo, Crewcuts, and Gap.

Cape Cod, Martha's Vineyard, and Nantucket

Cape Cod

Shaped like a bent arm and stretching 60 miles into the Atlantic, the peninsula of Cape Cod offers nearly 300 miles of beaches, along with acres of nature preserves, dozens of pretty villages, and an abundance of top-notch inns and restaurants that welcome families. Route 6A was designated a National Scenic Byway and runs almost 35 miles from Bourne to Orleans. Known as the King's Highway, it has evolved from a Native American pathway to a colonial road to the scenic byway that is one of the main routes for vehicle traffic today, the longest contiguous historic district in the country. For free information on the Cape, contact the **Cape Cod Chamber of Commerce,** with two visitor centers: 5 Patti Page Way (crossroads of Route 6 and Route 132) and on Route 25 South just before crossing the Bourne Bridge from the mainland; (888) 33-CAPECOD; capecodchamber.org or capecodtravelguide.com. For information on the traffic cameras monitoring the Sagamore and Bourne Bridges, and Greater Boston traffic, go to Mass511.com (**Mass511**). For traffic information, press 511 on your cellular phone and follow the prompts (this call is **free!**). At the fist of the Cape's arm, pulsating Provincetown surrounds the Pilgrim Monument, a replica of the Campanile in Siena. The spectacular view of the curving Cape and the surrounding ocean and bay is worth the climb up the tower's 116 steps. Regardless of the season, visit one or more of the first-class beaches along the Cape's eastern edge. A fun way to keep kids interested during the short drives from town to town is to make the trip into a lighthouse tour. There are seven working lighthouses on the Cape, from Provincetown all the way to Woods Hole. **Bed & Breakfast Cape Cod** (508-255-3824; bookcapecod.com)

CAPE COD, MARTHA'S VINEYARD, AND NANTUCKET

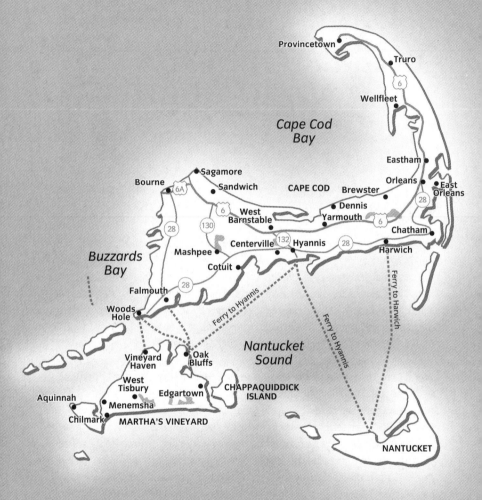

Cape Cod Bay

Provincetown

Truro

6

Wellfleet

Eastham

Orleans

East Orleans

CAPE COD

Brewster

28

Sagamore

Bourne

6A

Sandwich

Dennis

West Barnstable

6

Yarmouth

6

Chatham

28

130

Centerville

132

Hyannis

28

Harwich

Buzzards Bay

Mashpee

28

Cotuit

Falmouth

28

Ferry to Hyannis

Ferry to Hyannis

Ferry to Harwich

Woods Hole

Nantucket Sound

Vineyard Haven

Oak Bluffs

West Tisbury

Edgartown

CHAPPAQUIDDICK ISLAND

Aquinnah

Menemsha

Chilmark

MARTHA'S VINEYARD

NANTUCKET

is a great reservation service connecting you to outstanding properties on the Cape and the Islands.

Bourne & Sandwich

When you drive over the Sagamore Bridge, you end up on Route 6 in Sandwich, the oldest town on Cape Cod (settled in 1637). Few visitors stop here (a pity, since the Sandwich Boardwalk at Town Neck Beach is ranked one of the top ten in the country by National Geographic); most zip on by on their way to the beaches and cottages of the outer Cape. Considering how much there is to see and do here, try not to overlook this area. Grover Cleveland found Bourne so delightful that he made it his summer residence while president. For further information on this area, contact the **Canal Region Chamber of Commerce,** 1 Meetinghouse Ln., North Sagamore (visitor center at the base of the Sagamore Bridge), MA 02561 (774-413-7475, visitor center or 508-759-6000;

TopPicks on Cape Cod, Martha's Vineyard, and Nantucket

- **Cape Cod National Seashore**
- **Nauset Beach,** East Orleans
- **Cliffs and Beach at Aquinnah (Gay Head),** Martha's Vineyard
- **Children's Beach,** Nantucket
- **Woods Hole Science Aquarium,** Woods Hole
- **Flying Horses Carousel,** Martha's Vineyard
- **Whale-watching trips** from Provincetown
- **Chatham Break,** a **seal tour,** and the **Monomoy National Wildlife Refuge,** Chatham
- **Nantucket Shipwreck and Lifesaving Museum** and the **Whaling Museum,** Nantucket

capecodcanalchamber.org), the Sandwich Chamber, 4 Water St., Sandwich, MA 02563; (508-833-9755; sandwichchamber.com), or the **Cape Cod Canal Visitor Center** (run by the US Army Corps of Engineers), 60 Ed Moffitt Dr., Sandwich, MA 02563 (508-833-9678; capecodcanal.us or nae.usace.army.mil/Missions/Recreation/CapeCodCanal.aspx), open seasonally May through Oct. The Cape Cod Canal Visitor Center has rooms of interactive exhibits and hands-on activities, a retired 40-foot patrol boat (great for climbing), and the tracking of vessels on radar, camera, and computer screens that are traveling within the canal in real-time traffic. The Cape Cod Canal Visitor Center offers a variety of family-friendly programming throughout the summer for **free.** The visitor center functions as a museum and information center about the Cape Cod Canal.

Cape Cod Canal Bike Trail (all ages)

Access points along the Cape side of the canal: in Sandwich, at the left side of the Sandwich Marina on Freezer Road; Bourne Recreation Area off of Sandwich Road (right in the shadow of the Bourne Bridge); and the Tidal Flats Recreation Area off of Bell Road in Bourne. Access points along the mainland side of the canal: at the Buzzards Bay Recreation Area (beneath the railroad bridge) off of Main Street adjacent to Buzzard Bay Park, from the Bourne Scenic Park Campground (you may have to pay to park there for the day); Herring Run Recreation Area on Route 6 (the Scenic Highway) in Bournedale; at the Sagamore Recreation area on Canal Street; and at Scusset Beach State Reservation (fee to park in season); (508) 759-4431 (main office of the US Army Corps of Engineers); capecodcanal.us or nae.usace.army.mil/Missions/Recreation/CapeCodCanal.aspx. Free.
The well-maintained Cape Cod Canal Bike Trail (maintained by the Army Corps of Engineers) is a service road that borders the canal on both banks. Pick up a map in Sandwich at the Cape Cod Canal Visitor Center (60 Ed Moffit Dr.) or go to capecodcanal.us. The 6.5-mile-long trail along the Cape side is less hilly (both are fairly flat) and further removed from auto traffic than the 7-mile-long mainland-side trail. The mainland side is busier since it has more access areas in its mid-section. Families should avoid crossing either bridge with children, either on foot or on bicycle. If you must cross the canal on your bikes, use the Sagamore Bridge (its sidewalk is safer), and don't ride—walk. Because the bridges' auto lanes are so narrow, drivers aren't looking out for pedestrians or bikers—they're avoiding cars in adjacent lanes. Kids get a charge out of following the ships up close from the bike path as they go through the canal on their way to the open

sea. **Warning:** The Sagamore Bridge construction may be not completed and may restrict sidewalk access from time to time.

Green Briar Nature Center and Jam Kitchen (all ages)

6 Discovery Hill Rd., East Sandwich; (508) 888-6870; thorntonburgess.org. Open year-round, mid-Apr through Dec, Mon through Sat 10 a.m. to 4 p.m. and Sun 1 to 4 p.m., and Jan through mid-Apr, Tues through Sat 10 a.m. to 4 p.m. Closed July 4, Thanksgiving, Christmas, and New Year's. Admission is by donation.

The Green Briar Nature Center was established in 1980 by the Thornton W. Burgess Society. The Jam Kitchen, founded in 1903, is adjacent to the Briar Patch Conservation Area (owned by the town of Sandwich). The nature center houses natural-history exhibits and a collection of small live animals. The 57 acres of forests are laced with easy walking trails and include an award-winning wildflower garden. The Thornton W. Burgess Society runs a full program of nature walks and natural-history classes, mostly geared toward children and families, throughout the year. "Critter Capers" introduces one of the resident animals at the nature center every Fri, and the "Live Animals Story Time" on Sat introduces an animal featured in the story (both programs start at 10:30 a.m. and charge $2 per person). The Thornton W. Burgess Museum (4 Water St.), which housed books and memorabilia of the beloved author, is closed permanently. Their activities and programs have been moved to the Green Briar Nature Center. A gallery at the nature center will be converted into the Thornton Burgess room. Burgess penned the Mother West Wind stories about Reddy Fox, Peter Cottontail, and Paddy the Beaver, among many other animal characters. Burgess wrote enduring classics that focus on our delicate ecology and his love of nature and its creatures. After you explore the nature center, stop in at the Jam Kitchen, an old-fashioned kitchen in a pond-side building that looks like it's right out of one of Burgess's stories. The Jam Kitchen sells natural jams, jellies, relishes, and nature-related items; the sales in the shop help support the educational programs. Ask about classes on the fine art of making jam. The Cape Cod Cranberry Day in Sept, sponsored by the Green Briar Nature Center and Jam Kitchen, is quite popular.

Heritage Museums & Gardens (all ages)

67 Grove St., corner of Grove and Pine Streets, Sandwich; (508) 888-3300; heritage museumsandgardens.org. Open from mid-Apr through the end of Oct daily 10 a.m. to 5 p.m., reopening the day after Thanksgiving for Gardens Aglow (check

TopEvents on Cape Cod

January–August

- **St. Patrick's Day Parade,** Mar, Route 28, South Yarmouth; (508) 362-7239; capecodstpatsparade.com

- **Brewster in Bloom,** end of Apr/May, Brewster; (508) 896-3500; brewstercapecod.com

- **Wellfleet Blossoms,** Apr, Preservation Hall, 35 Main St., Wellfleet; (508) 349-2510; wellfleetchamber.com

- **Maritime Week,** Cape lighthouses open to the public, May; (888) 33-CAPECOD; capecodmaritimedays.com

- **Rhododendron Festival,** mid-May, Heritage Museums and Gardens, Sandwich; (508) 888-3300; heritagemuseumsandgardens.org

- **Figawi Race Weekend,** late May, Hyannis to Nantucket and back, Hyannis; (508) 221-6891; figawi.com

- **Harborfest,** late May/early June, Wellfleet's Pier; (508) 349-2510; wellfleetchamber.com

- **Father's Day Car Show,** Father's Day, Main St., Hyannis; (508) 775-2201; hyannis.com

- **Taylor Bray Farm Sheep Festival,** June, 108 Bray Farm Rd. North, Yarmouth Port; (508) 385-9407; taylorbrayfarm.org

- **Yarmouth Summer Celebration Kick-Off,** June, Yarmouth; (508) 778-1008; yarmouthcapecod.com or yarmouthsummercelebration.com

- **Auto Show,** June, Heritage Museums and Gardens, Sandwich; (508) 888-3300; heritagemuseumsandgardens.org

- **Portuguese Festival and Blessing of the Fleet,** MacMillan Wharf (blessing), late June, Provincetown; (508) 246-9080 (Provincetown Festival) or (508) 487-3424 (Provincetown Chamber of Commerce); provincetownportuguesefestival.com

- **Pops in the Park,** Aug, Eldredge Field, Orleans; (508) 362-0066; artsfoundation.org

- **Fourth of July Fireworks,** July 4, Hyannis, Falmouth Heights, Provincetown, Orleans, and Edgartown

- **Illumination Boat Parade,** July 4, Shawme Pond, Sandwich; (508) 888-4361; sandwichma.org

- **Mashpee Powwow,** beginning of July, Tribal Grounds, 483 Great Neck Rd. South, Mashpee; (508) 477-0208; mashpeewampanoag tribe.com

- **Pirate Palooza,** July, South Cape Village, Mashpee: (508) 477-0792; mashpeepiratepalooza.com

- **Barnstable County Fair,** July, Barnstable County Fairgrounds, East Falmouth; (508) 563-3200; barnstablecountyfair.org

- **Family Week for LGBT,** late July/early Aug, Provincetown; (617) 502-8700; familyequality.org/familyweek

- **Boston Pops by the Sea,** early Aug, Hyannis Village Green, Hyannis; (508) 362-0066; artsfoundation.org

- **Falmouth Road Race,** Aug, Woods Hole to Falmouth; (508) 540-7000; falmouthroadrace.com

- **The Festival of the Arts,** mid-Aug, Chase Park on Cross Street, Chatham; (508) 945-3583; capecodcreativearts.org

- **Peter Rabbit's Animal Day,** Aug, Green Briar Nature Center, 6 Discovery Hill Rd., East Sandwich; (508) 888-6870; thorntonburgess .org

- **La Tavola,** mid-Aug, South Cape Village, Mashpee; (508) 477-0792; mashpeechamber.com

- **Carnival Week Parade,** mid-Aug, Provincetown; (508) 487-2313 or (800) 637-8696; provincetown.com or ptown.org

the website). **Admission in season: $18 for adults, $8 for children 3 to 12, free for children 2 and under.**

The Heritage Museums & Gardens' collection concentrates on American art, history, and automobiles. The museum is comprised of three buildings: the Auto Gallery, the Special Exhibitions Gallery, and the American Art and Carousel Galleries (closed for renovations until the fall of 2014). The Auto Gallery holds an interesting collection of antique and vintage American cars in mint condition exhibited in a replica of a round Shaker stone barn (if you want to see the real thing, visit the Hancock Shaker Village near Pittsfield; see the "Berkshires" chapter). The Special Exhibitions Gallery building is a replica of a fort in New Windsor, New York; Washington and his men spent their last winter of the Revolutionary War in the original. The Special Exhibitions Gallery has rotating exhibits on a myriad of themes. Catch a ride on the restored antique carousel at the American Art and Carousel Gallery, which also houses the folk art galleries.

Gardening enthusiasts and kids with lots of energy love to roam the 100 acres of meticulously tended paths that wind through fantastic flower gardens and blooming shrubs (the gardens are the largest arboretum south of Boston) on the banks of Shawme Pond. The Old East Windmill was moved from its Orleans location to its new home on the Heritage Museum's grounds. A magnet for visitors in early spring, daffodils and tulips present a beautiful array of color. Rhododendrons bloom from the end of May to mid-June and are simply a gorgeous sight. Kids love to run around in the Hart Family Vine Maze Garden and the Labyrinth (made of crushed shell and pink granite, the Labyrinth has you trekking seven circuits of tighter and tighter circles to the center).

Hidden Hollow is a place set aside for children to play and explore nature. Kids can climb stepping stumps, balance on log beams, climb up the tree house, construct with blocks, create art, study plants, and manipulate interactive displays for hands-on fun. There are many activities geared for kids during the summer at the museum. There are live performances for kids and families on "Family Fun Fridays" in July and Aug that run the gamut from storytellers to giant puppets followed by a fun craft or garden project. The museum and gardens reopen during the holidays for the Gardens Aglow at Heritage. The Magnolia Cafe is great for a light meal or snack. Be sure to sign your kids up for the Summer Museum Adventures Day Camp, which offers art projects, outdoor games, and science projects.

Hoxie House and the Dexter Grist Mill (all ages)

18 Water St., Sandwich; (508) 888-1173. Open mid-June to mid-Oct, Mon through Sat 10 a.m. to 4:30 p.m. and Sun 1 to 4:30 p.m. Admission per site: $4 for adults, $3 for children 6 to 16; free for children under 6.

The oldest saltbox-style house on the Cape, restored to its original 1675 interior, contains furnishings on loan from the Boston Museum of Fine Arts. The Hoxie House has continuous tours full of social history and expressions of the day. One of many homilies that our tour guide explained was that most people didn't sleep in a bed until they got married, thus the expression "tie the knot" comes from the tradition of weaving a wooden frame with rope back and forth and on your wedding night, you tied the knot! Another Sandwich historical property, the Dexter Grist Mill, was built in 1640 (rebuilt in 1654) and is still in operation. Demonstrations of corn being ground into flour are fascinating to children. Buy a bag of cornmeal: They come with recipes—a great rainy-day project. Scenic Shawme Pond on the property attracts swans, ducks, and Canadian geese (bring bread to feed them). With the Hoxie House and the Dexter Grist Mill as a backdrop, the town of Sandwich has celebrated the Illumination Boat Parade at Shawme Pond on the Fourth of July for the past century. The evening begins with an old-fashioned band concert. Participants affix Japanese lanterns to their boats to outline elaborate displays—pirates, dragons, or whatever they can conjure up.

National Marine Life Center (all ages)

120 Main St. (edge of Cape Cod Canal), Buzzards Bay; (508) 743-9888; nmlc.org. Open daily 10 a.m. to 5 p.m. Memorial Day to Labor Day and then weekends until Columbus Day. Donations are welcome. Interim facility; fund-raising is in progress for a permanent facility.

The highest concentration of strandings in the US for whales, seals, dolphins, and sea turtles is on Cape Cod Bay, Nantucket Sound, and the coast of Maine. When fully opened, the National Marine Life Center will be a clearinghouse to address the needs of these marine animals through hospitalization and rehabilitation for future release (currently only stranded sea turtles and seals are treated). There is a live video feed from the hospital where the sea creatures (patients) are rehabilitating. You may also observe a treatment and diagnostic suite through a glass window, and you may be lucky enough to see a patient during an examination. The Marine and Science Center is open to the general public. It contains an interactive Discovery Center where kids can touch and feel bones, baleen, and shells, look into a critter tank, and see displays of whale bones and

TopEvents on Cape Cod

September–December

- **Scallop Fest,** Sept, Barnstable County Fairgrounds, East Falmouth; (508) 759-6000 (Canal Region Chamber) or (508) 563-3200 (Fairgrounds); capecodcanalchamber.org, scallopfest.org, or capecod fairgrounds.org

- **Food Truck Festival,** Sept, Barnstable County Fairgrounds, East Falmouth; (508) 563-3200; capecodfairgrounds.org

- **ClamBQ,** Sept, Orleans; (508) 255-1386; orleanscapecod.org

- **Cape Cod Cranberry Day,** Sept, Green Briar Nature Center, 6 Discovery Hill Rd., E. Sandwich; (508) 888-6870; thorntonburgess.org

- **Princess Tea,** Sept, Cape Cod Children's Museum, Mashpee; (508) 539-8788; visitcccm.org

- **Celebrate Our Waters,** Sept, Orleans; (508) 255-1386; orleanscape cod.org or orleanspondcoalition.org

- **The Dog Show,** Sept, Barnstable County Fairgrounds, East Falmouth; (508) 563-3200; capecodfairgrounds.org

- **Harwich Cranberry Festival,** mid-Sept, Harwich; (508) 430-1165; harwichcc.com

- **Yarmouth's Seaside Festival,** early Oct, South Yarmouth; (800) 732-1008; yarmouthcapecod.com or yarmouthseasidefestival.com

- **Oyster Fest,** Oct, downtown Wellfleet; (508) 349-2510; wellfleet chamber.com or wellfleetoysterfest.org

- **Oktoberfest,** early Oct, Mashpee Commons, Mashpee; (508) 539-1416; mashpeema.virtualtownhall.net

- **Halloween Family Fun Nights,** Oct, Heritage Museums and Gardens, Sandwich; (508) 888-3300; heritagemuseumsandgardens.org

- **Oktoberfest,** late Oct, Kate Gould Park, Chatham; (508) 945-5199 or (800) 715-5567; chathaminfo.org

- **Girls and Dolls Day,** Nov, Mashpee, (508) 477-0792; mashpee chamber.com
- **Lighting of the Pilgrim Monument,** eve of Thanksgiving, Province-town; (508) 487-1310; pilgrim-monument.org
- **Gardens Aglow,** end of Nov through mid-Dec, Fri through Sun, 67 Grove St., Heritage Museum and Gardens, Sandwich; (508) 888-3300; heritagemuseumsandgardens.org
- **A Seaside Christmas in Orleans,** Sat after Thanksgiving through Dec; Orleans; (508) 255-1386; orleanscapecod.org
- **Brewster for the Holidays,** Dec, Brewster; (508) 896-3500; brewster-capecod.com
- **Christmas Stroll,** mid-Dec, downtown Chatham; (508) 945-5199; chathaminfo.com
- **Christmas Parade,** Dec, Mashpee; (508) 477-0792; mashpeechamber .com or mashpeechamberchristmasparade.com
- **Falmouth Holidays by the Sea,** early Dec, Falmouth; (508) 548-8500; falmouthchamber.com
- **First Night Celebration** (only one on the Cape), Dec 31, downtown Chatham; (508) 945-5199; firstnightchatham.com

skeletons. Craft activities change daily and can include stamping T-shirts, making paper sea turtles, or painting a picture. Kids of all ages enjoy the National Marine Life Center.

Sandwich Glass Museum (all ages)

129 Main St. (Route 130), Town Hall Square, Sandwich; (508) 888-0251; sandwich glassmuseum.org. Open daily Apr through Dec 9:30 a.m. to 5 p.m. (glassblowing demonstrations 10 a.m. to 4 p.m. on the hour); Feb through Mar, Wed through Sun, 9:30 a.m. to 4 p.m. (glassblowing demonstrations 10 a.m. to 3 p.m. on the hour); closed Easter, Thanksgiving, Christmas Eve, Christmas Day, New Year's Eve, and the month of Jan. Admission: $8 for adults, $2 for children 6 to 14, free for children under 6. Museum gift shop.

On a bright day the Sandwich Glass Museum is a colorful sight to behold. Since much of the museum's collection is displayed in front of windows, sunlight is very much a part of the installation. Sandwich is internationally known for its glassware, made mostly during the 19th century. An excellent diorama explains the glassmaking process, and a multimedia presentation in the theater provides an overview of the first 200 years of glassmaking in Sandwich (on the half hour). Daily 20-minute glassblowing demonstrations, which kids can participate in, take place on the hour. The 1880 Hannah Rebecca Burgess Dining Room illustrates how the glass was used during mealtime, with holograms, music, and special effects. Kid activities include a treasure hunt throughout the museum (ask for the family guide—when the hunt is done, turn the guide in for a prize) and hands-on exhibits. A Contemporary Gallery with changing exhibits on local and nationally acclaimed artists depicts the glassmaking techniques of today. A wonderful 1.5-hour walking tour of Sandwich Village is given in the summer and fall at 10 a.m. (see schedule on website).

Scusset Beach State Reservation (all ages)

20 Scusset Beach Rd., Sandwich; (508) 888-0859; mass.gov/eea/agencies/dcr/ massparks/region-south/scusset-beach-state-reservation.html. Located north of the Cape Cod Canal. Open year-round 8 a.m. to 8 p.m. Parking is $7 per car.

On Cape Cod Bay at the east end of the Cape Cod Canal, Scusset Beach is a 380-acre park/beach area, which remains reasonably populated in the summer months. With 1.5 miles of frontage along the Cape Cod Canal, this is a prime location to watch the parade of boats and vessels passing through. The fishing pier at Scusset can be crowded at times with fishermen trying their luck at hooking a catch. Facilities include restrooms, access to the Cape Cod Canal Bike Trail, a snack bar, picnic tables, and 98 campsites. To reserve a campsite, contact Reserve America at (877) 422-6762; reserveamerica.com.

Other Things to See & Do

Aptucxet Trading Post, 24 Aptucxet Rd., Bourne; (508) 759-9487; bournehistorical society.org. Open Memorial Day to Columbus Day (check the website for hours), $5 for adults, $2 for ages 6 to 18. Pilgrims and Wampanoags traded here. Re-creation of a trading post with a collection of artifacts.

Butterflies of Cape Cod, 26 Herring Pond Rd., Bourne; (774) 413-9310; butterflies ofcapecod.com. Seasonal outdoor enclosure of butterflies and gift shop.

Lowell Holly Reservation, South Sandwich Road, Sandwich; (508) 679-2115; ttor .org. Open daily sunrise to sunset. Holly plants abound as well as rhododendrons and mountain laurel. There are two ponds great for water sports, such as canoeing, swimming, and fishing, and a sandy beach. Walking trails are an easy hike. **Free.**

Pairpoint Glass Works, 851 Sandwich Rd., Sagamore; (508) 888-2344 or (800) 899-0953; pairpoint.com. Watch glassware being made using methods that have been passed down for generations.

Sandwich Fish Hatchery, 164 Old Kings Hwy., Route 6A, Sandwich; (508) 888-0008. Open 9 a.m. to 3 p.m. daily. Free. Trout farm. Kids will love feeding the fish.

Where to Eat

Dunbar Tea Room, 1 Water St., Sandwich; (508) 833-2485; dunbartea.com. Open daily for lunch and afternoon tea from 11 a.m. to 5 p.m. (Sunday brunch served 8 a.m. to noon, lunch is noon to 5 p.m.). The *Zagat Guide for 2007 and 2008* rated the Dunbar Tea Room one of the top three spots for lunch on the Cape, the Cape Cod A List voted it #1 in 2012, and it has been voted the best lunch on the Upper Cape by *Cape Cod Life.* The afternoon tea (served all day) has assorted finger sandwiches, scones with jam and cream, and a mini-dessert selection. Mouthwatering! $

The Marshland, 109 Route 6A, Sandwich; (508) 888-9824; marshlandrestaurant .com. Open daily for breakfast, lunch, and dinner. Picturesque views of the marshes, great food. $–$$

The Mezza Luna Restaurant, 253 Main St., Buzzards Bay; (508) 759-4667; mezza lunarestaurant.com. Open for lunch and dinner, they do a fantastic job. A Bourne staple, rebuilt after a fire. Italian food is their specialty. Kids' menu. $–$$$

Where to Stay

Cranberry Manor, 50 Main St., Sandwich; (508) 888-1281; cranberrymanorbandb .com. Great location near local attractions. Deck and gazebo overlooking lovely garden. Children over 12 please. $$

Dan'l Webster Inn and Spa, 149 Main St., Sandwich; (508) 888-3622 or (800) 444-3566; danlwebsterinn.com. A traditional inn with canopy and four-poster beds and fireplaces in some of the rooms. Outdoor pool, full-service spa, and restaurant. $$–$$$$

The Fox Run Bed and Breakfast, 171 Puritan Rd., Buzzards Bay; (508) 759-1458; foxrunbandb.com. Lovely garrison in a residential neighborhood beautifully decorated, nice hosts, gazebo in the back. Children welcome; no charge for cribs. $–$$

Falmouth, Mashpee & Woods Hole

West of the town of Barnstable is Falmouth, a pleasant New England village that pulses with visitors throughout the summer. Its Nantucket Sound coast is lined with guesthouses, hotels, and summer homes. The downtown area has some good shopping and a few ice-cream parlors, but the main attraction of Falmouth is its coastline: The beaches are terrific, and the many inlets provide lots of space for private boat mooring. Of the four beaches that are open to nonresidents, the best are South Cape Beach, Surf Drive Beach, and Old Silver Beach. Woods Hole is home to the Woods Hole Oceanographic Institute, the National Marine

Fair Play

The Barnstable County Fair is the largest annual event on the Cape. Weeklong attendance exceeds 80,000 visitors every year.

Sneak This One In . . .

If you're in the Falmouth–Woods Hole area in mid-Aug, cheer on the runners in the **New Balance Falmouth Road Race,** an annual 7-mile race that attracts participants from all over New England. For more information, call (508) 540-7000 or visit falmouthroadrace.com.

Fisheries Science Aquarium, and the Steamship Authority. The village of Woods Hole is part of Falmouth; it's a fun place for kids to watch the boats going in and out of Eel Pond, which serves as a harbor and town center, of sorts. Walk around the pond to see the village's sites: the Aquarium, St. Mary's Bell Tower and Garden, the harbor, and the drawbridge. Many families see little more of Woods Hole, however, than the Steamship Authority parking lots and waiting area. For more information on Falmouth, contact the **Falmouth Chamber of Commerce and Visitor Information Center,** 20 Academy Ln., Falmouth, MA 02540; (508) 548-8500 or (800) 526-8532; falmouthchamber.com. For information on Mashpee, contact the **Mashpee Chamber of Commerce,** 17 Joy St., Mashpee, MA 02649; (508) 477-0792; mashpeechamber.com. Mashpee is still inhabited by the Wampanoag tribe, who gave the town its name.

Ashumet Holly Wildlife Sanctuary (all ages)
286 Ashumet Rd., East Falmouth; (508) 362-1426 or (508) 362-7475; massaudubon .org. Trails open dusk to dawn. Free.
Enjoy nature trails that wind among holly trees (more than 65 varieties) on 49 acres. The sanctuary sponsors ecology cruises to Cuttyhunk and other Elizabeth Islands; call for the schedule.

Barnstable County Fair (all ages)
Barnstable County Fairgrounds, 1220 Nathan Ellis Hwy., Route 151, East Falmouth; (508) 563-3200; barnstablecountyfair.org. Admission: $12 for adults, $3 for kids 6 through 12, free for children 5 and under. On Wristband Days the rides are unlimited for $22 per person.
In late July bring the kids to Barnstable for a real old-time county fair (since 1844). All profits are used to improve the fairgrounds and for scholarships for agricultural and home-economic careers. You'll enjoy livestock shows, oxen pulls, baking contests, a rollicking Demo-Derby, a busy midway, and lots of great food.

Cape Cod Children's Museum (under 10)

**577 Great Neck Rd. South, Mashpee; (508) 539-8788; capecodchildrensmuseum
.org. Open Mon through Sat 10 a.m. to 5 p.m., Sun noon to 5 p.m. Memorial Day
to Labor Day. From early Sept to to late May, open Mon through Fri 10 a.m. to
3 p.m., Fri and Sat 10 a.m. to 5 p.m., and Sun noon to 5 p.m. Closed on Thanksgiving, Christmas Eve, Christmas, and New Year's Day. Admission: $7 for ages 1
through 59, $6 for over age 60, free for children under 1.**

The Cape Cod Children's Museum is a good place to spend a rainy day. It has
a tree house, a post office, an interactive submarine, and a 30-foot pirate ship
(especially popular with toddlers). Visit the toddler castle in the toddler play
area; a big wooden train (perfect for climbing and exploration); a diner with play
food, utensils, and a cash register; a music room with handheld instruments and
a variety of drums; the puzzle table; and the science workshops. The arts-and-
crafts workshops, daily programs, field trips, and monthly museum activities are
fun for everyone. Children under 13 must be accompanied by an adult. This is a
great place for a toddler's birthday party.

Island Queen (all ages)

**75 Falmouth Heights Rd. (off Route 28), Falmouth; (508) 548-4800; islandqueen
.com. Operates late May to mid-Oct to Oak Bluffs. Price round-trip: $20 for adults,
$10 for children 5 to 12, free for children under 5. Bicycles cost $8 to transport.
Passenger ferry only; there is no car transportation. There is a charge of $15 per
calendar day for parking. *Note:* Only cash or traveler's checks are accepted as
forms of payment.**

If your family is in the mood for a pleasant boat ride, take the *Island Queen,* an
alternative to the Steamship Authority ferries to and from Martha's Vineyard,
departing from its own dock in Falmouth's Inner Harbor. Park the car at the
Island Queen parking lot on Falmouth Heights Road, and take the 35-minute ferry
over to the Vineyard for the day; it's less expensive, and the boat is smaller and

Family Fun Night

Your family can attend free movies under the stars on Wed nights
and summer musical concerts on Fri nights in July and Aug at Peg
Noonan Park, Main Street, in Falmouth.

Pow**wow**

The **Wampanoag Powwow** is held at the Tribal Grounds (483 Great Neck Rd. South, Mashpee) the first weekend in July in the Upper Cape. This three-day event features native crafts and foods. Native drumming, dancing, and singing demonstrations and contests are key to this colorful festival. The Fireball, on Saturday night, is a spiritual-healing medicine game, played like soccer with a ball on fire. It's a way for the warriors to take the pain that others have experienced, embrace it, and make it their own. The clambake dinner held on the last day of the powwow is a highlight. Admission is $13 for adults, $8 for seniors and children 6 to 12, free for children 5 and under. For more information, contact the Mashpee/Wampanoag Indian Tribal Council Office (508-477-0208; mashpeewampanoagtribe.com).

more comfortable than the Steamship Authority boats. No reservation is needed, but do try to get there 45 minutes before departure to get the time that you want.

Nobska Light (all ages)

Nobska Road, Woods Hole Harbor entrance, Woods Hole; lighthouse.cc/nobska. The grounds are open to the public year-round. Lighthouse tours are conducted by the US Coast Guard from 9:30 to 11:30 a.m. on select days (see website for the schedule). The lighthouse tower is accessible only during open houses. Children must be 6 years old and 45 inches tall.

Nobska Light sits on a bluff above winding Nobska Road between Woods Hole and Falmouth, overlooking Martha's Vineyard, Vineyard Sound, and the Elizabeth Islands. The lighthouse building that stands on this site today was built in 1876. Flashing every 6 seconds, Nobska's fixed-beacon light provides precise information to mariners: Seen head-on, the beam is white, indicating the safest route into Woods Hole Harbor; seen from either side, the red beam warns mariners against routes that could force them to go aground against the shoals. The light guides thousands of ships each year through the treacherous waters that lead to Woods Hole.

Old Silver Beach (all ages)

Off Route 28 on Quaker Road, North Falmouth; (508) 548-8623; falmouthmass .us/deppage.php?number=9. Parking is $20 per car in season. Lifeguards are on watch late June to Labor Day. No dogs are allowed May through Sept.

On Buzzards Bay, this crescent-shaped beach is a mecca for families, who are attracted to the fine white sand and shallow water. Lots of colorful sailboards, kayaks, and paddleboats are seen in the calm surf beyond the swim area. This town beach is lifeguarded and has restrooms, showers, a beach wheelchair, and a snack bar.

Shining Sea Bikeway (all ages)

North Falmouth to Locust Street to Steamship Authority Ferry Terminal Woods Hole Harbor access or pick it up near the intersection of Routes 28A and 151 in North Falmouth for the northern terminus at County Road; falmouthmass.us. or capecodbikeguide.com/shiningsea.asp. For a downloadable map, visit woodshole .com/documents/bikewaymap.pdf. Open year-round. Free.

The Shining Sea Bike Path is a 10.7-mile trail between North Falmouth and Woods Hole that's named for the last line of Falmouth native Katharine Lee Bates's beloved song, "America the Beautiful." The path can be crowded in the summer, and it's hilly in a few spots. From here it winds through a cranberry bog that is still farmed, breezes past West Falmouth Harbor with its many boats, stretching beyond scenic ponds and glacial moraines, marshlands and forests, goes past Nobska Lighthouse, and ends at Woods Hole Harbor. The path follows a prehistoric pathway of the Wampanoag Indians. *TIP:* The main parking area is in Falmouth Village off of Depot Road.

South Cape Beach State Park and the Waquoit Bay National Estuarine Research Reserve, and South Cape Beach

(all ages)

Great Oak Road, Mashpee; (508) 539-3288 (Waquoit Bay) or (508) 457-0495 (state park); mass.gov/eea/agencies/dcr/massparks/region-south/south-cape-beach-state-park.html or waquoitbayreserve.org. Between Columbus Day and Patriots' Day, the park's gates are locked; park at the Mashpee town Beach lot. Parking is $7.

Located between Waquoit Bay and Vineyard Sound, South Cape Beach is part of South Cape Beach State Park, which has several nice nature trails that lead behind dunes to a salt pond with great birding. In the summer see tern colonies, piping plovers, and other nesting shore birds. In the winter, loons, snowy owls, and winter ducks call it home.

The beach is the attraction here, though: It's a 2-mile-long barrier beach with nice warm water, gentle waves, a jetty where people go to fish, views to Martha's Vineyard on a clear day, and a big parking lot that rarely fills. The park is jointly managed by the State of Massachusetts Department of Conservation and Recreation and NOAA (National Oceanic and Atmospheric Administration), which oversees the Waquoit Bay National Research Reserve (of which South Cape Beach is a subset).

Steamship Authority (all ages)

1 Cowdry Rd., Woods Hole; (508) 548-3788 (Woods Hole general information) or (508) 477-8600 (vehicle reservation), (508) 693-9130 (Martha Vineyard's terminal general information), or (508) 548-5011 (administrative offices); islandferry.com or steamshipauthority.com. Directions: Follow the signs to the Woods Hole Steamship Authority off Route 28. Parking is $10 to $12 a day (depending upon the lot), mid-May to mid-Oct and is $8 for the rest of the year. Passengers and vehicles are accepted. Visit the website for rates for passengers, bikes, surfboards, sailboards, and vehicles.

If you want to visit Martha's Vineyard without a car, park in one of the Steamship Authority's parking lots and take the free shuttle bus to the harbor. You don't need a reservation if you're traveling without a car; simply purchase tickets for each person. The trip takes approximately 45 minutes for Martha's Vineyard, and there are numerous ferry departures for both Oak Bluffs (seasonal) and Vineyard Haven (year-round). The vehicle reservations for the Steamship Authority ferries go fast; the reservation lines open in late January (early Jan for Headstart customers), so plan early. The car ferry runs to both locations in Martha's Vineyard

Whisked **Away**

The **Whoosh Trolley** (800-352-7155; capecodrta.org) operates between the Falmouth Mall and the Woods Hole Steamship Authority, with stops in between, from late June to early Sept ($2 for adults and children; free for children 5 and under). Day passes are also available for unlimited rides, $6 for adults and children, free for 5 and under.

in season. ***Warning:*** This location services Martha's Vineyard only. Ferry passage to Nantucket is from Hyannis.

Surf Drive Beach (all ages)

Off Main and Shore Streets, Falmouth; (508) 548-8623; falmouthmass.us/deppage .php?number=9. Open late June through Labor Day, with lifeguards and parking attendants. Parking is $15. No dogs are allowed May through Sept.

On Vineyard Sound, Surf Drive Beach is popular with sailboarders and sunbathers. There are a lot of little stones as you enter the water, so water shoes are recommended, but with a bathhouse, restrooms, a beach wheelchair, and concession stand, this is still a great family beach. It's west of the main part of Falmouth, which keeps much of the summer crowd away. ***Beware:*** The water can be choppy!

Woods Hole Science Aquarium (all ages)

166 Water St., at Albatross Street, Woods Hole; (508) 495-2001 or (508) 495-2267; aquarium.nefsc.noaa.gov. Open Tues through Sat 11 a.m. to 4 p.m.; closed all federal holidays. Free.

The country's oldest public aquarium, the Woods Hole Science Aquarium preserves living sea creatures that are native to the Cape's waters or have reached our ocean via the Gulf Stream. The touch tanks are low to the ground so that even toddlers can reach in and feel the hermit, spider, and horseshoe crabs, lobsters, fish, sea stars (starfish), and other sea creatures. The whole place is child oriented, and the helpful staff love to answer kids' questions. A real treat is to watch the seal feeding and training session (at 11 a.m. and 4 p.m.) at the seal tank in front of the building.

Other Things to See & Do

Coonamessett Farm, 277 Hatchville Rd., E. Falmouth; (508) 563-2560. Animals to feed and pet, Little Sprouts Camp, ice cream and general store, Fri Night Farm Family Buffet, and Wed a Jamaican Buffet and Grill with steel-drum music in season.

Falmouth to Edgartown Ferry, Falmouth Harbor; (508) 548-9400; falmouth edgartownferry.com. Sailing from Falmouth Harbor to Edgartown. Pricing: Adults $25, kids $15, bikes $5. Seasonal.

Highfield Hall and Gardens, 56 Highfield Dr., Falmouth; (508) 495-1878; highfield hall.org. Kids and family events, art and cooking classes. Walking tours through Beebe Woods.

Mashpee Wampanoag Indian Museum, Route 130, Mashpee; (508) 477-9339 (museum) or (508) 477-6160 (Historic Preservation Office); mashpeewampanoagtribe .com. History and culture of the Wampanoags from the Stone Age to the present.

Oceanquest, Waterfront Park, 100 Water St., Woods Hole; (508) 414-1009; ocean quest.org. Price: $25 for adults, $20 for children 4 to 11, under 4 **free.** Lots of hands-on activities and learning opportunities about the ocean, science, and use of navigational tools for passengers. See website for parking tips.

Old Indian Meetinghouse, Meetinghouse Way near the Route 28 intersection, Mashpee; (508) 477-0208; mashpeewampanoagtribe.com. Built in 1684 for the Mashpee/Wampanoag tribe, the Old Indian Meetinghouse is the oldest surviving meetinghouse on the Cape.

Spohr's Garden, on Fells Road, off Oyster Pond Road, Falmouth; (508) 548-0623; spohrgardens.org. A 6-acre woodland garden overlooking Oyster Pond that's a lovely spot. Donations accepted.

Woods Hole Film Festival, late July through early Aug; (508) 495-FILM; woodshole filmfestival.com. Look for animation and comedies. None of the films are rated, so use caution in your choices.

Woods Hole Theater Company, 68 Water St., Woods Hole; (508) 540-6525; woods holetheater.org. Comedic and dramatic productions.

Where to Eat

Coonamessett Inn, 311 Gifford St., Falmouth; (508) 548-2300; capecodrestaurants .org/coonamessett. Fine dining in a country inn overlooking a pond. Appealing kids' menu. $–$$$

Landfall Restaurant, 9 Luscombe Ave., Woods Hole; (508) 548-1758; woodshole .com/landfall. Waterfront location next to the island ferry. The restaurant was built using recycled material from old buildings and shipwrecks. Specializies in seafood. Large selection of desserts for those with a sweet tooth. $–$$$$

Pie in the Sky, 10 Water St., Woods Hole; (508) 540-5475; woodshole.com/pie. Open daily year-round for breakfast, lunch, and dinner. Great muffins, juice, coffee, and sandwiches. $

Quarter Deck Restaurant, 164 Main St., Falmouth; (508) 548-9900; qdfalmouth .com. A quality restaurant in downtown, nautically themed with recycled decor. Kids' menu. $–$$

The Lanes Bowl and Bistro, Central Square, Mashpee Commons, Mashpee; (508) 833-1155; thelanesbowlbistro.com. Boutique bowling venue combining ten-pin bowling, full-service dining, and entertainment. Lane-side wait service. Sandwiches, pizzas and apps. Fun food in a fun place! $

Wicked Restaurant, 680 Falmouth Rd.,Mashpee; (508) 477-7422; wickedrestaurant .com. Organic ingredients are used in their pizza, made from scratch, and their entrees. Gluten-free specials. $–$$$

Where to Stay

Alexander Hamilton House, 9 Horseshoe Bend Way, Mashpee; (508) 419-1584; alexanderhamiltonhousecapecod.com. Beautiful, charming bed-and-breakfast overlooking a pond; the only one in Mashpee. Dog- and kid-friendly. Continental breakfast. $$$

Coonamessett Inn, 311 Gifford St., Falmouth; (508) 548-2300; capecodrestaurants .org/coonamessett. Fine country inn in picturesque setting; children welcome. $–$$$

Sea Crest Resort, 350 Quaker Rd., Falmouth; (508) 540-9400 or (800) 225-3110; seacrest-resort.com. Two-hundred-sixty-three-room resort on the beach with pool and snackbar. Family-night movies with popcorn, ice cream shop, children's fit camp, and activities in season. $–$$$$

Woods Hole Passage, 186 Woods Hole Rd., Woods Hole; (508) 548-9575 or (800) 790-8976; woodsholepassage.com. Open year-round. Quiet bed-and-breakfast in the northern part of Woods Hole. Rooms are spacious and comfortable, and the full breakfasts are delicious. Children of all ages welcome with notification. $$

Barnstable & Its Villages

Barnstable is the Cape's largest town; its 60 square miles include the villages of Barnstable and West Barnstable along Cape Cod Bay, and Cotuit, Marstons Mills, Osterville, Centerville, and Hyannis along Nantucket Sound. These villages differ greatly. Hyannis is the commercial center of the Cape, as well as its most crowded town. If you're coming to the Cape to get away from crowds, malls, and traffic, you should avoid Hyannis. If you like the bustle of a busy harbor town, however, you'll enjoy Hyannis—but be sure to get out into the quieter villages that border it on the north and west. By the way, while you're in Hyannis, don't bother looking for Kennedys: When they're at their private compound on the town's western edge, they're on vacation, too, and they keep well out of sight. The **Hyannis Chamber of Commerce** can be reached at 397 Main St., Hyannis, MA 02601; (508) 775-2201 (visitor center); hyannis.com (it's in the same building as the JFK Hyannis Museum), or visit their harbor visitor center at the Harbor Master's Office on Ocean Street (seasonal).

Cape Cod Central Railroad (all ages)

The train leaves from the station depot at 252 Main St. in downtown Hyannis, 70 Main St. in Buzzards Bay, or you can make a whistle stop at 28 Jarves St. in Sandwich; (508) 771-3800 or (888) 797-RAIL; capetrain.com. Open Apr through Dec; call for a schedule and prices.

The narrated scenic 2-hour train ride on the Cape Cod Central Railroad from Hyannis to Buzzards Bay is fun for kids. Views of the Cape's forests, salt marshes, sand dunes, and cranberry bogs line the route. If you want to shorten the train trip to 1 hour (round-trip), the train makes a whistle stop in Sandwich and you and your family can get off there; the small village of Sandwich is a nice place to

Hyannis **Ferries**

Fast ferries from Hyannis to Nantucket take approximately 1 hour and can zip along at a faster rate because they are smaller vessels, carry fewer people (in a more luxurious setting), and don't accept vehicles. The traditional Martha's Vineyard and Nantucket ferries take approximately 2 hours, with only the Steamship Authority accepting vehicles. All of the ferries offer restrooms, a snack bar, free shuttle service from their parking lots in Hyannis for the Steamship Authority (parking is on-site for the Hy-Line Cruises), and onboard carriage of bikes for a fee. Arrive 45 minutes before departure. Call or visit their website for prices and their daily operating schedule.

- **Hy-Line Cruises,** 220 Ocean St., Ocean Street Dock, Hyannis; (508) 778-2600, (508) 778-0404, or (800) 492-8082; hylinecruises.com. Fast ferry to Nantucket and Martha's Vineyard; traditional ferry service to both Nantucket and Martha's Vineyard, Oak Bluffs dock. The ferry ride takes just under 2 hours on the traditional service to either Martha's Vineyard or Nantucket. The speed ferry to Nantucket or Martha's Vineyard takes only 1 hour. No cars accepted (passengers only). A new service, Around the Sound, allows you to tour the islands of Nantucket and Martha's Vineyard all in one day for about 4 to 5 hours per island. The cost is $79 per adult and $44 for ages 5 to 12; free for children under 5. A charge for parking is collected when you drop off your car.

- **Steamship Authority,** 141 School St., South Street Dock, Hyannis; (508) 477-8600 (vehicle reservations), (508) 495-FAST (for fast ferry passenger reservations), (508) 771-4000 (Hyannis ferry terminal) or (508) 228-0262 (Nantucket ferry terminal); steamshipauthority.com or islandferry.com. Choice of traditional or fast ferry service to Nantucket only; passage to Martha's Vineyard is from Woods Hole. Check the website for the traditional, fast ferry and vehicle rates. Cars are accepted with reservations on the traditional ferry only. Parking in the main lot is $15 to $20 a day from mid-May to mid-Oct (depending upon your dates), $5 to $10 during the rest of the year.

stroll for a couple of hours while visiting the village's family-oriented attractions before catching the train back to Hyannis. The train (cited by *USA Today* as one of the top 10 in the nation) operates only in the summer and fall; the Cape Cod dinner train (featured on the Food Network as one of the top three dinner trains in America) or a selection of other dining options are available May through Oct, offering a vintage dining experience. Special themed trains operate for Thanksgiving dinner, a Murder Mystery (out of Hyannis), or to Christmas Town (out of Buzzards Bay). *TIP:* A pretty time to take the ride is at sunset.

Cape Cod Potato Chip Factory (all ages)

100 Breeds Hill (corner of Breeds Hill Road and Independence Drive), off Route 132, Hyannis; (508) 775-3358; capecodchips.com. Open weekdays year-round, 9 a.m. to 5 p.m. Free.
One of the highlights of a trip through busy Hyannis is a self-guided tour of the Cape Cod Potato Chip Factory, followed by **free** samples. As you approach, you can smell the chips. Cape Cod Potato Chip Factory produces potato chips and popcorn.

Craigville Beach (all ages)

Craigville Road, Barnstable; (508) 790-9888; town.barnstable.ma.us. Parking is $15 Mon through Fri, $20 weekends and holidays (parking fees are collected from 7 a.m. to 5 p.m.), Memorial Day through Labor Day; after 4 p.m. and the rest of the year, it's free. The beach is lifeguarded from 9 a.m. to 5 p.m. starting in late June through Labor Day (gates lock at 9 p.m.). The restrooms are open 7 a.m. to 6:30 p.m.
On Nantucket Sound, Craigville Beach is a busy place that's popular with teenagers as well as families with young children. The water is warmer here than on the north or east coasts of the Cape. Craigville Beach has lots of parking, clean changing rooms and showers, restrooms, lifeguards, and a snack bar across the street (and plenty of clam shack-type eateries within a few minutes' walk of the beach).

John F. Kennedy Hyannis Museum (all ages)

397 Main St., Hyannis; (508) 790-3077; jfkhyannismuseum.org. Check the website for the schedule. Price: $9 for adults, $5 for kids 8 to 17, free for kids under 8.
The museum focuses on JFK's life during his time on the Cape and how the Cape impacted his decision making. JFK was the only US president that got to sign a bill that he had written (the creation of the Cape Cod National Seashore). This

Land and Sea Tours in the Hyannis Area

- **Cape Cod Duckmobile,** 437 Main St., Hyannis; (508) 790-2111 or (888) 225-3825; duckmobile.com. Open in season 10 a.m. to 5 p.m. daily. Tours are every half hour. Price: $18 for adults, $15 for students and kids over 5, $5 for kids 5 and under. Land-and-sea tour of Hyannis on an amphibious duckmobile.

- **Catboat Eventide,** 146 Ocean St., Ocean Street Dock, Hyannis; (508) 775-0222; catboat.com. Harbor and sunset cruises; the price is $35 for adults and $10 for children under 90 pounds. Sailings daily mid-May through Columbus Day. A $2 per person discount for the bar and galley is found on the website. Salty tales, historical facts, and dish!

- **Hyannis Whale Watchers,** 269 Millway Rd., Millway Marina; (800) 287-0374; whales.net. Open May through Oct. Mid-Cape's only whale-watching adventure. Naturalists describe whales, their habits, and their habitat. Tidbits on local Cape history and environs. Spottings of dolphins and other marine creatures.

- **Hy-Line Hyannisport Harbor Cruises and Deep Sea Fishing,** 138 Ocean St., Ocean Street Dock, Hyannis; (508) 790-0696 or (888) 778-1132; hylinecruises.com. Specializing in fishing trips, harbor cruises, and Sundae Ice Cream "Float" cruises. Children sail for free on early-morning family harbor cruises. Check the website for pricing.

- **Pirate Adventures,** Ocean Street Docks, Hyannis; (508) 394-9100; capecodpirateadventures.com. Open Memorial Day through Labor Day. Price: $24 per person; must be over 1 year old. If your kids like pirate adventures à la *Peter Pan*, complete with painted faces, sailor sashes, sailor odes, and swashbuckling yarns, then all aboard! Follow the secret treasure map to claim your booty. Reservations a must. Arrive 20 minutes prior to sailing. Free eye-patch coupon and pirate-themed games for kids on the website.

museum is not as impressive as the one in Dorchester, but 60,000 people a year do visit. Ask for the map of the Kennedy Legacy Trail Hyannis.

Kalmus Park Beach (all ages)

670 Ocean St., Hyannis; (508) 790-9884; town.barnstable.ma.us. Parking is $15 Mon through Fri, $20 weekends and holidays (parking fees are collected from 9 a.m. to 3:45 p.m.) Memorial Day through Labor Day; after 4 p.m. and the rest of the year, it's **free.** The beach is lifeguarded from 9 a.m. to 5 p.m. starting in late June through Labor Day (gates lock at 9 p.m.). The restrooms are open 9 a.m. to 4:30 p.m.

Wide, scenic Kalmus Park Beach is a good spot for families. There are gentle waves, fine sand, designated fishing areas, lots of seashells to collect, and a sheltered area for toddlers, as well as ample restrooms, a picnic and volleyball area, lifeguards, and a snack bar. Kalmus, a peninsula, juts out into Lewis Bay and Nantucket Sound (one of the largest windsurfing areas on the Cape and in the country).

Long Pasture (all ages)

345 Bonehill Rd., Cummaquid (Barnstable); (508) 362-7425; massaudubon.org. Trails open sunrise to sunset, the visitor center is open daily Memorial Day to Columbus Day 9 a.m. to 5 p.m. Admission: $4 for adults, $3 for kids 2 to 12, **free** for under 2.

Located on Barnstable Harbor, Long Pasture is a 101-acre sanctuary with breathtaking views of the tidal flats and Sandy Neck Beach. The sanctuary encompasses pond, salt marsh, forest, and fields on 2.5 miles of trails. The Butterfly Trail was designed to attract numerous butterfly species. There are farm animals, and a summertime weekly goat walk will delight your child (the kids hold a leash and walk a goat down a trail). There are a lot of great family programs to choose from; bird walks, tidal flats exploration, natural history walks, kayaking, Barnstable Harbor, Elizabeth Islands, Cuttyhunk, and hands-on aquatic and marine-biology cruises out of Hyannis. Out of all the Audubon properties on the mid- and upper Cape, Long Pasture has the most programming, children's events, and activities.

Sandy Neck Beach (all ages)

425 Sandy Neck Rd., off Route 6A, West Barnstable; (508) 362-8300; town.barn stable.ma.us. Parking is $15 Mon through Fri, $20 weekends and holidays (parking fees are collected from 9 a.m. to 3:45 p.m.) Memorial Day through Labor Day;

after 3:45 p.m. and the rest of the year, it's free. The beach is lifeguarded from 9 a.m. to 5 p.m. starting in late June through Labor Day (gates lock at 9 p.m.). The restrooms are open 9 a.m. to 4:30 p.m.

At Barnstable's lovely beach on Cape Cod Bay, the dunes of 6-mile-long Sandy Neck Beach protect Barnstable Harbor from heavy surf. They also form one of the Cape's finest barrier beaches, and one that's rarely crowded. The beach has an adjacent parking lot, restrooms, convenient changing rooms, a picnic area, and a small snack bar. Off-roading is allowed on the beach with a permit pass.

Veterans Park Beach (all ages)

480 Ocean St., at the end of Gosnold Street, Hyannis; (508) 790-9885; town.barn stable.ma.us. Parking is $15 Mon through Fri, $20 weekends and holidays (parking fees are collected from 9 a.m. to 3:45 p.m.) Memorial Day through Labor Day; after 3:45 p.m. and the rest of the year, it's free.

Adjacent to the John F. Kennedy Memorial in Veterans Park, Veterans Park Beach has lots of picnic tables, grills, a bathhouse (open from 7 a.m. to 7 p.m.), a small playground, a mobile snack bar, and volleyball, and it is lifeguarded from 9 a.m. to 5 p.m. *TIP:* The water is shallow here so it's a great beach for families with young children.

Other Things to See & Do

Cahoon Museum of American Art, 4676 Falmouth Rd., Cotuit; (508) 428-7581; cahoonmuseum.org. Open Tues through Sat 10 a.m. to 4 p.m., Sun 1 to 4 p.m. Closed Jan, major holidays, and on Mon. Price: $8 for adults, and free for children under 12. Featuring the home and the art of Ralph and Martha Cahoon, antiques dealers who painted primitives on furniture and other folk-painting mediums. Ralph is the most famous artist the Cape has produced, and his paintings have been collected by Kennedys, Posts, Mellons, Merriweathers, and DuPonts.

Cape Cod Maritime Museum, 135 South St.; Hyannis; (508) 775-1723; capecod maritimemuseum.org. The region's maritime history is explored. Classes on boatbuilding (kayaks, skiffs, and dories), tying knots, lofting, and building a ship in a bottle.

Cape Cod Melody Tent, 21 West Main St., Hyannis; (508) 775-5630 (office) or call (800) 514-3849 to purchase tickets or book online; melodytent.org. Nationally known musical groups, concerts, and comedians. Children's theater productions on Wed during the summer.

Cape Symphony Orchestra, Business address is 1060 Falmouth Rd., Hyannis; (774) 470-2282 (office) or (508) 362-1111 (tickets); capesymphony.org. Third-largest orchestra in Massachusetts. Performances are at the Barnstable High School Performing Arts Center at 744 West Main St., Hyannis.

Sturgis Library, Route 6A, 3090 Main St., Barnstable; (508) 362-6636; sturgislibrary .org. Oldest public library building in the US.

Toad Hall Classic Car Museum, 288 Scudder Ave., Hyannisport; (508) 778-4934; toadhallcars.com. Open daily year-round from 11 a.m. to 5 p.m. Admission: $8 for adults, $4 for kids 10 to 16, free for kids under 10. Collection of more than 50 cars in mint condition, all in neon *red!*

The West Parish Meetinghouse, Corner of Route 149 and Meetinghouse Way, 2049 Meetinghouse Way, West Barnstable; (508) 362-4445; westparish.org. Second-oldest surviving meetinghouse on the Cape.

Zion Heritage Museum, 276 North St., Hyannis; (508) 790-9466; zionheritage museum.org. A Cape Verdean and African-American Museum.

Where to Eat

Four Seas, 360 South Main St., Centerville; (508) 775-1394; fourseasicecream.com. Open mid-May through mid-Sept. Rated number one in New England by *Gourmet* magazine. Serves some of the best ice cream on the Cape, along with sandwiches and lobster salad rolls. Seasonal. $

Gringo's, 577 Main St., Hyannis; (508) 771-8449; gringoshyannis.com. Features seafood, pizza, and Mexican dishes. Children's menu. Seasonal. $–$$

Paddock Restaurant, 20 Scudder Ave., Hyannis; (508) 775-7677; paddockcapecod .com. Steaks and seafood specialties. Open seasonally. $–$$$$

Tugboats, 21 Arlington St., Hyannis Marina, Hyannis; (508) 775-6433; tugboats capecod.com. Outside dining on a covered deck with great views of Hyannis harbor. Kids will love watching the water activity (especially the passing of the steamship). Seasonal. $–$$$

Where to Stay

Anchor-In, 1 South St., Hyannis; (508) 775-0357; anchorin.com. The only hotel in Hyannis with its own boat-docking facilities (people rent for a season); there is also a harborside outdoor pool. Family-friendly. $–$$$$

Captain Gosnold Village, 230 Gosnold St., Hyannis; (508) 775-9111; captaingosnold .com. Open May to Oct. Efficiency studios and large one-, two-, three-bedroom cottages with fully equipped kitchens. Outdoor pool, play yard, lawn-game equipment, and gas grills. Flags from the guest's country of origin are put by the door of their unit, a nice icebreaker for conversation! $–$$$$

Long Dell Inn, 436 S. Main St., Centerville; (508) 775-2750; longdellinn.com. Operating since 1929, the Long Dell is a newly renovated (2013), gracious Cape Cod–style home with a large lawn and 7 guest rooms. Four-course gourmet breakfast. Welcomes ages 12 and up. $–$$

Marston Family Bed and Breakfast, 70 Marston Ave., Hyannis; (508) 775-3334; catboat.com/b&b. Built in 1786, an antique Cape Cod house with four fireplaces. Weekly rental includes four bedrooms for up to eight people and a **free** ride on their catboat *The Eventide*. Call for pricing.

Simmons Homestead Inn, 288 Scudder Ave., Hyannisport; (508) 778-4999 or (800) 637-1649; simmonshomesteadinn.com. Views of Simmons Pond and lovely gardens. Toad Hall Classic Car Museum on property. Full breakfast served in the a.m. and wine in the p.m.! Both children and dogs are welcome. $$–$$$

Yarmouth, Dennis & Harwich

Yarmouth, Dennis, and Harwich cover both the bay and the sound coasts of the mid-Cape, as well as the congestion of Route 28 and the peaceful residential areas north of Route 6A and south of Route 28. The **Yarmouth Chamber of Commerce** is at 424 Route 28, West Yarmouth, MA 02673 (with a visitor center off Route 6 between exit 6 and 7); (508) 778-1008 or (800) 732-1008; yarmouth capecod.com. To contact the **Dennis Chamber of Commerce** (238 Swan River Rd., at the intersection of Routes 28 and 134, West Dennis, MA 02670), call (508) 398-3568 or visit dennischamber.com. The **Harwich Chamber of Commerce** (PO Box 34) is located at 1 Schoolhouse Rd., Harwichport, MA 02646; (508) 430-1165 or (800) 442-7942; harwichcc.com.

Beach Blanket Bingo on Nantucket Sound

Yarmouth has many fine beaches (with warmer waters streaming up from the Gulf of Mexico) popular with families. All have a $15 parking fee:

- **Bass River Beach,** 220 South Shore Dr. Your crew can watch the boats coming down the Bass River into Nantucket Sound. There are plenty of benches, a boat launch, a fishing dock, a bathhouse, a large parking lot, and a mobile concession stand.

- **Parker River Beach,** 157 South Shore Dr. Families love it here because of the playground. Facilities include a snack bar, outdoor showers, restrooms, and a small swimming area.

- **Seagull Beach,** 125 Seagull Rd. This beach is great for your teens and young adults. This is Yarmouth's largest beach with a bathhouse, a shower, a large parking lot, and food for purchase.

Bass Hole aka Gray's Beach (all ages)
400 Centre St. (off of Route 6A), Yarmouth Port; (508) 398-2231 or (508) 790-9133; yarmouth.ma.us. Life guarded from 8 a.m. to 4 p.m. May through Sept. Open parking, no fee.

A fine beach for families, albeit with cooler waters from Cape Cod Bay, Gray's Beach has another attraction—the long wooden Bass Hole Boardwalk, which stretches over a salt marsh. Kids love to scamper along the elevated walkway; it's also fun to peer out over the marshy grasses and flowers. The beach has calm water, lots of picnic tables, handy restrooms, walking trails, and a small playground. *Warning:* There is a strong current beyond the swimming area.

Cape Cod Rail Trail (all ages)
Running from Route 134 in South Dennis to the spar to Wellfleet. To pick up the trail, take exit 9A off Route 6 in Dennis, turn south on Route 134, and travel approximately 0.25 mile. The trail ends in Wellfleet, just east of Route 6, near the

Wellfleet Chamber of Commerce information booth; (508) 896-3491; mass.gov/eea/ agencies/dcr/massparks/region-south/cape-cod-rail-trail.html. Free. The Cape Cod Rail Trail is a 22-mile-long (one-way) asphalt biking path that follows the old (discontinued) railroad tracks that cut a swath through six towns (Dennis, Harwich, Brewster, Orleans, Eastham, and Wellfleet), passing through Nickerson State Park and the Cape Cod National Seashore. The trail is fairly flat and safe; however, short sections of the trail are on roads. There are lots of places to pull over for beach fun, buy a hard-earned snack, or use a restroom. Restrooms are located at Nickerson State Park in Brewster, the Cape Cod National Seashore Salt Pond Visitor Center in Eastham, or the National Seashore Headquarters, 99 Marconi Site Rd., Wellfleet. To rent a bicycle, contact **Barbara's Bike Shop,** 430 Route 134, South Dennis (508-760-4723), or at 3430 Main St., Brewster (508-896-7231; barbsbikeshop.com). The rental shop in South Dennis is at the beginning of the Cape Cod Rail Trail; the second location is just outside of Nickerson State Park. If you wish to bike to Chatham from the Cape Cod Rail Trail, take the Old Colony Rail Trail off of the bike rotary in Harwich (just after mile marker 3). If you want to continue on from Wellfleet to Provincetown, get a back roads map for Route 1 (Route 6 is too dangerous) from the Cape Cod National Seashore's Salt Pond Visitor Center in Eastham.

Cape Cod Center **for the Arts**

The **Cape Cod Center of the Arts** Campus in Dennis includes the Cape Cinema, the Cape Cod Museum of Art, and the Cape Playhouse located at 820 Route 6A:

- **Cape Cinema,** (508) 385-2503; capecinema.com. This is an art house movie theater. Simulcasts of performances from the National Theatre in London and the Metropolitan Opera in NYC.

- **Cape Cod Museum of Art,** (508) 385-4477; ccmoa.org. Work by Cape Cod artists. Special treasure hunt for children (Artquest).

- **Cape Playhouse,** (508) 385-3911; capeplayhouse.com. Many of the famous thespians of today cut their teeth here. The playhouse bills itself as America's Oldest Professional Summer Theater. Thurs and Fri morning live children's productions in July and Aug.

Amazing
Massachusetts Facts

- It is the law in Massachusetts for children 12 and under to wear protective helmets when operating or riding as a passenger on a bicycle.
- The tallest all-granite structure in the US is the Pilgrim Tower in Provincetown.

Cape Cod Waterways (all ages)

16 Main St., Route 28 (0.25 mile east of Route 134) on the Swan River in Dennisport; (508) 398-0080; capecodwaterways.com. Rent by the hour; price depends on boat chosen and number of participants. Open mid-Apr through mid-Oct 8 a.m. to 7:30 p.m. daily in season and 10 a.m. to 6 p.m. off-season.

Paddleboat or canoe, which to choose? Luckily, the rental is by the hour, and the owner allows you to change boats midstream. Our decision was to canoe the route to South Village Beach and change over to the paddleboat for the northerly trek to Swan Pond. The paddleboats can be electronically operated to help navigate the changing tidal currents, or you can switch over to manual and use foot power to propel you on your way. Single and double kayaks are also available. **Note:** Construction near Cape Cod Waterways will be completed by Labor Day 2014 but they are still open.

Freedom Cruise Line (all ages)

702 Main St., Route 28, Saquatucket Harbor Dock, Harwichport; (508) 432-8999; nantucketislandferry.com. Operates mid-June through late Sept, three times a day in season. Price round-trip: $74 for adults, $51 for children 2 to 11, $6 for children under 2. Parking is free for day-trippers only.

Eighty-minute high-speed cruise from Harwichport to Nantucket. Freedom Cruise Line's appeal is its location mid-Cape—less hustle and bustle here than leaving from Hyannis. Reservations are recommended; bikes allowed onboard for an extra fee ($14). No vehicles accepted. For overnight parking the charge is $17 per night.

Scargo Tower (all ages)

Route 6A, to Old Bass River Road, take the first left onto Scargo Hill Road, Dennis. Scargo Tower isn't that tall a tower—only 28 feet—but the high hill it sits on makes it a great place to take in a terrific view of Nantucket Sound, Cape Cod Bay, and the Cape's midsection. The top of Scargo Tower stands at 188 feet above sea level. Open sunrise to sunset.

West Dennis Beach (all ages)

Off Davis Beach Road, West Dennis; (508) 760-6162 or (508) 760-6159; dennis chamber.com. Parking is charged Memorial Day to Labor Day from 8 a.m. to 5 p.m. The price is $20 midweek (Mon through Fri), $25 weekends and holidays. One-mile-long West Dennis Beach, bordering a flat salt marsh and several tidal streams, is a busy place in the summer. The eastern end is for Dennis residents only; the rest of it is taken over by families, who park in the enormous parking lot that usually fills up in July and August. Enjoy the beach and its many facilities— good swimming, lots of lifeguard stations (manned Memorial Day through Labor Day), restrooms, showers, play areas with swing sets, and a snack bar in season.

Other Things to See & Do

Bass River Cruises and Kayaks, 116 Main St., Route 28, West Dennis; (508) 362-5555; capecodriverkayaking.com. Price for cruise: $20 for adults, $7 for children 1 to 11. Scenic cruise on the Bass Rivers showcasing fine homes, local lore, and the native wildlife. Kayak rentals. Seasonal.

Cape Cod Lavender Farm, Corner of Weston Woods Road and Route 124, then look for the signs to the farm, Harwich; (508) 432-8397; capecodlavenderfarm.com. Largest seller of lavender on the East Coast (Martha Stewart has been a customer). Children love the Enchanted Garden created especially for them.

Captain Bangs Hallet House, 11 Strawberry Ln. (off Route 6A), Yarmouth Port; (508) 362-3021; hsoy.org. Open June to mid-Oct and for special events. Fifty-acre sea captain's house and estate; hiking trails.

Cap'n Kids Fishing Adventures, Route 28, Saquatucket Harbor, Harwich Port; (508) 430-0066 or (508) 394-9100; capecodkidsfishing.com. Weekends late May to mid-June, then daily through early Sept. Two-hour fishing trips; includes all equipment and bait.

Cranberry Bog Tour, 1601 Factory Rd., Harwich; (508) 432-0790; cranberrybogtours.com. Open spring through fall. Adults $15, kids 6 to 18 are $10, free for under 6. Cranberry bog 1.5-hour guided tour. Visit farm animals.

Edward Gorey House, 8 Strawberry Ln., Yarmouth Port; (508) 362-3909; edwardgoreyhouse.org. Learn about the life and work of Edward Gorey, an animal rights activist and artist.

Harwich Junior Theatre, 105 Division St., Harwich; (508) 432-2002; hjt capecod.org. The first family theatre on the "straw hat" circuit. Summer theater productions for kids, classes, and winter productions for all audiences. On the Cape Cod A List for Best Theater. Previous pieces performed have been *The Wind in the Willows, Peter Pan, Dracula, Annie,* and *The Secret Garden.*

Old Colony Rail Trail, a spur just past Mile Marker #3 on the Cape Cod Rail Trail leads you to the Old Colony Rail Trail running from the bike rotary in Harwich to Main Street in Chatham, approximately 7.5 miles one-way. Glide past cranberry bogs, ponds, historic Harwich Center, and conservation areas with woods and fields until you reach Chatham. Fairly flat with short small hills interspersed. Easy biking for families.

Where to Eat

Breakfast Room, 675 Main St., West Dennis; (508) 398-0581; breakfastroomcape cod.com. Open in season for breakfast and lunch from 7 a.m. to 2 p.m. Always a line, very popular. Kids' menu. $

Dog House, 189 Lower County Rd., Dennisport; (508) 398-7774; doghousedennis .com. Best place to get an old-fashioned hot dog. Casual eating outside at picnic tables.

Captain Parkers Pub, 668 Main St. (Route 28), West Yarmouth; (508) 771-4266; captainparkers.com. Open year-round. A local favorite. Winner of the Cape Cod Chowder Festival five out of ten times in the last decade. ***Note:*** There could be a line. $–$$$

Clancy's, 8 Upper County Rd. (off of Route 134), Dennisport; (508) 394-6661; clancys restaurant.com. Outside deck overlooking Swan River. Seafood, pasta, steaks, gluten-free menu, kids' menu. Open 7 days a week for lunch and dinner. Voted best family dining by *Cape Cod Life* for the mid-Cape. $–$$$

Lobster Boat, 681 Main St. (Route 28), West Yarmouth; (508) 775-0486; thelobster boatrestaurant.com. Waterfront dining overlooking the Parker River and the marina open daily for lunch and dinner in season. Lobster and other seafood dishes, as well as hamburgers, fried chicken, and the like. Kids' menu. $$–$$$

Marshside Restaurant, 28 Bridge St., East Dennis; (508) 385-4010; themarshside .com. Serving lunch and dinner year-round. Lots of bird activity in the many bird-houses that are in the marsh and Sesuit Creek keeps kids' attention. Kids' menu. $–$$$

The Sundae School, 381 Lower County Rd. (off of Route 28), Dennisport; (508) 394-9122; sundaeschool.com. Homemade ice cream and sundaes in season. Other loca-tions in Harwich Port and East Orleans. $

The Weatherdeck, 168 Main St., West Harwich; (508) 432-8240. Family style, order seafood, burgers, or ice cream in season. A minigolf course on the property has sight-lines of the Herring River. $–$$

Where to Stay

By the Sea Guests B&B, 57 Chase Ave., Dennisport; (508) 398-8685 or (800) 447-9202; bytheseaguests.com. Right on the beach, views to Nantucket Sound, very casual and low key in decor and atmosphere. In business for over 50 years; repeat business from generations of families. No swimming pool. Full breakfast. $$–$$$

Clarion All Seasons Motor Inn, 1199 Main St., Route 28, South Yarmouth; (508) 394-7600 or (800) 527-0359; choicehotels.com. Indoor and outdoor pools; TV, VCR, restaurant for breakfast, fitness center, sauna; and refrigerator in every room. Open year-round. $–$$

Edgewater Beach Resort, 95 Chase Ave., Dennisport; (508) 398-6922; edgewater resorthoa.org. Open year-round. Suites, some oceanfront and some efficiency. Indoor and outdoor pools. $–$$$$

Holiday Hill Motor Inn, 352 Main St., Route 28, Dennisport; (508) 394-5577 or (800) 333-2569; holidayhillmotorinn.com. Ice-cream shops, Family Fun Center with a video game arcade, bumper cars, minigolf, and a heated pool on premises. Modest rooms are easy on the pocketbook (with many amenities). Open the first weekend in May to Columbus Day. $–$$$

The Lighthouse Inn, 1 Lighthouse Inn Rd., West Dennis; (508) 398-2244; lighthouse inn.com. Family-oriented resort on Nantucket Sound, near the Bass River. Accommodations include single rooms and cottages scattered across 9 well-maintained acres. On-site attractions include a working lighthouse, tennis courts, an outdoor heated pool, miniature golf, shuffleboard, a playground, a volley ball and basketball court, private beach, and lots of planned activities for kids. Breakfast included in rate. Open Memorial Day to Columbus Day. $$–$$$$

Red Jacket Inn, 1 South Shore Dr., S.Yarmouth; (800) CAPECOD; redjacketresorts .com. Great ocean views, family-friendly resort with 150 rooms on the beach, indoor and outdoor pools. $$–$$$$

The Tern Inn and Cottages, 91 Chase St., West Harwich; (508) 432-3714; thetern inn.com. Rural setting, quaint and comfortable. Amenities include swing sets, a pool, games, and a picnic area with a grill welcoming well-behaved children. Cottages are weekly rentals; the room rates are by the day. Buffet breakfast. $–$$$$

Chatham

Chatham is a village of shingled cottages, with a delightful Main Street full of shops and cafes and a variety of top-level summer accommodations for families. Several attractions are in the don't-miss category for families: the Fish Pier, Chatham Lighthouse, the Friday evening band concerts at Kate Gould Park, and the Railroad Museum. Contact the **Chatham Chamber of Commerce,** 2377 Main St., PO Box 793, South Chatham, MA 02633; (508) 945-5199 or (800) 715-5567; chathaminfo.com. There is also a visitor center information booth from May

Down by **the Sea**

A variety of water and seal tours in Chatham can be arranged by contacting one of the following boat tour operators:

- **Beachcomber** (508-945-5265; sealwatch.com)
- **Chatham Water Tours** (508-237-2564; chathamwatertours.info)
- **Rip Rider** (508-945-5450; monomoyislandferry.com)

Safety Tip

The road between Chatham and Orleans can be busy; take the time to drive the kids to the beach rather than allowing them to walk.

through Oct at the intersection of Route 137 and Route 28 in South Chatham and an information booth on Main Street by Town Hall.

Chatham Light, Chatham Break, and
Chatham Lighthouse Beach (all ages)

On Main Street between Shore Road and Bridge Street, Chatham; (508) 945-5175 (Chatham Parks and Recreation) or (508) 945-3830 (US Coast Guard Chatham Station); town.chatham.ma.us or uscg.mil/d1/staChatham.
Chatham Light sits across from a small parking lot, several sets of coin-operated binoculars, and a breathtaking view of the Chatham Break and Chatham Lighthouse Beach. The break was formed during a ferocious winter storm in 1987, when storm-pounded waves broke through the barrier beach that stretches south from Nauset Beach, forming a separate island (now called South Beach) and a break in the barrier that had protected Chatham's harbor and coastline from the full brunt of the Atlantic. The break is a spectacular example of the power of weather, wind, and ocean. There are strong currents and tides at Chatham Lighthouse Beach; please monitor your children and keep them away from the no-swim area (and if the red flag is up, swimming is forbidden). The present structure of the Chatham Light is one of a pair of towers that was built in 1877 (the light's twin was moved to Nauset in 1923). Chatham's original lighthouses were built in 1808. Heavy erosion, which is still a problem in Chatham, forced the Coast Guard to move the lights back from the coast to the spot where the light stands today. Chatham Light flashes twice every 10 seconds. Chatham Light is open Wed during the summer for visitation.

Chatham Railroad Museum (all ages)

153 Depot Rd., Chatham; (508) 945-5199 (Chamber of Commerce); chathaminfo.com/museums. Open mid-June through mid-Sept, Tues through Sat, 10 a.m. to 4 p.m., and then Sat 10 a.m. to 1 p.m. from mid-Sept to mid-Oct. Free; donations accepted.
The restored depot building of the Chatham Railroad Museum, with its Cheerio-like architectural details, holds an impressive collection of thousands of model

trains. Thomas the Tank Engine fans will enjoy the old caboose, which saw more than a million miles of track before its retirement and is most kids' favorite object. *TIP:* There's a great playground across the street.

Hardings Beach (all ages)

Hardings Beach Road (off of Route 28 to Barn Hill Road to Hardings Beach Road), Chatham; (508) 945-5100; chathaminfo.com/beaches. Lifeguarded from 9 a.m. to 4:30 p.m. from mid-June through Aug. Parking is $15 per day, $60 per week, and $125 for the season. Pay by the day at the beach, or obtain a sticker at the permit department at Town Hall.

The best family beach in Chatham is Hardings Beach. It's a long beach with warm water and gentle ocean waves (usually) with small dunes facing the Nantucket Sound. There are lifeguards, restrooms, snack trucks, and a large parking lot (arrive early; it can fill up before noon in the summer) with vistas of Stage Harbor, the Oyster River, Buck's Creek, and the Monomoy National Wildlife Refuge.

Kate Gould Park (all ages)

On Main Street, Chatham; chathaminfo.com/parks. Band concert every Fri night at 8 p.m. from early July through early Sept. Free.

Every Friday night there's a band concert at the bandstand in Kate Gould Park. Thousands of visitors and locals show up for these evenings to dance to old standards, Sousa marches, and the like. Arrive early to get a good spot; don't forget the blankets and chairs!

Catch as **Catch Can**

Watch the day's catch being unloaded from the observation deck at **Chatham Fish Pier** between 2 and 6 p.m. It's just north of town, on the corner of Bar Cliff Avenue and Shore Road. The local fishermen go an amazing 120 miles out to sea and when they arrive back, they process their catch at the fish pier. *TIP:* To get a close peek at the local seals, go to the fish pier. Local seals are likely to gather when the fish are being unloaded, hoping to get the leftovers!

Monomoy National Wildlife Refuge (all ages)

30 Wikis Way, Monomoy National Wildlife Refuge Visitor Center, Morris Island, Chatham; (508) 945-0594; fws.gov/refuge/Monomoy (literature and maps of Monomoy). The trails are open dawn to dusk year-round. Surf-fishing on Morris Island is allowed 24 hours a day. Free.

One of the true adventures left for Cape visitors is a trip to Monomoy National Wildlife Refuge, a 3,244-acre wilderness area on two islands (although the refuge extends beyond the islands to the waters around it, and thus it consists of 7,604 acres in total) that serve as a resting area for migratory birds and a home for as many as 300 species of birds. In addition, an amazing number of gray and harbor seals call the sandbars off this island home. On your tour of the islands (North and South Monomoy), you'll see acres of true seaside wilderness: There are no roads, no buildings (except for the light keeper's cottage on South Monomoy), and no electricity. To reach the island, you must visit by boat, paddle, or sail. Forty-two acres on Morris Island are accessible by vehicle, and then on foot, giving you a small taste of what you would see on the islands. Tour operators traveling to Monomoy (by reservation) are the Monomoy Island Ferry (508-237-0420) or Outermost Adventures (508-945-2030).

Do visit the Monomoy National Wildlife Refuge Visitor Center on Morris Island. They offer self-guided tours and a small exhibit area. The helpful staff will provide you with plenty of literature and will point you and the kids toward the 0.75-mile self-guided interpretive tour around Morris Island. The Morris Island Visitor Center also offers birding and naturalist hands-on programs and special family-fun days (call the refuge for more information). Leashed dogs only, please. Directions to the Morris Island Visitor Center: From Main Street in Chatham, make a right onto Shore Road, take the first left after Chatham Light. Take the first right; follow Morris Island Road to the visitor center (508-945-0594). *TIP: The Disappearing Island,* by Corinne Demas and illustrated by Ted Lewin, is a great book about this area and our fragile ecology.

Other Things to See & Do

Atwood Museum, 347 Stage Harbor Rd., Chatham; (508) 945-2493; chatham historicalsociety.org. Open mid-June through mid-Oct. Price: $6 per adult, $3 for ages 7 to 18, free for children 6 and under. Maritime and American antiques, shell collections, artwork by local artists, China trade, bird carvings by nationally known Elmer

Crowell, an 18th-century furnished house, and paraphernalia make for an eclectic museum.

Cape Aerial Tours Inc., 240 George Ryder Rd., Chatham Airport; (508) 945-2363; chathamairport.com/aerial_tours.php. Sightseeing rides to view Monomoy Island seals or Provincetown.

Chatham Marconi Maritime Center, 847 Orleans Rd., S. Chatham; (508) 945-8889; chathammarconi.org. History of wireless communication on Cape Cod and its impact on the world and world events. Kids enjoy the interactive exhibits and the films.

Grist Mill, 10 Grist Mill Ln., Chatham; chathamwindmill.com. Original old wind-powered mill built in 1797 to grind corn.

Where the Sidewalk Ends, 432 Main St., Chatham; (508) 945-0499; booksonthe cape.com. Toys, games, and adult and children's books are among the dizzying array found here.

Where to Eat

Buffy's Ice Cream, 456 Main St., Chatham; (508) 945-5990. Homemade ice cream made fresh daily in season. $

Chatham Bars Inn, 297 Shore Rd., Chatham; (508) 945-0096; chathambarsinn.com. Four restaurants, meals are served in spacious, elegant dining rooms or on the beach (most families prefer the Beach House Grill, where the kids can run off and play on the upper beach); clambakes take place on the beach Mon through Thurs in the summer. Kids' menu. $$–$$$$

Chatham Candy Manor, 484 Main St., Chatham; (508) 945-0825 or (800) 221-6497; candymanor.com. Hand-dipped chocolates and unusual candies.

Chatham Pier Fish Market, 45 Barcliff Ave. Ext., Chatham; (508) 945-3474; chatham pierfishmarket.com. Takeout from May to New Year's with outdoor picnic tables overlooking the pier and the water. Fried seafood, packed lobster rolls, fresh sushi, homemade clam chowder, and lobster bisque. Clambakes and steam lobsters by order. $–$$

Chatham Squire, 487 Main St., Chatham; (508) 945-0945; thesquire.com. A family restaurant with a roster of entertainment. A cross section of dishes for all tastes. $–$$

Breaker's Beach

If you're looking for a semi-deserted beach, try **South Beach,** which is the south part of Nauset Beach, which was separated by the Chatham Break in 1987. In the years since the Chatham Break, South Beach finally reconnected to the Chatham mainland (in 1992) in front of the Chatham Light and formed a sandy peninsula; now you are able to walk over to the tip (approximately 2.5 miles one-way) instead of relying on watercraft. There are no lifeguards and no facilities here; pack a lunch and plenty of water. You'll share the beach with lots of shorebirds, the overflow from Monomoy Island.

Where to Stay

Carriage House Inn, 407 Old Harbor Rd., Chatham; (508) 945-4688 or (800) 355-8868; thecarriagehouseinn.com. Historic inn and carriage house. Fresh fruit, beverages, and warm baked cookies. Full breakfasts. Children over 10 welcome. $$–$$$

Chatham Bars Inn, 297 Shore Rd., Chatham; (508) 945-0096 or (800) 527-4884; chathambarsinn.com. Open year-round. Select from suites, cottages, and rooms with balconies; there are 217 rooms in all on the 25-acre property. The inn has a private beach just across Shore Road, with planned complimentary activities (including all-day children's programs). $$$–$$$$

Pleasant Bay Village, Route 28, 1191 Orleans Rd., Chatham; PO Box 772, Chatham, MA 02633; (508) 945-1133 or (800) 547-1011; pleasantbayvillage.com. Open the end of Apr through the end of Oct. Large complex of buildings (58 bedroom suites) set on beautifully maintained grounds with 11 waterfalls. The atmosphere is quiet and peaceful—almost Zen-like! Efficiency units have well-equipped kitchens and grills. Heated pool and adult spa, playground for kids and koi pond. $$–$$$$

Brewster

Brewster was home to dozens of ship captains during the 19th century, many of whom built beautiful homes along what is now Route 6A. Today, when the tide is out, Brewster's beaches along the bay—Sea Street Beach, Paines Creek Beach, and

Point of Rocks Beach on Cape Cod Bay—are fun spots for kids to explore the miles and miles of sun-warmed tidal pools and skittering seaside animals, birds, and bugs (if you go, don't forget your net to scoop up some tidal booty!). If you need further information, contact the **Brewster Chamber of Commerce** at 2198 Main St. (PO Box 1241), Brewster, MA 02631; (508) 896-3500; brewster-capecod.com.

Cape Cod Museum of Natural History (all ages)

869 Route 6A, Brewster; (508) 896-3867; ccmnh.org. Admission: $10 for adults, $5 for children 3 to 12; **free** for children 2 and under. Check the website for the hours of operation, the hours change dramatically throughout the year.

The Cape Cod Museum of Natural History does a terrific job of teaching kids (and their parents) about the Cape's fragile ecology. Permanent and rotating exhibits focus on the Cape, its history, and the Cape's environment (and the work of environmental organizations that are based on the Cape). An osprey cam gives a live feed from the nest. There are three nature trails (guided trail walks to Wing Island are a treat and can take 1.5 hours) and marine tanks with live indigenous salt- and freshwater creatures. The tidal pools feature invertebrates such as crabs, mollusks, snails, frogs, and other local species and more than 65 saltwater, freshwater, and brackish water aquarium habitats. Set aside about 1 hour to completely digest the museum. Other family activities include kid-friendly programs with interactive games and crafts, and a STEM-based natural-history day camps for kids that runs from three days to a week in the summer months. A special program called Mud Flat Mania is intriguing—it's a guided trip to the tidal flats to learn about the creatures beneath your feet (summer only).

Nickerson State Park (all ages)

3488 Main St. and Route 6A, Brewster; (508) 896-3491; mass.gov/eea/agencies/dcr/massparks/region-south/nickerson-state-park.html. **Free.**

If your family would rather not swim in salt water, Nickerson State Park, Cape Cod's largest park, is a great place for you—it has several large freshwater

Row, Row, Row Your Boat!

Jack's Boat Rental (Nickerson State Forest; 508-896-8556 or 508-349-9808) can fix you up with canoes, kayaks, surf bikes, seacycles, Sunfish, and paddleboats.

kettle ponds with a small beach at one of the ponds. The park also features hiking trails, ponds stocked with trout, bike trails that connect to the Cape Cod Rail Trail, boating, summertime interpretive programs, and camping with more than 400 campsites (call Reserve America at 877-422-6762; reserveamerica.com).

Jack's Boat Rental (508-896-8556 or 508-349-9808; jacksboatrental.com) is located at both Flax's and Cliff Ponds in Nickerson State Park Skating and cross-country skiing (conditions permitting) are popular in the winter.

Other Things to See & Do

Barbara's Bike Shop, 3430 Main St., Brewster; (508) 896-7231; barbsbikeshop .com. Rental shop located outside the entrance to Nickerson State Park in Brewster. Close access to the Cape Cod Rail Trail.

The Brewster Store, intersection of Route 6A and Route124, Brewster; (508) 896-3744; brewsterstore.com. Opened in 1866. General merchandise, penny candy (but it's not a penny anymore!), and fresh ice cream in season.

Stony Brook Grist Mill and Museum at the Herring Run, 830 Stony Brook Rd., Brewster; (508) 896-1734. Corn mill still in use. Demonstrations and artifacts of Cape Cod life. Alewife (fish) run in season (Mar and Apr). Herring run in season (mid-Apr to early May).

Where to Eat

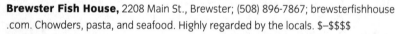

Brewster Fish House, 2208 Main St., Brewster; (508) 896-7867; brewsterfishhouse .com. Chowders, pasta, and seafood. Highly regarded by the locals. $–$$$$

Chills Bistro at Chillingsworth, 2449 Main St., Route 6A, Brewster; (508) 896-3640; chillingsworth.com. Don't confuse the bistro with the restaurant of the same name, unless you're up for a seven-course dinner in an antique-filled setting (not a good idea with kids). The bistro specializes in grilled food, has a contemporary setting with lots of glass and skylights, and will gladly do a pasta dish for the kids. $$–$$$

Laurino's Restaurant and Tavern, 3668 Main St., Rte. 6A, Brewster; (508) 896-6135;

laurinostavern.com. Next to Nickerson State Park. Grab a bite. Pizza, Mexican food, grinders, or more formal entrees. $–$$

Where to Stay

Ocean Edge Resort and Golf Club, 2907 Main St., Route 6A, Brewster; (508) 896-9000 or (800) 343-6074 (for room reservations); oceanedge.com. Open year-round. Located on a private beach with 2 indoor and 4 outdoor pools, tennis, bike trails, kids' programs, and 3 dining rooms (the most family friendly is Link's). You can opt to stay in a hotel room or a one-, two-, or three-bedroom villa. A Best of *Boston Magazine*'s pick for 2013 "Best Resort Cape Cod." $$–$$$$

Old Sea Pines Inn, 2553 Main St., Brewster; (508) 896-6114; oldseapinesinn.com. Family suites, cozy fireplace in the main area, and an inviting porch with rocking chairs. Step back in time (1930s estate) to a slower pace. Reasonable rates include a full breakfast and Wi-Fi. $–$$

Orleans & East Orleans

For families, Orleans's main attraction is actually in East Orleans—Nauset Beach. Other recreational opportunities take advantage of water locations. Orleans is bounded on the east by the Atlantic and on the west by Cape Cod Bay. For more information contact the **Orleans Chamber of Commerce** (PO Box 153), 44 Main St., Orleans, MA 02653; (508) 255-1386; orleanscapecod.org.

Nauset Beach (all ages)

250 Beach Rd., East Orleans; (508) 240-3700, ext. 465 or (508) 240-3780 (beach office); town.orleans.ma.us. Nonresidents fee (may be going up): $15; you can park at both Nauset and Skaket Beaches (see entry below) for the same price and try two beaches in one day! Directions: From exit 12 off Route 6, turn right onto Eldredge Park Way, right onto Main Street, then left at fork onto Beach Road, which leads to Nauset Beach. Nauset Beach has two beach chairs for the disabled to access the beach (no charge).

Nine miles long and backed by high dunes, this is one of the Cape's best beaches. If you're willing to walk a bit, Nauset Beach is so long that you will be able to stake out your own territory even on the busiest summer weekends. If you want to stay near the lifeguards, however, keep within the marked area. There's a large bathhouse with restrooms, changing rooms, and showers;

there's also a good snack bar with outdoor picnic tables. On Mon in July and Aug from 7 to 9 p.m., there are free bandstand concerts at the gazebo. Everything from folk to rock 'n' roll can be heard. Children like to dance down front, and couples can walk the beach and still hear the music.

Skaket Beach (all ages)

200 Skaket Beach Rd., Orleans; (508) 240-3700, ext. 465 or (508) 255-0572 (beach office); town.orleans.ma.us. Nonresidents fee: $15; you can park at both Nauset and Skaket Beaches (see entry above) for the same price and try two beaches in one day! Directions: Take exit 12; turn right off the exit and take the first left onto West Road. Follow West Road until the end (facing Skaket Beach Road). Take a left onto Skaket Beach Road for Skaket Beach.

With views to Provincetown, Skaket Beach (Orleans's bay beach) is popular with families who enjoy playing in tidal flats and warm, clear sea. Facilities include restrooms, lifeguards, two beach chairs for the disabled, changing rooms, outside shower, and a snack bar. Skaket Beach is a great place to watch the sunset!

How to Eat a **Lobster**

For the uninitiated in the fine art of eating a lobster, we offer this primer:

1. Assemble your tools: a nutcracker, a lobster pick or fork, and a lobster bib (eating lobster can be a very messy undertaking).

2. Twist off the claws, crack them open with the nutcracker, remove the meat, and dip in drawn butter.

3. Separate the tail from the body (bend it until it breaks away), then split the tail down the middle to get to the meat. You may see a green or red line in the center of the tail meat. This is the liver, or tomalley, and is a treat to some lobster connoisseurs. *Warning:* Eat the liver only if it is green.

4. Open the main body of the lobster and hunt down the lobster meat in the small pockets. Other sources of meat are the small claws (break them off the body) and the flippers of the tail.

Other Things to See & Do

French Cable Station Museum, corner of Cove Road and Route 28, Orleans; (508) 240-1735; frenchcablestationmuseum.org. Open June and Sept, Fri through Sun 1 to 4 p.m.; July through Aug, Thurs through Sun 1 to 4 p.m. Rare collection of undersea telegraph cables, instruments, and memorabilia. **Free.**

Goose Hummock Kayak, 15 Route 6A (off the Route 6 rotary) on town cove, Orleans; (508) 255-2620 or (508) 255-0455; goose.com. Canoe and kayak rentals and tours. *Note:* Nauset Beach is a challenging area to paddle, but if you stay in Town Cove or inside the estuary of Nauset Marsh, it's pristine protected waters—even from the wind!

Kid Kaboodle, 115 Route 6A, Orleans; (508) 240-0460; kid-kaboodle.com. Unique clothing for infants and children up to size 16.

The Playhouse, 120 Main St., Orleans (on the way to Nauset Beach); (508) 255-1963; apacape.org. Musical dramas, comedies, and original works. Children's theater series on Sat mornings in the summer and select shows during the year.

Where to Eat

Hot Chocolate Sparrow, 5 Old Colony Way, Route 6A, Orleans; (508) 240-2230 or (800) 922-6399; hotchocolatesparrow.com. Coffee and chocolate bar (specializing in drinks, chocolates, desserts, and ice cream). $

Joe's Bar and Grill at the Barley Neck Inn, 5 Beach Rd., East Orleans; (508) 255-0212; barleyneck.com. Casual, comfy, and kicked-back with a creative, highly acclaimed kitchen. Kids' menu. $–$$

Land Ho!, corner of Route 6A and Cove Road, Orleans (second, newer location in Harwich); (508) 255-5165; land-ho.com. The kale soup is a specialty here, but everything's good (from deli to fish and chips). Kids' menu. Open daily at 11:30 a.m. year-round. $–$$

Where to Stay

A Little Inn on Pleasant Bay, 654 South Orleans Rd., South Orleans; (508) 255-0780 or (888) 332-3351; alittleinnonpleasantbay.com. Sit in one of the Adirondack chairs overlooking Pleasant Bay during sunset and completely unwind. Nine air-conditioned guest rooms and exquisite gardens. European breakfast buffet. $$$–$$$$

The Nauset House Inn, 143 Beach Rd., East Orleans; (508) 255-2195 or (800) 771-5508; nausethouseinn.com. Fourteen guest rooms in an idyllic setting, including a magical turn-of-the-20th-century glass-enclosed solarium. Short half-mile walk to Nauset Beach. Children over 12 welcome. Full breakfast. $–$$

Eastham

Eastham, the gateway to the Cape Cod National Seashore, is where Myles Standish and his band first met Native tribes in 1620, after the Pilgrims' landing in Provincetown and before their settlement of Plymouth. The meeting spot is commemorated by a bronze marker at the top of the dunes of First Encounter Beach. Today most visitors go to Eastham, known as the "outdoor recreation area" for the Cape, to enter the Cape Cod National Seashore, which covers nearly 44,000 acres of the outer Cape. It is administered by the National Park Service (see listing below). For visitor information, contact the **Eastham Chamber of Commerce** at PO Box 1329, Eastham, MA 02642, or (508) 240-7211; easthamchamber.com. The visitor booth (508-255-3444) is at 1700 State Hwy. (Route 6); open May to mid-Oct.

Take Me Out to **the Ball Game**

Looking for something to fill your family's summer vacation evenings? Between mid-June and mid-August, the **Cape Cod Baseball League** is just the thing. Ten towns on the Cape field teams made up of the country's top college baseball players, who play before enthusiastic crowds and, more often than not, big-league scouts. Past players have included Kolten Wong, Mark Teixeira, Chase Utley, Carlos Peña, Justin Smoak, Evan Longoria, Tim Lincecum, Mike Lowell, Jackie Bradley Jr., Gordon Beckham, Alex Avila, Jacoby Ellsbury, and Eric Hinske. Eight of the MLB managers are from the Cape Cod Baseball League including John Farrell of the Boston Red Sox. Each of the teams on the league conducts weekly clinics for kids. For more information, contact the Cape Cod Baseball League at Box 266, Harwich Port, Ma 02646; (508) 432–6909; capecodbaseball.org. Free.

Cape Cod National Seashore's Coast Guard Beach, Nauset Lighthouse, and Nauset Light Beach (all ages)

50 Nauset Rd., off Route 6 and Nauset Road (Salt Pond Visitor Center), Eastham; (508) 255-3421; nps.gov/caco. Parking at Little Creek parking lot is $15 in season (the day pass is good for all six of the National Seashore Beaches) and includes a free bus shuttle to Coast Guard Beach. The National Park Service also provides tours of the original Three Sisters Lighthouses in Eastham during the summer; ask for a schedule at the Salt Pond Visitor Center information desk (open 9 a.m. to 5 p.m. in season and until 4:30 p.m. off-season). A Cape Cod National Seashore Seasonal Beach Pass is $45, good at all six National Seashore beaches. The Nauset Lighthouse is open May, June, Sept, and Oct on Sun, and Wed in July and Aug (508-240-2612; nausetlight.org/NLtours.htm). The National Park Service offers kids programs and a scavenger hunt.

Be sure to visit the Salt Pond Visitor Center in Eastham, where helpful guides offer complete information on the seashore and walking trails (the Nauset Marsh Trail is especially scenic), as well as orientation talks, films, a museum, and guided field trips. Respect the rules set forth by the Park Service; they are designed to protect this unique and fragile area. Major points of interest are Coast Guard Beach, Nauset Light Beach (not to be confused with Nauset Beach in East Orleans), and the Nauset Light.

Coast Guard Beach is one of the best beaches along the National Seashore and can be reached by shuttle bus. The bathhouse is one of the Cape's best. To reach Coast Guard Beach from the Salt Pond Visitor Center, continue on Nauset to Doane Road or take the 1.6-mile Nauset Bike Trail. The Little Creek Parking Area will be on the left; park and take the shuttle (in season).

Nauset Lighthouse (the top half is red and the bottom half is white) has a complicated history. In 1923 the building was moved from Chatham, where it was one of two lights. Because of soil erosion, the building was moved again to its current location in 1996. The site it now occupies was also the spot of the first of the three lighthouses that sat in a row on the cliffs of Nauset from 1838 to 1911. The original "Three Sisters" were moved to Cable Road at Cape Cod National Seashore, not far from the Nauset Light Beach. Nauset Light flashes red and white and helps mariners distinguish it from other Cape Cod lighthouses. The round ball at the top of the tower is called a ventilator ball; it allows air to circulate and cool the lantern room, where the lighthouse's beam rotates.

Nauset Light Beach, just off Ocean View Drive (which connects Nauset Light Beach with Coast Guard Beach), is a long sandy beach framed by cliffs (up the coast from the Coast Guard Beach access). Nauset Light Beach is lifeguarded, and there can be heavy surf at times—but the views are of raw nature at its best. Parking is right at Nauset Light Beach, which fills up quite early due to limited parking.

A 5-minute drive south of the Salt Pond Visitor Center brings you to the Fort Hill Area (off of Governor Prence Road in Eastham), undeniably one of the most picturesque points in the park. There are walking trails with scenic overlooks. The Fort Hill Trail, a 1.5-mile easy loop, is the most popular trail, winding through woodlands, fields, and along salt marsh; a fly-by for migratory birds.

First Encounter Beach (all ages)

Samoset Road, Eastham; (508) 255-3444 (town of Eastham) or (508) 240-7211 (Eastham Chamber of Commerce). Directions: From Route 6 North, turn left on Samoset Road at the first traffic light and follow it to the end. Parking is $15 midweek and $18 on weekends Memorial Day through Labor Day, free the rest of the year. *Warning:* No lifeguards are on duty.

First Encounter Beach, on Cape Cod Bay, is named for the site where the members of the *Mayflower* company led by Myles Standish and the Nauset tribe first encountered each other. The Pilgrims determined that the soil was too sandy to support farming. Look for the bronze plaque erected to commemorate the event. Restrooms and calm waters add to your family's comfort and safety (particularly the bay side of the beach). At low tide the water is way off shore; the little ones love to explore the sea life left behind in the tidal pools. This is the largest Eastham Bay beach, and it's managed by the town.

Other Things to See & Do

Eastham Windmill (oldest working windmill on the Cape), corner of Samoset and Route 6, Eastham; (508) 240-5900; easthamchamber.com. Original gristmill built ca. 1680; it still functions grinding corn.

Little Capistrano Bike Shop, 30 Salt Pond Rd., Eastham (also 1446 Rte. 6, S. Wellfleet); (508) 255-6515; littlecapistranobikeshop.com. Bike rentals.

Where to Eat

Arnold's, 3580 State Hwy., Route 6, Eastham; (508) 255-2575; arnoldsrestaurant .com. Delicious lobster, fried seafood, raw bar, and Richardson's ice cream; classic Cape Cod fare. Seasonal. Adventure minigolf next door. $–$$$

Hole in One Donut Shop and the Fairway Restaurant, 4295 State Hwy., Rte. 6, North Eastham (second location of the Donut Shop is in Orleans, serving breakfast and lunch); (508) 255 3893: fairwaycapecod.com. The Donut Shop is a local-yokel place, hand-cut donuts a specialty (all baking is done on the premises); the Fairway Restaurant serves breakfast and dinner. $–$$

Karoo Restaurant, 3 Main St., Eastham; (508) 255-8288; karoorestaurants.com. Traditional South African food, vegan, vegetarian, and gluten-free options. $–$$

Where to Stay   ⊖

Inn at the Oaks, 3085 County Rd., Eastham; (877) 255-1866; innattheoaks.com. Inviting Victorian inn with wraparound porch, 13 rooms. Children over age 2 and pets ($50 per stay) are welcome. $–$$$$

Midway Motel and Cottages, 5460 State Hwy., Rte. 6, North Eastham; (508) 255-3117 or (800) 755-3117; midwaymotel.com. Silver winner for a motel on the outer Cape by *Cape Cod Life*. Small and intimate, nestled in a pine grove. $–$$

Town Crier Motel, 3620 State Hwy., Eastham; (508) 255-4000; towncriermotel.com. Thirty-six rooms on beautiful grounds, indoor heated pool, abutting the Cape Cod Rail Trail. Poolside Restaurant does a very reasonably priced breakfast buffet. $–$$

Wellfleet

Wellfleet is the epitome of "Old Cape Cod"; no neon, no malls, no light pollution—the town tries to keep it as it was in the 1940s or 1950s, a simple summer resort. Known as "the gallery town," the focus in Wellfleet falls equally on the arts and the natural world. Many of the year-rounder's and summerhouse owners who live in or near Wellfleet's tiny, picturesque harbor are artists, writers, actors, and other arts-oriented people; under their influence several arts day camps are run each summer for children and families. Well over half of Wellfleet's area is conservation land. Much of it is in the care of the Cape Cod National Seashore; the rest is part of the 1,000-acre Wellfleet Bay Wildlife Sanctuary. Bordered by water to the east (the Atlantic Ocean) and to the west (Cape Cod Bay and Wellfleet Bay), it's the skinniest part of the Cape. Visit the **Wellfleet Chamber** Information Booth for vacation information at 1410 Route 6, South Wellfleet, MA 02667; (508) 349-2510; wellfleetchamber.com. *TIP:* Wellfleet is known for its oysters.

Wellfleet Bay Wildlife Sanctuary (all ages)

West side of Route 6, 291 State Hwy., South Wellfleet; (508) 349-2615; wellfleetbay
.org or massaudubon.org. Visitor and nature center open daily from Memorial
Day to Columbus Day, 8:30 a.m. to 5 p.m.; Nov through Apr, Tues to Sun, 9 a.m. to
4:30 p.m. Trails are open from dawn to dusk year-round. Admission: $5 for adults,
and $3 for children 2 to 12. Excursion costs vary, usually $25 to $45 per day per
program. If you've been a member of the Audubon Society for at least a year, you
and your family can camp here (but you need to reserve early).

Massachusetts Audubon Society's Wellfleet Bay Wildlife Sanctuary offers a myriad of nature-oriented activities for families: bird and bat watches; trips through
a sandy beach, field and pond, woods, and salt marshes; occasional guided trail
walks; several excellent self-guided walking trails, where you'll see a variety of
birds and coastal animals (watch for turtles); and arranged tours to Monomoy
National Wildlife Refuge. Visit the sanctuary's website for schedules and reservation information.

Wellfleet **Ocean Beaches**

- **Cahoon Hollow Beach**—1140 Cahoon Hollow Rd., a sticker-only
  beach for town residents to park; however, parking is available at
  the Beachcomber Restaurant for $20 with a $20 coupon toward
  food. The beach has restrooms, and there are lifeguards mid-June
  through Labor Day. The dune down to the beach is 85 feet, however, there is also a sand trail; the surf can be rough at times.

- **Marconi Beach**—Marconi Beach Road, off of Route 6, part of the
  Cape Cod National Seashore. Great bathhouse. Parking: $15 for the
  day (good for all six of the National Seashore Beaches), $45 for a
  seasonal pass.

- **White Crest Beach**—520 Ocean Beach Dr., town beach, broader
  than Cahoon Hollow; restrooms, surfing is allowed, lifeguarded
  mid-June through Labor Day. The path leading to the beach is
  down a 100-foot dune. Parking: $20.

The Wellfleet Drive-In (all ages)

On Route 6 just north of the Eastham-Wellfleet line, Wellfleet; (508) 349-7176 or (508) 349-0541; wellfleetcinemas.com. Check the website for the flea market and drive-in schedule.

The Wellfleet Drive-In wears two hats: It's a flea market by day, and in the evening it's a 700-car first-run drive-in movie theater with dairy bar, minigolf, playground, and snack bar. An indoor cinema theater (open year-round) with four screens ensures that the whole crowd is pleased, no matter what the weather.

Other Things to See & Do

Marconi Wireless Site, at the end of Marconi Site Road, South Wellfleet. Site of first transatlantic communication, beautiful observation deck. The markers have been removed due to erosion.

Square Dancing on the Chatham Town Pier, Kendrick Avenue, Wellfleet Harbor; (508) 349-0314; wellfleetma.org. Wed nights in July and Aug from 7 to 9:30 p.m. Swing your partner! **Free.**

Chatham Skateboard Park, 70 Kendrick Ave., Baker's Field, Wellfleet; (508) 349-0314; wellfleetma.orgchamber. Skateboarding only from 9 a.m. to dusk; helmets required. No fee.

Where to Eat

The Beachcomber, 1120 Cahoon Hollow Road, Wellfleet; (508) 349-6055; thebeachcomber.com. One of the only restaurants on the beach (Cahoon Hollow Beach) on Cape Cod. Order lunch or dinner; Young Minnows menu. Seasonal. $–$$

The Lighthouse, 317 Main St., Wellfleet; (508) 349-3681; mainstreetlighthouse.com. Hearty breakfasts (seasonal) are particularly good. Every Thurs night is Mexican night. Kids' menu. Closed the month of Mar, open for lunch and dinner the rest of the year. $–$$$

Mac's On the Pier Seafood, Town Pier, 265 Commercial St., Wellfleet; (508) 349-0404; macsseafood.com. Fun, casual, family restaurant with picnic tables in the sand overlooking Wellfleet Harbor and next to Mayo Beach serving local seafood, burgers, and ice cream. $–$$

Moby Dick's, 3225 Route 6A, across from Gull Pond Road, Wellfleet; (508) 349-9795; mobydicksrestaurant.com. Seafood in the rough. Sit inside at picnic tables with interesting nautical artifacts scattered about. Overlooks marshland. Open May through Columbus Day. Gluten-free choices. $–$$$

VanRensselaer's, 1019 Route 6, South Wellfleet; (508) 349-2127; vanrensselaers .com. Opposite the entrance to the Marconi Area of the Cape Cod National Seashore. Bright and airy, family-oriented restaurant serving breakfast and dinner only, with a breakfast buffet on the weekends. Something for all tastes. Seasonal (open mid-Apr through mid-Oct). $–$$$

Where to Stay

Inn at Duck Creeke, 70 Main St., Wellfleet; (508) 349-3450; innatduckcreeke.com. Historic inn facing the creek with panoramic ocean views in a central location near town and beaches. Children welcome. Continental breakfast. $–$$

Wellfleet is a cottage colony mecca. One of the best is:

Surfside Cottages, 50 Ocean View Dr., along the Cape Cod National Seashore, South Wellfleet; (508) 349-3959; surfsidevacation.com. One-, two-, and three-bedroom cottages are available steps from the beach on the Atlantic side on a weekly basis in the summer, off-season a shorter stay is allowed, all with kitchens, fireplaces, and screened-in porches; some have roof decks as well. $$$$

Truro

Truro is best known for its beaches and the plethora of summer houses and cottages that dot its high hills and dunes. For such a beautiful place (over half of the town is park or conservation land), it's remarkably untouristy. It has the distinction of being the least densely populated community on the Cape. To reach the town center of Truro, take the Pamet Road exit off Route 6. The **Truro Chamber of Commerce** is on Route 6A, Truro (508-487-1288; trurochamberofcommerce .com).

Cape Cod Light/Highland Lighthouse and the Highland Museum (all ages)

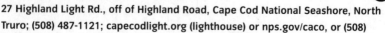

27 Highland Light Rd., off of Highland Road, Cape Cod National Seashore, North Truro; (508) 487-1121; capecodlight.org (lighthouse) or nps.gov/caco, or (508)

487-3397; trurohistorical.org (museum). The lighthouse is open mid-May to mid-Oct from 10 a.m. to 5:30 p.m. daily and charges $4 for all ages. There is a 48-inch height requirement for children in the lighthouse. The museum is open June through Sept, Mon through Sat from 10 a.m. to 4:30 p.m. The museum fee is $5 for adults; free for children under 12.

The first light that sailors see when they make the trip from Europe to Boston is that of Cape Cod Light, the oldest lighthouse on the Cape. Because it was built on the highlands of Truro, it is also known as the Highland Light. The present buildings date from 1857, but the first lighthouse constructed on this spot went up in 1797. Highland Light's precarious position on eroded cliffs made it likely that it would tumble into the ocean, so the Truro Historical Society successfully spearheaded efforts to move it to its present site 453 feet back in 1996. Ownership of the Cape Cod Light was transferred from the Coast Guard to the Cape Cod National Seashore.

At night children will enjoy looking for the light's bright white beam, which is visible during the drive on Route 6 from Truro to Provincetown. Highland is the highest (182 feet above sea level) as well as the tallest (66 feet) lighthouse on the Cape. The museum gives you a peek into the past and is operated by the Truro Historical Society. There are 13 rooms of artifacts, art, and memorabilia covering Truro's history and families. Of special interest to kids are tools and furniture used by the early settlers and their descendents and Wampanoag objects (a growing collection). The museum has a tremendous amount of shipwreck artifacts and items relating to marine history. There have been 100 shipwrecks in the Truro area in the last century (the winds drive the ships into the shallows). Kids love to explore in the archaeological dig box and try their luck with the scavenger hunt.

Corn Hill Beach (all ages)

Castle Road, Truro. Take Castle Road from the center of Truro (follow signs from Route 6), then follow it to Corn Hill and Corn Hill Beach. Parking is $10 for the day.

Corn Hill Beach (on Cape Cod Bay side) is the place where Myles Standish and his desperately hungry group "borrowed" their first corn from the natives. A marker on the cliff at the edge of the bay indicates the spot where the event took place.

A great place for shelling, this is also a great walking beach; walk to the jetty or along the low tide flats (they go out pretty far almost to the sandbars). ***Note:*** No lifeguards here.

East Harbor Sand Dunes (all ages)

Highhead Road (off of Route 6), at the south end of Pilgrim Lake/East Harbor, Truro; (508) 487-1256 (Province Lands Visitor Center, Provincetown), or (508) 255-3421 (Salt Pond Visitor Center, Eastham); nps.gov/caco. Free. Park at the Highhead parking lot at the Cape Cod National Seashore.

The Pilgrim Lake Sand Dunes area of the Cape Cod National Seashore is the only place along the National Seashore where visitors can legally walk over the enormous sand dunes that roll across this part of the Cape. Previous visitors have worn away much of the sand and, with it, the beach grass that covers and preserves the dunes; therefore, the National Park Service restricts foot traffic on the dunes to this area.

Head of the Meadow Beach (all ages)

Head of the Meadow Road (off Route 6), North Truro; (508) 487-1256 (Province Lands Visitor Center, Provincetown), or (508) 255-3421 (Salt Pond Visitor Center); nps.gov/caco. Parking is $15 for the day good for all six National Seashore Beaches, $45 for the seasonal national seashore pass.

The part of the Head of the Meadow Beach that's maintained by the Cape Cod National Seashore (the town of Truro manages the remainder) has lifeguards, restrooms, and outdoor showers. On a calm day this beach is one of the best along the national seashore. For bicycle enthusiasts, there's a 2-mile path from Head of the Meadow Beach parking lot that passes the Pilgrim Heights area and stops near High Head Road.

Pilgrim Heights Area (all ages)

Off Route 6, North Truro; (508) 487-1256 (Province Lands Visitor Center, Provincetown), or (508) 255-3421 (Salt Pond Visitor Center, Eastham); nps.gov/caco. Free.

The Pilgrim Heights area of the national seashore has a nice trail to the place where the Cape's first European visitors found freshwater. Take the Pilgrim Spring Walk from the interpretive shelter. The Small Swamp Trail is a short, fairly flat loop through a densely forested area.

Where to Eat

Montano's Restaurant, 481 Rte. 6, North Truro; (508) 487-2026; montanos.com. Italian cuisine and New England sea fare. Dinner only, early-bird specials. Kids' menu. Open year-round. $–$$$

Savory and Sweet Escape, 316 Rte. 6, Truro; (508) 487-2225; savorysweettruro .com. Pizza, sandwiches, salads, and ice cream. $

Whitman House, 5 Great Hollow Rd., Rte. 6, Truro; (508) 487-1740; whitmanhouse .com. Traditional Cape Cod setting, in business since 1961, fifth place for the Cape Cod A list. Known for fresh seafood. Open seasonally. Early-bird specials. Childrens menu. $$–$$$

Where to Stay

Kalmar Village, 674 Shore Rd., North Truro; (508) 487-0585 (in season) or (617) 277-0091 (in winter); kalmarvillage.com. Cottage colony on private Beach Point with a swimming pool, grills, and picnic tables outside each room. Across from the National Seashore. Open May through Oct. $–$$$$

Provincetown

At the fist end of the Cape, Provincetown is an eclectic collection of open-minded artists, fishermen, wind worn buildings, and seaside moors. Go here for the beaches, the whale watching, and the people-watching, which is especially good in this, New England's most gay-friendly seaside community. For more information, contact the **Provincetown Chamber of Commerce,** 307 Commercial St., Provincetown, MA 02657; (508) 487-3424; ptownchamber.com.

Herring Cove Beach (all ages)

At the end of Route 6, Provincetown; (508) 487-1256 (Province Lands Visitor Center, Provincetown), or (508) 255-3421 (Salt Pond Visitor Center, Eastham); nps.gov/ caco. Parking is a one-time day pass fee of $15 per car (accepted at all National Seashore beaches). A Cape Cod National Seashore pass for the season is $45, good for all six beaches.
One of Provincetown's best beaches for families is Herring Cove Beach with gentler waves than Race Point (see entry below) and warmer water because it is

A Whale of a Trip

You'll find whale-watching trips advertised everywhere along the Cape (and in Boston and on the North Shore, too, for that matter), but the best place to leave from is Provincetown. Why? Because it's closest to Stellwagen Bank, the whales' feeding ground, which is only 6 miles from Provincetown; other trips take much longer to reach the same spot. Most of the whale-watching expeditions from Provincetown are about 3.5 hours long, but some last all day. Regardless of the weather on shore, be sure to bring a warm sweater and long pants for everyone in your party—even at the height of the summer, the wind on the open ocean can be downright cold.

between the bay and the ocean. A snack bar, showers, and restrooms are available here. To be sure of a parking place in the summer, arrive early. **Caution:** Nude bathing has been reported on the stretch of beach to the left of the bathhouse, even though it is prohibited. Families should seek the beach to the right of the bathhouse.

Long Point Lighthouse and Wood End Lighthouse
(ages 12 and up)

Commercial Street, Provincetown; (207) 594-4174; lighthousefoundation.org. Not appropriate for young children or for anyone without sturdy footwear and good balance; best walked at low tide.

When it was built in 1827, Long Point was the center of a busy fishing community on the tip of the Cape. Now isolated at the end of a long breakwater, Long Point Lighthouse (and its companion, Wood End) can best be viewed from the rotary at the end of Commercial Street (while you're here, look for the plaque that commemorates the first landing place of the Pilgrims). If your family is up for a long walk, park the car at the rotary and walk along the rocky breakwater for about half an hour to reach Long Point. Another half-hour walk, to the end of the breakwater, will lead to Wood End Lighthouse. The unusual tower is square; most lighthouses are circular. Wood End was built in 1873. It flashes a red light every 15 seconds, whereas Long Point flashes a green light; together they mark Provincetown Harbor's entrance. **Caution:** It's a long walk—bring something to drink and watch the tides.

Whale-Watching Tours

The best of the many whale-watch cruises are:

• **Alpha Whale Watch,** McMillan Wharf, Provincetown; (508) 221-5920; alphawhalewatch.com. Year-round whale watching on the *Dixie II*, a 32-foot Blue Hill Marine. The captain prefers to take a maximum of six people for a more customized whale watching or deep-sea fishing tour. You can choose your own tour, departure day and time, length of cruise, snacks, and itinerary. Price upon request.

• **Provincetown Whale Watch,** Fisherman's Wharf, Provincetown; (508) 487-1102 or (508) 747-3434, or (800) 225-4000; ptownwhale watch.com. Buy your tickets at the Whale Watch Store, 308 Commercial St., Provincetown or at Fisherman's pier. Prices: $40 adults, $25 age 6 to 12, under 6 free. A naturalist is onboard with running commentary to help enhance the experience, identify marine life, and add local color.

• **Dolphin Fleet,** McMillan Pier, Provincetown; (508) 240-3636 or (800) 826-9300; whalewatch.com. The ticket offices are located in the Chamber of Commerce building at Lopes Square as well as a ticket booth on McMillan Pier. The *Dolphin* operates from Apr through Oct. Rates are $44 for adults, $29 for children 5 to 12, free for children under 4. A $2 discount is given to seniors and AAA members; ticketing online will save you $2. Guaranteed whale sightings or you will receive a free ticket toward a future trip. This fleet originated whale watching on the East Coast. Scientists and naturalists guide every cruise and are available to answer questions. The *Dolphin* is associated with many worldwide educational and research institutions.

The Pilgrim Monument and the Provincetown Museum
(all ages)

1 High Pole Hill Rd., Provincetown; (508) 487-1310; pilgrim-monument.org. Open daily, Apr through Nov, 9 a.m. to 5 p.m.; until 7 p.m. in May through mid-Sept. The last admission is 45 minutes before closing. Admission: $12 for adults, $4 for children 4 to 14; free for children under 4.

The Pilgrim Monument and the Provincetown Museum are worth a visit for the view from the 252-foot-high tower (Pilgrim Monument) that was modeled after the Campanile, or bell tower, in Siena, Italy. The tower was built to commemorate the landing of the Pilgrims and the signing of the Mayflower Compact. On a clear day the view of the curving Cape is breathtaking. The museum focuses on maritime history, Provincetown's diverse history, and the whaling industry.

Provincetown Library (all ages)

356 Commercial St., corner of Commercial and Center Streets, Provincetown; (508) 487-7094; ptownlib.com. Check the website for the schedule.

Art collection and half-scale model of the vessel *Rose Dorothea* are on display.

Race Point Beach (all ages)

End of Race Point Road, off Route 6, Provincetown; (508) 487-1256 (Province Lands Visitor Center) or (508) 255-3421 (Salt Pond Visitor Center); nps.gov/caco. Parking is a one-time day fee of $15 (good for all the National Seashore beaches) or $45 for a seasonal sticker (accepted at all National Seashore beaches).

Race Point has large sand dunes and smaller crowds, making it a great family beach. Race Point Beach is sheltered since it's the middle ground between the bay and the Atlantic Ocean beach. The beach actually got its name from the interaction of the water between Cape Cod Bay and the Atlantic Ocean commingling and causing a wave reaction called a race (a strong current). It's a great spot for fishing because the fish are attracted to the churning of the water. The waves are a little bigger, and the water is a little colder than Herring Cove Beach. Public showers and restrooms are available. Arrive early to get a parking spot.

Race Point Lighthouse (all ages)

Race Point Beach, Provincetown; (508) 487-9930; nps.gov/caco (National Park Service), or (855) 722-3959 or (207) 594-4174; lighthousefoundation.org or race pointlighthouse.org (American Lighthouse Foundation). Open for touring on the first and third Sat, June to Oct from 10 a.m. to 2 p.m. Free but donations are encouraged (money raised helps to preserve Race Point Lighthouse). You can arrive on foot or by a four-wheel-drive vehicle.

The 2-mile walk to reach Race Point Lighthouse is along the Cape Cod National Seashore's Race Point Beach (bring refreshments, especially drinks; the long sandy walk back to the car can be tough for kids). The original Race Point Lighthouse was constructed in 1816, but the current tower was erected in 1876. The lighthouse was built to help ships navigate around the treacherous "knuckles" of the Cape to Provincetown. Between 1816 and 1946 more than a hundred shipwrecks were recorded in this area. Race Point Lighthouse has a white light and a foghorn that warns ships of low-visibility conditions. Race Point Lighthouse is managed by the Coast Guard, although it's on Cape Cod National Seashore grounds. If your family doesn't have the energy to take the long walk to Race Point, Race Point Lighthouse is also visible from Herring Cove Beach.

Other Things to See & Do

Art's Dune Tours, 4 Standish St. (departure location), Provincetown; (508) 487-1950 or (800) 894-1951; artsdunetours.com. Price changes seasonally (open mid-Apr through fall), but it's approximately $28 per adult and $18 per child ages 6 to 11 for the 1-hour tour. Reservations recommended. Go to the heart of the Cape Cod National Seashore. The dune tour traverses the sand, the shore, and the Atlantic. Each truck holds 6 to 8 passengers.

Commercial Street Shopping, Commercial Street, Provincetown. Commercial Street is 3 miles long, but the center mile and a half has art galleries and artsy boutiques, with restaurants and eateries peppered in.

Expedition Whydah Museum, 16 MacMillan Wharf, Provincetown; (508) 487-8899; whydah.com. Authentic pirate treasure discovered from the sunken ship *Whydah* off of Cape Cod (the only pirate shipwreck ever found).

Ghost Tours, Lopes Square, Provincetown; (508) 487-4810; provincetownghosttours .com. Narrated 90-minute haunted ghost tour, about 1 mile of walking.

P-town Pedicabs, Provincetown; (508) 487-0660; ptownpedicabs.com. Unique way to get around town. Drivers can be pure transportation, or better yet give a history, shopping, or guided scenic tour. Maximum of 3 passengers and/or 500 pounds.

Provincetown Trolley, in front of Town Hall, Provincetown; (508) 487-9483; province towntrolley.com. Forty-minute tour of Provincetown with 4 stops to get on or off.

Where to Eat

Bayside Betsy's, 177 Commercial St., Provincetown; (508) 487-6566; bayside betsys.com. Casual fine dining and menu; gorgeous water views. Open in season for breakfast, lunch, and dinner, off-season check the schedule. The owner, Betsy is very friendly. $–$$$

George's Pizza, 275 Commercial St., Provincetown; (508) 487-3744. Greek-style pizza, sandwiches, and fresh ingredients. Outdoor on the patio (the people-watching is unsurpassed!) and indoor dining. $–$$

Lewis Brothers Ice Cream, 310 Commercial St., Provincetown; (508) 487-0977; lewisbrothersicecream.com. Seasonal. $

The Lobster Pot Restaurant, 321 Commercial St., Provincetown; (508) 487-0842; ptownlobsterpot.com. Open seasonally Apr through Nov. Voted one of the top 100 restaurants in New England in a *Phantom Gourmet* dining poll. Two water-view dining rooms. Extensive menu. $$–$$$

Napi's, 7 Freeman St., Providence; (800) 571-6274; napis-restaurant.com. In business for generations; beloved by the locals. Varied menu, artsy setting. Try the Brazillian shrimp. Open year-round. $–$$

Where to Stay

Harbor Hotel, 698 Commercial St., Provincetown; (855) 447-8696 or (800) 442-4224; harborhotelptown.com. Newly renovated, retro 1950s and '60s style (think *Mad Men*), outdoor pool, views of the harbor by the outdoor fire pit. $–$$$$

Provincetown Inn, 1 Commercial St., Provincetown; (508) 487-9500 or (800) WHA-LEVU; provincetowninn.com. Private beach and outdoor pool. Rates include continental breakfast for two. Kids under 12 eat and stay for free. $–$$$$

Race Point Lighthouse Keepers House and the Whistle House, Race Point Beach, Provincetown; (855) 722-3959; racepointlighthouse.net or mybnbwebsite .com/racepointlighthouse/accommodations.htm. Bring your own food and water, linens, and towels. The Keeper's House (open May to Nov) can be rented by the night. The Whistle House is rented weekly Sat to Sat Memorial Day weekend to early Sept, and from early Sept to closing for a 2-night minimum. You need a 4-wheel-drive vehicle to access these Coast Guard properties. Money raised from rentals goes to the restoration of Race Point, Long Point, and Wood End Lighthouses. Reservations required. $$–$$$$

Martha's Vineyard

Martha's Vineyard provides more spectacular beaches and seaside atmosphere with less stress and fewer visitors than you'll see on the Cape. Only 7 miles from Falmouth at its closest point, the island is more populous and cosmopolitan than neighboring Nantucket. The Vineyard boasts large expanses of deep forest and acres of rolling farmland. The colorful cottages and Flying Horses Carousel in Oak Bluffs are beloved by the lucky children who live on the island as well as those who visit. Annual visitors treat their island vacations as sacred family rituals, booking their reservations as far as six to eight months ahead. Try to make your family's ferry reservation (see the "South of Boston" chapter for the Seastreak from New Bedford or this chapter for the *Island Queen* and Steamship Authority from Woods Hole or the Hy-Line from Hyannis) and accommodations plans as early as possible. A great resource for availability, the **Martha's Vineyard Chamber of Commerce**, 24 Beach Rd., Vineyard Haven (508-693-0085 or 800-505-4815; mvy.com), has a sophisticated telephone messaging system for ordering visitor information. They man visitor booths by the Steamship Authority dock in Vineyard Haven, on Circuit Avenue in Oak Bluffs, and on Church Street in Edgartown (open 8 a.m. to 8 p.m. in season). The main office is open Mon through Fri year-round.

Trust the **Trustees**

Trust the trustees to do things right! The Trustees of Reservations offer tours that focus on Martha's Vineyard's fragile wildlife as well as natural-history tours of Martha's Vineyard. If you are in the mood for more adventurous active touring, the trustees have canoeing, fishing, lighthouse, snorkel discovery, and kayaking guided tours (and an "eerie creatures of the night" family hike!). You can reach the Martha's Vineyard Regional Office at (508) 693-7662.

Destination Insider has a reservoir of rooms and represents most hotels and inns. They are a reservation and concierge service for dining, lodging (vacation homes, resorts, cottages, hotels, inns, B&Bs), transportation, and activities. Contact them at PO Box 1651, Vineyard Haven, MA 02568, (508) 696-3900 or (866) 696-3900; destinationinsider.com.

Vineyard Haven

Vineyard Haven has great restaurants and shopping in a more relaxed setting than some of the other Vineyard towns. Vineyard Haven Harbor is a more romantic setting than bustling Oak Bluffs.

Things to See & Do

Black Dog General Store, 9 locations on Martha's Vineyard (12 locations more on the East Coast); (508) 696-8182 or (800) 626-1991 (customer service and mail order); theblackdog.com. Here's where you can buy those Black Dog T-shirts, sweatshirts, and hats that everyone seems to be wearing.

Island Cove Mini Golf, 386 State Rd., Vineyard Haven; (508) 693-2611; island coveadventures.com. Minigolf, rock-climbing wall, grill, and ice cream. *TIP:* Ask the Park n' Ride shuttle bus at the Vineyard Haven Ferry to drop you off at the minigolf course—it's free.

Martha's Vineyard Film Center, 79 Beach Rd., Vineyard Haven (at the Tisbury Market); (508) 696-9369 or (774) 392-2972; mvfilmsociety.com. Showing independent, classic, and foreign language films. Special events include live poetry readings, children's movies, and educational programming.

Martha's Bike Rentals, 4 Lagoon Pond Rd. (at Five Corners), Vineyard Haven; (508) 693-6593 or (800) 559-0312; marthasvineyardbikes.com. Children's mountain and hybrid bikes. For families with small children, they have baby seats, joggers, and Burley trailers. Will deliver to any location.

Vineyard Playhouse, 24 Church St., Vineyard Haven; (508) 696-6300 (Playhouse) or (508) 687-2452 (box office); vineyardplayhouse.org. Family classics, recent hits, world premieres, and holiday shows. The Fabulists produce theater for children outdoors on Sat at 10 a.m. at the Tisbury Amphitheater during the summer. Summer Stars Theater Arts Camp for kids.

The **Black Dog**

You will see Black Dog T-shirts everywhere. Children will probably enjoy reading *The Story of the Little Black Dog* picture book by J. B. Spooner and Terre Lamb Seeley to help explain the popularity of the Black Dog!

Winds Up, 199 Beach Rd., Vineyard Haven; (508) 693-4340 or (508) 693-4252; winds upmv.com. Rent kayaks, sailboats, canoes, stand-up paddle boards, Windsurfers, and other water-related equipment. Lessons can be arranged.

Where to Eat

Art Cliff Diner, 39 Beach Rd., Vineyard Haven; (508) 693-1224. Considered the best place on the island for breakfast, with an enormous menu; can have long lines. Try the almond French toast. $–$$

Black Dog Bakery and Cafe, two locations: 509 State Rd. and 3 Water St., Vineyard Haven; (508) 696-8190 (State Road) or (508) 693-4786 (Water Street); theblack dog.com. Delectable desserts and baked goods all day, with sandwiches served at lunchtime. Open year-round. $

Black Dog Tavern, 20 Beach St. Ext., Vineyard Haven Harbor, Vineyard Haven; (508) 693-9223; theblackdog.com/tavern.html. Full menu serving breakfast and lunch year-round and dinner daily in season; limited hours off-season. Fun and salty atmosphere. Open year-round. $–$$$$

Blue Canoe Grill, 52 Beach Rd., Vineyard Haven; (508) 693-3332; bluecanoegrill .com.

Large portions, locavores delight, waterfront location, indoor and outdoor seating. Specializing in seafood, their crabcakes have received great reviews. $–$$$$

Waterside Market, 76 Main St., Vineyard Haven: (508) 693-8899; watersidemarket .com. Prices are great and portions are huge. Breakfast all day. Baked goods made fresh that day. $

Where to Stay

Mansion House, 9 Main St., Vineyard Haven; (508) 693-2200 or (800) 332-4112; mvmansionhouse.com. Rooms have different amenities ranging from soaking tubs, fireplaces, and ocean views to suites with fridges and microwaves. At the health club and spa, there is a chlorine-free, mineral-spring-fed, 75-foot pool (swimming classes in season). Grab and Go breakfast and complete use of the health club and classes comes with the room. The **Copper Wok,** a pan-Asian Restaurant, is just off the lobby. $–$$$$

Martha's Vineyard Family Campground, 569 Edgartown Rd., Vineyard Haven; (508) 693-3772; campmv.com. Open mid-May through mid-Oct. One and a half mile from the Vineyard Haven ferry; only campground on Martha's Vineyard. A limited number of one- and two-room cabins are available. Tent sites (maximum of one family per site) and RV sites are also available, complete with campfire area. The main building has hot showers, restrooms, a laundry room, a rec hall, a playground, and a grocery store. $–$$

Vineyard Harbor Hotel, 60 Beach Rd., Vineyard Haven; (508) 693-3334; vineyard harbormotel.com. Only waterfront motel on Martha's Vineyard, with a small beach attached. Every room is an efficiency. It's not fancy, but it's adorable, within walking distance from the ferry and the market, and across the street from restaurants. A great place for families. $$–$$$

Oak Bluffs

The colorful gingerbread cottages of the Wesleyan Grove Campground were built here during the late 19th century to replace the tents used by Methodist parishioners who camped and worshiped here every summer. Observe the no-bicycles rule and quiet time, which begins at dusk and ends at sunrise.

Cottage Museum (all ages)

1 Trinity Park, Oak Bluffs; (508) 693-7784; mvcma.org/museum.htm. During the summer, open Mon through Sat 10 a.m. to 4 p.m., Sun 1 to 4 p.m. Price: $2 for adults, 50 cents for ages 3 to 12, free for children under 3.
View a typical gingerbread cottage house complete with period furnishings and vintage photographs that explain the history of the Martha's Vineyard Camp Meeting (established by the Methodists in the 1800s).

Do You Know **the Score?**

Community sings are held weekly at 8 p.m. on Wed during July and Aug at **The Tabernacle,** Oak Bluffs Cottage Colony Campground. Hymns, folk songs, rounds, spirituals, and patriotic songs are the standard. Donations accepted.

Flying Horses Carousel   (all ages)

15 Lake Ave. (Bottom of Circuit Ave.), Oak Bluffs; (508) 693-9481; mvpreservation .org. Open Easter Sat through Columbus Day, check the website as the schedule varies. Price: $2.50 per ride.

An old wooden red building houses the Flying Horses Carousel, a National Historic Landmark that's wonderfully alive with merry-go-round lovers of all ages. It's the oldest operating platform carousel in the country; the horses were carved in 1876. There's even a brass ring; if you catch it, your ride is free!

Hy-Line Cruises Interisland Ferry Service   (all ages)

The information line is (508) 778-2600 or (800) 492-8082; hylinecruises.com. Price: $36 one-way for adults, $24 one-way for children 5 to 12; free for children 4 and under. Fee for bikes is $7 one-way. Seasonal (May-Sept).

Hy-Line Cruises has the only interisland ferry service between Oak Bluffs in Martha's Vineyard and Straight Wharf in Nantucket. The 70-minute, high-speed cruise has a snack bar and plenty of restrooms onboard. Departures are once a day, and reservations are not necessary (but recommended).

Island Alpaca   (all ages)

1 Head of Pond Rd. (off of Edgartown/Vineyard Haven Road) Oak Bluffs; (508) 693-5554; islandalpaca.com. Open daily: 10 a.m. to 4 p.m. and extended hours until 5 p.m. mid-Mar through Oct and for special events.

The alpaca are super-friendly animals, and kids (and adults!) really enjoy observing and petting them. Self-guided walking tours of the farm let you meander at your leisure. Every morning there is an Alpaca Discovery Program; for $25 you can feed the alpacas, manage their pasture, and walk them (by preregistration only). Island Alpaca was voted one of the "Best Children's Activities on Martha's Vineyard in 2012" by *Cape Cod Life*. There are knitting and spinning classes,

TopEvents on Martha's Vineyard

- **Shearing Day Festival,** Island Alpaca, 1 Head of Pond Rd., Oak Bluffs; (508) 693-5554; islandalpaca.com

- **Sheepapalooza,** Apr, 14 Aero Ave., Edgartown; (508) 627-7007; farminstitute.org

- **Oak Bluffs Harbor Festival,** June, Oak Bluffs, Martha's Vineyard; (508) 693-3392; oakbluffsmv.com

- **West Tisbury's Summer Farmers' Market,** June through Sept, Grange Hall, West Tisbury, Martha's Vineyard; (508) 693-9561; thewesttisburyfarmersmarket.com

- **Fourth of July Fireworks,** July 4, Edgartown Harbor/Lighthouse, Edgartown; (508) 693-9561; mvy.com

- **Edgartown Regatta,** mid-July, Edgartown, Martha's Vineyard; (508) 693-0085; mvy.com (Martha's Vineyard Chamber of Commerce) or (508) 627-4361; edgartownyc.org (Edgartown Yacht Club)

- **Oak Bluffs' Fireworks,** mid-Aug, Oak Bluffs Harbor, Martha's Vineyard; (508) 693-0085; mvy.com

- **Grand Illumination Night,** mid-Aug, The Tabernacle, Oak Bluffs, Martha's Vineyard; (508) 693-0085; mvy.com (Martha's Vineyard Chamber of Commerce) or (508) 693-0525; mvcma.org (Martha's Vineyard Camp Meeting Association)

- **Moshup Pageant,** Aug, Aquinnah; (508) 645-9265; wampanoagtribe .net

- **Martha's Vineyard Fair,** late Aug, Fairgrounds, West Tisbury; (508) 693-4343 or (508) 693-9549; mvas.vineyardMartha's Vineyard International Film Festival, Sept, Martha's Vineyard; (508) 696-9369 or (774) 392-2972; mvfilmfest.com

- **Annual Aquinnah Wampanoag Powwow,** Sept, Aquinnah; (508) 645-9265; wampanoagtribe.net

- **Striped Bass and Bluefish Derby,** mid-Sept through mid-Oct, Martha's Vineyard; (508) 693-0085; mvy.com

- **Fall for the Arts,** Oct, Island wide Arts and Cultural events, Martha's Vineyard; (508) 693-0085; artsmarthasvineyard.org

- **Martha's Vineyard Food and Wine Festival,** Oct, Martha's Vineyard Island wide; (508) 693-0085; mvy.com (Martha's Vineyard Chamber) or (508) 280-0080; mvfoodandwine.com (Martha's Vineyard Food and Wine Festival)

- **West Tisbury Winter Farmers' Market,** mid-Oct through Dec, Agricultural Society, 35 Panhandle Rd., West Tisbury; (508) 693-9561; thewesttisburyfarmersmarket.com

- **Christmas in Edgartown,** second weekend in Dec, island-wide in Martha's Vineyard; (508) 693-0085; mvy.com/calendar

many fun family-style events, or you can rent an alpaca for a party. A live alpaca cam allows you to watch the alpacas during daylight (there are no lights set up for nighttime viewing). *TIP*: Don't miss their gift shop, where you can find locally grown garments from their herd.

Other Things to See & Do

Island Spirit Kayak, on Sengekontacket Pond, Oak Bluffs; (508) 693-9727; island spirit kayak.com. Tours of Sengekontacket Pond by kayak and paddleboarding by day and night.

WIMP Comedy IMPROV, Alex's Place, 111 R Vineyard Haven–Edgartown Rd., Oak Bluffs; (508) 939-9368; imp4kids.com. Original improv comedy show on Tues nights in season by a highly regarded Teen and College Troupe (which performed at the Chicago Improv Festival 2013, the only youth group invited). Year-round performances. Summer camp.

Where to Eat

Giordano's, 18 Lake Ave., Oak Bluffs; (508) 693-0184; giosmv.com. Open for lunch and dinner May to mid-Sept. Serves up enormous portions of spaghetti, fried clams, fried chicken, and the like. Pizza by the slice at their take-out window or a pie to go. Cash only. $–$$$

Nancy's Restaurant, 29 Lake Ave., Oak Bluffs; (508) 693-0006. An island institution for six decades. Two restaurants: a street-level snack bar and an upstairs restaurant with a deck offering Oak Bluffs Harbor views. President Obama ate here! Specializing in fresh seafood. $$–$$$$

Where to Stay

A Bed and Breakfast Afloat, Oak Bluffs Harbor Marina, Oak Bluffs; (508) 650-0466; abedandbreakfastafloat.com. Welcome aboard the MS *Resolute* bed-and-breakfast, a 40-foot Island Cutter that sleeps up to four people. Galley kitchen, living room with a flat-screen TV, a head with a shower, and continental breakfast served daily. You have the deck and the entire boat to yourself! $$–$$$$

The Dockside Inn, 9 Circuit Ave. Ext, Oak Bluffs; (508) 693-2966; vineyardinns.com. Easy walk from all the Oak Bluffs ferries, very family friendly. Newly renovated in 2013, a large gingerbread cottage on the exterior but modern inside. Children welcome. Continental breakfast. A *Yankee Magazine* Editors' Choice in 2013. $–$$$$

Oak Bluffs Inn, 64 Circuit Ave., Oak Bluffs; (508) 693-7171 or (800) 955-6235; oakbluffsinn.com. Open mid-Apr to end of Oct. Rates include continental breakfast. A cupola-topped, three-story, pink building; 10 comfortable rooms (including three in the carriage house). Great location. $–$$$$

Cycle Around . . .

An 11-mile round-trip flat bike path shuttles cyclists between Edgartown and Oak Bluffs. The heavily traveled scenic path parallels the Edgartown-to-Oak-Bluffs road (aka Beach Road) and Nantucket Sound, passing by Bend in the Road Beach, Joseph Sylvia State Beach, and Sengekontacket Pond (which touches the eastern end of Edgartown and the western end of Oak Bluffs). *TIP:* Be careful of the sand blown on the path—it can be hazardous and cause a spill.

I Scream, **You Scream**

Mad Martha's is a Martha's Vineyard institution (closed Oct through Apr) serving 23 great homemade ice-cream flavors and 7 kinds of nonfat yogurt. My favorite is the red, white, and blueberry pie ice cream. Try one of their unique to-die-for chocolate lover's dream sundaes, such as the Sinful Chocolate Sundae or the 12-scoop Pig Sundae (ordered by saying "oink"). There are several locations on the island:

- 12 Circuit Ave., Oak Bluffs; (508) 693-9151 (ice-cream and coffee shop)
- 20 Union St., Vineyard Haven; (508) 693-5883
- 12 North Water St., Edgartown; (508) 627-8761

Edgartown

Stately homes line the narrow streets of this seaport village. A great yachting center, Edgartown attracts seafarers today. Walk to Edgartown Lighthouse from North Water Street. In 1828 the lighthouse was built on what was then an island in Edgartown Harbor; after a storm in the early 20th century, a sandbar emerged from the water and attached the smaller island to the Vineyard. The **Chappaquiddick Passenger and Vehicle Ferry,** (508) 627-9427 or (508) 627-6965 (hotline); chappyferry.com, operates year-round (from 7 a.m. to midnight in season). Catch it at Dock Street in Edgartown for a short 5-minute crossing.

Farm Institute (3 and up)

14 Aero Ave., Edgartown; (508) 627-7007; farminstitute.org. Year-round educational programs. Check the event schedule.

The Farm Institute is a private nonprofit educational farm, and a favorite place for kids and their families. A variety of programs are offered. A popular Saturday program for younger children is "Wee Farmers" for ages 2 to 4 (accompanied by an adult). "Wee Farmers" has circle time, story time, and visiting the farm animals. In the summer the institute runs a full- or half-day camp for ages

4 to 17 and "Farmer for the Day" for ages 5 to adult ($50 a day for the first child and $25 for each additional person). The "Farmer for the Day" does a farm tour, spends time working in the garden or tending to farm chores, and cares for the animals (children can attend unaccompanied, but family groups are also welcome). Samantha the goose greets you upon your arrival; cows, chickens, goats, guinea hens, lambs, sheep, and one rabbit (in the field) all enhance the farm experience. Don't miss the family-friendly "Barnyard Movie Nights" (movies are shown on the side of the barn) in the summer or bring a carload for pumpkin picking in the fall.

Felix Neck Wildlife Sanctuary (all ages)

100 Felix Neck Dr., Off Edgartown–Vineyard Haven Road to Felix Neck Drive, Edgartown; (508) 627-4850; massaudubon.org (click on sanctuary). Open year-round. Trails open daily from dawn to dusk. The visitor center is open daily year-round (check the website for the schedule). Admission: $4 for adults, $3 for seniors and children 2 to 12; free for children under 2.

A preserve that's affiliated with the Massachusetts Audubon Society, Felix Neck Wildlife Sanctuary comprises 350 acres of forests, salt marshes, ponds, shoreline, grasslands, fields, and an excellent interpretive center that conducts guided nature walks year-round. Many pleasant hiking trails leave from the sanctuary's exhibit building (there are 4 miles of trails). A magnet for birders; sightings have included ospreys, American oystercatchers, and swallows. A live-feed cam can be viewed from the visitor center, giving you a bird's-eye view of nesting barn owls. Don't miss the Discovery Room with hands-on activities and exhibits for all ages. Sign up for their land and sea programs and Summer Camp.

Children's **Favorites**

Delightful children's books with island settings are:

- *Morning Beach* by Leslie Baker. Set in Martha's Vineyard.

- *Nat, Nat the Nantucket Cat* by Peter W. Barnes, illustrated by Susan Arciero. Set in Nantucket.

Joseph Sylvia State Beach (all ages)

Beach Road, Edgartown to Oak Bluffs. Open year-round. Free.
This 2-mile-long narrow beach between Oak Bluffs and Edgartown is owned by
the state and maintained by the county. The section of Joseph Sylvia State Beach
known as Bend-in-the-Road Beach in Edgartown is a nice spot for kids; there are
no facilities, although there are lifeguards in season. Even though Joseph Sylvia
State Beach is popular, it never feels crowded. Parking can be difficult, so you
may want to ride your bike here.

Martha's Vineyard Museum (all ages)

**59 School St. (corner of Cooke Street), Edgartown; (508) 627-4441; mvmuseum
.org. Open mid-May through mid-Oct, Mon through Sat 10 a.m. to 5 p.m.; and
from mid-Oct to mid-May, Mon through Sat 10 to 4 p.m. Winter pricing: $6 for
adults, $5 for kids. Summer pricing: $7 for adults, $6 for kids 6 to 15; free for
kids under 6.**
The Vineyard Museum is a campus of five buildings: the Cooke House, the Carriage Shed, the Pease House, the Gale Huntington Research Library, and the
Fresnel Lens Tower. Everything on display relates to the history of Martha's
Vineyard.

The Cooke House is a colonial home built in 1765 with 11 rooms of exhibits
relating to the life and history of Martha's Vineyard and its residents. In the
attached Tool Shed, various tools and equipment are on display.

The Carriage Shed displays seagoing vessels and land vehicles, including
a boat used during whaling days, pieces of shipwreck found off the coast, a
hearse, a 19th-century fire engine, and a wagon.

The Pease House is a 19th-century home with six gallery spaces: a permanent exhibit, a Native American Wampanoag exhibit, and an ever-changing
exhibit done by local students. Changing exhibits are drawn from their vast
collection of over 30,000 objects of art and artifacts, photography, scrimshaw,
the life of islanders, and the oral histories of island residents. A museum shop is
located in this building.

The Gale Huntington Research Library is an archive library with genealogical
records and ephemera.

The Fresnel Lens Tower, with the original Fresnel lens from the Gay Head
Lighthouse, is the last structure on the campus. The lens, a series of more than
1,000 prisms, was replaced by an electric light. The lens is lighted up for a few
hours every evening.

No Sour Grapes Here

Martha's Vineyard was discovered in the 1600s by Bartholomew Gosnold, who named the island after his beloved daughter and all the wild grapes that grew here.

Mytoi and East Beach (all ages)

51 Dike Rd., Chappaquiddick; (508) 627-3599 (Mytoi office) or (508) 627-7689 (Trustees of Reservations). The garden is free and open daily year-round. Admission for East Beach: $3 per person; free for children under 15. Directions: From the Edgartown/Chappaquiddick Ferry, take Chappaquiddick Road for 2.5 miles to Dike Road (a dirt road on the left at the curve). The gatehouse at the refuge is open from 9 a.m. to 4:45 p.m.

The property comprises a Japanese-style garden with native and exotic plantings. Picturesque features of the garden are ornamental bridges arching over ponds (one of which leads to a serene island). Travelers find Mytoi a reflective calming space away from the hustle and bustle of the island. Farther down the road is East Beach, part of Cape Poque Wildlife Refuge and Wasque Reservation (thetrustees.org), a quiet rustic beach and natural wildlife area with no lifeguards. The Trustees run tours from Mytoi to the remote Cape Poque Lighthouse via kayak or oversand vehicles in season.

South Beach (older children and strong swimmers)

End of Katama Road, south of Edgartown. Restrooms and changing rooms in season only. Free.

Also known as Katama Beach, South Beach is a 3-mile-long barrier beach; the most popular beach on the island. There is heavy surf on one side and a protected salt pond on the other. Lifeguards patrol about three-quarters of the beach. There are no public facilities off-season. South Beach is not appropriate for younger children or weak swimmers, since the undertow can be treacherous, but surfers love it! It's accessible by shuttle bus from Edgartown.

Where to Eat

Among the Flowers, 17 Mayhew Ln., off North Water Street, Edgartown; (508) 627-3233. Open May through June and Sept through Oct for breakfast and lunch; July and Aug for breakfast, lunch, and candlelit dinner. Cafe serving PBJ and other regular fare. $

Atria, 137 Main St., Edgartown; (508) 627-5850; atriamv.com. Open year-round. A very "in" place in Edgartown with great food. $$$–$$$$

The Seafood Shanty, 31 Dock St., Edgartown; (508) 627-8622; theseafoodshanty .com. On the harbor, next to Memorial Wharf. Great family restaurant, serving lunch and dinner, specializing in local seafood. Seasonal. Kids' menu. $$$

The Wharf Pub and Restaurant, 5 Lower Main St., Edgartown; (508) 627-9966; wharfpub.com. Open year-round for lunch and dinner. Great family-style restaurant. Kids' menu. $–$$$$

Where to Stay

Clarion Martha's Vineyard, 227 Upper Main St., Edgartown; (508) 627-5161; clarion mv.com. Open year-round, large rooms all with a fridge and a microwave. Located just out of the town center, by a bike path and public transportation, one of the few hotels with 2 queen-size beds in the room (so it's very family friendly). Close to restaurants and a food store. $–$$$

Edgartown Commons, 20 Pease Point Way, Edgartown; (508) 627-4671 or (800) 439-4671; edgartowncommons.com. Family-oriented, 35 units. Playground, outdoor swimming pool, grills, and kitchen facilities in the rooms. Close to town and a public transportation stop. Loyal following. Seasonal. $–$$$

Amazing
Vineyard Facts

Martha's Vineyard bike paths cover about 44 miles of paved and off-road bike trails going past picturesque villages and scenic views down island, about 60-plus miles to bike the perimeter of the entire island.

Harborview Hotel and Resort, 131 North Water St., Edgartown; (508) 627-7000 or (800) 225-6005; harbor-view.com. Prime Edgartown location, 8 cottages, a renovated main building, and the Mayhew building. Ocean views. Open year-round. $–$$$

Victorian Inn, 24 South Water St., Edgartown; (508) 627-4784; thevic.com. Rates include breakfast, tea, and cookies in the afternoon (in the garden!). Open Apr through Nov 1. Located a block away from the harbor and in the center of the shopping district. Each charming room has its own personality (some with four-posters and harbor views). Children 8 and older welcome; no cots. $$–$$$$

West Tisbury

West Tisbury is a typical New England village, with a prerequisite white church, general store, and fine clapboard homes.

Cedar Tree Neck Wildlife Sanctuary (all ages)
200 Obed Daggett Rd. (off of Indian Hill Road), West Tisbury; (508) 693-5207; sheriffsmeadow.org. Open 8:30 a.m. to 5:30 p.m. daily.
Four hundred acres with trails through forests, dunes, and beach. Scenic trails and gorgeous hilltop views of Vineyard Sound and the Elizabeth Islands. No picnicking or swimming allowed (very strong undertow). Owned and managed by Sheriff's Meadow, a Martha's Vineyard land trust.

Manuel Correllus State Forest (all ages)
Off Edgartown–West Tisbury Road and Barnes Road; (508) 693-2540; mass.gov/ eea/agencies/dcr/massparks/region-south/manuel-f-correllus-state-forest.html. Open year-round dawn to dusk. Free.
The 5,343 acres of Manuel Correllus State Forest were created to save the rare heath hen (which is now extinct). The forest is crisscrossed with 14 miles of bike, equestrian, and hiking trails. The most popular is the paved bike paths, but steer clear of the rabbits, deer, skunks, and raccoons! Park near the Barnes Road entrance to the park.

Martha's Vineyard Fair (all ages)
35 Panhandle Rd., West Tisbury; (508) 693-4343 or (508) 693-9549; mvas.vineyard .net. Held in late Aug. Admission charged: $10 per adult, $5 for children 5 to 12, under 5 are free.

Oldies but Goodies

The Tabernacle, Trinity Park in Oak Bluffs, shows family-friendly films on select Tues nights July through Aug; admission is free but donations are encouraged. Movies can be a mix of children's classics to those more current.

This old-fashioned four-day fair is a bit more upscale than other state fairs. There are typical showcases of fruit and vegetable displays, livestock (oxen and draft horses, sheep, alpaca, and llamas), creative arts (quilts, painting, demonstrations of spinning, weaving, shearing, and photography), and local food and crafts. Unique to the Martha's Vineyard Agricultural Society Fair are some of the contests: oyster shucking, antique tractor pulls, dog shows, a woodsman contest with 12 different events, the skillet throw, smoked fish, and the unusual pet. The midway features rides, games, and fried food. Performances are by local musicians and there are puppet shows for the kids.

Polly Hill Arboretum (all ages)

809 State Rd., West Tisbury; (508) 693-9426; pollyhillarboretum.org. The arboretum is open year-round from dusk to dawn. The visitor center is open from 9:30 a.m. to 4 p.m. daily Memorial Day to Columbus Day and guided tours are offered at 10 a.m. Suggested donation: $5 for adults; free for children 12 and under. Ask for the Family Explorer's Backpack.

This property was initially a sheep farm; in 1926 the Butcher family (Polly's parents) purchased 40 acres of the farm. Polly eventually inherited the property, and she acquired 20 more acres, increasing the size of the piece to its present 60 acres. Polly planted seeds and nurtured plants that weren't native to the Vineyard, and through natural selection and crossbreeding, she got a hardier stock that was able to survive the harsh conditions of the Vineyard soil and climate. Your family is free to roam and discover the famous North Tisbury azaleas, the Tunnel of Love, the Monkey Puzzle Tree, the Julian Hill Magnolia, and the Dogwood Allee. No pets please.

Other Things to See & Do

Alley's General Store, 1045 State Rd., West Tisbury; (508) 693-0088. Old-fashioned country store.

Crow Hollow Farm, Tiah's Cove Road, West Tisbury; (508) 696-4554; crowhollow farm.com. English horseback-riding lessons.

Long Point Wildlife Refuge, Edgartown–West Tisbury Road, Two entrances: 330 Hughes Thumb Rd. or 300 Long Point Rd., West Tisbury; (508) 693-3678; thetrustees .org. Price: $10 per car, plus $3 per adult. Six hundred thirty-two acres, 2 miles of trail, woodlands, dunes, and a beach. Boating and swimming activities, and tours are offered. (Call 508-693-7392 for tour reservations.) The beach here is considered by many to be the best on the Vineyard.

Menemsha Hills Reservation, 1 Trustees Ln. off of North Road, Chilmark; (508) 693-3678; thetrustees.org. Free. Two hundred eleven acres, 3 miles of trails. Views of Menemsha Harbor, Gay Head Lighthouse, Vineyard Sound, and the Elizabeth Islands.

Nip N' Tuck Farm, 39 Davis Look Rd., West Tisbury; (508) 693-1449. Hayrides by reservation only.

Where to Eat

State Road Restaurant, 688 State Rd., West Tisbury; (508) 693-8582; stateroadmv .com. Green restaurant, uses local produce and foodstuffs. Open for breakfast lunch and dinner. Charming decor. Open year-round. $–$$$$

Where to Stay

Hostelling International, 525 Edgartown/West Tisbury Rd., West Tisbury; (508) 693-2665 or (888) 901-2087; capecodhostels.org. Sixty-seven beds, 4 private rooms, and 4 large dorms. Open mid-May to Columbus Day. Children are welcome. Credit cards accepted. $–$$

The Red Hat Bed and Breakfast, 629 Edgartown/West Tisbury Rd., West Tisbury; (508) 696-7186; theredhat.com. Three rooms with shared bath; quaintly decorated. Large yard and gardens. Reasonably priced for families (children welcome). Continental breakfast included in room rate. Weekly rates during the summer, daily rates off-season. $–$$

Aquinnah (formerly known as Gay Head), Menemsha & Chilmark

Aquinnah, or Gay Head, is known for its breathtaking cliffs and views of the ocean. It's a more remote, sparsely populated area of Martha's Vineyard. The **Aquinnah Cultural Center,** 29 Black Brook Rd. (508-645-7900; wampanoagtribe .net), opened a traditional longhouse behind the tribal office. The Edwin D. Van-Derhoop's Homestead Museum is downstairs in the visitor center and sponsors events, programs, and exhibits relating to tribal culture. If you've seen the film *Jaws,* you may recognize the Chilmark village of Menemsha and Dutcher's Dock, which served as a backdrop in many of the film's harbor shots. It's truly a quaint seaside spot with a wonderful beach (Menemsha Beach) and fresh seafood straight from the docks. Don't miss Chilmark's Community Center weekly films and family events.

Aquinnah/Gay Head Beach (all ages)

65 State Rd. near Aquinnah Circle, Aquinnah; (508) 645-2300 (Town Hall); aquinnah-ma.gov. Parking is $15.

Below the colorful clay cliffs, Aquinnah/Gay Head Beach (commonly known as Moshup Beach after a Wampanoag legend) is very popular during the summer. Because parking is limited and the beach extends south for several miles, it's rarely crowded. **Note:** There are no lifeguards here, and the closest restrooms (50-cent charge—bring change) are on the center of the circle. You'll probably see people climbing up the cliffs. Resist the temptation; if caught, you will be fined. The worst of the cliffs' erosion is a direct result of foot traffic. Moreover, the cliffs are the private property of the Wampanoag tribe, which runs the town of Aquinnah/Gay Head. **Caution:** There is nude bathing on some stretches of beach, and heavy surf.

Gay Head Lighthouse (all ages)

9 Aquinnah Circle, Aquinnah; (508) 627-4441; mvmuseum.org or gayheadlight .org. Open Sat and Sun from 10 a.m. to 5 p.m. the end of May to mid-June, then opening daily mid-June to mid-Sept from 10 a.m. to 5 p.m. In addition, Gay Head lighthouse open Fri and Sat evenings from mid-June to mid-Sept.; 7 to 9 p.m. in June and July; and 6 to 8 p.m. in Aug and Sept. Price: $5 per person, 12 and under admitted for free.

Lighthouse Tours of Martha's Vineyard

The lighthouses of Aquinnah/Gay Head (9 Aquinnah Circle, Aquinnah), East Chop (229 East Chop Ave., Oak Bluffs), and Edgartown (121 N. Water St., Edgartown) are maintained by the Martha's Vineyard Museum (508-627-4441; mvmuseum.org). The museum opens the lighthouses in the late spring through early fall for tours and views. Check the Martha's Vineyard Museum website for the schedule. Don't miss the Cape Poge Lighthouse in Edgartown at the tip of Chappaquiddick (information on tours is in the Edgartown section of this book) or the West Chop Lighthouse on Main Street in Vineyard Haven (a historic lighthouse that is a gorgeous place for sunsets, but not open for tours). The price is $5 per person (under 12 free) for these gorgeous views.

The redbrick Gay Head Lighthouse is a spectacular setting. On Fri and Sat evenings during the summer, you can go up to the lighthouse's observation deck to watch the sun setting over the sound. The National Trust for Historic Preservation has called the Gay Head Lighthouse one of America's 11 Most Endangered Places because of eroding cliffs. Efforts are under way to save this historic lighthouse and relocate it to a safer place.

Where to Eat

Aquinnah Shop Restaurant, 27 Aquinnah Circle, on the cliffs, Aquinnah; (508) 645-3867. Open late May through Columbus Day, seven days a week. Serving breakfast, lunch, and dinner in season. Beautiful views and bountiful food. Fresh seafood and pasta specialties; children's menu. *TIP:* As the sun sets, the local, friendly, and curious skunks make their way to the outside deck. Moral: Go early! $$–$$$$

Home Port, 512 North Rd., Menemsha (in Chilmark); (508) 645-2679; homeportmv .com. Open mid-May to mid-Sept for dinner. Casual seafood restaurant just steps from the water. Reservations are recommended. Bike delivery of your order to Menemsha Beach is available. $$$$

Where to Stay ⊖

Duck Inn Pigout, 10 Duck Pond, off State Road, Aquinnah; (508) 645-9018; duckinn
onmv.com. Open year-round. Comfortable, health-oriented bed-and-breakfast. The
kids will enjoy the 5-minute walk to the private beach; parents will love the hot tub,
infrared sauna, ionic-cleanse foot bath, and massages. Children are welcome, and one
room is available to guests with pets. Organic breakfasts. $$–$$$

Menemsha Inn and Cottages, 12 Menemsha Rd., Menemsha (Chilmark); (508)
645-2521; menemshainn.com. Voted the best cottage colony on Martha's Vineyard
by *Cape Cod Life.* Short walk to Menemsha Beach (with spectacular striped-bass fly
fishing and surfcasting), kayaks, bikes, a tennis court, a gym, and more. $$–$$$$

Nantucket

Nantucket's unique character has much to do with its distance from the main-
land—it's a good 30 miles out to sea. Unlike cosmopolitan Martha's Vineyard,
Nantucket (which means "faraway island" in the Wampanoag language) is more
traditional and less crowded, even during the summer. Moors cover a large
percentage of the island, and its bike paths and long beaches make for wonder-
ful family vacations. The stocky Brant Point Lighthouse is one of New England's
shortest beacons (it's just 31 feet high); it's also one of Massachusetts's most
photographed spots. When you leave the island by ferry, you'll see lots of visi-
tors throwing pennies overboard as the ship rounds Brant Point. This tradition
supposedly ensures that they will return to the island.

For a visitor packet, contact the **Nantucket Island Chamber of Commerce,**
0 Main St., second floor, Nantucket, MA 02554 (508-228-1700; nantucketchamber
.org). Also helpful is the **Nantucket Visitor Service Center,** 25 Federal St.,

Fun Facts

Nantucket is 14 miles long by 3.5 miles wide (at its narrowest
width)—and nearly 40 percent is protected conservation land. Nan-
tucket is the only place in America to have a town, a county, and an
island all with the same name.

Surf's Up

Always be on a lifeguarded beach when traveling with children. Due to fiscal crunches, a beach may be left unguarded when staff is pulled to other areas of rougher surf!

Nantucket, MA 02554 (508-228-0925; nantucket-ma.gov and click on "Visitors Services"). Open daily in season (9 a.m. to 5 p.m.), and Mon through Sat off-season (9 a.m. to 5 p.m), they have the latest availability status for every lodging on the island, dining, things to do and see, last-minute reservations, and so forth. For information on hotels, B&Bs, condos, and rental properties, contact **Nantucket Accommodations,** 2 Windy Way, Suite 162, Nantucket, MA 02554; (508) 228-9559 or (866) 743-3330; nantucketaccommodations.com. **Note:** This is a private reservation service and they only represent the establishments that pay them to do so. For information on the ferry service between Nantucket and the Cape, see the Hyannis Ferries sidebar or the Freedom Cruise Line in Harwichport in this chapter. For interisland ferry service provided by Hy-Line Cruises, see the Martha's Vineyard section in this chapter.

Children's Beach (all ages)

Off South Beach Street on 15 Harbor View Way (on the bottom by the harbor), Nantucket; (508) 228-0925 (visitor services), (508) 228 7244 (Parks and Recreation), or (508) 228-7230 (beach manager). Free.

Children's Beach on Nantucket Harbor is appropriately named because it's perfect for very young children. There is no surf. It's very scenic, and your kids can watch the harbor activity and wave at the steamship passengers as they pass by. It offers a wheelchair-accessible restroom, lifeguards, an excellent snack bar and restaurant with a Mexican flair, a bandstand, a playground, a grassy play area, picnic tables, and organized activities for kids such as yoga, puppet shows, and dance programs. (Bring your own shirt for Tie-Dye T-Shirts Fridays). On Sun evenings, band concerts are held in July and Aug; performances on Tues night (Tues with Tony) and Fri evenings there are movies. Children's Beach is well located and is a short 2 blocks from town, limited parking.

Children's Theatre of Nantucket (ages 8 to 18)

Nantucket High School Auditorium, 10 Surfside Rd., Nantucket; (508) 228-8513. Children's theater program from end of June through mid-Aug.

Children perform in adaptations of popular and widely known plays and musicals. Plays are mounted with professional sets and costuming. This children's summer theater (since 1996) is by children, for children. One-week sessions make it doable for visitors. The *Inquirer and Mirror* (local newspaper) voted the Children's Theatre of Nantucket the best theater on Nantucket in 2007.

Cisco Beach (ages 7 and up)

268 Hummock Pond Rd., bear to the left just before the end of Hummock Pond Road, Nantucket; (508) 228-7244 (Parks and Recreation) or (508) 228-7230 (beach manager). Free.

Heavy-surf beach on the south side of Nantucket with beautiful raw views of the untamed sea. Lifeguarded but recommended for children and adults who know how to swim. Limited parking; you may wish to consider riding your bike the 4 miles from town. You can sign up for surfing lessons here.

Dionis Beach (all ages)

9 Dionis Beach Rd., off Eel Point Road, Nantucket; (508) 228-7244 (Parks and Recreation) or (508) 228-7230 (beach manager). Free.

Beach swimming is safe for children because there is no surf. Lifeguard on duty in season; wheelchair-accessible restrooms. Limited parking.

Light Up My Life

Three memorable Nantucket lighthouses are:

- **Brant Point Lighthouse** (Nantucket Harbor entrance; second-oldest lighthouse in the nation)
- **Great Point Lighthouse** (northern tip)
- **Sankaty Head Lighthouse** (eastern tip)

First Congregational Church and Tower (all ages)
62 Centre St., Nantucket; (508) 228-0950; nantucketfcc.org. Open mid-June to mid-Oct, Mon through Sat 10 a.m. to 4 p.m. (weather permitting). Admission: $5 for adults and **free** for under age 12.

The tower offers magnificent views of Nantucket on a clear day (Nantucket is only 14 miles long, and the tower is located near the midpoint of the island). There are 94 steps to climb to the top of the tower!

Francis Street Beach (all ages)
76 Washington St. Ext., Nantucket; (508) 228-7244 (Parks and Recreation) or (508) 228-7230 (beach manager).

Francis Street Beach is a small beach located on Nantucket Harbor. The waves are mild enough for children to play around the water. The beach has a public restroom, a turtle climb, and kayak rentals and is located a short 4 blocks from the center of town. *Caution:* No lifeguards!

Jetties Beach (all ages)
4 Bathing Beach Rd., Nantucket; (508) 228-7244 (Parks and Recreation) or (508) 228-7230 (beach manager). **Free.** Ample parking.

Lots of facilities—tennis courts; wheelchair-accessible restrooms; showers; a snack bar; a volleyball net; kayak, sailboat, and windsurfing rentals and lessons; beach-accessible wheelchair (requires another person to push it, it's not motorized); tennis lessons by the week; boardwalk onto the beach; and a

Jetties Beach

The most kid-friendly restaurant on the island is **Jetties Restaurant** at Jetties Beach (4 Bathing Beach Rd.; 508-228-2279; thejetties.com). It is right on the beach with picnic tables under an awning and it has a full-scale restaurant at night (after 5 p.m.) with a liquor license with fairly reasonable prices by Nantucket standards. The best part is that when the little rascals get restless, they can scamper onto the beach and play under your watchful eye as you relax with a glass of wine and a good meal! This is not a place to be missed with young children.

playground—plus rental chairs and lifeguards make this Nantucket's best beach for families. Since Jetties Beach is approximately a mile from the center of town, the NRTA (Nantucket Regional Transit Authority) summer shuttle is recommended over walking and dragging the children and assorted paraphernalia (pick it up downtown). Jetties Beach is where the annual Sandcastle and Sculpture Day contest is held in mid-Aug.

Madaket Beach (all ages)

338 Madaket Rd., Nantucket; (508) 228-7244 (Parks and Recreation) or (508) 228-7230 (beach manager). Free.

Madaket Beach, on the south shore, is one of the most beautiful beaches on the islands. Sunsets are to be savored here. The surf can be rolling and heavy at times, so it's best to keep a firm grip on children. Restrooms and lifeguards. Occasional erosion due to weather and surf (erosion lost 130 feet of the bank). There is limited parking, and Madaket is quite far from town (relatively speaking), so take the NRTA shuttle from town or ride the 5.5-mile bike path. There is a snack bar near the bus stop.

Maria Mitchell Association (all ages)

The Maria Mitchell Association is headquartered at 4 Vestal St.; (508) 228-9198; mariamitchell.org. Properties include the Aquarium, the Natural Science Museum, the Maria Mitchell Birthplace (aka the Mitchell House), the Loines Observatory, and the Vestral Street Observatory. The properties are at various locations just beyond Main Street in Nantucket. Properties are open seasonally Mon through Sat from 10 a.m. to 4 p.m. (except for the two observatories). A visitor pass for all association properties is $10 for adults, $8 for children, and includes the Aquarium, the Natural Science Museum, the Mitchell House, and the Vestral Street Observatory (the Loines Observatory is not included). This is the most cost-effective way to buy tickets for the museum because individual locations charge.
Maria Mitchell was the first professional woman astronomer to discover a comet (the Maria Mitchell Comet), and she did it on Nantucket, from the roof of the Pacific Bank located downtown. Her father constructed an observatory on top of his bank building on Main Street. The **Vestral Street Observatory** (3 Vestal St.; 508-228-9273) is a research facility but conducts daytime tours for daylight observation of the sun and sunspots. There are also permanent exhibits on display. The tours are at 2 p.m. Mon through Sat during the summer season. Later, the **Loines Observatory** (59 Milk St. Extension; 508-228-9273) was constructed;

TopEvents on Nantucket

- **Daffodil Festival,** late Apr, Nantucket; (508) 228-1700; nantucket chamber.org

- **The Nantucket Food and Wine Festival,** mid-May, Nantucket, (617) 527-9473; nantucketwinefestival.com

- **Figawi Race Weekend,** late May, Hyannis to Nantucket and back, Hyannis; (508) 221-6891; figawi.com

- **Nantucket Film Festival,** late June, Nantucket; (508) 325-6274 or (646) 480-1900; nantucketfilmfestival.org

- **Fourth of July Fireworks and Events,** July, Nantucket; (508) 228-1700; nantucketchamber.org

- **Antiques and Design Show,** Aug, Whaling Museum, 15 Broad St., Nantucket: (508) 228-1894; wha.org.

- **Boston Pops Concert,** Aug, Jettie's Beach, Nantucket; (508) 825-8100; nantuckethospital.org

- **Sandcastle and Sculpture Contest,** mid-Aug, Jetties Beach, Nantucket; (508) 228-1700 (Nantucket Chamber); nantucketchamber .org, or (508) 325-6659; nisda.org

- **Nantucket County Fair,** Sept, Tom Nevers Fairgrounds, Nantucket; (508) 228-7244; nantucket-ma.gov/parksandrecreation

- **Egan Maritime Festival,** Sept, Nantucket; (508) 228-2505; egan maritime.org

- **Conservation Foundation Cranberry Harvest Festival,** Oct, Milestone Cranberry Bog, Milestone Rd., Nantucket (508) 228-2884; nantucketconservation.org

- **Festival of Wreaths,** Thanksgiving Week, Whaling Museum, 15 Broad St., Nantucket; (508) 228-1894; wha.org.

- **Christmas Stroll,** first Sat in Dec, downtown Nantucket; (508) 228-1700; nantucketchamber.org

- **Festival of Trees,** Dec, Whaling Museum, 15 Broad St., Nantucket: (508) 228-1894; nha.org.

it is known for its nighttime tours held on Mon, Wed, and Fri at 9 p.m. mid-June through mid-Sept (weather permitting). The visitor pass doesn't include the nighttime tour, which charges $10 per adult and $7 per child. Maria Mitchell was the librarian at the Nantucket Athenaeum for twenty years before becoming an astronomy professor at Vassar College. The **Maria Mitchell Administrative Offices** (4 Vestal St.; 508-228-9198; open by appointment) has a fascinating collection of Maria's 19th-century papers and shares space with the administration offices. Next door is **Maria's birthplace,** aka the **Mitchell House** (1 Vestal St.; 508-228-2896), which has the telescope she was using when she discovered "her" comet. The **Aquarium and Gift Shop** (28 Washington St.; 508-228-5387) gives visitors an insider's look at the marine life of the island through its many displays and sponsors field trips. The **Natural Science Museum and Shop** (7 Milk St., corner of Milk and Vestal; 508-228-0898) is a natural-history museum focusing on Nantucket's natural habitats. The Maria Mitchell Association offers adult walks and field trips, many "Feed and Meet" the Animals Series (prices range from $5 to $10 per person), a Discovery Camp for kids, and a Teen Naturalist Program. This is also a great place to have a birthday party. And heads up: A new Aquarium and Science Center is slated to open in 2015 on the Maria Mitchell Campus!

Miacomet Beach (ages 7 and up)

GPS address is 36 West Miacomet, end of Miacomet Road (paved road turns to dirt, go about 0.5 mile to the end for Miacomet Beach. Warning: Do not take any of the branch turns, or you may end up at a nude beach—not a family-oriented outing for most people!). Nantucket; (508) 228-7244 (Parks and Recreation) or (508) 228-7230 (beach manager). Free.

Even though this is a south-side beach with heavy surf, there is a freshwater pond that is great for swimming, especially for beginners. Lifeguards on duty and a parking lot are your only amenities.

Nantucket Shipwreck and Lifesaving Museum (all ages)

158 Polpis Rd., Nantucket; (508) 228-1885; nantucketshipwreck.org or eganmaritime.org Open daily Memorial Day to Columbus Day 10 a.m. to 5 p.m. Admission: $6 for adults, $4 for children 5 to 17, free for children under 5 (guided tours of the museum are included in the cost of your admission). The museum is right off the bike path, just 3.5 miles from town.

The museum, part of the Egan Maritime Institute, is a reproduction of an original lifesaving station on Nantucket. If it wasn't for whaling, shipwrecks would be the big island story. In a span of 60 years, there were more than 700 shipwrecks off the shoals (a big sandbar) of Nantucket's waters. Back then it was like I-95 out there in the sea lanes, without the aid of GPS or weather satellites, so it was quite easy to run amuck! When a ship did run aground, the local motto was "You have to go out, but you don't have to come back." The people of Nantucket were herculean in their efforts and heroism to save the crew and the passengers of the sinking vessels. Many Nantucket volunteers lost their lives trying to help. Memorabilia includes lifesaving equipment (a rare surfboat and an authentic beach cart), original photographs, artifacts from shipwrecks (the *Andrea Doria,* a luxury cruise ship with registry from Italy, went down in Nantucket waters in 1956), and remains from Island lighthouses (the Fresnel lens that came off of the Great Point Lighthouse during the 1984 storm was moved to the museum's property). A new exhibit on maritime lifesaving practices, procedures, and pastimes will be showcased in 2014. Tied in with the exhibit will be a lot of hands-on activities (both inside the museum as well as outside) for children of all ages. Children's programs are offered in July and Aug including family days. Check the museum's schedule for lectures, films, events, and concerts. Be sure to pack a lunch; the museum has a wonderful picnic area atop a knoll with views of Folgers Marsh. *TIP:* A great children's reading book with wonderful illustrations is *Marshall: A Nantucket Sea Rescue* by Whitney Stewart.

'Sconset Beach (all ages)

Siasconset Road to the end of Gulley Road (#2 GPS address), Nantucket; (508) 228-7244 (Parks and Recreation) or (508) 228-7230 (beach manager). Free.

'Sconset Beach, a long, remote, narrow stretch, can be a bit seaweedy, but your family may overlook the inconvenience if you enjoy having lots of room to yourselves (artists and rich folks hang out in this part of the island). There's a swing set here (100 feet to the left of the beach entrance) too. There are no restrooms or snack facilities here, but the beach is lifeguarded in season, and restrooms are nearby. Occasional erosion due to weather. In fact, more homes have been lost to the sea here since 1998 than on the entire East Coast! Luckily, the erosion has stopped recently. *TIP:* It is approximately a 6.5-mile bike ride on a paved path.

Nantucket Island **Biking Paths**

The Nantucket Visitor Service Center has all the bike paths consolidated onto one easy-to-use map (nantucket-ma.gov).

- **Hummock Pond Bike Path.** The newest bike path is a 2.75-mile-long trail from town to Cisco Beach (it's fairly flat and very scenic, passing by fields and lots of open meadowland). Directions: Starting at Main St take a left onto Milk Street (just outside of town). The path starts at the intersection of Milk and Hummuck Pond Road ending at Cisco Beach.

- **Madaket Bike Path.** The prize at the end of the path (approximately 5 miles) is Madaket Beach, great for sunsets but dangerous swimming for kids. The path can have some inclines and sharp curves. A 1-mile extension off this bike path goes on to Dionis Beach. Directions: Follow Main Street to the top until it turns into Madaket Road. Follow it to the end.

- **Polpis Bike Path.** This is the longest bike path (8 miles), with some gradual hills and curving corners. Directions: From town (Main Street) take a left onto Washington Street, at Orange Street take a right, follow to the rotary, go halfway around the rotary and take a left onto Polpis (following the signs for the Polpis Bike Path). The path goes to the left at the split (it is marked).

- **'Sconset Beach Bike Path.** Families enjoy biking to 'Sconset Beach via the 7-mile trail that parallels Milestone Road. There are some mild hills. It's approximately 1 hour to 'Sconset. Directions: From town (Main Street) take a left onto Washington Street. At Orange Street take a right, follow to the rotary, go half way around the rotary and take a left onto Polpis (following the signs for Madaket) and then go straight to 'Sconset.

- **The Surfside Bike Path.** A 3-mile-long, flat trail that leads from the town of Nantucket to its best beach. Directions: Take Main Street in town to Pleasant Street; turn right on Atlantic Avenue and proceed to Surfside. The path can be crowded.

The Black Heritage Trail, Downtown Nantucket and New Guinea

The African Meeting House (29 York St., Five Corners, Nantucket; 508-228-9833; maah.org) is the second-oldest structure in the US built by and for free Africans. It was used as a church, a school, and a meeting place. This historic building is now owned by the Museum of African American History, Boston. Call or visit their website for the schedule. Prices for the guided walking tour of the Black Heritage Trail's 10 sites, which starts at the Whaling Museum (13 Broad St., Nantucket) and ends at the African Meeting House are: $5 for adults, $3 for ages 13 to 17, and free for under age 12.

Surfside Beach (ages 7 and up)
166 Surfside Rd., Nantucket; (508) 228-7244 (Parks and Recreation) or (508) 228-7230 (beach manager). Free.

Surfside's heavy surf, typical of the south side of the island, makes it inappropriate for families with younger children, but strong swimmers who love bodysurfing will enjoy it. But, on calm days, with gentle surf, it is great for children. This beach can be crowded with college kids and surf casters, but Surfside is long enough to accommodate everyone. Facilities include a large parking lot, accessible restrooms, showers, a beach accessible chair, rental chairs and umbrellas, and a snack bar. Lifeguards are on duty. This beach is available via the Nantucket Regional Transit Authority, which can be boarded in downtown Nantucket or consider hiking or biking the 2-mile-plus trek.

Theatre Workshop of Nantucket (all ages)
2 Centre St. (the Box Office is at the Methodist Church), Nantucket; (508) 228-4305; theatreworkshop.com. Productions are at either the Centre Stage (2 Centre St.) or Bennett Hall (62 Centre St.).

The Theatre Workshop of Nantucket has been a tradition in Nantucket since 1985. The summer season repertoire can range from the dramatic to the comedic; from readings to a short-play festival; from an improv comedy group to a family matinee!

Whaling Museum and Historic Sites (all ages)

13 Broad St., Nantucket; (508) 228-1736 (whaling museum) or (508) 228-1894 (main number); nha.org. Check their website for the schedule. All-Access Pass: $20 for adults, $5 for children 6 to 17, under 6 free for the Whaling Museum and to all the historical sites (open seasonally Memorial Day to Columbus Day). The historic sites are $6 for adults and $3 for kids 6 to 17; free for kids 5 and under. The Walking Tour is $10 for adults and $4 for kids 6 to 17; free for kids 5 and under. Nantucket in its heyday was the whaling capital of the world. Visit the Whaling Museum to see a vivid explanation of the phrase "Nantucket sleigh ride." That's what happens when your harpoon gets stuck in a whale's back, and the whale decides to take you and your companions for a ride through the waves. Start your visit with one of the two daily presentations before touring the Whaling Museum. Don't miss the 46-foot sperm whale skeleton, the rooftop observation deck, and the restored spermaceti candle factory. A staffed children's discovery room (in season) offers hands-on learning interactive opportunities, plus projects and crafts. The historical properties consist of:

- Greater Light, 8 Howard St.—Summer home of sisters Gertrude and Hanna Monaghan, art collectors and artists with gardens out back. Set aside a half hour; staff are present to answer questions.

- Jethro Coffin House, 16 Sunset Hill Rd.—Oldest surviving home in Nantucket (1686). Don't overlook the self-guided period kitchen garden in the back. Allow 30 minutes for the guided tour.

- Old Mill, 50 Prospect St.—Oldest operating mill in the country (built in 1746). Corn-grinding demonstrations are held, weather permitting (the mill is wind-driven). Guided tour lasts for half an hour.

- Old Gaol, 15 R Vestal St.—Defunct jail built in 1806. Last resident prisoner was in 1933. Set aside 15 minutes for the self-guided tour with an interpreter on-site and a good 20 minutes to find it (you are now being challenged to do it in less time!).

A Great Read for Kids

If your kids love to explore the outdoors, pick up a copy of the book *Where Does the Trail Lead* by Burton Albert and Brian Pinkney.

Readers' Choice

The Nantucket Atheneum at 1 India St. (508-228-1110; nantucket atheneum.org). Open Tues through Sat from 10 a.m. to 5 p.m., with extended hours on Tues and Thurs until 7:30 p.m. This is one of the oldest continually operating libraries in the US. It contains many artifacts, including scrimshaw, figureheads, paintings, sculpture, and ship models. There's a children's wing, as well as an adjoining garden and park where kids like to run around in and activities are held. The first librarian, Maria Mitchell, was the first woman to discover a comet. Tons of children's programming ranges from story hours, films, visiting authors and illustrators, and dance, craft, and music activities.

- Quaker Meetinghouse, 7 Fair St.—This is the first museum acquired by the Nantucket Historical Association. Early Quaker meetinghouse built in 1838 used as both a school and a church. Brochure on-site will be your guide (budget 15 minutes).

- Fire Hose Cart House, 8 Gardner St.—This house is the last firehouse on Nantucket dating back to the 1800s. Rare firefighting equipment is on display as well as interactive exhibits on the history of firefighting on Nantucket. Self-guided tour (taking about 10 minutes); however, a staff member is on-site to answer your questions. Watch the videos on the Great Fire of 1846 that destroyed most of Nantucket.

Other Things to See & Do

Brant Point Beach and Lighthouse, end of Easton Street, Nantucket. Great spot for viewing the ferries rounding the bend into Nantucket Harbor. **Warning:** Strong undertow and big drop-off.

Coskata Coatue Wildlife Refuge, Wauwinet Road, Nantucket; (508) 228-5646 or (508) 228-0006 (Gatehouse) thetrustees.org. Free to pedestrians and boaters. Trustees of Reservations property; scenic trails, abundant wildlife, saltwater fishing, and the Great Point Lighthouse. **Warning:** Dangerous swimming. Stop at the Guard House to get your four-wheel-drive permit ($65 for a day pass, $140 for a season pass for a private vehicle). It is 5.5 miles to the lighthouse or the point. Natural-history, fishing, and seal tours are offered.

Endeavor Pirate Cruise, on Straight Wharf, Nantucket; (508) 228-5585; endeavor sailing.com. Ahoy mate! Don your pirate hat and cruise around the harbor on a sloop. Watch a small cannon being fired, hear the history of local pirates, and sing sea shanties. Ask about their Walking Pirate Tour of town.

Nantucket Babysitters' Service, 5 Windy Way, Nantucket; (508) 228-4970; nantucketbabysitters.com. Babysitter service, rental of baby equipment, and Home Helpers.

Nantucket Lightship Basket Museum, 49 Union St., Nantucket; (508) 228-1177; nantucketlightshipbasketmuseum.org. Collection of baskets from pre-lightship times to the present. A cottage industry for the seamen stationed on the lightships.

Nantucket Bike Shop, 4 Broad St., Steamboat and Straight Wharves, Nantucket; (508) 228-1999 or (800) 770-3088; nantucketbikeshop.com. Free delivery on multiple-day bike rentals; rent adult and kids bikes and scooters. You can also reserve online.

Nantucket Community Sailing, 4 Winter St., PO Box 2424, Nantucket, MA 02554; (508) 228-6600 or (508) 325-7757 (Jetties Beach Office); nantucketcommunitysailing .org. Lessons for adults and kids. Rentals of kayaks, Windsurfers, paddleboards, and boats.

Nantucket Ghost Walk, top of Main St., Nantucket; (508) 332-0953. For older kids that enjoy being scared. One-and-a-half-hour walking tour of haunted places in Nantucket town.

Sesachacha Heathlands, Polpis Road to Barnard Valley Road, Nantucket; (508) 228-9208; massaudubon.org. Free. Audubon Wildlife Sanctuary on 875 acres; trails open dawn to dusk. Part of the middle and eastern moors which is 5,000 acres of conservation, foundation, and land bank properties.

Sea Nantucket Kayak Rentals, 76 Washington St., Nantucket; (508) 228-7499. Short lessons, single and double kayaks, and stand-up-paddle rentals.

Shearwater Excursions, Straight Wharf, Nantucket; (508) 228-7037; explorenantucket .com. Seal, whale-watch, 1-hour harbor cruise (daily on the hour), ice-cream cruise, and ecotours. Private charters. Other sea adventures by reservation only.

Where to Eat

The Boarding House, 12 Federal St., Nantucket; (508) 228-9622; boardinghouse-pearl.com. Patio and dining room dining. Bills itself as "farm-to-table dining. Voted Best of Boston for brunch. $$–$$$$

Fog Island Cafe, 7 South Water St., Nantucket; (508) 228-1818; fogisland.com. Known for its extensive breakfast menu, sandwiches, burgers, and tacos. $–$$

Le Languedoc, 24 Broad St., Nantucket; (508) 228-2552; lelanguedoc.com. Upscale French restaurant that caters to all tastes in an old whaling home. Popular with locals who savor the Traditional French Steak Frites avec sauce béarnaise. $–$$$$

Pi Pizzeria, 11 West Creek Rd., Nantucket; (508) 228-1130; pipizzeria.com. Pizza made in a wood-fired brick oven from stone ground flour and organic toppings. Pasta based dishes. $–$$$

Slip 14, 14 Old South Wharf, Nantucket; (508) 228-2033; slip14.com. Voted best water view restaurant by readers of Cape Cod Life. Nautical casual vibe. Fresh fish. Outdoor covered patio. $–$$$

Sweet Inspirations/Nantucket Clipper Chocolates, 26 Centre St., Nantucket; (508) 228-5814 or (888) 225-4843; nantucketchocolatier.com. Chocolate lovers don't need inspiration, just the address. $–$$

Where to Stay

The Beachside, 30 North Beach St., Nantucket; (508) 228-2241 or (800) 322-4433; thebeachside.com. Open early May to the end of Oct. Double-decker motel near Jetties Beach; standard rooms and 3 two-room suites are available. Children under 16 stay free in their parents' room. Pet friendly. Complimentary breakfast. $$–$$$$

Brant Point Courtyard, 15 Swain St., Nantucket; (508) 228-0241 or (800) 228 2968 (Reservations); brantpointcourtyard.com. Little apartments with kitchenettes (some with fireplaces and patios) off of the main street. Near Jettie's and Children's Beach and a short walk to town. $–$$$

Brant Point Inn, 6 North Beach St., Nantucket; (508) 228-5442 or (508) 228-5451; brantpointinn.com. Post-and-beam inn; traditional country decor. Guest suites with kitchens work well for families with children (over 6 only, please). Great location, walking distance to town and Children's Beach. Continental breakfast included in price. $$–$$$$

The Cliffside Beach Club, 46 Jefferson Ave. (on Cliffside Beach), Nantucket; (508) 228-0618; cliffsidebeach.com. Panoramic views of Cliffside beach, lap and leisure pool, whirlpool, spa, fitness center, hotel rooms, suites, and cottages. $$$$

The Cottages and Lofts/Boat Basin, 1 Old South Wharf, Nantucket; (508) 325-1499 or (800) 475-2637; thecottagesnantucket.com. Waterfront cottages with kitchens and patio decks overlooking the wharf area. Units range from a studio to three bedrooms. The Boat Basin is next door (at the marina) with 240 boat slip rentals with concierge service. Nantucket Island Resorts also manages:

The White Elephant, White Elephant Village, the Jared Coffin House, and the **Wauwinet.** A prearrival concierge prebooks dining, transportation, and tours for no additional fee. $$$$

#3 Hussey Street Guest House, 3 Hussey St., Nantucket; (508) 228-4298; languedocinn.com. Budget-minded guests can share a bathroom or pay extra for a private bath. Clean and tidy, located in the historic part of town, 3 blocks from the main street. ***Warning:*** steep stairs leading to guest rooms. $–$$$

Index

THE BRADT STORY

In 1974, my (former) husband George and I spent three days sitting on a river barge in Bolivia writing our first guide for like-minded travellers: *Backpacking along Ancient Ways in Peru and Bolivia*. The 'little yellow book', as it became known, is now in its sixth edition and continues to sell to travellers throughout the world. Since 1980, with the establishment of Bradt Publications, I have continued to publish guides for the discerning traveller, covering more than 100 countries and all six continents, and winning the 1997 *Sunday Times* Small Publisher of the Year Award; *Guide to Zanzibar* (3rd edition) is the 137th Bradt guide to be published.

The company continues to develop new titles and new series, but in the forefront of my mind there remains our original ethos – responsible travel with an emphasis on the culture and natural history of the region. I hope that you will get the most out of your trip, and perhaps have the opportunity to give something in return.

Travel guides are by their nature continuously evolving. If you experience anything which you would like to share with us, or if you have any amendments to make to this guide, please write; all your letters are read and passed on to the author. Most importantly, do remember to travel with an open mind and to respect the customs of your hosts – it will add immeasurably to your enjoyment.

Happy travelling!

Hilary Bradt

41 Nortoft Road, Chalfont St Peter, Bucks, SL9 0LA, England
Tel/fax: 01494 873478 Email: bradtpublications@compuserve.com

THE BRADT STORY

In 1974, my (former) husband George and I spent three days sitting on a river barge in Bolivia writing our first guide for like-minded travellers: *Backpacking along Ancient Ways in Peru and Bolivia*. The 'little yellow book', as it became known, is now in its sixth edition and continues to sell to travellers throughout the world. Since 1980, with the establishment of Bradt Publications, I have continued to publish guides for the discerning traveller, covering more than 100 countries and all six continents, and winning the 1997 *Sunday Times* Small Publisher of the Year Award; *Guide to Zanzibar* (3rd edition) is the 137th Bradt guide to be published.

The company continues to develop new titles and new series, but in the forefront of my mind there remains our original ethos – responsible travel with an emphasis on the culture and natural history of the region. I hope that you will get the most out of your trip, and perhaps have the opportunity to give something in return.

Travel guides are by their nature continuously evolving. If you experience anything which you would like to share with us, or if you have any amendments to make to this guide, please write; all your letters are read and passed on to the author. Most importantly, do remember to travel with an open mind and to respect the customs of your hosts – it will add immeasurably to your enjoyment.

Happy travelling!

Hilary Bradt

Hilary Bradt

41 Nortoft Road, Chalfont St Peter, Bucks, SL9 0LA, England
Tel/fax: 01494 873478 Email: bradtpublications@compuserve.com